THE LAWFUL AND THE UNLAWFUL

Kitāb al-ḥalāl wa'l-ḥarām

BOOK XIV of
THE REVIVAL OF THE RELIGIOUS SCIENCES
Iḥyā' ʿulūm al-dīn

OTHER TITLES IN THE ISLAMIC TEXTS SOCIETY
AL-GHAZĀLĪ SERIES

FROM *The Revival of the Religious Sciences*

Al-Ghazālī on Invocations & Supplications

Al-Ghazālī on the Manners Relating to Eating

Al-Ghazālī on Disciplining the Soul & Breaking the Two Desires

Al-Ghazālī on Patience & Thankfulness

Al-Ghazālī on Love, Longing, Intimacy & Contentment

Al-Ghazālī on Intention, Sincerity & Truthfulness

Al-Ghazālī on the Remembrance of Death & the Afterlife

OTHER WORKS

Al-Ghazālī on the Ninety-Nine Beautiful Names of God
(*al-Maqṣad al-asnā fī sharḥ asmā' Allāh al-ḥusnā*)

Al-Ghazālī Letter to a Disciple
(*Ayyuhā'l-walad*)

AL-GHAZĀLĪ
ON THE LAWFUL & THE UNLAWFUL

Kitāb al-ḥalāl wa'l-ḥarām

·BOOK XIV· of THE REVIVAL OF THE RELIGIOUS SCIENCES

Iḥyā' ʿulūm al-dīn · translated with an INTRODUCTION & notes by YUSUF T. DELORENZO

This first edition published 2014 by
THE ISLAMIC TEXTS SOCIETY
MILLER'S HOUSE
KINGS MILL LANE
GREAT SHELFORD
CAMBRIDGE CB22 5EN, U.K.

British Library Cataloguing-in-Publication Data.
A catalogue record for this book is
available from the British Library.

ISBN: 978 1903682 241 cloth
ISBN: 978 1903682 258 paper

CONTENTS

THE BOOK OF THE LAWFUL AND THE UNLAWFUL

PREFACE

A narration of dubious authenticity but unquestionable wisdom says that before undertaking a journey one must first give thought to the choice of an appropriate guide and travelling companion: *al-rafīq qabl al-ṭarīq*. From the moment he set pen to paper, Abū Ḥāmid al-Ghazālī has been considered by the scholars of Islam to be one of the best of all guides and companions. Whether the journey is to be of the nature of a flighty philosophical excursion or a plodding theological discourse, a soaring spiritual exercise or a pedestrian legal lesson, Abū Ḥāmid is the one to have alongside you. If you are capable and well prepared, you might even keep pace with him. Moreover, whatever the nature of your peregrinations, the likelihood is that somewhere along the way Abū Ḥāmid will try your patience. Even so, as the sort of indefatigable companion who will ever urge you onward, he cannot fail to win your admiration, however grudging; and in the end, you will not regret your choice.

To quote from the contemporary Moroccan philosopher, M. ʿAzīz al-Ḥabbābī, whose own travels with Abū Ḥāmid have been considerable:

> With al-Ghazālī, we shall disembark from the express train, with its clearly-defined tracks and familiar landmarks. Indeed, we know at exactly which station we boarded; but we have no idea about where we are to arrive. Our journey is not going according to plan, and we no longer have a map. For, with al-Ghazālī there are countless question marks. It is as if every cell in his brain is a resting place for a legal problem, or a philosophical, or a theological, or a spiritual one.

> Apparently, his mind is always set to boil!
> So who are you, Abū Ḥāmid? You who are as bothersome to yourself as you are to others! Your genius will never let you rest; and your personality is so ambiguous that it too leads only to more questions. This is why it is so difficult to deal with you.
> Are you a philosopher?
> 'Yes. And no.'
> Are you a theologian?
> 'No. But, to an extent, I am an Ashʿarite.'
> Are you an ascetic?
> 'Yes. But...'
> Every 'yes' of yours is linked to a 'no'. Just like every 'no' is linked to a 'yes'. The sum of your heretical utterances, your intellectual departures, and your self-contradictions is greater than the power of even your own intellect to encompass! This fact alone explains why your rivals have no alternative but to respect you, and to follow in your footsteps.[A]

The path chosen for travel in this volume would appear at first glance to concern few other than the mendicant residents of Sufi retreats. Moreover, the subject of this work would appear to concern the Sufi in only the most mundane of his affairs, that of keeping himself fed, sheltered and clothed. Add to this that the book is essentially a work of jurisprudence (*fiqh*), and most readers would be ready to close it and place it back on the shelf!

Allow me, then, to attempt to persuade you to do otherwise. In this modest volume, Abū Ḥāmid will take us to the courts of potentates, to dusty roads and covered bridges, to battlefields and plunder, to the inner sanctums of Islam's most celebrated ascetics and scholars. He will discourse for us on the meaning of government, and he will dare to call the sultan a thief! He will expand on the subtleties of the law, and he will disparage mercenaries, tax

[A] M. ʿAzīz al-Ḥabbābī, *Waraqāt ʿan falsafāt Islāmiyya* (Morocco, 1988), p. 6.

collectors, courtiers and all manner of ignorance and greed. Most importantly, however, he will discuss the fundaments of finance in Islam. The lawful and the unlawful of which Abū Ḥāmid speaks in this volume are the legal categorizations for the ways in which people earn their livings, acquire and manage their wealth and enter into trade and exchange with others. It is for this reason that this volume is as vital to Muslims today as it was to the mendicant residents of Sufi retreats for whom it was originally written nearly a thousand years ago.

Before proceeding any further, however, I would like to acknowledge my debt of gratitude to several learned individuals whose guidance and companionship have assisted me in no small manner to understand and appreciate Abū Ḥāmid al-Ghazālī and his work. It was my teacher, the late Mawlānā ᶜAbd Allāh Kākā Khayl, son of Mawlānā Nāfiᶜ Gul of Peshawar and Deoband, with whom I first formally studied the works of Ghazālī. Equally as important for myself and for this project, it was Mawlānā ᶜAbd Allāh who first urged me to consider the art of translation as a vocation. On reflection, it was very likely by design that he never requested to see the fruits of my labour. Notwithstanding his excuses that his English was rudimentary at best (to my recollection we never once conversed in this language), it was plain to me that he wished never to dampen my growing enthusiasm with even the most perfunctory sort of criticism. How I wish now, with the benefit of hindsight, that I had better understood his example during my years as a teacher. May God bless him and have mercy on his soul.

The late Mawlānā Muḥammad Yūsuf al-Bannūrī, also of Peshawar and Deoband, was the living example to me of what Abū Ḥāmid represented. Indeed, Mawlānā Bannūrī too had the temerity to call the sultan a thief! He was a scholar's scholar,[A] known far

[A] One day as I sat studying in the mosque, a man approached and asked me where the Mawlānā was. As the term Mawlānā is an honorific that students commonly used for all of their teachers, I naturally asked, 'Which Mawlānā?'

and wide for his learning. At the same time, he devoted himself to worship and his relationship with the Almighty. Mawlānā's lessons to his students, inside and outside of the classroom, were filled with references to the works of Ghazālī; it was, perhaps, Mawlānā's facility with, if not mastery of, the entire spectrum of Islamic sciences that brought home to me the idea that a single scholar might indeed be as rounded and, at the same time, as spiritually accomplished as the ideal envisioned and embodied by Abū Ḥāmid.

A more practical and direct contribution to the work at hand was made by my friend and colleague, Shaykh Nizam Yaqubi of Bahrain, who is presently completing his own work on the subject of the unpublished *fatwā* literature produced by Ghazālī. Shaykh Nizam's enthusiasm for the subject, like his enthusiasm for all topics related to the Islamic sciences, is boundless; as is his energy in pursuing knowledge, wherever it is to be found. I am particularly indebted to him for his insights regarding the *fiqh* of Ghazālī, and for his help in tracing Ghazālī's *fatwās* to their sources in unpublished manuscripts. In addition, Shaykh Nizam was particularly generous in helping me to translate some of the more difficult passages in the text.

While I never consulted directly with Dr. Bernard Weiss in regard to this work, I feel nevertheless that I owe him a considerable debt of gratitude for the groundbreaking work he has done to 'build up a terminological apparatus with which to be able to talk about issues in *uṣūl al-fiqh* in English.'[A] It was not until I had

The visitor looked down at the book in my hand, a work of *uṣūl-al-fiqh*, and said to me, 'If you understand the contents of that book, you'll know the one I seek,' adding in Arabic, '*al-ʿāmm idhā uṭliqa fa-yurādu bihi al-fard al-kāmil.*' When I realized what he had meant, I directed him to Mawlānā Bannūrī's home. What he had said to me in Arabic was straight from the pages of a work of *uṣūl*, and it means that a term of general reference, if expressed without qualification, will indicate the most perfect individual in its class, i.e., 'The Mawlānā'.

[A] Quoted from a letter by Dr. Weiss to the translator following my review of his book, *The Search for God's Law* (Utah, 1995).

familiarised myself with Dr. Weiss' work that I was able to consider translating a work from this discipline, with its specific and complex terminology, into English. In particular, his work on key terms opened the way for much of the material in Chapters Two and Three of this translation.

In addition, I am indebted to Dr. Ahmad Alwani and his sister Zaynab Alwani; the former for allowing me access to his huge library, and the latter, whom I am proud to count among my students, for her mature thinking about the contributions of Ghazālī to the development of Islamic legal methodology.

My friend, the historian Dr. Bashir Nafi first introduced me to the work of the contemporary Moroccan philosopher, M. ʿAzīz al-Ḥabbābī, author of *Waraqāt ʿan falsafāt Islāmiyya*. As a historian with a particular interest in the classical scholars of Islam, Dr. Bashir engaged me in many fruitful hours of conversation concerning the stars in that particular firmament!

Yusuf Talal DeLorenzo
West Palm Beach, Florida 2014/1435

INTRODUCTION

ISLAMIC JURISPRUDENCE has always been a shared endeavour. From one perspective, it is shared between man and God, such that God is the Lawgiver or Divine Legislator and man, the jurist, is responsible for receiving and interpreting, and then doing all of the things necessary for implementing the spiritual, legal and other requisites of that revelation. Given that no further revelation may be expected, as it was terminated when the Messenger of God's mission concluded, Muslim jurists are charged with taking a finite body of revelation, the Qur'ān and the *Sunna*, and applying it to ever changing circumstances. The first few centuries of Muslim history resulted in a huge body of practical and theoretical jurisprudence derived from the revelational sources and, as Muslim society expanded and developed, Muslim jurists were called upon to produce relevant solutions from those sources to the continually changing circumstances in which they lived. Such judicial lawmaking, though clearly based on revelation, or what came to be known as Sharīʿa, remained an effective and dynamic part of Muslim society in most parts of the world until the colonial incursions of the eighteenth and nineteenth centuries. In the fourth century of the Hijra, the century in which Ghazālī produced this work, this process was very much a part of the mainstream in society. It was Ghazālī's perception, however, that the other element in the two-part equation described above, the element of the Divine, had become an abstraction for most legal practitioners in his times.

Abū Ḥāmid al-Ghazālī was a man of God. In the Islamic tradition, what this means is that he was a man of this world and the next; and what that means is that Abū Ḥāmid al-Ghazālī was as much concerned, in his capacity as a scholar, with the Sharīʿa as a way of dealing with the affairs of this world, as he was with the Sharīʿa as a way that leads to the next. In his own understanding and practice of Islam, in his orthodoxy and his orthopraxy, he had managed to bridge what others perceived as the gulf between the legalistic practice and ritual encompassed by *fiqh* and the spiritual discipline and experience encompassed by Sufism. To the mind of the Master, it was all one and the same thing. If others perceived contradictions, Abū Ḥāmid explained them away, or he waxed eloquent on how those could be reconciled. But the crux of the matter is that in order to travel the road to the Afterlife, one's feet need to come in contact with the earth, even while one's head might remain in the air. The Sharīʿa, literally 'the Way', led Abū Ḥāmid in all of his travels, and at every level. Indeed, it is difficult to imagine how anyone who has approached his *Revival* with any degree of gravity can fail to discern this simple truth. Consider what Zayn al-Dīn al-ʿIrāqī had to say about the book (and not only the volume in your hands right now): 'Verily, it is among the most sublime of all the books in Islam in regard to knowledge of the lawful and the unlawful. In it he combines the outer aspects of the law and then delves into secrets too subtle for general discernment. He neither limits himself to the two sciences of theoretical and practical jurisprudence, nor does he so lose himself in the depths of the [spiritual] ocean that it is impossible to return to shore. On the contrary, he blends the sciences of the exoteric and the esoteric such that their meanings conjoin in the most exquisite manner.'[A]

When Islam is understood to mean 'commitment', that means that a life lived in accordance with Islamic norms is a life of commitment; and the Sharīʿa may be said to be the divine

[A] Quoted in ʿAbd al-Ḥalīm Maḥmūd, *Taḥlīl kitāb al-Iḥyā'*, reprinted as an appendix in the Dār al-Arqam edition of *Iḥyā' ʿulūm al-dīn*, v.15.

delineation of the life of commitment.[A] Then, if one is truly to live that life, one must come to terms with how that life is actually delineated by the Divine. It is precisely that 'coming to terms' that is known in classical Muslim scholarship as '*fiqh*'. This is what Abū Ḥāmid did throughout his life, and he did it with equal facility for the exoteric and the esoteric. This, more than any other explanation, clarifies the meaning of the statement that, 'The *fiqh* of Ghazālī is in his *Revival*.'[B] Thus, while *fiqh* explains things like marriage, prayer and inheritance, it also explains things like hope, repentance and prudence. And so, while it may be convenient for some to classify the *Revival* as a work of *taṣawwuf*, it is in fact just as much a work of *fiqh*.

Having spent his life in the systematic attempt to classify human behaviour, whether under the heading of *fiqh* or *taṣawwuf*, it is not surprising that Abū Ḥāmid thought about classifying humans as well. Indeed, such classifications were already an established part of the Islamic academic and legal tradition. For example, within each of the four Sunni schools of jurisprudence there were carefully constructed hierarchies that clarified whose opinions, and in what order of precedence, were to be valued. Likewise, volumes and volumes of the biographies of *Ḥadīth* narrators had been written to establish who among them could be considered reliable or unreliable, or belonging to any of the several categories in between. In the same way, in the traditions of the grammarians, the poets, the philosophers, the Sufis, there were masters and there were masters! By Abū Ḥāmid's times, clearly the golden age of Islamic civilization, the hierarchies of the learned were both well established and commonly known.

[A] Weiss, *The Spirit of Islamic Law*, p. 18. Note that I substitute 'commitment' for Weiss' 'submission'.

[B] While I have heard this statement ascribed variously, notably to Shaykh ʿAbd al-Ḥalīm Maḥmūd and others, I am unable to trace it to a definite source. I suspect that this is one of those sayings that, owing to its resonance, has literally taken on a life of its own. And God knows best.

So, even if there was no ecclesiastical hierarchy in Sunni Islam, everyone knew who the imams were.

In addition, there was a certain hierarchy for spiritual accomplishment that was clearly of great significance for Abū Ḥāmid. As this volume, *The Lawful and the Unlawful*, deals specifically with issues related to the maintenance of Sufi retreats, themselves a clear manifestation of the level of organization attained by the Sufi community in those times, it is well that the reader give some consideration to this matter so as to be able to place this work in its proper context. Retreats, after all, like colleges, provided the institutional framework for the development of human abilities and, in particular, for taking the best and the brightest and preparing them for the challenges of leadership when and if they were fortunate enough to be placed in positions of leadership. So, in the same way that the chief justices (*qāḍī al-quḍā*) of the future were prepared in the colleges of law (*madāris*), the Sufis developed their future masters in their system of retreats. Then, in a very clear sense, those likely to become the most accomplished in their practice of the religion of Islam, who combined in their persons both knowledge and practice, *fiqh* and *taṣawwuf*, were those who had undergone the discipline of formal education in the *madāris* and who had then given themselves over to a life of simple devotions in the retreats.

The very first generations of Muslims had lived their lives in the attempt to emulate the Prophet's example, may God bless him and grant him peace. *Verily you have in the Messenger of God a good example for everyone who looks forward to God and the Last Day and remembers God continually.*[C] And, at a very early date the Sufis began speaking of the perfect human (*al-insān al-kāmil*), and it was not long before Sufis began to speak in terms of a saintly hierarchy presided over by one or more temporal heads (*aqṭāb*, pl. of *quṭb*). I will leave it to others to decide to which school Abū Ḥāmid prescribed in the details of his beliefs regarding such *aqṭāb*; I mean

[C] Q. XXXIII.21

here only to point out how Abū Ḥāmid viewed the Sufi retreats and the people who populated them. In doing so, however, I hope that the reader may gain a better understanding of the world that he lived in and how he viewed it. Indeed, as there is much in this volume that has to do with society and how it is organized, it is important to develop an appreciation for the author's particular perspective.

In Chapter Two of this volume, Abū Ḥāmid wrote, 'The way of true religion, however, may only be tread by those few who are capable of it.'[A] This is the first line in one of the most important and revealing passages in the entire book. It is in this passage that the author gives the reader a glimpse of his unique perspective; and one that might be labelled today as decidedly elitist in nature. For Ghazālī, however, Islam is everything because Islam is The Religion. God said: *Today, I have perfected for you your religion, and I have bestowed upon you the full measure of My favour, and willed that Islam shall be your religion.*[B] And He said: *Behold, the only true religion in the sight of God is Islam!*[C] Moreover, religion is what the world was created for. *Nor have I created the jinn and humankind except to worship Me.*[D]

But for Abū Ḥāmid and his contemporaries, religion was not a simple matter; it required accomplishment, intellectual accomplishment first of all, and then spiritual accomplishment. Neither of these was to be attained easily. Indeed, the sheer numbers of those who set out on the path of attainment in those days were considerable. Owing to the patronage of the Emirs and princes, the incentives for success in the colleges were also considerable; and competition for spaces, for both students and faculty, was high. It is clear from his biography that Abū Ḥāmid knew this as well as or better than anyone else. Likewise, within the Sufi orders, and

[A] See below p. 76.
[B] Q.v.3.
[C] Q.iii.19.
[D] Q.li.56.

within the inner circles of the Sufi masters, the numbers of highly accomplished aspirants (*murīdūn*) were equally considerable.

To return to the passage, Abū Ḥāmid followed his opening remark by stating, 'If all of humankind were to involve themselves with it [exclusively], all order would fail and the world would be destroyed. This would be to seek the great domain of the next world. Likewise, if all people were to seek the domain of the present life and forsake all the humble professions and lowly industries, the world-order would fail. Then, with the failure of that order, the domain will fail also.' Abū Ḥāmid understood very well that the world had its place in the order of things. It was not a very nice place, perhaps, but it served a purpose... as did those who maintained its natural order, from simple farmers and labourers to privileged elites, mercenaries and tyrants. Everyone played a part. For the world was the platform from which the true servants of God, the accomplished ones, sallied forth in devotion to Him. Moreover, in the same way that the world order requires the humblest of professions in order to remain operative, the order of the Hereafter requires the presence of the temporal world. Indeed, it might be supposed that the Almighty would be satisfied with the worship of the angels alone; but He Himself refuted that assumption. *And lo! Your Lord said to the angels: 'Behold, I am going to establish on earth a vicegerent! They [the angels] said, 'Will You place on it those who will corrupt it? and shed blood? While we praise You in thanksgiving and sanctify You?' He answered, 'Surely, I know that which you know not!'*[A]

When the purpose of creation is worship, and it is God's will that He be worshipped by humans on earth, Abū Ḥāmid goes further and states, 'Thus, the peoples of the professions have been reconciled to their professions so that the domain [of the present life] may fall into order for the rulers.' In other words, if God is to be worshipped on earth, there must be order; and for there to be order, there must be rulers. The people who, by means of their

[A] Q.II.30.

toil and labour, perform the tasks that make the system work, they too are essential for that order. Moreover, in Abū Ḥāmid's view, the Almighty caused such people to be content with their lot in life: 'Likewise, those who seek the world have been reconciled to their quest so that the way of religion remains open to the people of religion; religion being the domain of the Afterlife.' And he concludes the argument thus: 'Were it not for this kind of reconciliation there would be no religion for the people of religion. Thus, the condition for the well being of their religion is that the rest of the people neglect it and concern themselves instead with worldly matters. All of this, of course, is an allocation (*qisma*) that has been determined by the divine will. This is what is alluded to in the verse: *We have divided among them their livelihood in the life of this world, and we have elevated some of them over others in degrees.*'

In short, to Abū Ḥāmid's way of thinking, the Sufi retreats were among the most important of all human institutions. Indeed, if the Almighty is to be worshipped in the most perfect manner, that worship is to be undertaken by the most perfect humans. Human life being what it is, a certain order must be maintained in the world so that the most perfect ones may engage in their devotions. That order must accommodate every sort of human necessity. Consider, for example, what the author writes in Chapter Five of this volume: 'Furthermore, while there is no religious matter that depends on the knowledge of a doctor, physical health does, and religion follows the body. Therefore, it is clearly in the interests of the Muslim public that the treasury should also support medical practitioners and all those whose professions are similarly required for the maintenance of health and society.'[A]

So the professions, from the most humble to the most advanced, are given to those who have reconciled themselves to them. By this logic, the maintenance of order is given to those who are capable of maintaining it. Then, while it is not necessary

[A] See below p. 193.

to approve of their methods, it is clear that the early generations of Muslims grew accustomed to tolerating their excesses.

In one of the most famous and widely-discussed passages authored by Abū Ḥāmid, also from this volume, he writes: 'The conditions to be satisfied and the attributes to be possessed by a ruler lead to the expectation that he will rule in the interests of the public. If we rule today that his authority is illegitimate, the interests of the public will immediately be compromised. So why squander one's capital in pursuit of profit? Authority nowadays depends on nothing other than power (*shawka*). Thus, whoever receives the allegiance and support of the powerful becomes the Caliph. And whoever is himself powerful and is loyal to the Caliph by giving the Friday sermon (*khuṭba*) and minting coins in his name will be deemed a legitimate ruler whose judgment and government will have the force of law throughout the land.'[A]

Nor was Abū Ḥāmid's position on this matter anything out of the ordinary. For, indeed, the classical *muḥaddithūn* and jurists were in general agreement on this point. 'The kingdom, then, or the state is evil; but it is a necessary evil whose status in the matter is that of the laws of nature... While it is correct that they did not join the ᶜAbbasid reign at the time, they did not [seek to] remove the veil of its legitimacy either...'[B]

In explaining all of this my intention is simply to show how, for the author, the Sufi retreats were so important. It was for that reason that he included this volume in his magnum opus, *The Revival of Religious Sciences*. Even so, and regardless of the author's worldview, and regardless of his immediate intentions in writing the book, the fact remains that, by virtue of its *fiqh*, the book is of significant relevance to Muslims in the modern world, particularly in view of the revival of Sharīᶜa-based and Sharīᶜa-compliant finance.

At the core of Islamic finance are the religious precepts governing what is good and permitted, or lawful, and what is harmful

[A] See below p. 196.

[B] Riḍwān al-Sayyid, *al-Umma wa'l-jamāᶜ wa'l-sulṭa*, pp. 168-170.

and forbidden, or unlawful. The Sharīʿa may be said to govern every aspect of a Muslim's life. It is also concerned with social justice. In the marketplace, the role of the Sharīʿa is a prominent one because the business of earning a living is one that concerns everyone, as individuals, as groups within society, and as citizens of nations and the world. The logic of Islamic teachings on the subject is that when people earn their livings in a wholesome and lawful manner, everyone will benefit. There is no end to the examples that might be used to illustrate how, when even a small portion of society earns its living by harmful and unwholesome means, the impact on the rest of society is negative in the extreme. While the specific economic environment may differ from one society to another, and during different historical periods, the principles articulated by the Qur'ān and the *Sunna* are of universal relevance. The Qur'ān exhorts Muslims to: *Partake of the good things and work righteousness.*[A]

In this verse, 'the good things' refer to all things that are lawful. In many verses of the Qur'ān, Muslims are urged to avoid partaking of what is unlawful, whether in the form of earnings, or food, or relationships, or social activities. In the Qur'ān there are many verses that caution the faithful against what is impure, evil, or inherently detrimental. In fact, the Qur'ān describes the message of Islam to the believers as one that: *...makes lawful to them the good things and forbids the impure.*[B]

Following the example of the Messenger of God (may God bless him and grant him peace everlasting) who was himself an honest and successful trader, Muslims have always turned to the marketplace for their livelihood. Through their trade and commerce in the Middle Ages, Muslims spread over the continents of Asia and Africa and into Europe, bringing with them their religion and their culture. From the earliest days of the expansion of Islam to the present day, Muslim businesses have been models of

[A] Q. XXIII.51.
[B] Q.VII.157.

success and integrity. In today's world, with its capital markets orientation, Muslims are beginning anew to assert their growing economic independence and strength, as well as their particular religious and cultural identities, through doing business in a Sharīʿa-compliant manner. Indeed, by means of business transacted in this way, Muslims offer their business partners and clients worldwide a glimpse of what is best about Islam.

Even so, there are Muslims in the world today who harbour misgivings on the subject of such finance in the modern world. These misgivings are attributable in many ways to the centuries of stagnation endured by Islamic institutions in the Muslim world. Indeed, if it is true that Islamic jurisprudence has not kept abreast of developments in the modern world, it is because in order to do so it needed to be involved in the day-to-day workings of society. This provides us with another perspective on how Islamic jurisprudence is a 'shared endeavour'. Thus, during the centuries in which Islam's political, legal, educational, charitable, financial, social and economic institutions were marginalized by colonial and other powers, it is not surprising that *fiqh*, with no place to apply its dynamic of *ijtihād*, was relegated to a long confinement in exclusively academic settings. Moreover, in order for it to break out of the confines of academia, it required practitioners who were not only conversant with the classical discipline but, in addition, cognizant and appreciative of the changes the world had undergone in the intervening centuries. It also required a subject on which it might focus its attention.

Then, if there is a success story to be associated with the revival of *fiqh* in modern times, that story will certainly include mention of Islamic Finance. From little more than a concept in the first decades after most Muslim countries regained their independence following the Second World War, Islamic Finance took the form of Islamic banks and investment houses in the seventies and eighties, and a growing body of scholarship was generated by the practical needs of those institutions as they began to proliferate. Then, as deposits accumulated, and demands for product diversity grew more insistent, especially when Islamic institutional investors became involved in the new market, *fiqh* and its new practitioners had no alternative but to rise to the challenge. Indeed, without Sharīʿa expertise the banks would never have acquired the sophistication required to become both feasible and profitable. In other words, without the assistance of qualified and informed Sharīʿa scholarship, our modern Islamic banks, funds, home finance companies, *takāful* companies and investment houses would never have achieved compliance with the regulations in the various financial jurisdictions in which they operate while, at the same time, complying with Sharīʿa principles and precepts.[A] Even so, the misgivings remain.

Many Muslims today have simply decided for themselves that modern finance and the economies of the modern world are based on interest and thus incompatible with, and inimical to, anything Islamic. Interest, they point out, is so pervasive in modern society that it is to be found on one's utility bills. Adjustments in the prime rate or LIBOR warrant immediate coverage in the media worldwide! Then, to these Muslims, there is no point in even attempting to transact in ways that accord with the Sharīʿa. Even if it were possible to do so (and they suppose it not to be possible), the attempt to do so would be counterproductive because it would run outside of accepted norms and could potentially spell ruin for the entire system! When pressed to cite evidence in favour of their opinions, such people generally mention either legal necessity (*ḍarūra*), or the legal principle that grants license under extraordinary and all-enveloping circumstances (*ʿumūm al-balwā*). Abū Ḥāmid would term all such thought as delusional and extremist in nature. 'They suppose that all the wealth in the world is unlawful, and so they extend their involvement without even trying to distinguish

A See my introductions to vols. I and II of my *Compendium of Legal Opinions on the Operations of Islamic Banks*.

[between lawful and unlawful]. Obviously, this is precisely what delusion is.'[A]

Today, too, there are those who resist Islamic Finance because it is not based on a general theory of Islamic Finance, claiming instead that it is merely a patchwork of disparate and uncoordinated initiatives. These critics are often connected in one manner or another with academia and the social sciences; and to their way of thinking Islamic jurisprudence is little more than a footnote in the history of thought. Even if Islamic jurisprudence did have relevance for the modern world, it would only be from the standpoint of its methodologies. Eager to 'Islamize' everything from modern Muslim thought to grade school curricula, they appear reluctant to transact in accordance with Sharīʿa norms until the ideas and principles behind that transacting have been articulated in the language of the modern academy, and propounded in the form of a comprehensive theory based on a scientific definition! Then, even if it takes these academics another fifty years to agree on such a definition, much less a general theory, they will prefer to observe (which means to criticize!) rather than to participate in the practical development of Islamic Finance. Abū Ḥāmid likened people with such an attitude to those (*muwaswisūn*) whose suspicious natures cause them to be ever doubtful about everything, including their own ritual purity. 'In the same way, people with unfounded suspicions regarding purity (*ṭahāra*) will often neglect it entirely. The same thing is true of people with unfounded suspicions regarding what is lawful.'[B]

Another group of modern Muslims insists that Islamic Finance is entirely incompatible with modern financial and economic systems, especially capitalism, and that true Islamic Finance means a return to the golden ages of Islam and the 'Islamic Dirham'! One wonders how, in the face of the mercantile tradition established by the Messenger of God (may God bless him and grant

[A] See below p. 85.
[B] *Ibid.*

him peace) and his Companions, anyone making a serious call to Islam could suppose that the concepts of investing capital, of having professionals manage those investments, of free and open markets, of transparency and accountability...how any of these concepts could possibly be at odds with Islam? If their purpose is to urge Muslims to achieve economic independence, then that is surely admirable. But if, in doing so, they alienate Muslims to the extent that they refuse to have any dealings in what they consider a corrupt financial system, then they are doing themselves and others a grave disservice. Islamic Finance, by working within the system and still maintaining its own integrity, thereby operating on its own terms (e.g., free of *ribā*, free of *gharar*, etc.), has much to contribute in the long run, and even in the short term, for the reform of the present, interest-based system of finance prevalent in the world today. Given the level of professionalism among practitioners of Islamic Finance at the present time, it may be expected that the new sector will soon begin to extend its influence to all those who recognize sound economics and prudent business practices, regardless of their religious or cultural orientations.

Moreover, the call for a return to any sort of 'Islamic' currency betrays a profound lack of appreciation for Sharīʿa principles regarding currency. For indeed, whether a dinar, or a dirham, or a dollar, the important thing from a Sharīʿa perspective is that currency be understood as no more than a means to an end, and not an end in itself. Money, in other words, is not a commodity; it cannot be marked up, or rented out, or even bartered at a higher price. It is a medium of exchange and a measure of value only. The Sharīʿa categorizations of exchange (*ṣarf*) are thus intrinsically tied to the prohibition of *ribā*.

It must be admitted, however, that the global economy, based as it is on both *ribā* and the fractional reserve banking system, is far removed from the prudent, value-based system envisioned by Islam.

Finally, the modern apologists for the Islamic Dirham appear not to have any sort of reasoned approach for the accomplishment of their goal. So, in calling for a return to that currency, they urge Muslims to do the impossible! In this, they resemble those described by Abū Ḥāmid in the following terms, 'If they find something to be difficult, they simply abandon it.'[A] The result, if one were to combine all of the misgivings described here, would be that Muslims would have to keep their money in mattresses... which is, in itself, in contravention of Sharīʿa precepts requiring that money be kept in circulation for the good of society! Abū Ḥāmid wrote, 'The Messenger of God (may God grant him peace and blessings) said, "Extremists will come to ruin." Beware, then, of such exaggeration because while it may not be harmful to you, it may give others the impression that it is important. Indeed, when others find themselves incapable of such prudence, they may abandon prudence altogether. In our own times, this is the way of most people. If they find something to be difficult, they simply abandon it. In the same way, people with unfounded suspicions regarding purity (*ṭahāra*) will often neglect it entirely. The same thing is true of people with unfounded suspicions regarding what is lawful. They suppose that all the wealth in the world is unlawful, and so they extend their involvement without even trying to distinguish [between lawful and unlawful]. Obviously, this is precisely what delusion is.'[B]

Then, while it is clear that Abū Ḥāmid was indeed a keen observer of the human condition, what may be said of the relevance of this present work to modern Islamic Finance? How is the jurisprudence of Ghazālī of value in the present?

Let us begin by examining what Abū Ḥāmid had to say about one of the most fundamental and indeed essential elements in modern Islamic Finance, the Sharīʿa Supervisory Board. Unless a business has qualified Sharīʿa supervision, it has no way of

[A] *Ibid.*
[B] *Ibid.*

certifying to the public that its services, products and operations are actually Sharīʿa-compliant. Moreover, by assuming responsibility for the Sharīʿa compliance of a financial institution or for what it offers, Sharīʿa supervision places itself in a position of directly representing the religious interests of the Muslim investor or consumer; and by making every possible effort to ensure that an Islamic financial product is lawful (*ḥalāl*), the services performed by Sharīʿa supervisors are directed toward the investor, or consumer. Undoubtedly, as a result of these efforts, financial institutions and their management will derive benefits. But certainly the primary beneficiary is the Muslim consumer who can rest assured that his/her money is being put to use in ways that accord with the teachings of Islam. It is for this reason that Sharīʿa supervision may also be characterized as consumer advocacy.[A]

In regard to the need for such scrutiny in financial matters, Abū Ḥāmid has included an entire chapter in this volume, Chapter Three 'On Scrutiny and Enquiry or Silence and Disregard and their Indications'. With regard to its relevance to the modern institution of the Sharīʿa Supervisory Board, consider the following passage from that chapter. 'When you know that someone's wealth is intermixed with the unlawful, and that person has some ulterior motive in having you attend his function, or accept his gift, his word is not to be trusted and there is no point in questioning him. In such a case, you should inquire of another [about him]. The same will be true if the person is trying to sell you something so as to realize a profit. His word is not to be trusted, so there is no point in questioning him [about whether or not what he intends to sell to you is lawful]. Instead, you should question another [about him, or about the product he is offering].'[B]

This passage is of particular relevance to the products offered by conventional financial institutions through their 'Islamic

[A] DeLorenzo, 'Shariah Supervision in Modern Islamic Finance,' *ABANA Review*, 2002, vol. XIX, no. 2.

[B] See below p. 136.

windows', but is certainly inclusive of all products and services that claim to be compliant with Sharīʿa norms, regardless of who, or what institution, is offering them. The point here is not necessarily that such institutions are not to be trusted, but that in regard to matters of Sharīʿa-compliance it is necessary to have specialized experts perform that task. Sharīʿa Board Certification, generally documented in a formal *fatwā* (Sharīʿa position paper), may be thought of as a form of due diligence. In effect, the Sharīʿa supervisor, or supervisory board, performs this due diligence on behalf of consumers who are without access to the details of what is offered to them and, likewise, without the experience or qualifications to evaluate those details in light of Sharīʿa teachings. When a company offers such certification, it should be clear to Muslim consumers and/or investors that the company takes the matter of compliance seriously; and its submitting to the certification process, much like an audit, should be understood as another level of transparency.

Another of the most essential elements of modern Islamic Finance is purification, or the concept of segregating or cleansing impure wealth from wealth that is pure, like purifying tainted earnings from an investment portfolio. Chapter Four, entitled 'Extricating the Repentant from Financial Iniquity', deals specifically with problems of this nature. Not only does the author deal with the question of segregating the unlawful, he also discusses in great detail the matter of how to dispose of such wealth, including discussions of whether it might be given to one's family, or parents, or to charity. But, to return to the matter of segregating the unlawful portion, there are a number of issues regarding purification in modern Islamic Finance that remain open to debate and discussion, including whether or not non-permissible earnings from a publicly-traded company should be purified if the investor does not receive dividends. And whether or not capital gains on shares in companies in which a small percentage of revenues come from non-permissible sources should be purified and, if so, to what degree?[A] Abū Ḥāmid's discussion of preponderant opinion and legal presumption in this chapter provides a framework for further consideration of these questions. Indeed, here Abū Ḥāmid may truly be seen to be in his element, as he advances an opinion, then questions himself, answers his questions, objects to his answers and then moves on to new questions!

A further issue of importance, and one that Abū Ḥāmid deals with at length in Chapter Two, is that of commingling or, as I translate it in the book, intermixture (*ikhtilāṭ*). In the modern world, the transaction of business, even by the most prudent practitioners, will sometimes involve contact with unlawful earnings or practices. For example, regulators in most jurisdictions will consider it a breach of fiscal responsibility if a publicly-owned company holds cash for any length of time without at least collecting interest on it because, by neglecting such interest earnings, the officers of the company have squandered an opportunity to earn for the shareholders. Then, if the company's primary business is acceptable from a Sharīʿa standpoint, like healthcare, or telecommunications, or information technology, and its revenues from those sources are lawful, Muslim investors may purchase and hold shares in that company. But what of the tiny percentages of earnings from cash held in interest-bearing accounts and instruments? Will such earnings disqualify the company from consideration by a Muslim investor? The same questions may arise in regard to corporate debt. However, in considering all of these matters, Muslim jurists have a rich heritage of jurisprudence to which they may refer. Chapter Two, 'The Degrees of the Dubious, its Causes and How it is Distinguished from the Lawful and the Unlawful', provides one of the most exhaustive and informative studies of the matter of intermixing. Ghazālī looks at intermixing from a number of different angles and, in doing so, clarifies many matters related to modern finance. Of course, while the true value of Abū

[A] Dr. Mohammed Elgari, 'Islamic Equity Investing' in Archer and Abdel Karim, *Islamic Finance: Innovation and Growth* (London, 2003) p. 157.

Ḥāmid's work is in his discussions of legal principles, the modern jurist cannot fail to appreciate his indirect contributions to the realities of modern Islamic Finance.

Before closing this discussion, it will be appropriate to mention Abū Ḥāmid's thinking on another matter of significance for modern Sharīʿa scholarship as it relates to Islamic Finance; even though this is taken from another of his works. Abū Ḥāmid wrote, 'I do not consider *ijtihād* to be a level of scholarship that excludes specialization (lit. 'that is beyond division'). On the contrary, a scholar may be said to have attained the level of *ijtihād* in certain areas of the law, but not in others. Then, those who have mastered the methods of legal analogy may perform *ijtihād* in regard to issues involving legal analogy, even if they are not authorities on the subject of *ḥadīth*. Likewise, it will suffice for a scholar who considers the issue of joint inheritance to be a competent jurist (*faqīh al-nafs*) who is learned in the jurisprudence of inheritance and its meanings, even though he has not memorized all the reports narrated concerning the prohibition of intoxicants, or the issue of marriage without a guardian. This is because the issue [he is concerned with] has nothing to gain from these [narrations], as they have no relevance to it. Thus, how can one's lack of knowledge in regard to these, or one's superficial knowledge, be considered a shortcoming?'[A]

This opinion is especially important for the development of Islamic Finance because without *ijtihād*, the process of judicial lawmaking that allows Sharīʿa to remain relevant under changing circumstances, Islamic Finance would never be able to advance or develop. Obviously, without the ability to adjust, Islamic Finance would be unable to keep up with its competitors. Therefore, it is of the utmost importance to Islamic Finance to have the support of informed and expert Sharīʿa scholarship. In today's world of specialization, it is near to impossible to expect that any other than a Sharīʿa scholar who has specialized in the study of finance,

[A] *Al-Mustaṣfā min ʿilm al-uṣūl*, p. 345.

or economics, could be capable of more than token assistance in the development of complex financial instruments and structures. Indeed, as the industry itself grows increasingly more specialized, it would be very restrictive if Sharīʿa experts were required to be anything but specialists themselves. Of course, the other way that Islamic Finance meets these challenges is by employing the collective skills and expertise of a group of Sharīʿa scholars in the form of a Sharīʿa Supervisory Board (SSB); and this has now become the accepted industry standard.[A]

The Book of the Lawful and the Unlawful

The *Iḥyā'* consists of four quarters, each of which is made up of ten books. The first quarter is the Acts of Worship (*ʿibādāt*), the second is the Norms of Daily Life (*ʿādāt*), the third quarter is the Mortal Vices (*muhlikāt*) and the fourth quarter is the Saving Virtues (*munjīyāt*). Thus the *Iḥyā'* is forty sections, each called a *kitāb* (literally, a book), and each able to stand on its own.

The book at hand, *Kitāb al-ḥalāl wa'l-ḥarām*, is the fourth book of the quarter of the Norms of Daily Life, or the fourteenth book of the whole *Iḥyā'*. As a subject, the lawful and the unlawful in Islam is generally a part of traditional *fiqh* manuals that are divided topically; for example, marriage and the legal aspects of who one may marry and what is required and so forth. In contrast to this, Ghazālī organized his work by discussing the theory of what is lawful and what is unlawful, then relating topics to this, thereby comprehensively approaching the subject in a subtle yet noticeably different way.

Ghazālī begins the *Book of the Lawful and the Unlawful* with a key theme, that of balance and moderation: it can be extremely

[A] According to the standards set by AAOIFI (Auditing and Accounting Organization of Islamic Financial Institutions), a business offering Sharīʿa-compliant products and/or services must have a Sharīʿa Supervisory Board of at least three members.

difficult to establish what is lawful or be satisfied with what one can be absolutely certain is lawful, but the difficulties of this undertaking do not justify unlawful transactions. Rather one must strive to attain the knowledge necessary to enable him to distinguish the lawful from the unlawful. The Book is made up of seven chapters:

Chapter One: *On the Excellence of the Lawful and the Reprehensibility of the Unlawful with an Exposition of the Kinds of Lawful and their Rankings and of the Categories of Unlawful and the Degrees of Caution Exercised in Relation to These*
Ghazālī explains at the outset of Chapter One the virtues of lawful transactions and the iniquities of unlawful transactions by citing numerous verses from the Qur'ān and narrations from the *Sunna*. This is followed by examples of the Companions, the Successor generations and the pious Predecessors.

Ghazālī carefully lists the categories of the lawful and the unlawful, then further divides unlawful wealth based on what causes it to be unlawful: something may be unlawful because of its substance or because of the method by which it was acquired. He then examines and defines the idea of prudence (*waraʿ*) in all aspects of one's life and explains the degrees of prudence. In emphasising its importance, Ghazālī cautions the reader, saying, 'Now, if you have understood the truth of this matter, you have a choice; if you like, be as cautious [or prudent] as you possibly can; and if you like, use license with yourself. But remember, it is for yourself that you are wary; and it is against yourself that you use license.'

Chapter Two: *The Degrees of the Dubious, Its Causes and How it is Distinguished from the Lawful and the Unlawful*
Chapter Two begins with an explanation of the meaning of the *ḥadīth* that the lawful and the unlawful are self-evident while between the two is a category known as the dubious. It is this middle category, says Ghazālī, that is most difficult to discern; it

is occasioned by four factors, each with subcategories. The first factor occasioning it is doubt concerning legitimising and prohibiting factors. This factor may be sub-divided into four categories. Abū Ḥāmid explains each of these in detail, making use of examples and legal principles including the presumption of the continued existence of a known state (*istiṣḥāb al-ḥāl*). The second factor that can cause doubt is intermixture, which Ghazālī divides into three categories. Here, Ghazālī makes a persuasive and important argument, namely, that even if we were to suppose a time in which the greater part of all wealth were to be unlawful, it would still be lawful to partake of it. In his explanation of the third factor occasioning doubt, when a legitimising factor is compromised by sin, Ghazālī discusses the three degrees of legal disapproval, after which he cautions that most people should refrain from the subtleties of prudence unless they do so under the guidance of an accomplished scholar. The fourth and final factor is that of contradictory indicators and it is sub-divided into three categories: when indicators conflict with one another, when signs in the indicators are contradictory, and when appearances are contradictory. In explaining the third of these categories, Ghazālī discusses the importance of one's heart of hearts in deciding about these matters, explaining that, 'the sort of heart that can be relied on is the heart of certainty that regards attentively the subtleties of one's [spiritual] state and acts as a touchstone that tests what is normally hidden. How precious is such a heart among hearts! Then, those who cannot fully trust their own hearts, let them seek the light from a heart in possession of these attributes. To such a heart they may relate their experiences.'

Chapter Three: *On Scrutiny and Inquiry or Silence and Disregard and their Indications*

Ghazālī opens this chapter by declaring that people are not at liberty to question anyone who offers them something, whether for sale, or as a gift, or for whatever purpose. Nor may people neglect to scrutinise what they are offered, though there are occasions on which such scrutiny is disapproved. He then explains that it is the element of doubt that leads to questioning; and doubt may arise either as a result of the circumstances of the possessor, or as a result of the possession itself. The circumstances of the possessor are three, while the circumstances of the possession itself once again centre on the subject of intermixture of the lawful and the unlawful. Throughout the chapter, Abū Ḥāmid presents examples in illustration of the points he wishes to clarify. He closes the chapter with a series of questions and answers that bring further clarity to the principles and precepts articulated at the outset.

Chapter Four: *Extricating the Repentant from Financial Iniquity*
This chapter consists of two parts: the first concerns the segregation and removal of what is unlawful from what is lawful; and the second concerns what is to be done with the part that is unlawful. Here, too, the matter of intermixture is considered yet again, as it is not always a simple matter to separate the lawful from the unlawful. Moreover, in the absence of certainty, varying degrees of prudence are required. Ghazālī explains all of these matters in detail, finishing his exposition with a series of practical examples.

Chapter Five: *Grants and Gifts made by Rulers and which of these may be Considered Lawful and which Unlawful*
The acceptance of gifts from rulers requires that the recipient ascertain the provenance of such largesse. Ghazālī explains that a ruler's wealth may originate with the believers or the disbelievers; he then discusses in some detail the eight different sources of this wealth. Following this, he explains that those who allow the acceptance of gifts from the wealth of rulers when these are composed of both the lawful and the unlawful—and when it is known that the gift itself is not unlawful—do so on the basis that it is impossible to establish whether the gift came from lawful or unlawful funds. Thereafter, Ghazālī turns to the example set by the early generations of Muslims in this regard, citing example after example of pious Muslims who accepted gifts from rulers.

Abū Ḥāmid further explains that the instances of refusal recorded in history were based on prudence. Following this, Abū Ḥāmid defines four degrees of prudence in regard to rulers; and for each degree he gives examples from recorded history. Ghazālī concludes the matter with a discussion of how gifts given by tyrants in his own times differ fundamentally from those given in the early days of Islam. At the end of the chapter, Abū Ḥāmid deals with a further consideration: the quantity of what is accepted and the attributes of those who accept it. This involves an important discussion of public welfare and those deserving of support from those who govern, as well as an examination of authority, injustice and the distribution of funds among the deserving.

Chapter Six: *What is Lawful in Regard to Socialising with Despotic Rulers and Others; and the Categorisation of Attendance at their Courts, of Calling on them and of Showing them Respect*
Chapter Six continues the subject of the previous chapter, and examines in further detail one's relations with rulers. While it is lawful in many cases to receive gifts from rulers, the aspect of sin may arise when the recipients begin to serve the ruler, or to assist him, or to regularly visit him, or to praise him in his presence, or to do the kinds of things that are usually required of those who expect to receive gifts from rulers. Briefly, there are three possible relationships one could have with rulers. The first relationship is one's visiting rulers; and here Ghazālī cites several *ḥadīth* and reports to show the dangers of such a relationship, and follows this with a legal discussion of how the prohibited in this regard may be distinguished from the disapproved and merely permissible. Abū Ḥāmid explains that one who associates with rulers is in danger of sinning either by means of deeds, or words, or silence. The second possible relationship is that of one's receiving a visit from a ruler; Ghazālī clarifies the responsibilities of the visited in such an instance, and cites the examples of the pious in this regard. The third possible relationship is avoidance; here Abū Ḥāmid cites several examples of how the early generations of Muslims managed

to avoid contact with unjust rulers. Before closing the chapter, however, Ghazālī discusses the difference between scholars of this world and scholars of the next and explains how foolish scholars are particularly susceptible to two fallacies of self-deception. The chapter closes with a discussion of seven issues related to the subject of receiving, and dealing with, wealth from rulers.

Chapter Seven: *A Variety of Issues of Such Importance that Questions Concerning them are Asked in the* Fatwā *Literature*
In this chapter, Ghazālī records four questions and his legal edicts (*fatāwā*) to the same. Each of these is related to lawful and unlawful wealth; the first three concern the inhabitants of Sufi retreats, and the fourth question deals with the matter of bribes and seeks to identify the difference between a gift and a bribe when both are motivated by a desire to attain or to acquire something from the recipient. Ghazālī's response includes a list of five purposes one may have in spending money.

Note on Legal Terms

The reader will note that throughout this work, the translator uses the specific legal terminology developed by the classical jurists of Islam to categorize the acts of humans. Such Sharīʿa categorizations (*aḥkām sharʿiyya*) are five in number and pertain to the values placed on the acts of humans by the Sharīʿa. These are obligatory (*wājib*), recommended (*mandūb*), permitted (*mubāḥ*), disapproved (*makrūh*), and forbidden (*maḥẓūr*).

The difference between obligatory and recommended acts is that obligatory acts are peremptory under the Sharīʿa and recommended acts are non-peremptory. The same applies to the difference between acts that are disapproved of by the Sharīʿa and acts that are forbidden; the first are non-peremptory and the second peremptory. Finally, when the Sharīʿa allows a choice in the matter of performance or non-performance of an act, then it is 'permitted' (*mubāḥ*) in a neutral sense.

The reader will note that at times the translations of these terms will be preceded by the qualifying term 'legally' so as to clarify and emphasize the nature of the terminology. However, to prevent excessive repetition, the terms are mostly given without the qualifier and readers should familiarize themselves with the terms and understand that they are used with a specific purpose.

Editions of the Iḥyā'

There are hundreds of manuscript copies of the *Iḥyā'*. Badawī, in his work *Mu'allafāt al-Ghazālī* attempts to list all of these, thereby highlighting the fact that there is not a centre of learning, a capital, or a country of the Muslim world that does not have manuscript copies of the *Iḥyā'*. With the diffusion of printing technology, editions of the book have increased. It is studied by scholars and students alike; its wisdom has been also summarized and its material reworked by every generation since Ghazālī's time. The *Iḥyā'* has been translated into all the primary languages of the Muslim world, in many cases more than once. It has also been summarised and condensed countless times over the centuries. Although Ghazālī wrote many other successful works in almost all fields of Islamic knowledge, including philosophy and logic, the *Iḥyā'* remains his most pertinent and lasting work, his magnum opus. To state that Ghazālī is one of the most studied personalities of the Muslim world, second only to the Prophet (may God bless him and grant him peace), is not an exaggeration, but a fact.

The *Iḥyā'* has been reprinted in countless editions since the earliest printing by Būlāq (Amīriyya) in Cairo in 1269/1853. In 1957, an edition by ʿĪsā al-Bābī al-Ḥalabī (known as the Ṭabana edition) became the definitive edition; it is the most accurate and popular edition to date and has been reprinted in facsimile by scholarly publishers throughout the Muslim world.

The translation of this work is based on the following published texts: (1) The Amīriyya edition of 1289/1894 that is printed in the margins of al-Zabīdī's commentary, *Ithāf al-sāda al-muttaqīn*, abbreviated A. (2) The text of the *Iḥyā'* as reproduced in the commentary itself, also from the Amīriyya edition of 1289/1894, abbreviated Z. (3) The text in the Dār al-Arqām edition of 1419/1998, edited by Dr. ʿAbd Allāh al-Khālidī; he has taken certain liberties with the text (as explained in his introduction to the same[A]) and this has resulted in the omission of entire passages at several places in the text of the volume. This work is abbreviated D. (4) The Beirut edition of book fourteen of the *Iḥyā'*, published by Dār al-Kutub al-ʿIlmiyya in 1414/1993 is abbreviated B. No editor is named. The edition carries the *takhrīj* (or *ḥadīth* verification) of al-Ḥāfiẓ Zayn al-Dīn al-ʿIrāqī as footnotes.

Brackets are used throughout the translation to indicate the original Arabic in instances in which the specialist reader may appreciate such indications. In some cases, these are used when the text requires explanation. I have chosen to use my own translations of Qur'ānic texts; in these, however, I have attempted to convey the meanings perceived by the author, who cited the texts for one purpose or another in the course of his work. Readers will also notice that care has been taken to trace all references to issues with legal significance to their sources in the corpus of the classical *fiqh* literature. Certain key issues of import have been researched rather more exhaustively than others; and in such cases, care has been taken to refer to the opinions of each of the major Sunni schools of jurisprudence. Finally, references by the author to matters unrelated to the sciences of *fiqh* or *ḥadīth* have also been carefully traced to their sources in works of history or literature. In regard to this last category, however, success has

[A] See ʿAbd Allāh al-Khālidī's Introduction to *Iḥyā' ʿulūm al-dīn* in which he explains, among other things, the need to 'liberate' the work from unreliable narrations!

not always been achieved. Readers who locate such references are encouraged to share their findings with the translator so that future editions may be more complete.

And it is God who causes us to prosper and assists! He Alone is our sufficiency!

THE BOOK OF THE LAWFUL AND THE UNLAWFUL

Being the Fourth Book of the Quarter of the Norms of Daily Life

[PROLOGUE]

In the name of God, Most Compassionate and Merciful

PRAISED BE GOD, who created every human being from dry and sticky clay; who fashioned humankind's appearance in the best of molds and proportioned it in the most complete way; who nourished humankind at the start of their development with milk, purified from waste and blood, like limpid water flowing; who then protected humankind, by means of pure provision, from all that occasions weakness and decline ongoing; who restrained their devious passions from ascendancy and domination; who subjected these [passions] to seek—as He required of humankind—for lawful preservation; and who defeated, by breaking these passions, the army of Satan ready for divagation. For indeed, Satan's intrigues run through the children of Adam as blood courses through their veins. Even so, it is the power of the lawful that restrains Satan's machinations and legerdemains; so that overriding and abandoned passion is all that remains to propel Satan to the most abysmal domains. Thus, when bridled with the reins of the lawful, Satan is rendered frustrated and woeful, with no one to accompany him or to be helpful.

May peace and many blessings be invoked upon Muḥammad, the Guide against deviations, and upon his Family, the Best of all Relations!

As to what follows: The Messenger of God (may God bless him and grant him peace) said, 'Seeking the lawful is the legal obligation (*farīḍa*) of every Muslim.'[1] This was related by Ibn Masʿūd (may God be pleased with him). Among all legal obligations, this obligation is the most difficult for peoples' minds to comprehend, and the most burdensome for their bodies to perform. It was for this reason that it disappeared completely, in theory and in practice; such that the obscurity of its knowledge became a reason for the disappearance of its practice. For the ignorant ones supposed that the lawful was forever lost, and that the road to its recovery had been blocked, and that the only pure things remaining are rainwater and grass that grows on unclaimed meadows. All else [they claim] has been spoiled by the hands of transgression and ruined by vitiated transactions. Then, since it is impossible to be satisfied with no more than grass, there is nothing left but for the prohibited to proliferate. So, they have abandoned this pivotal node of religion, and discern no distinction between wealth of one sort or another.

How ridiculous! Indeed, how ridiculous [is what they suppose]! For the lawful is self-evident. And the unlawful is self-evident. And between the two are matters that give rise to confusion. These three [categories] continue to apply regardless of how situations change. However, since the negative consequences of this negligence have spread throughout the religion, and since its sparks have drifted throughout creation, it has become necessary to expose the face of its corruption by explaining the differences between the lawful (*ḥalāl*), the unlawful (*ḥarām*), and the dubious (*shubha*) in a manner that verifies and clarifies. And, while there may be constraints, the task is not impossible. Thus, we shall explain all of this in the following seven chapters:

Chapter One: The Excellence of the Lawful[2] and the Reprehensibility of the Unlawful, and the Degrees of the Lawful and the Unlawful.[A]

Chapter Two: The Degrees of the Dubious, its Causes, and How it is Distinguished from the Lawful and the Unlawful.

Chapter Three: On Scrutiny and Inquiry, or Silence and Disregard, and where these may be appropriate in regard to the Lawful and the Unlawful.

Chapter Four: Extricating the Repentant from Financial Iniquity.

Chapter Five: Grants and Gifts made by Rulers and which of these may be Considered Lawful and which Unlawful.

Chapter Six: Socialising with Rulers and Mixing with Them.[3]

Chapter Seven: A Variety of Issues.[4]

[A] Some of the chapter headings given here vary slightly from how Ghazālī gives them in the text.

CHAPTER ONE

On the Excellence of the Lawful and the Reprehensibility of the Unlawful with an Exposition of the Kinds of Lawful and their Rankings and of the Categories of Unlawful and the Degrees of Caution Exercised in Relation to These

The Excellence of the Lawful and the Reprehensibility of the Unlawful

GOD (EXALTED IS HE!) has said, *Partake of the good things and work righteousness;*[1] such that He gave the command to consume good things before He commanded the working of righteousness. Furthermore, it is said that the meaning of 'good things' (*ṭayyibāt*) is the lawful.

God (Exalted is He!) also said, *And do not wrongfully appropriate one another's wealth,*[2] and He said, *Those who wrongfully appropriate the wealth of orphans appropriate fire in their stomachs.*[3]

God (Exalted is He!) also said, *O you who have faith! Heed God, and give up what remains of interest,*[4] and then He said, *If you do not, then take notice of war from God and His Messenger.*[5] He then said, *But if you repent, you may have [back] your principal [sums].*[6] And He said, *Those who revert, those are the companions of the Fire; those will abide therein forever.*[7]

Thus, the Almighty began by declaring war on those who consume interest (*ribā*), and finished by banishing them to the Fire.

There is no counting the number of verses revealed concerning the lawful and the unlawful in the Qur'ān.

Ibn Masᶜūd related that the Prophet (may God bless him and grant him peace) said, 'Seeking the lawful is the legal obligation of every Muslim.'[8]

In commenting on the *ḥadīth* [of the Messenger of God] (may God bless him and grant him peace) 'Seeking knowledge is the legal obligation of every Muslim,'[9] certain scholars said that the meaning was seeking knowledge of the lawful and the unlawful; so that the meaning of the two narrations is the same.

He (may God bless him and grant him peace) said, 'Whoever goes out and earns for his family in a lawful manner is like a soldier (*mujāhid*) in the path of God; and whoever seeks the worldly in a lawful manner, and with continence (*ᶜafāf*), shall attain the rank of the martyrs.'[10]

He (may God bless him and grant him peace) said, 'For whomsoever eats the lawful for forty consecutive days, God will enlighten his heart and cause fountains of wisdom in his heart to flow from his tongue.'[11]

In another version of the same narration, the wording is thus, 'God will make him yearn for the next world while he is still in this world.'[12]

It is related that Saᶜd [b. Abī Waqqāṣ] asked the Messenger of God (may God bless him and grant him peace) to request the Almighty to make him, Saᶜd, one whose every prayer is answered. He (may God bless him and grant him peace) replied to him, 'Ensure that what you consume is good, and your petitions will be answered.'[13]

In mentioning those greedy for the life of this world, he (may God bless him and grant him peace) said, 'Many an unkempt and dusty person, a wandering traveller whose provision is unlawful, whose clothing is unlawful, and who is sustained by the unlawful, will raise his hands and say, "Lord, O Lord!" Now, how can someone like that expect to have their prayer answered?'[14]

In a narration related by Ibn ᶜAbbās, the Prophet (may God

bless him and grant him peace) said, 'God has an angel at the Sacred Mosque in Bayt al-Maqdas [Jerusalem], who calls out every night, "Whoever consumes the unlawful will have neither deeds nor justice accepted."'[15] It is said that the meanings of 'deeds' and 'justice' are the superogatory (*nafl*) and obligatory (*farḍ*) categories of worship.

He (may God bless him and grant him peace) also said, 'Whoever buys a garment for ten dirhams, even one [dirham] of which is unlawful, will not have his prayers accepted by God for as long as he wears that garment.'[16]

He (may God bless him and grant him peace) said, 'Meat (from an animal) nourished by the unlawful, the Fire is more deserving of it!'[17]

He (may God bless him and grant him peace) said, 'Whoever cares nothing for where he earns his living, God will care nothing for where He throws him in the Fire.'[18]

He (may God bless him and grant him peace) said, 'Worship (*ʿibāda*) is made up of ten parts; nine of which concern seeking the lawful.'[19] There are versions of the same narration that attribute it to certain of the Companions.

He (may God bless him and grant him peace) said, 'Whoever sleeps exhausted because of his efforts to seek the lawful will awaken forgiven of his wrongdoing, and God will be pleased with him.'[20]

He (may God bless him and grant him peace) said, 'If one gains wealth through wrongdoing, and then uses it to improve family ties, or gifts it as charity, or spends it in the way of God; God will gather it together, and then He will throw it into the Fire.'[21]

He (may God grant him peace) said, 'The best of your religion is your fearing God (*waraʿ*).'[A22]

He (may God bless him and grant him peace) said, 'Whoever

[A] The term *waraʿ* has been translated here as 'fearing God' and elsewhere as 'prudence'. Its meaning is 'fearing God in everything one does' which explains the choice of 'prudence' and 'the prudent' (*wariʿūn*) where applicable.

meets God as a God-fearing person will be granted by God all the blessings of Islam.'[23]

It is related that God (Exalted is He!) has said in one of the books He revealed, 'As to the God-fearing (*wariʿūn*), I will be too embarrassed to take them to account.'[24]

He (may God bless him and grant him peace) said, 'A single dirham from interest (*ribā*) is more heinous to God than thirty instances of adultery in Islam.'[25]

In a narration related by Abū Hurayra (may God be pleased with him) it is said, 'The stomach is the watering place of the body, and the veins go down to it. Then, if the stomach is healthy, the veins carry health out from it; and if the stomach is ailing, the veins carry illness out from it.'[26]

The example of a morsel in Islam is as the foundation of a building. If the foundation is stable and secure, the building will stand. But if the foundation is weak, the building will sway and collapse. God (Exalted is He!) said, *Is he who lays his foundation on heeding God and His pleasure better than one who lays his foundation on a shifting sand dune, so that it crumbles with him into the Hellfire? God guides not the people who do wrong.*[27]

In a narration it is said, 'Whoever earns wealth from the unlawful and then gives it away in charity, will not have it accepted of him. And if he leaves it behind him, it will be his provision in the Fire.'[28]

Several other narrations, all of which illustrate the excellence of lawful earning, are mentioned in the book on *The Manners Relating to Earning*.[A]

As to the narrative examples [left by the Companions and the pious Predecessors]; it is related that al-Ṣiddīq [Abū Bakr] (may God be pleased with him) drank milk that his servant had earned, and then asked the servant how he had earned it. The servant replied, 'I did some soothsaying for a tribe, and this is what

[A] This is *Kitāb ādāb al-kasb wa'l-maʿāsh*, Book XIII of the *Revival of the Religious Sciences*.

they gave me in return.' Thereupon, he [Abū Bakr] put his fingers in his throat and forced himself to vomit until the narrator of this example, ʿĀ'isha, thought his life would go out of him. Afterwards he said, 'O Lord! I apologise to You for what was carried by the veins and was mixed in the stomach.'[29]

In some versions of this narrative, when [the Messenger of God] (may God bless him and grant him peace) was told of what had happened, he said, 'Didn't you know? Nothing goes into al-Ṣiddīq [Abū Bakr] unless it is good.'[30]

Likewise, by mistake, ʿUmar (may God be pleased with him) drank milk from a camel given in charity (*ṣadaqa*)[31] and then put his fingers down his throat and vomited.[A][32]

ʿĀ'isha (may God be pleased with her) said, 'Surely you neglect the most important form[33] of worship; fearing God.'[34]

ʿAbd Allāh b. ʿUmar (may God be pleased with him) said, 'If you were to pray for so long that your backs bent like bows, and if you were to fast for so long that you became as thin as bowstrings, none of that would be accepted of you unless you protected [yourselves by being] God-fearing.'[35]

Ibrāhīm b. Adham (may God have mercy on him) said, 'Those who attained [success] would never have attained [that success] had they not known what was going to go inside[B] of them.'[36]

Fuḍayl (may God have mercy on him) said, 'One who knows what is going to go inside of him will be considered by God righteous (*ṣiddīq*). Take care, then, as to those with whom you break your fasts!'[37]

Once, Ibrāhīm b. Adham (may God have mercy on him) was asked why he did not drink water brought from the well of Zamzam. 'I would,' he replied, 'if I had drawn it with my own bucket.'[38]

Sufyān al-Thawrī (may God be pleased with him) said, 'One

[A] The reason for ʿUmar's rejection of what is given in *ṣadaqa* is that *ṣadaqa* can be given as a form of purification for sins. .

[B] i.e., what they were consuming.

who spends unlawful earnings in acts of devotion to God is like one who attempts to purify an unclean garment with urine. An unclean garment may not be purified except by means of pure water, and wrongdoing may not be rectified except by means of the lawful.'

Yaḥyā b. Muᶜadh said, 'Devotion (*ṭāᶜa*) is a treasury from the treasuries of God. The key to that treasury is supplication (*duᶜā'*), and the teeth [of the key] are lawful morsels [of food].'

Ibn ᶜAbbās (may God be pleased with him) said, 'God will not accept the prayer of one in whose innards there is anything unlawful.'[39]

Sahl al-Tustarī said, 'A servant will not attain the reality of faith (*īmān*) until he possesses four qualities: performance of the obligatory duties in the manner prescribed by the *Sunna*, fearing God in consuming only the lawful, avoiding the prohibited both internally and externally, and persevering in these until death.'[40]

[Sahl] also said, 'One who would like to manifest the signs of the righteous (*ṣiddīqūn*) must not eat except that which is lawful, and must not act except in accordance with the *Sunna*, unless out of necessity.'[41]

It is said that anyone who eats what is dubious for forty days will cause his heart to grow dark. This is the explanation of the verse, *By no means! Rather, on their hearts is the stain of what they earn.*[42]

Ibn al-Mubārak said, 'To return a dirham of dubious origin is preferable to me over my gifting as charity a hundred thousand dirhams, and a hundred thousand thousand dirhams, and...' He continued until he had named a total of six hundred (thousand) dirhams.[43]

One of the Predecessors said, 'Sometimes it happens that a person will eat his meal and it will cause his heart to change so that it festers just as skin festers. After that, he is never the same again.'[44]

Sahl (may God be pleased with him) said, 'Whoever eats what is unlawful will find that his extremities disobey him, regardless of whether he wants them to or not, and regardless of whether he knows about it or not. Whoever eats the lawful will find that his extremities obey him, and that they engage in doing good.'[45]

One of the Predecessors said, 'The first lawful morsel eaten by a person causes his previous wrongdoings to be forgiven; and one who places himself in a position of insignificance, solely in order to be able to earn the lawful, his sins will fall away from him like the leaves of a tree [in autumn].'[46]

It is recorded from one of the Predecessors that, 'Whenever someone stood up to give advice to the people, and exhort them to do good, the learned would say, "Look for three things about him. Firstly, see if his beliefs are free of wrongful innovation (*bidʿa*). If not, then do not sit and listen to him, for he will speak with the tongue of Satan. Then see if his daily bread comes from the lawful; if not, he will speak his own desires. Lastly, see if his mind is disciplined. If it is not, his words will do more harm than good; so do not sit and listen to him."'[47]

A well-known saying attributed to ʿAlī (may God be pleased with him), and to others [of the Predecessors], is, 'The lawful of the world will have to be accounted for, and what is unlawful of the world will be punishable.' Certain others added, 'And the dubious of the world is met by reprimand.'[48]

It is related that a certain traveller[49] gave food to one of the spiritual masters who then refused to eat it. When the traveller questioned him as to why he had refused, the master replied, 'We eat nothing but what is lawful. That is why our hearts remain steadfast, and our spiritual states remain constant. And that is why we glimpse the Eternal, and witness the life of the Hereafter. If we were to partake of what you eat, even for three days, nothing would remain of our certain knowledge; and both the fear and the witnessing would go from our hearts.' Then the traveller said to him, 'But I fast every day, and I complete the recitation of the Qur'ān thirty times every month.' The master replied, 'This drink, the one I drink every night, is more important to me than thirty recitations of the Qur'ān in three hundred cycles (*rakʿa*) of your prayer.' His drink was the milk of a wild mountain goat.[50]

Aḥmad Ibn Ḥanbal and Yaḥyā b. Maᶜīn were friends for many years until, one day, Yaḥyā said, 'I would never ask anyone for anything. If [I were desperate and] Satan offered me something to eat, I'd take it [rather than beg].' Thereafter, Aḥmad refused to meet Yaḥyā, until Yaḥyā said he was sorry, explaining that he had only been joking. At that, Aḥmad replied, 'Do you joke about religion? Do you not know that eating is a part of religion that God has given precedence over good deeds?'[51] Then he recited the verse of the Qur'ān, *Eat of the good things and work righteousness.*[52]

There is a narration to the effect that it is written in the Torah, 'Those who are unconcerned about where their daily bread comes from, God will be unconcerned about which of the doors to the Fire He sends them through.'[53]

It is related that ᶜAlī (may God be pleased with him), after the murder of ᶜUthmān and the pillaging of his house,[A] ate only marked and stamped food, so as to avoid consuming the dubious.[54]

When Fuḍayl b. ᶜAyyāḍ, [Sufyān] Ibn ᶜUyayna, and Ibn al-Mubārak went to visit Wuhayb b. al-Ward in Mecca, they mentioned dates. Wuhayb said, 'It is the food I most prefer to eat, except that I do not because the dates of Mecca were mixed with those of Zubayda and others.'[B] Ibn al-Mubārak replied, 'If you are so strict about where your food comes from, you'll have trouble eating even bread.' [Wuhayb] said, 'And why is that?' [Ibn al-Mubārak] replied, 'Because the landed estates have become mixed with the lands granted by feudal tenure.' At that, Wuhayb

[A] As the disturbances in Medina at the time were widespread, many of the goods taken by plunderers from the house of the martyred caliph ᶜUthmān, including stores of food, were openly put to use, both in homes and in the marketplace. Thus, in order that he consume only what he was sure of, ᶜAlī determined to mark his own stores.

[B] Zubayda was Harūn al-Rashīd's queen and the mother of more than one ᶜAbbāsid caliph. Being of a pious and charitable nature, she purchased many gardens and wells and turned them over to the people as charitable trusts (*waqf*). However, as the money used to purchase these properties was considered 'dubious' by Wuhayb, he would not eat or drink from the *waqf* gardens.

swooned and became unconscious. So Sufyān [b. ʿUyayna] said, 'You've killed the man!' Ibn al-Mubārak replied, 'I meant only to make things easier for him!' When he regained consciousness, the first thing that Wuhayb said was, 'By God! I shall never eat bread again, not until I meet Him [my Maker]!'[55]

As [Wuhayb] was in the habit of drinking milk, when a woman[56] brought it to him he asked her from where it had come. She replied, 'It comes from the goats of a certain tribe.' Then he asked her how much it had cost, and how the tribe had come to have the goats. To all of his questions the woman had an answer. Then, when he had brought the cup close to his lips, he asked, 'And where does the tribe pasture their goats?' At that, the woman was silent; and Wuhayb did not drink, because he realised that the goats were pastured on public lands. The woman said to him, 'Go ahead and drink. God will forgive you!' Wuhayb replied, 'I do not want that I should be forgiven after I drink, so that I gain His forgiveness only through disobedience to Him!'[57]

Bishr al-Ḥāfī (may God have mercy on him), was among those who practised fear of God (*wariʿūn*). Once he was asked what he ate. He replied, 'I eat what you eat. But there is a difference between one who eats while he is crying, and one who eats while he is laughing.'

[Bishr] also said, 'Some hands are longer than others. And some morsels are smaller than others.'[58]

And in this way they used to guard against the dubious.

Categories of the Lawful and the Unlawful[59] *and the Means of their Attainment*

Know that details regarding the lawful and the unlawful are to be found in the books of jurisprudence (*fiqh*). The true aspirant (*murīd*), however, will not need to pursue the subject at length if he has a regular diet that he is certain, by means of a legal edict (*fatwā*), is lawful;[A] and if he consumes nothing else. Those, however, who are liberal in the variety of food they consume will need to have complete knowledge of the lawful and the unlawful, as we have explained in detail in the books of jurisprudence.[B]

We shall point out the essentials of this matter by means of a division. Thus, wealth is unlawful either because of a reason related to its substance, or because of something wrong in the way that it was acquired.

THE FIRST DIVISION: WHAT IS UNLAWFUL OWING TO AN ATTRIBUTE OF ITS SUBSTANCE; LIKE WINE, PORK, AND OTHERS

The edible substances on the face of the earth are no more than three kinds: minerals like salt and clay, plants and animals.

MINERALS: these include the elements of earth and all that comes from it. None of these are unlawful to eat unless they are harmful to the consumer. Certainly, some minerals act in the same manner as poison. Now, if bread were injurious, it would be unlawful. Likewise, the clay that some people are in the habit of eating will not be unlawful unless it is harmful.[C] The benefit in our mentioning something that would not be unlawful if it were

[A] If an aspirant knows that something has been declared lawful by a competent legal authority, like a *muftī*, there will be no need for further inquiry into the matter. In our own times, this equates to *ḥalāl* certification by an official or otherwise recognised agency or, with regard to financial products and services, by a reputable *Sharīʿa* supervisory board.

[B] The author was himself a recognised legal authority within the Shāfiʿī school of jurisprudence, having authored at least ten books on the subject of *fiqh*, or practical jurisprudence, and two volumes of *fatāwā*, or case law. On the subject of *uṣūl al-fiqh*, or theoretical jurisprudence, he wrote at least six books including *al-Mustaṣfā*, perhaps the most masterly of all his legal works. See the introduction by Muʿawwaḍ and ʿAbd al-Mawjūd to their edition of *al-ʿAzīz sharḥ al-Wajīz*, by ʿAbd al-Karīm al-Rāfiʿī (Beirut, 1417/1997), I.82; and '*Qirā'āt fi-fikr al-Ghazālī al-uṣūlī*' by Zaynab Ṭāhā al-ʿAlawānī in *Islāmiyyat al-maʿrifa*, no. 27 (Winter 2001), 121–140.

[C] Zabīdī explains that pregnant women are sometimes known to eat clay. He follows with a discussion of different sorts of clay, including two with allegedly beneficial effects. See Z.VI.15.

not [generally] eaten is to show that if something of that nature were to fall into a soup, for example, or any other edible liquid, it would not cause that soup to become unlawful.[A]

PLANTS: No plant is unlawful unless it does away with reason, life, or health. Examples of the things that do away with reason are cannabis (*banj*), wine, and all other intoxicants. What is lethal is poison. What does away with health is medicine administered at the wrong time. Thus, all of this would seem to revert to a single reason for being unlawful: that these are harmful, except wine[B] and other intoxicants.

In the case of wine and other intoxicants, even amounts that are not intoxicating are unlawful for reasons related to their attribute of producing extreme unnatural states. Small, harmless amounts of poison, however, or poison mixed with something else and thus rendered harmless, are not unlawful.

ANIMALS: These are divided into what is edible and what is not. Details, of course, may be found in the book of *Edibles*,[C] for their discussion is a lengthy matter; particularly in reference to exotic birds and beasts from land and sea.

The lawful for consumption among these becomes lawful when it is slaughtered according to the *Sharīʿa*; so that all

[A] The soup would not become unlawful, per se. The mixture of the soup and the poison, however, would be unlawful because it would be harmful. For a discussion of the consumption of harmful substances, see Rāfiʿī, *al-ʿAzīz sharḥ al-Wajīz*, II.157–158. See also Ghazālī, *al-Wasīṭ fī'l-madhhab* (Beirut, 1422/2001), IV.245.

[B] The notion that intoxicants may not be intrinsically harmful is supported by the verse at Q.II.219, *They ask you about intoxicants and games of chance. Say: 'In both there is great evil as well as some benefit for people; but the evil they bring is greater than the benefit.'* This verse has occasioned many legal discussions among the classical commentators and jurists.

[C] Here, the author refers in a general way to the works of jurisprudence on the subject. Book XI of the Quarter of Norms of Daily Life is entitled *On the Manners Relating to Eating* (trans. D. Johnson-Davies); it deals with the social aspects of eating. Evidently, then, the author intends to refer to works outside the present work.

conditions are met concerning the one doing the slaughtering, the instrument used, and the place of slaughter. All of these matters are explained in detail in the book of *Game and Slaughtering*.[A]

That which is not slaughtered in the manner specified by the *Sharīʿa* or which dies a natural death [carrion] is therefore unlawful. There are, however, two kinds of carrion that may be eaten; fish and locusts. Similar to these two, are things that are transformed,[B] like worms in [cooked] apples, vinegar,[60] or cheese, and because it is impossible to avoid them. When these are separated and eaten on their own, however, the same ruling will apply to them as applies to flies, beetles, spiders, and all other bloodless creatures.[61]

Moreover, there is no reason for it being unlawful to consume these things, other than that they are considered filthy. Were it not for this, there would be no disapproval (*yukrah*)[C] [of their consumption]. Yet, if someone should be found who does not consider these creatures filthy, no attention will be paid to his particular nature.[D]

[A] Here, the likelihood is that the author is directing the readers to chapters on both the subject of game and the subject of slaughtering in the works of *fiqh* or practical jurisprudence.

[B] Two reasons are given here for the lawful categorisation of these substances. The first is indicated by the word transformation (*istiḥāla*) and the second is that the substances are unavoidable. In fact, the first of the two reasons is the one with the greatest legal credence. It is on the basis of the theory of transformation that gelatin, for example, may be considered lawful, even if it is made from pork or beef that has not been slaughtered lawfully. For general references to the theory of transformation, see Ibn Taymiyya, *Majmūʿat al-fatāwā al-kubrā* (Riyadh, 1398/1978), xxi.7, 481, 611; Ibn Ḥazm, *al-Muḥallā bi'l-āthār* (Beirut, n.d.), i.138, 161; and Ibn ʿĀbidīn, *Radd al-muḥtār ʿalā al-durr al-mukhtār sharḥ tanwīr al-abṣār* (Egypt, 1386/1966), i.217. In the examples cited here, the substance and attributes of the worm are transformed in the process of cooking or preparation. A worm in an uncooked apple, however, will retain its original characteristics and must be considered outside this ruling.

[C] Like the legal term *makrūh*, *yukrah*, and *karāha* in the next paragraph, both derive from *kariha* 'to detest, to disapprove, to be repugnant'. For the five legal definitions, see Note on Legal Terms in the Introduction.

[D] This is in accordance with the legal maxim that 'What is rare is like what

Rather, all such creatures are legally categorised with the unclean for the reason that they are generally considered to be filthy. Thus, their consumption is disapproved (*makrūh*) in the same way that collecting mucus and then drinking it is disapproved.

Nor is the disapproval (*karāha*) owing to any inherent impurity; for the sound legal ruling is that these creatures, when they die, do not cause anything to become impure. This is because the Messenger of God (may God bless him and grant him peace) ordered that a fly should be immersed if it falls into food.[A62] Of course, if the food is hot, it will cause the insect to die. Thus, if an ant or a fly falls into a cooking pot, it will not be necessary to discard its contents. This is because the thing that is considered filthy is its body, if it remains intact, and its body will not make something else impure so that it becomes unlawful owing to contamination by the impure. All of this indicates that the reason for it being unlawful to consume these things is that they are generally considered filthy.[B]

is nonexistent.' See ʿĀlī Ḥaydar, *Durar al-ḥukkām fi-sharḥ majallat al-aḥkām* (Beirut, 1991); Haytamī, *al-Fatāwā al-kubrā al-fiqhiyya* (Cairo, 1357/1938).

[A] The *ḥadīth* is related variously on the authority of Abū Hurayra that the Messenger of God (may God bless him and grant him peace) said, 'If a fly falls in your drink, immerse it and then take it out; for in one of its wings there is disease, and in the other there is its cure.' In another version, the text reads, 'If a fly falls in your food. . .' And in another version it reads, 'If a fly falls in one of your vessels…' Modern Muslims who are puzzled by this seemingly unsavoury teaching of the Messenger of God (may God bless him and grant him peace) may take notice here. The teaching has to do with a legal issue and not with sanitation. The situation described is one in which the fly has already contaminated the food. The purpose of the teaching is to say that a fly is not impure in a religious/legal sense. Otherwise, people might have deduced that there was a need to perform new ablutions every time a fly alighted on their persons, or to cleanse their water supply if a fly fell into it, or to wash their places of prayer whenever a fly was detected on it. And God knows best.

[B] The sixth of the ten principles postulated by the author regarding food is that anything considered filthy by the early generations of Arabs is unlawful. See Rāfiʿī, *al-ʿAzīz sharḥ al-Wajīz*, XII.143–148; Ghazālī, *Wasīṭ*, IV.243–244.

Thus, we may say: If a part of a dead human being were to fall into a cooking pot, even a small piece of flesh, all the contents of the pot would become unlawful. This would not be for the reason that the dead human flesh is impure, for the authentic *Sharīʿa* ruling is that death does not make human flesh impure.[A] Rather, the reason would be that its consumption is unlawful out of respect [for all that is human], and not because it [human flesh] is generally considered filthy.

In regard to edible animals slaughtered in accordance with the conditions prescribed by the *Sharīʿa*, not all parts of such animals are lawful. Rather, the blood and the contents of the bowels and intestines are unlawful, as are all other parts that are clearly impure.[B]

Thus, the consumption of anything impure is unlawful. But there is no substance that is impure other than from among the category of animals.[63] Among the category of vegetables, the only thing impure is that which intoxicates; as opposed to that which deprives one of reason yet does not intoxicate, like cannabis. The only reason for the impurity of intoxicants is in order to emphasise prevention of their abuse; for the assumption is that these substances lead to all manner of wrongdoing.

Whenever a drop of impurity, or a part of an impure solid falls into a soup, or food, or oil, it is unlawful to consume any of it.[C] It is not unlawful, however, to make use of it otherwise. Thus, oil contaminated by an unlawful substance may be burned in an oil lamp, or mixed in with other ingredients to make paint for a boat, and so on.[D]

[A] Certain of the Iraqi jurists, however, held otherwise. For discussions of the matter, see Nawawī, *al-Majmūʿ sharḥ al-muhadhdhab* (Egypt, 1352/1933), I.301.

[B] Mujāhid related that the Prophet disliked seven parts of a goat; the gall bladder, intestines, anus, penis, testicles, ganglion and blood. Abū Ḥanīfa, *Kitāb al-āthār*, p. 588; Manāwī, *Fayḍ al-qadīr*, v.245.

[C] See, for example, Jaṣṣāṣ, *Aḥkām al-Qur'ān* (Istanbul, 1335/1917), I.127; Ibn Ḥazm, *Muḥallā*, VI.117; Sharbīnī, *Mughnī al-muḥtāj* (Egypt, 1355/1958), I.586.

[D] See, for example, Anṣārī, *al-Ghurar al-bahiyya sharḥ al-buhja* (Beirut, 1997),

These, then, are the essentials of what is unlawful owing to the characteristics of its substance.

THE SECOND DIVISION: WHAT IS UNLAWFUL OWING TO AN IRREGULARITY IN THE ESTABLISHMENT OF ITS OWNERSHIP

This is a subject that [deserves] extensive consideration. Therefore, we shall begin by saying that wealth (*māl*) is obtained either by means of one's volition (*ikhtiyār*), or without it.

The example of wealth acquired without one's choosing [to acquire it] is inheritance.

If wealth is obtained by means of one's volition, the wealth will either not have an owner, as in when a mine is discovered [in the desert], or it will have an owner.

Then, wealth that is obtained from an owner will either be obtained forcibly or by mutual consent.

Wealth obtained forcibly will be obtained either as a result of the owner's loss of protection, like [wealth taken as] the spoils of war, or because others have a right to it, as in the case of those who withhold payment of the *zakāt*[A] or [obligatory] payments of support.[B]

Wealth obtained by mutual consent will either be obtained in exchange for something else, as in sales, dowry and wages; or it will be obtained without exchange, like a gift or a bequest.

From the above explanation, we may distinguish six categories, as follows:

Firstly, wealth that has no owner: This includes mines that are newly discovered, arable lands that have been reclaimed, [wealth obtained through] hunting, gathering, or drawing water from rivers, or harvesting wild fields. All of this is lawful, on the condition that what is taken has not already been claimed by someone with rights (*dhī ḥurma*). If such a claim has lapsed, for whatever

II.43; Nawawī, *Majmūʿ*, IV.335; and Ibn ʿĀbidīn, *Radd al-muḥtār*, I.316.

A *Zakāt* is understood to be the right of the poor. See Q.LI.19.

B i.e., for their families, when ordered to make such payments by a *qāḍī*, or judge. For a general outline of the rules of support see Ghazālī, *Wasīṭ*, IV.3–26.

reason, the wealth becomes the property of the one who takes possession of it. Details may be had from the book of *Reclaimed Land* (*iḥyā' al-mawāt*).[A]

Secondly, wealth that is obtained forcibly from one who has no rights: This includes booty and the spoils of war taken from disbeliever combatants. Such wealth is lawful for Muslims as long as they deduct one fifth (*khums*) of it, and divide that equitably among the deserving; and as long as it is not taken from a disbeliever with rights, or protection, or immunity through treaty. Details of these matters may be had from the relevant chapters in the book of *Campaigns* (*siyar*),[64] from the book of *Spoils of War and Booty* (*fay' wa-ghanīma*), and the book of *Tribute* (*jizya*).

Thirdly, wealth taken forcibly from one who witholds what he is legally obliged to pay, so that it is taken without his approval: This is lawful when a reason for payment is legally established, when the one with the right to the payment is clearly identified as deserving, when the amount taken is no more than what is owed, and when the collection is undertaken by a legally empowered authority, such as the judge, the sultan, or the one with the right to the payment. Details may be had from the book of *Distributing Charity* (*tafrīq al-ṣadaqāt*), the book of *Charitable Trusts* (*waqf*) and the book of *Payments for Expenses* (*nafaqāt*), because they explain the ways that one comes to deserve *zakāt*, *waqf* monies, support payments, and other rights. Only when all of these conditions are satisfied is the wealth itself considered lawful.

Fourthly, wealth obtained by mutual consent for a consideration (*muʿāwaḍa*): This is lawful as long as the conditions relevant to the values exchanged, to the parties of the exchange, and to the expression of offer and acceptance in the exchange are [all] met in full; and as long as the requirements of the *Sharīʿa* avoiding conditions that invalidate are also met. Details may be had from the book of *Trade* (*bayʿ*), the book of *Forward Sale* (*salam*), of *Leasing*

[A] Here, again, the author intends to refer to works outside the present work. See, for example, Ghazālī, *Wasīṭ*, II.387–395.

(*ijara*), of *Transfers* (*ḥawāla*), of *Guarantees* (*ḍamān*), of *Commenda* (*qirāḍ*), of *Partnership* (*shirka*), of *Watering* (*musāqā*), of *First Refusal* (*shufʿa*), or *Settlement* (*ṣulḥ*), of *Divorce for Consideration* (*khulaʿ*), of *Manumission for Consideration* (*kitāba*), of *Bride Gifts* (*ṣadāq*), and of all the other commutative contracts.

Fifthly, wealth obtained by mutual consent but without exchange: This is lawful when all the conditions pertaining to the object of transaction, the conditions pertaining to the transactors, and the conditions pertaining to the transaction itself are met in full, and when the transaction of this nature does not lead to the detriment of an heir, or of anyone else. Details may be had in the book of *Gifts* (*hibāt*), *Bequests* (*waṣāyā*), and *Charitable Giving* (*ṣadaqāt*).

Sixthly, wealth obtained without one's choosing [to acquire it], like inheritance: This is lawful if the wealth to be inherited was obtained in a lawful manner, by means of one of the five categories [mentioned above]. Of course, [the transfer of] this [wealth] will take place only after the debts of the deceased's estate are honoured, the bequests [if any] are paid out, the portions [of the inheritance] are divided among its recipients, *zakāt* is deducted, pilgrimage (*ḥajj*) expenses are paid, and monetary expiation (*kaffāra*), if necessary, is discharged. Details may be had in the book of *Bequests* (*waṣāyā*), and *Legal Divisions of Inheritance* (*farā'iḍ*).

These are the collective means to the lawful and the unlawful. We have done no more than point out the main features here in order that the aspirant may know that, if his daily bread comes from different sources, rather than a single known[A] source, then he cannot do without knowledge of these matters. Thus, before he consumes anything, from whatever source, he should question those in possession of knowledge about these matters, rather than undertake anything in ignorance.[B]

[A] i.e., one that is known by the aspirant to be lawful.

[B] The logic of this argument describes perfectly the need in modern times for certification from qualified authorities, whether in the matter of lawful

For, as it may be asked of a scholar, 'Why are your actions inconsistent with your knowledge?' it may be asked of an ignorant person, 'Why are you adhering to your ignorance?', and, 'Why do you not learn about these things when it has been said to you that seeking knowledge is an obligation for every Muslim?'

Degrees of the Lawful and the Unlawful

Know that what is unlawful, all of it, is iniquitous. Still, some of it is more iniquitous than the rest. Likewise, what is lawful, all of it, is good; but some of it is better and purer than the rest.

For example, when a doctor tells us that all sweet things are 'hot', he also tells us that some sweet things are hotter than others.[A] Sugar, for example, is of the first degree; sweetmeats of sugar cane juice and starch are of the second degree; date treacle is of the third degree; and honey is of the fourth degree.

With the unlawful it is the same. Some of it is 'iniquitous' to the first degree; and some to the second, third and fourth degrees. Likewise, the lawful is of different degrees, according to its attributes and virtues. We shall, therefore, determine our own terminology after that of the medical profession by specifying four degrees; though, of course, such a division is arbitrary and certainly not binding. Indeed, there is no end of ways that one might measure the differences between the kinds of deeds that constitute each degree. Even different types of sugar differ in relation to the degree of heat they produce in the body. The same is true of

food sold in supermarkets, or in the matter of Islamic financial products and services offered by financial institutions. Indeed, by means of such certification (the result of a process of scrutiny and oversight), modern *Sharīʿa* supervisory boards essentially perform a collective obligation (*farḍ kifāya*) that relieves consumers of the responsibility of determining these matters for themselves.

[A] The system of medicine with which Ghazālī was familiar was a modified version of the ancient Greek system in which physiology was based on the four cardinal humours in the body. The figurative temperature of what the body ingested played an important part in this system.

all other substances. We may therefore hypothesise that there are four degrees of prudence in regard to the unlawful:

[The Prudence of the Upright] The first degree of such prudence is the Prudence of the Upright (*wara*ᶜ *al-*ᶜ*adūl*).[A] This is prudence in regard to acts that constitute actual wrongdoing, undermine one's competence as a witness, make one deserving of the name 'wrongdoer', and make one eligible for the Fire. Essentially, then, this is prudence in regard to all that is prohibited by means of legal edicts (*fatāwā*) issued by the jurists.

[The Prudence of the Pious] The second degree is the Prudence of the Pious (*wara*ᶜ *al-ṣāliḥīn*). This is abstinence from something for which there exists a possibility that it is prohibited; although the legal authorities, basing their decisions on literal considerations (*al-ẓāhir*), permit it. Generally speaking, then, these are doubtful matters; and we may call the discomfort one feels about them the Prudence of the Pious. So this is the second degree.

[The Prudence of the Heedful] The third degree is [abstinence from] what is not prohibited by a *fatwā*, and which may not possibly be categorised as unlawful; but which may possibly lead to something else which *is* unlawful. Essentially, this degree of prudence amounts to one's abstention from something that is acceptable for fear of [committing] something that is not acceptable. This [degree of prudence] is called the Prudence of the Heedful (*wara*ᶜ *al-muttaqīn*). [The Messenger of God] (may God bless him and grant him peace), said, 'A worshipper will not attain the rank of the heedful until he abstains from the acceptable out of fear of the unacceptable.'[65]

[The Prudence of the Saintly] The fourth degree is [abstinence from] that which is completely acceptable, and about

[A] ᶜ*Adūl* in Sharīᶜa terminology is someone who combines a reputation for honesty and truthfulness with a moral, law-abiding and principled lifestyle and is therefore suitable as a witness in a Sharīᶜa court. That Ghazālī has chosen this term as the first degree of prudence demonstrates his desire to show that a Muslim who intends to travel the road of prudence must possess, at the very least, the characteristics required of a witness in a Sharīᶜa court.

which there is no fear that it may possibly lead to something unacceptable. Rather, this is [abstinence from] something that is done for other than God, or that is done, or consumed, without the intention of either heeding or worshipping God by means of it, or might be something in which an aspect of wrongdoing has been introduced through the conditions facilitating its performance. Abstinence in such cases is called the Prudence of the Saintly (*waraᶜ al-ṣiddīqīn*).[A]

These are the degrees of the lawful, in very broad terms, and we shall further explain them later on by means of examples and illustrations.

As to the category of unlawful mentioned in the first degree[B] as that which must be avoided for the reason that it undermines one's competence as a witness and earns for one the name of 'wrongdoer',[66] then it, too, may be classified in varying degrees of iniquity.

Thus, gaining possession of something by means of a vitiated (*fāsid*) transaction, as when a simple give and take exchange (*muᶜāṭā*)[C] takes place, is not of the same degree of iniquity as usurping property by forceful means. Rather, usurpation is far

[A] Though the usual translation for *ṣiddīqūn* is 'the righteous' or 'the truthful', and we have used 'the righteous' for *ṣiddīqūn* above, we have chosen to translate it here as 'the saintly' as what Ghazālī is describing is a most elevated level of perfection.

[B] i.e., in the Prudence of the Upright.

[C] Such an exchange has been the subject of debate among scholars for the reason that neither buyer nor seller expresses either an offer or its acceptance, two elements deemed essential for the validity of any sales contract. See Ibn Qudāma, *al-Mughnī* (Riyadh, n.d.), for the positions taken by the major jurists. It would appear that Ghazālī's opinion on the matter is in opposition to that of his imam, Shāfiᶜī, who held the give and take exchange to be void. See Ghazālī, *al-Mustaṣfā min ᶜilm al-uṣūl*, I.280. Ghazālī, however, was not the only jurist of the school to differ with the imam on this issue. See Ibn ᶜAbd al-Salām, *Qawā'id al-aḥkām fī maṣāliḥ al-anām* (Beirut, 1990), II.121; and Ramlī, *Nihāyat al-muḥtāj fi-sharḥ al-minhāj* (Beirut, 2003), II.18. See also the first issue in Chapter Seven of the present work.

more iniquitous because it involves both rejection of the ways approved by the *Sharīʿa* for earning, and detriment to another. The give and take exchange, on the other hand, may take place with no detriment [to either party]; so, at the most, it involves only the omission of something stipulated by the *Sharīʿa*.[A] And then the kind of omission that takes place in such a transaction is certainly less iniquitous than the omission of *Sharīʿa* precepts that occurs in interest-based transactions (*ribā*).[B]

These variations in degree may be discerned through a comparison of the severity of expression in the *Sharīʿa* texts in which the different prohibitions occur. This will be discussed at some length in *Kitāb al-tawba* [On Repentance][C] where the differences between major and minor wrongdoing are explained.

Moreover, taking something unjustly from a poor person, or a pious person, or an orphan is certainly more repulsive and more iniquitous than taking something from a strong, wealthy, or even an evil person. Obviously, the degree of detriment will differ in proportion to the status of the one afflicted.[67]

These, then, are fine points added to the explanation of what is iniquitous, and they should not be ignored. For, were it not for differences in the ranking of wrongdoers, there would be no differences in the degrees of [punishment in] the Fire.

Now, if you have understood the occasions for the use of severity, there should be no need to confine it to three or four categories. Indeed, the attempt to do so would be subjective and

[A] i.e., offer and acceptance (*ījāb wa-qubūl*).

[B] The literal meaning of *ribā* is increase, while it is widely understood to mean interest which is clearly prohibited in several emphatic verses of the Qur'ān, including II.275–280, III.130 and XXX.39. Generally speaking, a transaction in which there is *ribā* will ignore the principle that revenue must be accompanied by responsibility or exposure to risk (*al-kharāj bi'l-ḍamān*), and that increase not balanced by a corresponding increase in a countervalue may not be stipulated in a contract for only one of the contracting parties.

[C] This is Book XXXI of *The Revival of the Religious Sciences*, in the Quarter of the Saving Virtues.

the result arbitrary, as there is no limiting what is essentially incapable of being limited.

You will see the differences in the degrees of iniquity in the unlawful when we discuss conflicting prohibitions and the preference of one over another; as in the case of one forced by circumstances to eat either the flesh of a dead animal, or food belonging to another, or game taken within the sacred precincts [of Mecca or Medina], because then we must prefer one over another.

Examples of the Four Degrees of Prudence[68]

THE FIRST DEGREE: The Prudence of the Upright is prudence in regard to all that may be pronounced unlawful by means of a *fatwā*,[A] including the six categories[B] of the unlawful we mentioned above, which did not satisfy even one of the conditions for lawfulness. Such things are strictly unlawful; and those who commit them are corrupt and wrongdoers. This is what we mean when we speak of the strictly unlawful (*al-ḥarām al-muṭlaq*); and there is no need to give examples or parallels.

THE SECOND DEGREE: [The Prudence of the Pious] includes, for example, every dubious thing the avoidance of which is not essential but preferred, as shall be explained later in the chapter on 'The Degrees of the Dubious'. This is because the dubious includes both what must be avoided, and is therefore linked to the unlawful, and what should not be avoided, so that prudence in regard to it is as the prudence of the overly suspicious. The example of the latter is that of one who avoids hunting for game

[A] N.B. The reference here is to whatever has been clearly prohibited by the texts of the Qur'ān or the *Sunna* and may therefore be mentioned as unlawful in a *fatwā*. This does not mean that everything prohibited by means of a *fatwā* is automatically unlawful. This is because, when *ijtihād* is involved, or when the competence to pronounce a *fatwā* is in doubt, not every *fatwā* will be correct.

[B] These were the six categories that were unlawful because of something wrong in the ways that they were acquired. See the previous section of this chapter.

out of fear that it might have run away from someone who had earlier caught it and made it his own possession. This is no more than unfounded suspicion (*waswās*).

Included in this degree is what should be avoided, but not necessarily. It is to this degree that the tradition of [the Messenger of God] (God bless him and grant him peace) refers: 'Forsake what makes you doubtful in favour of what does not make you doubtful.'[69]

Our understanding of this text leads us to view it as indicating a sort of purifying prohibition (*nahy al-tanzīh*).[A] An example of this is the tradition [of the Messenger of God] (may God bless him and grant him peace), 'Eat of the game you kill before you; and avoid the game[B] that is wounded and runs.'[70] The word used in the tradition denotes the hunter's losing sight of the animal and then finding it dead, so that there is a possibility that the animal died from some other cause.

In such cases we prefer to say that it is not unlawful [to eat the game]; abstinence, however, may be considered the Prudence of the Pious.

On the other hand, the [Messenger of God's] saying, 'Forsake what makes you doubtful' is a purifying command. In another tradition, [the Messenger of God] said; 'Eat of it, even though you lost sight of it, so long as you find no wound other than that made by your arrow.'[71]

It was for this reason that the Messenger of God (may God bless him and grant him peace) said to ʿAdī b. Ḥātim, concerning his hunting dog, 'If it eats from the carcass, then do not eat the game; for I fear that the dog will have killed it for himself.'[72]

[A] Ghazālī uses 'prohibition' (*nahy*) here and 'command' (*amr*) below with the same meaning. Such a prohibition or command is not binding, but merely recommended as an act that is spiritually edifying.

[B] The meaning of this narration is that game killed before one's eyes will clearly be the property of the hunter. If the stricken animal runs off and is discovered at a later time, the possibility will exist that it was finally brought down by another hunter and may therefore be his property.

The purifying prohibition was given because of this fear.

But he (may God bless him and grant him peace) said to Abū Thaʿlaba al-Khushanī, 'Eat of it.' When Abū Thaʿlaba replied, 'Even if [the hound] has eaten of it?' [The Messenger of God] said, 'Even if it has eaten from it.'[73] The reason for all of this was that Abū Thaʿlaba was a poor man, and his personal circumstances did not permit him that kind of prudence; ʿAdī's circumstances, however, did.[A]

The story is told of Ibn Sīrīn and how he left four thousand dirhams to his partner because, in his heart, something about it was troubling to him.[74] Yet, he did this in spite of the agreement of the jurists that there was nothing wrong with it. [B]

We shall mention examples of this degree [of prudence] in our discussion of the Degrees of the Dubious [where we speak] of what is dubious yet need not necessarily be avoided.

THE THIRD DEGREE: The Prudence of the Heedful is attested to by the saying of [the Messenger of God] (may God bless him and grant him peace) that 'A servant will not attain the rank of the

[A] According to the commentator, Ibn Ḥajar, 'In reconciling the two narrations, the jurists took several different approaches. Among these, certain of the jurists who held the game to be unlawful explained the narration by Abū Thaʿlaba to refer to a situation in which the hunting dog kills the game and leaves it for a time before returning to it and then eating from it. Other jurists, however, consider the narration of ʿAdī preponderant [as evidence] owing to its inclusion in the two most authentic collections [Bukhārī and Muslim], whereas the narration of Abū Thaʿlaba is mentioned in other than the two most authentic collections and there is some difference of opinion regarding its authenticity.' The commentator continues, 'Certain jurists have also pointed out that ʿAdī was wealthy, so that the ruling chosen in his case was prohibition; whereas Abū Thaʿlaba was the opposite case.' Ibn Ḥajar al-ʿAsqalānī, *Fatḥ al-bārī bi-sharḥ Ṣaḥīḥ al-Bukhārī* (Beirut, 1414/1994), IX.233. See also, Rāfiʿī, *al-ʿAzīz sharḥ al-Wajīz*, XII.11–26; Ghazālī, *Wasīṭ*, IV.219.

[B] In the complete version of the story it is explained that Ibn Sīrīn bought some property and then, for whatever reason, felt uneasy about it and signed it over to his partner. At the end of the story, Ibn Sīrīn said, 'I have given it up owing to something that all the jurists consider lawful.' See Z.VI.25.

heedful until he forsakes what makes him doubtful in favour of what does not make him doubtful.'[75]

ʿUmar (may God be pleased with him) said, 'We used to forgo nine tenths of what was lawful out of fear of committing something unlawful.' The same is also ascribed to Ibn ʿAbbās.[A]

Abū al-Dardā' said, 'It is the height of God-consciousness (*taqwā*) for the servant to be wary about the smallest of quantities, so that he forgoes some of what he considers lawful out of fear of becoming involved in something unlawful. This will be as a screen between him and the Fire.'[76]

A creditor was owed one hundred dirhams by another. When the time for repayment came, the creditor exercised prudence and took back only ninety nine dirhams, rather than the full amount, out of fear of taking more than his share. Another was so wary that whenever he collected, he would be sure to collect a measure less; and whenever he repaid, he would be sure to repay a measure more, so that he could be screened from the Fire.[77]

Included in this degree is one's abstention from what most people are lax about. For although such things may be condoned by the letter of the law, if the door to them is opened, it is to be feared that others too will be drawn to them, that people will become accustomed to license, and prudence will be laid aside.

By way of example it is related that ʿAlī b. Maʿbad said, 'I was living in a rented house when I wrote a letter and thought to take dust from the wall in order to dry and blot the ink. But then I said to myself, "This is not my wall." My self answered, "What can the dust on a wall be worth?" So I took as much as I needed, and no more. But that night, when I had gone to sleep, I saw a man standing before me, and he was saying, "Tomorrow, ʿAlī b. Maʿbad, you'll learn what the dust on the wall is worth!"'[78]

A likely interpretation of this dream is that he would see how

[A] A similar saying is related in Makkī, *Qūt al-qulūb* (Beirut, 1417/1997), II.493, from Abū Bakr. Obviously, among the Companions, this was something quite commonplace. See Z.VI.25.

he was to be lowered in his station, for certainly God-fearing is of degrees that decrease or increase in proportion to the degree of one's devotion and prudence. Certainly, however, the meaning was not that he was going to be punished in any way.

Another example of the same is that of ʿUmar (may God be pleased with him) when he received a quantity of musk [perfume] from Bahrain and said to those gathered, 'I would like a woman to come forward and weigh this musk so that it may be distributed evenly among the Muslims.' But when his wife, ʿĀtika, said, 'I am good at weighing such things,' ʿUmar was silent for a while and then repeated his question. His wife repeated her answer. So ʿUmar said to her, 'I do not want you to place it with your hands on the weighing scales and then scratch your neck, so that your share of the perfume becomes greater than the shares to be distributed to the Muslims!'[79]

Once, musk to be distributed among the Muslims was being weighed in front of Caliph ʿUmar b. ʿAbd al-ʿAzīz. All the while, however, the caliph held his nose closed with his fingers, so that he would not smell the musk. When questioned as to the reason for doing so, he replied, 'One's profiting from it is one's smelling it.'[80]

Ḥasan b. ʿAlī (may God be pleased with them both) took a date from among dates given as charity when he was yet a small boy. The [Messenger of God] (may God bless him and grant him peace) said, 'Put it back! Put it back!'[A][81]

Another example of the same is how, when a pious man had gone to the home of one known to be dying, and the sick person died, the pious man said, 'Blow out the lamps! The oil in them is now the property of the heirs.'[82]

Sulaymān al-Taymī related from Nuʿaym al-ʿAṭṭār[83] who said, "ʿUmar used to give his wife perfume to sell among the Muslims. So I bought some from her, and she began weighing it and

[A] The reason for the Messenger's action here is that charity (*ṣadaqa*) was prohibited for the Messenger and his family; *ṣadaqa* being considered a form of purification for sins.

increasing and decreasing it, and biting it with her teeth,[A] so that some of it got on her fingers. When that happened, she wiped it off on her headscarf. Just then ʿUmar (may God be pleased with him) walked in and asked what it was he smelled. When she told him, he took her scarf from her head and, taking water, began washing the scarf, and then rubbing it with dirt, and then washing it again, until at last the scent had left it.' Nuʿaym related, 'I went to her another time and, while she was weighing out the perfume, some of it stuck to her finger. So she immediately put it in her mouth and then rubbed it in the dirt.'[84]

This, then, is the example of ʿUmar's prudence, the Prudence of the Heedful, owing to his fear of something leading to something else. Otherwise, his washing the scarf did nothing to return the perfume to its rightful owner. Rather, he did so to rebuke his wife, and in order to prevent the matter from leading to something else.[85]

Similarly, Aḥmad Ibn Ḥanbal was asked about a man whose job it was to take burning incense into mosques for a certain nobleman. 'He should wait outside the mosque while the incense burns, for one's profiting from it is one's smelling it.'[86] In fact, this is close to the unlawful for the reason that the amount of incense that might collect on the clothing of the man were he to remain in the mosque might be ignored [by the nobleman] as insignificant, or it might not be.

Aḥmad Ibn Ḥanbal was also asked about one who loses a paper on which *ḥadīth* narrations had been written. In particular, he was asked if the finder might copy the narrations for himself before returning the paper? [Ibn Ḥanbal] replied, 'No. You must first take permission [from the owner]. Then you may copy the narrations.'[87] In this case as well there is doubt as to whether the owner will agree or not. And when there is doubt about something, and that something might be unlawful, then it is better to avoid it altogether.[88]

[A] This must have been a solid form of perfume.

A similar matter is prudence regarding adornment, because while adornment in and of itself is permitted (*mubāḥ*), it is to be feared for what it might lead to.

Aḥmad Ibn Ḥanbal was asked about [wearing] *sabtī* sandals.[A] In reply, he said, 'Myself, I do not wear them. If they are to be worn for protection from mud, then I hope for the best for the wearer. But if they are to be worn out of ostentation, then no.'[B]

When ʿUmar (may God be pleased with him) assumed the office of caliph he had a wife he loved very much. But ʿUmar divorced the woman out of fear that she might advocate [for something] that was without merit, and that he might approve her recommendation merely in order to please her. This is another example of one's abstaining from something that is acceptable out of fear of something that is not acceptable.[C]

In fact, most of what is permitted can lead to what is forbidden (*maḥẓūr*). Even overeating is like this. Likewise, an unmarried person's use of perfume is something that stirs up passion, and passion leads to imagination, and imagination leads to watching, and watching leads to other things.

[A] *Sabtī* sandals were smooth sandals free of animal hair. Thus, it would seem that they were sandals of superior quality, soft and smooth, when the general run of footwear was rough and utilitarian (Z.vi.28).

[B] It is also related that when Imām Ibn Ḥanbal was asked about Sindhi sandals, he said, 'Do you want to look like the children of royalty?' According to Ibn Ḥanbal (*al-Warā*ʿ, pp. 183–184), Sindhi sandals were *makrūh*, or disapproved, for men, women and children. Obviously, such a ruling, given the changes in norms regarding dress today, must be understood in a different light. The principle, however, remains the same. See Makkī, *Qūt*, ii.468.

[C] I have been unable to find any historical references to this event that might somehow explain why a man of the stature of ʿUmar would divorce his wife solely on these grounds. The likelihood, if the story is authentic, is that the wife had family ties to people that had made it apparent to him that they would seek favours from him once he attained the office of caliph. Otherwise, it is barely conceivable that a man would so entirely disregard the feelings and the interests of his wife and family, whose care is obligatory, for the sole purpose of what he perceived to be his own spiritual growth. And God knows best.

Likewise, one's gazing at the homes of the wealthy, or at how the wealthy adorn themselves, all of this is permitted in and of itself. At the same time, however, it arouses greed and prompts people to seek the same for themselves. Such longing may incite people to commit what is not lawful, solely in order that they may obtain what they desire.

This is true in relation to all the permitted things, unless they are used or partaken of only as required, and only when there is a real need for them, and with prudence in regard to their dangers. So, first of all, knowledge is required, and then prudence. For, indeed, it is rare that the end result will be free of peril. The same is true of anything that is done as a result of aroused passion. In such instances, it is rare indeed that the end result will be free of peril.[89]

Aḥmad Ibn Ḥanbal even pronounced that the application of gypsum[A] to walls was disapproved. He said, 'Applying gypsum to floors keeps them clean. But on the walls it is no more than beautification, and of no practical value.'[90]

He even ruled out the application of gypsum to mosques, as [he considered] that to be ostentation.[91] In this, he cited the *ḥadīth* of the Prophet (may God bless him and grant him peace) when he was asked if the floor of the mosque might be treated. 'No,' he replied, 'Let it be an enclosure[B] like the enclosure of Moses.'[92]

The treatment suggested was simply the application of something like alcohol that would harden the surface of the

[A] Gypsum was used at that time as plaster on walls that were generally made of rough earthen brick. Evidently, smooth walls were considered a luxury. Here, too, note that changes in norms may lead to changes in rulings.

[B] I have translated the word used in the *ḥadīth*, *ʿarīsh*, as enclosure on the basis of a reference in *Tāj al-ʿarūs* that indicates the meaning to be an enclosure of the sort used to protect animals from the cold. Otherwise, the more widely used meaning is the roof-like trellis of a grapevine, or a sort of rough canopy. As the question concerned the floor of the mosque, the first meaning would seem the more appropriate one. In a *ḥadīth* related by Dārimī (*Sunan*, I.182 [Cairo, 1420/2000]) the word is used to mean something like a pulpit.

floor. But the Messenger of God (may God bless him and grant him peace) did not allow it.[93]

Our Predecessors did not like thin clothing either. They used to say, 'One whose clothes are flimsy will have a flimsy religion as well.'[94]

Of course, all of this came about as a result of their fear that the following of one's desires in regard to what is permitted will lead one to do what is otherwise. For indeed, the self will desire equally what is forbidden and what is permitted. If the passions are constantly being aroused, God-consciousness requires that one exercise prudence in regard to all of these things. Then, every sort of lawful thing that comes about as a result of this kind of fear is the good sort of lawful [referred to] in the third degree of prudence; and that is everything for which there is no fear that doing it will definitely lead to wrongdoing.

THE FOURTH DEGREE: the Prudence of the Saintly. For them, the strictly lawful (*al-ḥalāl al-muṭlaq*) is that in which the lawful is considered only to be that in which even the means are in no way connected to wrongdoing, that which itself may not contribute to wrongdoing, and that which in no way, either in the present or in the future, will lead to the satisfaction of one's desires. Thus, whatever is done or partaken of is done or partaken of solely for the sake of God, and for heedfulness in worship of Him, and in order to maintain life solely for Him.

This is the lawful of the people who see as unlawful everything that is not done solely for God, in accordance with the verse, *Say [to yourself], 'God (Allāh);' Then let others play at what absorbs them.*[95] This is the rank of the people of God's unity (*muwaḥḥidūn*), people who are free of the desires of the self, and whose only purpose is God, Exalted is He!

Certainly, one who is cautious about what may be used as a means to wrongdoing will be careful to avoid everything that, if performed, might be associated with wrongdoing or something disapproved.

In this vein it is related concerning Yaḥyā b. Yaḥyā,[96] that one day he drank medicine, and his wife suggested that he walk around the house until it began to work. Yaḥyā replied, 'That is a kind of walking I do not know; and I've been taking myself to task for the past thirty years.'[97] Evidently, because no religious intention attached to such a walk, he shunned it.[98]

Of Sarī [al-Saqaṭī] (may God have mercy on him), it is related that he said, 'I found myself by some vegetation at the side of a mountain from which there flowed water. So I stopped to eat and drink, and I said to myself, "If ever a day I have eaten the lawful, then that day is today." But then I heard a voice saying, "And what of the strength that enabled you to reach this place? Where do you suppose it came from?" So I returned and repented.'[99]

Likewise, it was related about Dhū'l-Nūn al-Miṣrī that he was starving in jail, and that when a pious woman sent him some food with one of the guards, he refused to eat it.[A] Instead, he excused himself by saying, 'It came to me in the hand of an oppressor.'[100]

Similarly, it is recounted concerning Bishr (may God have mercy on him) that he never drank water from a canal dug at the personal expense[B] of a ruler.[101] This was because a canal is a means for the movement of water and for bringing it to people. So, even though the water was in and of itself perfectly lawful, in drinking it Bishr would have benefited from the labour of those who dug the canal, when their wages had been paid from unlawful money.

It was for the same reason that a certain person refrained

[A] The explanation given by Zabīdī for Dhū'l-Nūn's incarceration is that certain rulers had arrested him on the basis of a *fatwā* issued by certain scholars who heard something that Dhū'l-Nūn was alleged to have said. See Z.IV.30. The version related by Makkī (*Qūt*, II.474) is that the authorities had arrested him when the citizenry became outraged at certain esoteric issues he had discussed in public.

[B] Oftentimes, rulers would use their own funds for charitable purposes. Then, even though tainted funds, when given as charity, are perfectly lawful (as will be explained in the following chapter of this book), many Sufis would avoid such charity for the reasons given here. Obviously, all of the examples cited here represent extreme instances of prudence.

from eating lawful grapes from lawful vines, and then said to his companion, 'They were spoiled when they were watered from the canal dug by the oppressors.'[102] This shows even more prudence in regard to oppression than refusal to drink water from their canals, because the grapes grew from the water the vines drew sustenance from.

Certain of those who travel to the pilgrimage (*ḥajj*) refrain from drinking water on the way from wells and tanks constructed by tyrannical rulers. This is in spite of the fact the water itself is lawful; but the devices for containing it have been constructed with unlawful funds. Thus, drinking water from those wells and tanks is as if one were to benefit from what is unlawful.

Still, Dhū'l-Nūn's refusal to eat food delivered by a guard was even greater than all this, in terms of prudence. This is because the hand of a guard may not be described as unlawful; in contrast to food delivered on a stolen plate. But the food reached Dhū'l-Nūn by means of energy that endowed the food with the quality of being unlawful. It was for the same reason that al-Ṣiddīq [Abū Bakr] (may God be pleased with him) vomited up the milk, out of fear that the unlawful would create energy within him. Of course, his doing so was not necessary. But ridding the stomach of the foul and impure was an example of the sort of prudence practised by the saintly.

Another example is avoidance of lawful earnings made by a tailor who sews while sitting in a mosque. This is because Aḥmad [Ibn Ḥanbal] (God have mercy on him) opined that such earnings are disapproved.[A][103]

[Ibn Ḥanbal] was also asked about a spinner who worked under a dome at a graveyard when it was raining. 'This has to

[A] The opinion of the Mālikī and Shāfiʿī schools in regard to economic activity in a mosque is that it is disapproved for the reason that it is contrary to the sacred nature of the mosque. The Ḥanafī and Ḥanbalī schools held all such activities to be unlawful. See *al-Mawsūʿa al-fiqhiyya* (Kuwait, 1983–2000), xxii.362 and Ibn Ḥanbal, *Waraʿ*, p. 59.

do with the next world,' he replied, 'The spinning done there is disapproved.'[104]

One of the masters went so far as to blow out a lamp that his servant had lit from the fire of a tribe whose wealth was from questionable sources.[105]

Another refused to fire his oven for bread with a coal that had come from wood that was legal but disapproved.[106]

Still another refused to lace up his sandals in the light of a sultan's torch.[107]

These are the finer points of prudence for the wayfarers to the path of the Ḥereafter.

The truth of this matter is that prudence has a beginning: it is refusal to transgress in what has been declared unlawful by a *fatwā*. This is the Prudence of the Upright. Likewise, prudence has an end, and it is the Prudence of the Saintly; it is to refrain from all that is not done for God [alone], whether it be something in which the passions are involved, or something that may lead to wrongdoing, or something that is even remotely connected to what has been categorised as disapproved.

Then, between these two, there are several degrees of prudence. The stricter one is with oneself, the more likely it is that on the Day of Judgement one's burden will be lighter, one's walk across the bridge [to Paradise] will be quicker, and that one's good deeds will outweigh one's bad deeds on the scale.

Moreover, the stations in the Hereafter will differ on the basis of the different degrees of prudence exercised in this world. Likewise, the stations in Hell will differ for tyrants on the basis of the different degrees of the unlawful [they committed or consumed].

Now, if you have understood the truth of this matter, you have a choice: if you like, be as cautious as you possibly can; and if you like, use license with yourself. But, remember, it is for yourself that you are wary, and it is against yourself that you use license.

Peace!

CHAPTER TWO

The Degrees of the Dubious, Its Causes and How it is Distinguished from the Lawful and the Unlawful

THE MESSENGER OF God (may God bless him and grant him peace) said, 'The lawful is self-evident and the unlawful is self-evident; but between the two are dubious matters not well understood by very many people. Those who avoid the dubious will protect their honour and their religion. But those who engage in the dubious will eventually commit something unlawful; in the same way that a shepherd who grazes his herd on the edge of a preserve will eventually trespass on it.'[1]

This tradition represents clear evidence for the existence of three distinct categories, the middlemost of which is the only problematic category among them—the one not well understood by very many people—the dubious. It is essential, therefore, that this category be explained, and that its veil be removed; for what may not be understood by the many, may yet be understood by the few.

Thus, we may say that: the 'strictly lawful' (*al-ḥalāl al-muṭlaq*) is that in which there are no intrinsic attributes that make it unlawful in and of itself, and in which there are no extrinsic reasons for it to be unlawful either. An example [of the strictly lawful] is water collected from rain before it falls on anyone's property, when the collector himself is standing either on his own [property], or on public property.

The 'strictly unlawful' (*al-ḥarām al-maḥḍ*)[A] is that in which there is an undoubted attribute of the unlawful; like intoxication in wine, or impurity in urine; or in which such an attribute came about owing to a clearly unlawful cause; like oppression, or interest (*ribā*), or the like.

These, then, are two self-evident opposites.

The same applies to whatever is connected to either category while admitting of the possibility that [a thing] may change [from one category to the other], even though there is no reason that indicates the possibility of this occurrence. Game taken on land or from the sea is lawful.[B] But a gazelle taken as game may possibly have been taken by another hunter before it ran away in a wounded condition. Likewise, a fish caught from the sea may have slipped away from another fisherman's hand or net. This kind of possibility, however, does not occur in regard to falling rainwater gathered from the air. Nonetheless, these others are as the rainwater in terms of their categorisation as lawful.[2]

To attempt to avoid or to abstain from such things must be considered unfounded suspicion (*waswās*). I will label the propensity [to do so anyway] 'the Caution of the Overly Suspicious' (*wara*ʿ *al-muwaswisīn*),[C] so that everything of this nature may be understood in the same way. Obviously, this is pure delusion without the least basis in fact.

Certainly, if there should be evidence to indicate [a change], and if this evidence is incontrovertible, like for example if the gazelle had an [owner's] tag in its ear,[3] or if the fish had a hook in

[A] Earlier Ghazālī used *al-ḥarām al-muṭlaq*; *muṭlaq* and *maḥḍ* are here used as synonyms and are not intended as different levels of prohibition.

[B] See Q.v.1 and Q.v.96. It should be noted that game is considered slaughtered in a lawful manner as long as its death results either directly or indirectly by something that is done by the hunter, even if he is unable to reach it in time to slaughter it in the prescribed way.

[C] We have chosen to translate *wara*ʿ here as 'caution' to differentiate it from the more positive degrees of *wara*ʿ ('prudence') that Ghazālī discusses in the previous chapter.

its mouth; or even if the evidence indicates a mere possibility [of a change], like if the gazelle were wounded or marked in a way that could be taken as a branding, then that becomes a situation for prudence. But when the evidence is negated in every way, then a possibility for which there is no evidence is as a possibility that does not exist.

This is like someone leasing a house assuming, if the landlord were to be absent for a time, that the landlord had died and the rights to the house had passed to the heirs.[A] This would be no more than unfounded suspicion because there is neither incontrovertible proof nor anything to occasion reasonable doubt; reasonable doubt being uncertainty caused by two conflicting convictions. That which has no cause (*sabab*) cannot be the reason for a conflict with another conclusion and thus occasion doubt.

It is for this reason that we say that someone who has doubts as to whether he has prayed three or four cycles (*rakʿa*) of prayer should proceed as if he had prayed three, because the only certainty is that he has prayed three.[B]

[A] The unfounded assumption on the part of the lessee here is that since the landlord is no more, rent for the house will have to be paid to the heirs.

[B] According to the *Kuwait Fiqh Encyclopedia* (*al-Mawsūʿa al-fiqhiyya*), a habitual possessor of unfounded suspicions is one who has doubts during worship, and whose doubts continue to increase until he doubts whether or not he has actually performed the act of worship once he has performed it. Doubt, in principle, requires that what is omitted be repeated. This is like someone's lifting his head (during prayer) and then having doubts as to whether or not he had performed a cycle of the prayer (*rukūʿ*). In such a case, the cycle must be performed (perhaps again) because the principle is that what is doubted may not be supposed to have occurred. Instead, one must proceed from certainty, i.e., from whatever one is certain of having performed. So, if one has doubts about whether one performed three or four cycles in the prayer, one must proceed from the certainty of having performed three by praying another cycle and then doing a prostration of negligence (*al-sahw*). If, however, one is a possessor of unfounded suspicions, then he may not pay attention to his suspicions because to do so will lead to hardship, and the *Sharīʿa* denies hardship. See *al-Mawsūʿa al-fiqhiyya*, xiv.233. See also, Ibn

Likewise, if someone were asked if the midday (*ẓuhr*) prayer he performed ten years before was three or four cycles (*rakʿa*s), and there was no way that he could be absolutely sure his prayer was four cycles, then such a possibility will not be called reasonable doubt[A] because it is not accompanied by a cause that would bring about the conviction that he had prayed only three.

Thus, understand the difference between reasonable doubt (*shakk*) and unfounded suspicion (*waswās*) and a possibility that is only imagined (*wahm*) as these may apply to the strictly lawful.

Likewise, something clearly unlawful, but which admits of the possibility of being lawful even though there is no evidence to indicate the validity of a legitimising factor, may apply to the strictly unlawful.

This is illustrated by the case of a person in whose possession there is produce belonging to a testator from whom he is to inherit as the sole heir. If the testator should absent himself, and the heir supposes him dead and that the ownership of the produce had passed on to himself, the heir would be committing the strictly unlawful [if he then disposes of the produce] because there is no reason for such an assumption [of ownership, without evidence].

This example, then, should not be counted among the different categories of reasonable doubts. By doubt we mean something we are unable to decide about, owing to two conflicting convictions; both of which come about for reasons that give rise to the two convictions.

There are five reasons for such uncertainties.[B]

al-Humām, *Fatḥ al-qadīr* (Beirut, 2003) 1.534; Fārisī, *al-Fatāwā al-hindiyya* (Beirut, 1986), 1.128.

[A] Meaning: his inability to remember how many *rakʿa*s he performed falls under the category of 'reasonable' not 'unreasonable' doubt.

[B] The discussion that ensues covers a significant portion of the book and yet mentions only four reasons. While it may be speculated that the fifth reason was ignored by a copyist, or that the author simply lost count, a simpler explanation is that he meant to say that there are four reasons for such uncertainties, and not five. In our estimation, it is difficult to imagine a classification of

Chapter Two

The First Reason for Doubt: Doubt Concerning Legitimising and Prohibiting Factors

In this there are two possibilities: either that the two factors are equally valid, or that one outweighs the other.[4]

If the two factors are equally valid, then the legal categorisation will be made on the basis of what was previously known, by means of presuming the continuing existence of a known state of affairs (*istiṣḥāb al-ḥāl*). The original legal categorisation [under such circumstances] may not be abandoned on the basis of doubt.

If one of the factors, owing to its substantiation[5] by considered evidence, should outweigh the other, the ruling will go to that factor.

None of this, however, will be clear except by means of examples and illustrations. We shall therefore divide the matter into four categories:

THE FIRST CATEGORY: When the prohibition is known beforehand, and then something happens to occasion doubt concerning a legitimising factor.

This is the kind of doubt that must be avoided, and it is unlawful to act upon [anything about which there is this kind of doubt].

An example of this kind of doubt is when a hunter shoots game and wounds it so that it falls into water. Later, if the hunter should come across the animal dead in the water, and does not know whether it had died from his arrow or from drowning, the game will be unlawful.[A]

The reason for this is that the legal presumption (*aṣl*) will always be for prohibition, unless the animal dies in a particular

reasonable doubt beyond the four, each with its own set of degrees and categories, discussed here by the author. The commentator, Zabīdī, makes no mention of the matter at all. One can only say that God knows best.

[A] In the case of a wounded animal falling into the water and being found dead later by a hunter, the certainty is that it is dead, and the doubt is in regard to the legitimising factor or, in this case, the way in which it died. See Ghazālī, *Wasīṭ*, IV.221; Rāfiʿī, *al-ʿAzīz sharḥ al-Wajīz*, XII.34–35.

way; and in this case there is doubt regarding the way it died. And certainty may not be discarded for doubt, as in cases of the breaking of ritual purity, unclean substances, the number of cycles one has prayed, and so on.

This is the principle upon which the following ruling [of the Messenger of God] (may God bless him and grant him peace) was based, when he said to ʿAdī b. Ḥātim, 'Do not eat the game; for I fear that the dog will have killed it for himself.'[6]

This also explains why [the Messenger of God] (may God bless him and grant him peace) would ask questions when he was unsure about whether he had been given something as charity (*ṣadaqa*) or as an outright gift.[7] It is related that the Messenger of God (may God bless him and grant him peace) spent a sleepless night. When one of his wives said to him, 'You didn't sleep at all last night,' he replied, 'Yes, I found a date yesterday, and I couldn't sleep because I was afraid it might have come from charity.'[8] Another version of the same *ḥadīth* reads, 'I ate it, and was concerned that it might have been charity.'

Another example was narrated by certain of the Companions. 'We were on a journey with the Messenger of God (may God bless him and grant him peace) when we were overtaken by hunger. So we made camp at a place where there were many sand lizards. Then, while the pots were still boiling with them, the Messenger of God (may God bless him and grant him peace) said, "There was once a tribe from the Children of Isrāʾīl that was transformed by God to animals. I am afraid that these might be them." So we overturned the pots.'[9] Later, God revealed to him that He had not allowed the transformed people to procreate.[10]

The prohibition [by the Messenger of God] (may God bless him and grant him peace) was based on the principle that the ruling in such matters is their prohibition. Accordingly, he had doubts about whether slaughtering them in the prescribed manner would make them lawful.[A]

[A] The Messenger of God (upon him be peace) had a personal dislike for

The Second Category: When there is doubt concerning a prohibiting factor in something known to be lawful.

The presumption in regard to the legal categorisation of things is that they are lawful [unless there is evidence to the contrary], and thus goes the legal ruling.[A] For example, two men marry two women and then, upon seeing a bird fly overhead, one of the men says, 'If that bird is a crow, my wife stands divorced.' Then the other man says, 'If it is not a crow, then mine is divorced,'[11] and it was impossible to ascertain whether or not the bird was [a crow].[12]

In each case, the ruling is for the lawful; that the divorce does not take place. Thus, neither man will be required to stay away from his wife. Prudence, however, dictates that they do so[B] and that they both divorce their wives so that the women may become lawful for whomever else would marry them.[C]

In a similar case, Makḥūl ordered that the men never again approach their wives.

Shaʿbī decided the same in a case in which two men had disputed. One said to the other, 'You are jealous.' The other replied, 'The wife of the one among us who is the most jealous is divorced.' Then the first man said, 'Yes.' Thereafter it was impossible to determine which of the two was indeed the more jealous.[13] So,

sand lizards, saying that they were not of the land of his tribe. It is nonetheless recorded that sand lizard was served on his table on more than one occasion, as will be mentioned later in this book.

[A] The understanding among jurists is that the law divides human actions into two different spheres: worship and transactions. Since the first is prescribed by the Almighty in accordance with specific directions, the legal presumption in such matters is that unless there is proof to the contrary (through revelation) if the the act is changed it will become prohibited. With regard to transactions, since these take place all the time between humans, the legal presumption will be that unless there is proof to the contrary, all such doings will be considered lawful.

[B] i.e., that they stay away from their wives in the sense of refraining from conjugal relations.

[C] See Ibn Taymiyya, *Majmūʿat al-fatāwā*, IV.493; Haytamī, *al-Fatāwā al-ḥadīthiyya* (Cairo, 1937) III.147.

in that case, if [Shaʿbī] had ruled with the intention that their not approaching their wives was a matter of caution, his decision was correct. But, if he intended that their doing so would be unlawful, there was no basis for deciding on such a ruling.[A] This is because it is an established legal principle in cases of water, impurities, ablutions and prayer that certainty may not be displaced by doubt. And this case is similar.

If you were to ask what the relationship between this case and that [case] could be, you should know that there need not be a relationship because the ruling will be the same without [a relationship], at least in most versions of a case like this. For, as long as the purity of the water is a matter of certainty, even if one were to doubt its purity, it would still be lawful to perform ablutions with that water. So how could it be unlawful to drink it? And if it is lawful to drink, then the principle is upheld that certainty may not be displaced by doubt.

There is, however, a subtlety here. The parallel to the question of the water is for the man to doubt whether or not he divorced his wife, so that it may be said that the legal presumption there is that he did not divorce his wife. The parallel of the case with the bird is for impurity to be ascertained in one of two vessels, without knowing exactly which one.[B] In such a case, it will not be lawful to use any one of the two without attempting to determine which one holds the impurity because the certainty that one is impure controverts the certainty that the other is pure. So, in such cases, the presumption of continuing

[A] Shaʿbī ruled on the side of prudence in a similar case. See ʿAbd al-Razzāq, *al-Kitāb al-muṣannaf*, Kitāb al-ṭalāq (Beirut, 1970–72) VI.374.

[B] The 'bird' here refers to the first case in this section in which the divorce pronounced by the two men is, in both cases, condition: if the 'bird' is a crow the divorce is pronounced and if it is not, the divorce will not be pronounced. 'Vessels' here is generic and does not refer to previously mentioned vessels in particular. This is a completely new case, but one that is similar to the case of the bird/crow because of the inability in both instances to identify one that would lead to a clear ruling.

existence [i.e., that the water is still pure] is rendered invalid.

Here too, in the same way, divorce was definitely pronounced over one of the two wives. But it is impossible to determine which one of the two women was actually divorced.[A]

The Shāfiʿī jurists differed on the question of the two vessels, taking three different legal positions. One group opined that the presumption of continuing existence (*istiṣḥāb*) was sufficient proof, so that no further attempt to determine the matter (*ijtihād*) was called for. Another group held that once it is ascertained that the purity of one is contravened by the impurity of the other, it is essential that both be avoided, and there is no point in attempting to determine which is which. The most reasonable group among them said that it is essential to make the attempt to determine which is which. And that is the correct position.[B]

The parallel to this, however, is for a man to have two[14] wives, so that he may say, 'If that bird is a crow, then Zaynab is divorced. And if it is not, then ʿAmara is [divorced].' In that case, surely, he may not have relations with either of the two, by presuming continuing existence. It is not permitted in such a case to attempt to determine (*ijtihād*) the case because there is no evidence. Therefore, both of the man's wives become unlawful for him. If he were to have sexual relations with both of them, he would definitely be committing an unlawful act. And if he were to have relations with only one of them, saying that he would restrict his sexual activity to her alone, then he would

[A] In the same way that one of the two vessels definitely contained impurities, divorce was definitely pronounced. However, while it is impossible to know which of the two women is divorced owing to the impossiblity of knowing whether or not the bird was a crow (with the result that recourse is had to a presumption of continuing existence, i.e., that the wives remain lawful to their husbands), it may be possible to ascertain which of the two vessels contains the impurities, which circumstance renders the presumption of continuing existence invalid.

[B] The author discusses this matter in some detail in his works of jurisprudence. See Rāfiʿī, *al-ʿAzīz sharḥ al-Wajīz*, 1.72–78; Ghazālī, *Wasīṭ*, 1.64–66.

only be guessing, specifying one rather than the other for no valid reason.

In such a case, then, there is a difference between the ruling for one person and the ruling for two, because there is no certainty about which of the two had actually become unlawful.

It might be possible to object that since the two water vessels belonged to two persons there should be no need to make the attempt to determine which was pure and which was not. Rather, each person should make ablutions from his own vessel because each is certain that his vessel was pure before that, and the doubt occurred afterwards.

We admit that this is a possibility, at least from the perspective of jurisprudence. However, the preponderant opinion[15] is prohibition [i.e., for both to abstain] because the plurality of persons[16] here is the same as there being only one. The reason for this is that the lawfulness of ablutions has nothing to do with ownership. Indeed, insofar as the removal of impurity is concerned, one's performance of ablutions from another's water is the same as one's performance of ablutions from one's own water. So it makes no difference if the vessels are owned by one or by two persons. But it is certainly unlawful to have sexual intercourse with another's wife.

Furthermore, evidence does play a part in matters concerning impurity, so there is scope for an attempt to determine its occurrence. But divorce is another matter. Thus, the presumption of continuing existence needs to be fortified by other evidence, so that the strength of the conviction that there is impurity may be countered by the conviction that there is purity.

The chapters on presumption of continuing existence and on the reasons for legal preponderance are among the most abstruse and demanding in the study of jurisprudence. While I have written at length on these subjects in other books,[A] my intention here is only to draw attention to some of the basic principles.

[A] In addition to references to the author's discussion of the subject above, see Ghazālī, *Mustaṣfā*, 1.217–220.

The Third Category: When the legal presumption is that something is unlawful, and something occurs that, in all probability, renders it lawful; such that it becomes dubious, and is probably lawful, and the situation becomes one that requires scrutiny.

If the probability is based on a legally valid reason, then the preferred ruling is that it is lawful, though it will be prudent for one to abstain from it.

An example of this is when one shoots game that then runs out of sight and is later found dead with no other sign [as to the cause of death] than the hunter's arrow. This situation admits of the possibility that the animal died as a result of a tumble or any other reason. If there should be a sign, however, of its having collided with something, or its having been wounded in another way, then the ruling concerning it will have to be the same as in the first category.[A]

There is some difference of opinion regarding the ruling given by Shāfiʿī (may God have mercy on him) in such cases. The preferred ruling, however, is that it will be lawful because a wound is clear evidence; and the legal presumption is that nothing else should have happened to it; nothing that would give rise to doubt, or that would be displaced by doubt.[B]

It might be objected[17] that Ibn ʿAbbās (may God be pleased with him) said, 'Eat of the game you kill before your eyes, and avoid the game that is wounded and runs.'[18]

It might also be objected that [Abū] ʿĀ'isha (may God be pleased with him) said, 'A man went to the Prophet (may God bless him and grant him peace) with a rabbit and said, "This is my game because I recognise my arrow in it." He [upon him be peace] asked the man if the rabbit had remained in sight after he shot it,

[A] See Rāfiʿī, *al-ʿAzīz sharḥ al-Wajīz*, xii.34–35; Zakariyyā Anṣārī, *Asnā al-maṭālib sharḥ rawḍ al-ṭālib*, (Egypt, 1313/1896), ii.558; Ibn ʿĀbidīn, *Radd al-muḥtār* v.469; Bahūtī, *Kashshāf al-qināʿ* (Riyadh, n.d.) vi.221.

[B] See Nawawī, *Majmūʿ*, v.131 in which he quotes the position of his imam, Shāfiʿī, and then states his preference for Ghazālī's opinion in the *Iḥyā'*.

or if it disappeared for a while. When the man replied that it had disappeared for a time, [the Messenger of God] (peace be upon him) said, "The night is one of God's creations. No one can appreciate its creation save the one who created it. Perhaps there was something else that contributed to the killing of the rabbit."'[19]

Likewise, it might be objected, [the Messenger of God] (peace be upon him) said to ʿAdī b. Ḥātim concerning his hunting dog, 'If it has eaten from the flesh of the game, then do not eat the game; for I fear the dog will have taken the game for itself.'[20] So here the probability is that the hound will not have forgotten[21] its training, and will have made the kill only at the bidding of its master. Even so, it was forbidden.[A]

Now, strictly speaking, it must be explained that something proves to be lawful where there proves to be a complete reason for it to be lawful. The complete reason here is the arrow's leading directly to the death of the game, without there being any other reason for the death. Doubt about this is doubt about there being a complete reason; such that it is unclear as to whether the death of the animal occurred in a lawful or in an unlawful manner. So, this is not the same as when the death proves to have occurred in a lawful manner at one time, and then there is doubt about something that occurs later on.

Thus, the answer to this question is that the forbidding by Ibn ʿAbbās and by the Messenger of God (may God bless him and grant him peace) should be understood as prudence, because of what was related in a certain tradition when [the Messenger of God] said, 'Eat of it, even if it disappears from sight; so long as you find no sign other than your arrow.'[22]

So this is to emphasise the point mentioned earlier that if other evidence is found [on the carcass], the two reasons will conflict, so that the two convictions will also conflict. Then, if nothing other than the one wound is found, there will be a probability,

[A] i.e., the Messenger of God (may God bless him and grant him peace) forbade the eating of the game.

and we may rule on the basis of it, overruling the presumption of continuing existence; in the same way that we may overrule the presumption of continuing existence on the basis of an individual's testimony, or by legal analogy (*qiyās*), or on the basis of whatever general principles may apply, or by other means.

As to the objection that its death did not prove to be under lawful circumstances at the time, so that there is doubt as to the cause of death; this is not the case. Rather, the cause is proved because the wound was the cause; and the doubt is in regard to the possibility of something else.

The correctness of this is attested to by the consensus of the scholars that if one person wounds another, and then the wounded person disappears only to be found dead [sometime later], retaliation (*qiṣāṣ*)[A] will be exacted from the one who inflicted the wound. Furthermore, even if the wounded person does not disappear, it is possible that his death takes place as a result of trauma caused by the wound; in the same way that some people die suddenly.

So, in other words, retaliation (*qiṣāṣ*) should not be exacted unless the wound is such that the neck is notched, or that the wound otherwise leads very quickly to death because the actual cause of death is something about which there can be little certainty; and quite often a perfectly healthy person will fall down dead. Yet, no one would say that retaliation should not be exacted for that reason, even though retaliation is based on reasonable doubt.

Likewise, the foetus in a slaughtered animal is lawful.[B] Yet, it is possible that it died before the slaughtering, for some reason other than the slaughtering.[23] . Then, because it never received the breath of life, blood money (*ghurra*) must be paid to the animal's

[A] *Qiṣāṣ* is legally prescribed retaliation for which details may be found in the legal commentaries of the Qur'ān at xvii.33–35 and the manuals of *fiqh*. See, for example, Rāfiʿī, *al-ʿAzīz sharḥ al-Wajīz*, x.117–288; Ghazālī, *Wasīṭ*, iv.103–107.

[B] See Shāfiʿī, *Kitāb al-umm* (Cairo, 1321/1903), iii.258; Anṣārī, *Ghurar*, i.41; Sharbīnī, *Mughnī al-muḥtāj*, vi.159.

owner.[A] Or maybe it never was alive, or maybe the man died for some other reason just before the wound was made.

So, the ruling must be based upon the outward causes. If there is no reliable evidence to back up the other possibility, then to rule on it would amount to ruling on mere notion and suspicion (*waswāsa*), as was mentioned earlier. The same is true here.

Shāfiʿī (may God be pleased with him) has two interpretations of the saying [of the Messenger of God] (peace be upon him), 'I fear that the dog will have killed it for itself.'[B] The one I prefer is the unlawful ruling because the reason was contravened.

This is because a hunting dog is like a tool, or an agent who acts on behalf of his principal. Thus, what it kills is lawful. But if a hunting dog were to proceed on its own and kill, the game will not be lawful because the legal presumption in that case will be that the dog was hunting for itself. If it sets out at the command of its master, however, and still eats of the game's flesh, its setting out on command indicates that it acts as the master's tool, and that it proceeds as his agent, and on his behalf. At the same time, however, its eating indicates that it is acting on its own behalf, and not for its master. Thus when the indicative factors are contradictory, the legal presumption, that to consume the game is unlawful, will continue to exist (*istiṣḥāb*) and will not be erased by doubt.

This is like one's appointing an agent to buy a slave-girl, and then the agent dies before he is able to explain whether the girl he bought was for himself or for his principal. In such a case the principal may not have intercourse with the girl because the agent had the power to make the purchase for himself as well as for his principal. Since there is no decisive evidence, and the legal presumption is that it is unlawful [to have intercourse with a slave-girl

[A] See Ibn al-Humām, *Fatḥ al-qadīr* x.306; Muḥammad b. Qāsim al-Raṣṣāʿ, *Sharḥ Ḥudūd Ibn ʿArafa* (Tunis, 1350/1932), pp. 483–484; Ḥaṭṭāb, *Mawāhib al-jalīl fī sharḥ Mukhtaṣar al-Khalīl* (Beirut, 1995), VIII.33.

[B] See Nawawī, *Majmūʿ*, V.131.

owned by another], this case, then, falls under the first category[A] and not the third.

THE FOURTH CATEGORY: When something is known to be lawful but it then becomes probable that, for a reason that is likely to be legally valid, there is a prohibiting factor such that the presumption of continuing existence is invalidated and a ruling of unlawful is given because when it appears that the presumption of continuing existence is weak, the original ruling no longer stands up to the new probability.

The example of this is when one's reasoning leads him to believe that one of two vessels is impure based on specific evidence [like the proximity of a thirsty dog] which brings about a preponderant opinion [on the matter] such that to drink from it becomes unlawful and, likewise, to use it for ablutions.[24] A similar example is when one says, 'If Zayd kills ᶜAmr, or if Zayd kills game by himself, then my wife is divorced,' and then [Zayd] only wounds [ᶜAmr] or the game, following which [ᶜAmr] or the game disappears, until he or it is found dead. In such a case one's wife will stand divorced because what is apparent is that [Zayd] alone killed [ᶜAmr] or the game, as discussed earlier.

Shāfiᶜī (may God have mercy on him) stated that if one finds water with changed characteristics in a well, there is a possibility that the changes occurred as a result of stagnation, or owing to impurities. Therefore, one may not use that water. If one witnesses a gazelle urinating in the water, and then discovers that it has changed [i.e., the attributes of the water have changed], so that there is a possibility that it changed either as a result of the urine or by stagnation, then its use will be unlawful.[B] This is because the witnessing of the gazelle urinating becomes a dominant indica-

[A] i.e., the category in which the prohibition is known to have been in place when doubt occurs in regard to a legitimising factor. In the third category, however, prohibition is in place when something occurs which, in all probability, requires legitimisation. See Z.VI.39.

[B] See Rāfiᶜī, *al-ᶜAzīz sharḥ al-Wajīz*, I.50–52; Anṣārī, *Asnā al-maṭālib*, I.26-27; Anṣārī, *Ghurar*, I.71 and Bujayramī, *Tuḥfat al-Ḥabīb fī sharḥ al-khaṭīb*, I.91.

tion of the possibility that impurity caused the changes; and this is an example of what we mentioned.

This is in reference to a probability that is based on evidence concerning the substance of something. In reference to probability that is not based on evidence concerning something's substance, Shāfiʿī's opinions are at variance as to whether, if the principle is that something be lawful, then will that be invalidated by such a probability? The reason for this is that his opinions differ on the question of the legality of performing ablutions from vessels belonging to idolaters or habitual wine drinkers,[C] and on the question of praying in excavated graves, or in the dust[D] of well-travelled roads; and I mean here in measures, or to degrees, greater than it would normally be possible to avoid.

His adherents [the jurists of the Shāfiʿī school] explained that the differences of opinion originated from the question of which is to be given consideration (i.e., preference) when the legal presumption and the probability are mutually contradictory. This difference extends to the question regarding whether or not it is lawful to drink from the vessels of idolaters and habitual drinkers of wine, because it is unlawful to drink what is impure.[E] Then the source [from which a legal ruling] of impurity [is derived] and [the source of a] lawful [ruling] is one; and uncertainty about [that derivation in] one will occasion uncertainty about the other.

My own preference is that the legal presumption is the more valid [of the two], and that evidence not concerning the substance of what is to be used does not necessitate invalidation of the legal presumption. An explanation of this matter will be given in [the

[C] While there may be no evidence to indicate that the water in such vessels is impure, the fact remains that they belong to drinkers of wine and may have had wine in them.

[D] Here, too, there is ambiguity about impurities. Not all the dirt from an excavated grave would be contaminated with impure substances, nor would all the dirt on a well-travelled road (over which animals would have passed and perhaps have left excrement).

[E] See Nawawī, *Majmūʿ*, 1.322; Sharbīnī, *Mughnī al-muḥtāj*, 1.139.

section below entitled] The Second Reason for Doubt: the Doubt of Intermixture.

From the above, the ruling of lawful when there is doubt concerning something being affected by a prohibiting factor, or the likelihood of one, and the ruling of unlawful when there is doubt concerning something being affected by a legitimising factor, or the likelihood of one, will have become clear. Likewise, the difference between a probability based on evidence concerning the substance of something and a probability that is not based on such evidenc should also be clear.

Furthermore, everything we ruled to be lawful in these four categories is lawful in the first degree, although prudence dictates their avoidance. Thus, one who would proceed with these things would not be numbered among the people of heeding (*muttaqīn*), or piety (*ṣāliḥīn*), but rather of the people of equilibrium (*ʿudūl*) who would not be declared by a *fatwā* either wrongdoers or sinners or deserving of punishment—save for that which we described as unfounded suspicion because one's refraining from [unfounded suspicion][A] is not really a matter of prudence.

The Second Reason for Doubt: Doubt Predicated Upon Intermixture

This is the doubt of intermixture, and it occurs when something unlawful becomes intermixed with something lawful[25] and the matter becomes uncertain such that one can no longer be distinguished from the other.

Such intermixing will occur either when both lawful and unlawful are in unlimited number or measure, or when one of the two is limited, or when both are limited. Then, when intermixture takes place in a limited measure, the intermixing will either

[A] The sense here is that refraining from unfounded suspicion is more a matter of common sense. Those given to unfounded suspicion often delude themselves into thinking that they are living a life of piety and heeding.

be a blending where there is nothing to demarcate what is unlawful and what is lawful; as when liquids mix. Or the intermixing will be an ambiguous[26] intermixing of distinguishable objects, like slaves, or buildings, or horses. The ambiguous intermixing, furthermore, will occur either with reference to something sought for itself, like merchandise; or to something that is not sought for itself, like hard currency.[A]

From the explanation above it is evident that there are three categories here:

THE FIRST CATEGORY OF INTERMIXTURE is when an object becomes indistinguishably intermixed among a limited number, as when a slaughtered animal becomes intermixed with a carcass,[B] or with ten [other animals],[27] or when a nursed sister is not distinguished from[C] with ten other women,[D] or if a man were to marry one of two sisters and then become confused as to which one was his wife. By consensus of the scholars, in such situations abstinence is essential because there is no scope either for legal reasoning (*ijtihād*) and there is no evidence. When something becomes intermixed with a limited number, the entire lot becomes as one,[E]

[A] i.e., gold or silver. Currency in the time of the author was not interchangeable or standardised, and was therefore classified as distinguishable. In our own times, currency would fall under the first heading, i.e., there is nothing to demarcate what is unlawful and what is lawful in it. Clearly, there is no way of knowing precisely which unit of currency was involved in which transaction. Transactions of significant volume are seldom carried out by means of cash.

[B] The meaning of carcass here is an animal not slaughtered in the lawful manner.

[C] i.e., in the sense that her identity as a nursed sister would be lost among a group of ten others, each of whom may have been nursed by the same woman.

[D] Note here that the problem would be in regard to the legality of marriage to a woman from the group, when one is known to be a nursed sister to the suitor and therefore prohibited to him. See the legal commentaries on verse (IV.23) in the Qur'ān for details of this prohibition. See also Ghazālī, *al-Wasīṭ*, IV.224.

[E] What this means is that the ruling for one becomes the ruling for all.

and the certainty of its being lawful is contradicted by the certainty of its being unlawful.

In such cases it makes no difference if something is first known to be lawful, and then is intermixed with something unlawful. This is like the case of a man pronouncing divorce on one of [his] two wives [in the example given above] of the bird; or like when something is intermixed before it is known to be lawful; or like when a nursed sister is mistaken for an unrelated (*ajnabiyya*) woman, and a nursed brother wants to make either of them [his] lawful [wife]. In such a case doubt arises[28] regarding the unlawful, as in the case of divorce of one of two wives, as mentioned above, even when continuing existence may be presumed.

We have already drawn attention to the reason behind the answer, and the continued existence [of this situation], that the certainty of the unlawful contravened the certainty of the lawful, so that the presumption of continuing existence [for the lawful] was rendered ineffective. Then, as the aspect of danger is more significant in the view of the *Sharīʿa*, preference is given to the unlawful ruling.

This is the case when the intermixing takes place between a limited quantity of the lawful and a limited quantity of the unlawful. Now, if a limited quantity of the lawful were to become intermixed with an unlimited quantity of the unlawful, the necessity to avoid it should be all the more obvious.

THE SECOND CATEGORY OF INTERMIXTURE is when a limited quantity of something unlawful intermixes with an unlimited quantity of something lawful. This would be like a nursed sister, or even ten of them, intermixing in a big city. Such circumstances would not mean that he [a nursed brother who knew only that several nursed sisters were in the city, without knowing exactly who they were] would have to refrain from marrying in that city. On the contrary, he may marry whomsoever he desires to marry [in the city].

The reason for this, however, must not be understood as being simply because of a surfeit of the lawful. For that would mean that marriage would be lawful if one unlawful marriage partner were to be confused among nine who were lawful. And no one would allow that. Rather, the reasons are [the existence of] *both* prevalence (*ghalaba*) and necessity (*ḥāja*). Indeed, it is impossible to close the door to marriage on everyone who loses track, for whatever reason, of relatives, nursed [brothers and sisters] or in-laws. Likewise, one who knows for a certainty that the wealth of the world has definitely had the unlawful intermixed with it need not abstain from buying and selling, or from eating, because that would be an undue hardship. And Islam is not a hardship.[A]

This is attested to by the fact that in the time of the Messenger of God (God bless him and grant him peace) when a shield[29] was stolen, and when a robe (*ʿabā'*)[30] was misappropriated from among the spoils of war, no one refrained from buying shields or robes. The same applies to anything stolen.

Likewise, it was known at that time that certain people were making usurious transactions in dinars and dirhams, yet neither the Messenger of God (may God bless him and grant him peace), nor his Companions refrained from using dinars and dirhams in their dealings.[B] Essentially, then, the world will be free of the unlawful only when people stop doing wrong, and that is impossible. So, when it is not stipulated that all people stop doing wrong in the world in order for anything to be lawful, it is not stipulated in a city either, unless the city be entirely cut off. Therefore, such abstinence is no more than the prudence of the overly suspicious, as it was never recorded from the Messenger of God (may God bless him and grant him peace) or any of his Companions.[31] Nor, for that matter, is it imaginable among any people anywhere, or at any time.

Someone might object that every quantity is limited in the knowledge of God, and then ask 'What is the definition of

[A] Allusion to Q.LXXVIII.22.

[B] There is an allusion to this in a *ḥadīth* related on the authority of Jābir that will be mentioned later.

limited?' Or state that if one wanted to count the number of inhabitants in a city, one could do so, if given the means.

Then, know that it is impossible to be precise in numbering any of these things, or their likes. Rather, they are determined on the basis of approximation. So, we can say that any number which is difficult for a viewer to arrive at, as when one or two thousand people are standing in an open space, may be considered unlimited. Whereas, what is simple to count, like ten or twenty people, may be considered limited. Between these two, however, there is a great and ambiguous middle ground which may, on the basis of probability, be legally aligned with either one of the two extremes.

Should any kind of doubt occur on this matter, one's heart should be consulted; for surely wrongdoing pricks the heart.[A]

It was in a situation such as this that the Messenger of God (may God bless him and grant him peace) said to Wābiṣa, 'Inquire of your heart;[B] even though others may answer you with *fatwā* after *fatwā*.'[32]

[A] These words are actually from a *ḥadīth* that was related by Bayhaqī in his *Shuʿab al-imān*, VII.307 and IX.410. When the Messenger of God (may God bless him and grant him peace) was asked about the meanings of piety and sin he replied, 'Piety is what your heart is comfortable with, and sin is what pricks your heart.'

[B] The word used in the text of the *ḥadīth* comes from the same root as *fatwā*; and this is why I have translated it in the way that I have: '...even though they may answer you with *fatwā* after *fatwā*.' Certainly, this is the sense of the *ḥadīth*. Moreover, considering that the pronoun 'they' refers to the Prophet's Companions, and probably to the most learned of the Companions, it is obvious that a very important point about the instincts and feelings of the individual believer is being made here. Even so, no one should imagine that the *ḥadīth* is in any way anti-authoritarian. Rather, in the same way that the opinions of the learned have their place, so also with one's heartfelt instincts. Likewise, there is no validity to the notion held by many, especially Sufis, that only a purified heart may be listened to and trusted. The heart, or the conscience, of a believer will always be true. But the believer must be honest enough with him or herself to know when it is the heart that is doing the urging, and when the source of the urging is something other than the heart. The author discusses this *ḥadīth* again later in this chapter. And God knows best.

Likewise, in regard to the four categories we mentioned in the *First Reason for Doubt*, there are clearly contradictory opposites that are either positive or negative, and between them lies a vast middle ground of ambiguity.

So, just as the *muftī* answers on the basis of probability, the questioner must [equally] consult his heart. Later, if his conscience is pricked by something he has done, then, between God and himself, he is the wrongdoer. Certainly, no *fatwā* from any *muftī* can protect him in the Afterlife because the *muftī*'s rulings are based on what is apparent; whereas God knows all that is hidden.

THE THIRD CATEGORY OF INTERMIXTURE is the intermixing of unlimited quantities of both lawful and unlawful, as is the case with wealth in our times.[33]

Now, those who derive rulings from externals only will opine that since the relationship between one unlimited quantity and another is the same as the relationship between one limited quantity and another, and as we already have a ruling of unlawful there, the ruling here should be the same. My own preference in the matter, however, is other than this. In fact, this kind of intermixing will not make it unlawful to consume something that, in itself, may be lawful or may be unlawful, unless the substance of that something should contain evidence to indicate that it is actually unlawful. If such evidence should not, however, be present, the way of caution and prudence will be abstention from the substance. Nonetheless, it will be lawful to consume it, so that one who does so will not be a wrongdoer.

An example of the kind of evidence pertinent to such cases is that the substance comes from the hand of a despotic ruler. Other forms of evidence will be discussed later on.

Now, the evidence [in support of the opinion towards which I have inclined] comes from both narrative (*athar*) and analogy (*qiyās*).

The narrative evidence is that in the time of the Messenger of God (may God bless him and grant him peace) as well as in the time of the Rightly-Guided Caliphs (may God be pleased with them) money belonging to the disbelievers living under the protection of Islam, money taken in exchange for wine or invested in usurious transactions or misappropriated from the spoils of war, was intermixed with all the other money [in circulation at the time].

Moreover, from the time that he (may God bless him and grant him peace) announced the prohibition against interest (*ribā*), when he said, 'The first interest I write off is the interest owed to ᶜAbbās,'[34] not all of the people discontinued their usurious transactions. The same was true in regard to the drinking of wine, and all the other misdeeds [prohibited by Islam]. Even some of the Companions of the Messenger of God sold wine. So ᶜUmar[35] (may God be pleased with him) said, 'May God curse so-and-so! He was the first to establish the sale of wine,'[36] for he had not understood then[A] that the prohibition against wine was actually against receiving the price of wine.[37]

He [the Messenger of God] (may God bless him and grant him peace) said, 'So-and-so will drag over Hellfire the hem of the long robe he stole from the spoils of war.'[38]

Likewise, a man from the Companions was killed in battle; and when his belongings were gathered it was discovered that he had misappropriated some pearls from the Jews, though their value was no more than two dirhams.[39]

Moreover, several of the Companions of the Messenger of God (may God bless him and grant him peace) lived to see tyrannical rulers. When the city of Medina was pillaged for three days by the army of Yazīd,[40] not one of the Companions refused to buy and sell in the marketplace [when it reopened].[B] Such participation

[A] At this point in the text, Zabīdī says the following: 'This is an excuse by the author for the deed of that particular Companion.' Zabīdī also explains that ᶜUmar's cursing the man was not to be taken literally, but was meant as an emphatic rebuke. See Z.vi.43.

[B] Among the tyrants listed by Zabīdī in his commentary were Yazīd b. Muᶜāwiya, ᶜUbayd Allāh b. Ziyād, Marwān b. ᶜAbd al-Mālik, Yazīd b. ᶜAbd al-Mālik, Yūsuf b. Ḥajjāj, and their ilk. Zabīdī then went on to explain the

is remarkable because in those days anyone who refrained from dealing in the pillaged goods was held as an example of piety. So, in spite of the obvious intermixing and the surfeit of plundered goods in the times of the despots, the majority [of Muslims] did not avoid the markets.

Anyone who imposes upon himself what the pious Predecessors did not, and who supposes himself to have a more complete understanding of the *Sharīʿa* than they [the Predecessors] had of it, that person is surely deluded and mentally unbalanced. Therefore, if it were lawful to outdo them in matters such as these, it would be lawful to contradict them in questions in which their only authority was their agreement; as in the case of considering a grandmother to be equally as unlawful as a mother,[A] or a grandson to be the same as a son,[B] or the hair and fat of swine to be as unlawful as its flesh, though only the flesh is mentioned in the Qur'ān,[41] or in considering the prohibition against interests to be valid in cases involving substances other than the six expressly mentioned.[C] Clearly, all of that is impossible, as they [the pious Predecessors] certainly had a better understanding of the *Sharīʿa* than others did.

Evidence [in support of my opinion comes] from analogy, for

following: 'Those sent by Yazīd to Medina were led by Muslim b. ʿUqba, known as "The Excessive". He laid siege to the city, cutting it off with great cruelty and then ordering it to be pillaged (by his troops). For three days and three nights, he ordered all manner of outrage and iniquity and murder. Cattle were tethered in the mosque. Acts of such depravity were committed during that period that their very mention is shameful. Thereafter, he granted the inhabitants immunity on condition that they become the slaves of Yazīd (upon whom be whatever he deserves from the Almighty!).' See Z.VI.43.

[A] i.e., in relation to a man married to the daughter, or granddaughter; so that his marriage to the mother or grandmother, while still married to the daughter or granddaughter, is unlawful.

[B] i.e., in certain cases of inheritance.

[C] The six substances are gold, silver, wheat, barley, dates and salt. For an excellent discussion of the six and their significance, see Nabil A. Saleh, *Unlawful Gain and Legitimate Profit in Islamic Law* (London, 1992), pp. 17–34.

if this door were to be opened, the door to all dealings would close. Then the world would truly come to ruin. This is because people in general are easily overcome by iniquity, and thus lax in adhering to what is stipulated by the *Sharīʿa* in their transactions. And that, no doubt, leads to intermixing.

It might be objected that a tradition about [the Messenger of God] (may God bless him and grant him peace) was related in which he refused to eat sand lizards, saying, 'There was once a tribe from the Children of Israel that was transformed by God into animals. I am afraid that these might be them.'[42] And that is a case in which a limited amount[A] was intermixed with an unlimited amount.[B]

My answer to this objection is to explain that his refusal was merely a matter of caution or prudence.[C] We might also say that that the sand lizard's appearance is, indeed, strange; and that the unnatural appearance of the substance in question may be an indicator of its [potential] unlawfulness.

An objection might be raised that it is well known regarding the times of the Messenger of God (may God bless him and grant him peace) and the times of his Companions after him, that intermixing took place as a result of usury, theft, plunder, misappropriation of the spoils of war, and the like. Even so, compared with the lawful the unlawful was quite uncommon. In our own times, however, the unlawful is pervasive owing to corrupt dealings in business, negligence in regard to conditions in contracts, the widespread use of interest, and the great wealth[43] of despotic rulers. What is the case then of a person who acquires wealth concerning which there appears to be no specific evidence to indicate its prohibition? Is it lawful or not?

[A] i.e., of transformed souls.

[B] i.e., of sand lizards.

[C] Ghazālī's opinion, like that of Shāfiʿī and others, was that it is not unlawful to eat sand lizards. Abū Ḥanīfa and his companions, however, held it to be unlawful. See Sarakhsī, *al-Mabsūṭ* (Beirut, 1409/1989), XI.221; Shawkānī, *Nayl al-awṭār sharḥ muntaqa al-akhbār* (Cairo, 1297/1880) XIII.289.

My answer is to say that it is not unlawful, but that caution dictates abstention from it. Moreover, caution under such circumstances is more important than caution when quantities are limited.

Still, the answer to the objection is to point out that it is an outright mistake to assume that the unlawful is pervasive in our times. This is because [such an assertion] overlooks the difference between what is common or commonplace and what is prevalent. Most people, even most jurists, assume that what is not rare is prevalent, thinking that these are two opposite categories between which there can be no third. This, however, is not the case. Rather, there are three categories: uncommon (*qalīl*), which is rare (*nādir*), common (*kathīr*), and prevalent (*akthar*). For example, hermaphrodites are rare among people. Furthermore, in relation to illness, health will be found to be prevalent; so much so that illness and travel are considered ordinary excuses, whereas *istiḥāḍa*[A] is considered an extraordinary excuse. It is well known that illness is not uncommon, nor yet is it prevalent. Instead, it is commonplace.

So, if a jurist is lax in his choice of words and says that illness and travel are prevalent and may therefore be considered ordinary excuses, when he means to say that these are not uncommon, then this is right in the sense that what is prevalent is not uncommon. But if he means other than this, he will be wrong. People who are healthy and non-travellers are prevalent, while unhealthy people and travellers are commonplace, and hermaphrodites and women with *istiḥāḍa* are uncommon.

Having explained this, we may go on to affirm that the statement that 'the unlawful is prevalent' is a faulty one. The reason for this is that the basis of such an assumption can either be the prevalence of unjust rulers and their minions, or the pervasiveness

[A] *Istiḥāḍa* is the term used to denote the appearance of blood after the usual number of days of a woman's period have passed, or after ten days if she does not have a usual number of days for her menstrual periods.

of usurious and corrupt transactions, or the inestimable number of hands through which, from the beginning of Islam to the present, the contemporary supply of money has passed.

The first basis is unsound because while unjust rulers may be commonplace, they are not prevalent. This is because injustices are committed by armed and outfitted soldiers and they, in relation to the rest of the population, constitute even less than one percent[44] of the total. For example, every ruler with a hundred thousand soldiers will rule over a territory in which a thousand thousand or more civilians live. Even the populace of one city, among the many that the ruler controls, may be greater than the ruler's army.

If, however, there were more rulers than subjects, everyone would be destroyed. The reason for this is that each subject supports the lavish lifestyle of a ruler. In fact, it takes a thousand or more subjects to support a single ruler. The same is true of thieves, for their numbers are insignificant when measured against the populace of a big city.

The second basis for such an assumption is the widespread practise of transacting usuriously or corruptly. This too, however, is commonplace but not prevalent. Indeed, most Muslims transact in accordance with what is stipulated by the *Sharīʿa*, so that the number [of sound transactions] are far greater. Even those who transact usuriously, if all of their transactions were counted, the number of their lawful and proper transactions would surely be greater than the number of their corrupt dealings. Of course, one might seek to estimate, in a given city, the particular dealings of the insane, the depraved, and the irreligious; and then speculate that the majority of those dealings would be corrupt. But such instances are truly rare.

Moreover, if those who transact usuriously or corruptly are commonplace, they are not prevalent. How can they be when the majority, or at least half, of their own dealings are lawful? This will be an obvious fact to anyone who cares to consider it. The reason for this sort of popular assumption is simply that people are prone to exaggerate the instances of corruption, and are repelled by it such that they find even a little of it intolerable. Therefore, [in the eyes of most people] corruption seems far greater, and far more prevalent, than it actually is. In fact, it is atypical. One might assume that interest (*ribā*)[45] and the drinking of wine are rife [in contemporary society], or as widespread as anything else that is unlawful. Then, the result of such thinking is that one will assume these things to be prevalent. Nonetheless, that assumption is incorrect because these things occur in the general populace only rarely, even if they are prevalent among certain circles in particular.

The third basis for such an assumption, and the one most commonly thought of, is to say that money comes from minerals, plants, and animals; and that animals[46] reproduce themselves. So, if we consider a goat, and that it gives birth maybe once yearly, then the number of goats originating from a single goat in the time of the Messenger of God (God bless him and grant him peace) would be about five hundred.[A] It is not inconceivable that, in the case of at least one goat out of the original number of goats, a theft occurred, or a misappropriation, or an improper exchange. How may it be supposed that the entire line [of transactions in goats] could have escaped some manner of corruption up to our own times? Likewise, the seeds of vegetables and fruit will have five hundred or a thousand for each one from the time the law [of Islam] was first revealed. And none of that will be lawful unless its seed was lawful, and unless all the seeds from which it sprang were lawful, all the way back to the time of the revelation.

As to minerals, they are substances that may be taken as if from the very beginning; and they represent, moreover, the rarest form of wealth. Then, among these what is used the most are dinars and dirhams,[B] though these come only from mints, and those are con-

[A] At the rate of one per year, by the time of the author, who died in 505 AH, the total would be about five hundred. See Z.VI.45.

[B] Dinars were coins based on gold, while dirhams were based on

trolled by the unjust. Indeed, the mines themselves are controlled by the unjust such that they prevent people from going there, and use the poor to dig them under great hardship, and then usurp from them [what the poor have so laboriously extracted]. So, in view of all this, for a single dinar to remain lawful, one that is free of injustice at the time of its being mined, and at the time of its being minted, and is afterwards never used in corrupt exchanges or usurious transactions, is either very rare or impossible.

There remains nothing, then, that is absolutely lawful except game, or grass from the open spaces and plains, or wood taken lawfully from the forest. Then, whoever obtains these things cannot eat them, but is forced to sell them for grain or animals that are produced either by reproduction or growing, so that the seller, in essence, exchanges the lawful for the unlawful. This, then, is the worst sort of notion to assail the mind.

The answer [to this objection] is that the [supposed] pervasiveness did not occur as the result of the prevalent unlawful intermixing with the lawful. As such, then, this is other than the model we have been considering here and is, in fact, more closely related to the case that we had alluded to earlier in which a legal presumption conflicts with what is probable. This is because the legal presumption in regard to these forms of wealth is that they may be accepted in dealings, and agreed over [in transactions]. In this instance, however, that principle is overruled by contradictory evidence that acts to negate the validity of the presumption. This is the basis of the two opinions held by Shāfiʿī (may God be pleased with him) on the question of impurities.[A]

The correct ruling in my opinion, however, is that prayer performed in the streets is lawful so long as there are no impurities there. The dust in the streets, after the rains, is pure. Likewise, [it

silver. See Abū al-Fatḥ al-Ṭarazī, *al-Mugharrib fī-tartīb al-muʿarrib* (Aleppo, 1402/1982), p. 163.

[A] i.e., that it is not lawful to perform prayer in the dirt of the streets, or use water kept in vessels owned by idolaters, etc., as discussed earlier.

is my opinion that] ablutions performed with water from the vessels of idolaters[A] are permitted, as is prayer in excavated graves.[B]

So, to begin with, this is the ruling that we affirm. Then we use analogy to compare this to the subject we are dealing with at present. Evidence in support of this position is that[47] the Messenger of God (upon him be peace and blessings) performed ablutions from an unbeliever's leather water-bag.[48] Likewise, ʿUmar (may God be pleased with him) performed ablutions from the vessels of Christians, even though they were known to drink wine and consume the flesh of swine, and thus never known to abstain from the kinds of impurities prohibited by the *Sharīʿa*. How, then, could anyone suppose that their vessels were kept free from contact with impurities?

On the contrary, we say that we know for a fact that they used to wear cured hides and dyed clothing, and everyone who knows tanners and dyers knows that impurities abound with them, and that it is either very rare or impossible that the garments they make ever remain pure.

We can say for a fact that they used to eat bread made from barley and wheat which, as grain, they did not wash; even though it had been trampled underfoot by cattle and domestic animals that urinated and excreted over it, so that very little of it escaped contamination. Moreover, they used to ride their perspiring mounts bareback; and they never washed the backs of those animals even though the animals used to roll in all manner of impurities, and quite often at that. In fact, every one of those animals, when born, emerged from its mother's womb covered in impurities that may or may not have been washed away by the rain later on.

Anyway, people have never bothered to avoid any of these things. They even went shoeless in the streets, though sometimes

[A] Ibn ʿĀbidīn, *Radd al-muḥtār*, 1.205–206.

[B] For a complete discussion of the matter of conflict between legal presumption and probability based on appearances, see Zarkashī, *al-Manthūr fī'l-qawāʿid* (Kuwait, 1402/1982), 1.313–315.

they did wear shoes. Then they would go and perform prayer. They would walk in the dirt and mud even if there was no particular need for doing so. They did not, however, deliberately step in urine or excrement, or sit in it. Rather they avoided these things.

So when were the streets ever free of impurities? There has always been an abundance of dogs and their urine, and of so many other animals and their dung! Nor should one suppose that time or place ever made any difference in these matters; as if they used to wash the streets in the old days! Or prevent animals from using them. No, indeed! That is something that custom tells us is obviously impossible.

This indicates that they avoided only apparent impurities, or signs of impurities. They did not, however, give consideration to probabilities that arose as a result of comparing conjecture to actual conditions.

This is the opinion of Shāfiᶜī who held that a small quantity of water would not become impure unless an actual change[A] took place in it. This is because the Companions continued to enter the public baths [after the conquests] and perform ablutions there from pools and basins in which there was little water. Even so, many hands would continually be dipped in that water.[B]

So this is conclusive evidence in this regard. When the permissibility of performing ablutions in the vessels of the Christians has thus been established, so also is the permissibility of drinking from them; where the ruling of permissibility parallels the ruling on impurity.

The objection might be made that an analogy between permissibility and impurity is an invalid analogy and that, furthermore, the Companions are known to have been very particular in matters of purity (*ṭahāra*) as they avoided everything that might have been unlawful. How, then, can the one be compared to the other?

[A] i.e., a change in the water's characteristics, like smell, or color, or taste. See Shāfiᶜī, *Kitāb al-umm* 1.3–4; Ghazālī, *Wasīṭ*, 1.54.

[B] i.e., and thus create the suspicion that the water would become impure.

We would reply that if it is being suggested that they performed prayer in the presence of impurities (either on their persons or on the places where they prayed), then performance of prayer in the presence of impurities is a sin; when prayer is one of the pillars of the faith. So, perish the thought!

On the contrary, it is essential that one believe of them that they avoided all the impurities that needed to be avoided, and that they tolerated them only when there was no need to avoid them. Thus, among the things they tolerated was this particular instance when the legal presumption and the probability seemed to contradict one another. It should be obvious, then, that a probability not based on evidence related to the substance of something dubious is null and void.

Their prudence in matters of the lawful, then, had to do with their extreme God-consciousness (*taqwā*) which is essentially one's abstaining from the seemingly innocuous so as not to become involved in the truly detrimental. This is because financial affairs can be dangerous and, unless restraint is exercised, people are naturally drawn towards them.

The matter of purity, however is not like this. Many people avoided things that are completely lawful, simply in order to ensure that their hearts never developed any sort of interest [in anything other than God]. Yet, was it ever reported that even one of them avoided performing ablutions with seawater,[49] even though nothing could be purer?[50] Thus, the difference in this case should not in any way be considered contrary to my decision here to answer this question on the basis of the answer I have given to the two preceding questions.

Moreover, I do not accept the point they make about the unlawful being prevalent. This is because even if the sources of today's wealth are [both far-reaching and] numerous, it is still not essential that the unlawful was present in those sources. Rather, today's wealth consists of both that which has injustice in its roots and that which does not. Just as there is less wealth usurped or stolen today than there is wealth that is not, the same was true for all times. Thus, the quantity of usurped wealth in the world, or the wealth in which corruption has been a factor, has in every age been relatively less than the quantity of untainted wealth.

Then, since we cannot know if a particular branch of wealth has come from one sort [of root] or the other, we cannot agree that the probability is that it will be unlawful. After all, in the same way that usurped wealth begets more of the same, so also [untainted wealth] grows and prospers, so that the branches put out by the predominant form of wealth will certainly outnumber, in all places and at all times, the branches put out by [tainted wealth]. In fact, the general rule is that usurped grain is consumed straight away and is very rarely used for planting. The same is true in regard to stolen livestock, most of which is consumed and only rarely acquired for breeding.

How, then, can it be supposed that the branches of the unlawful are more numerous when the roots of the lawful are clearly more numerous than the roots of the unlawful? Let the one seeking guidance, then, understand well the way to knowledge of what is prevalent. This is a subject concerning which many of the learned make mistakes. So what then of the common people?

This, of course, has been in regard to renewable commodities from the animal and vegetable worlds. Minerals however are perfectly unrestricted and may be taken from the lands of the Turks or others[A] by anyone who has the inclination to do so. Some minerals, however, are undoubtedly taken by rulers; though what they take is surely the smaller portion and not the greater. Still, when a sultan takes control of a mine, the obvious injustice in the matter will prevent people from having anything to do with it.

Furthermore, that which is taken by labourers from such mines is taken for the ruler in return for wages. The authentic *Sharīʿa* position here is that delegation is permitted in establishing possession, and that such delegation may take place through

[A] The commentator, Zabīdī, adds, 'and from the lands of the Franks.' See Z.vi.48.

one hired for wages. Thus, water drawn by one hired for wages becomes the property of the one who hired him to draw the water. The same is true of what is taken from mines.

Now, to expand on this principle, the substance of gold taken from a mine will not be unlawful, unless we consider that injustice has been done to the miners [in that they are paid extremely low wages]. That, however, is not relevant here; and we cannot say that [for this reason] the gold is unlawful. Rather, the owner is unjust, and the [unpaid] wages of the miners remain his responsibility.

Furthermore, the gold that comes out of a mint is not necessarily the same gold substance that was usurped by the sultan. Rather, traders bring gold [in the form of jewellery, etc.] and worn out coins to the mint and then hire those [at the mint] to [melt it and then] make ingots of it and new coins. Indeed, they take out as much as they put in, leaving a small share to the mint in payment for the service. This is certainly permissible. Then, even if it were supposed that some coins were minted from gold usurped by the sultan, these would undoubtedly amount to a mere pittance in comparison to the wealth brought in by traders.

Yes, it is true that the sultan does injustice to the hired help at the mint by forcing them to pay him a tax, because he singled them out for this from among all the people. But this, too, is a mere pittance in comparison to what comes out of the mint. In fact, what goes to the mint and the sultan from all that the mint produces is not even one part in a hundred, a mere tenth of a tenth. So how could this be [considered] prevalent?

These [objections], then, are simply suspicions that have found their way to people's hearts by means of suggestion. Still these thoughts have been entertained by a group of people whose religion is so weak that they find fault with prudence and close the door on it; and fault the discriminative powers of those who differentiate between one form of wealth and another. Obviously, this is exactly what wrongful innovation (*bidʿa*) and deviation (*ḍalāl*) are all about.

Here, another question might be asked. Suppose that the unlawful was actually prevalent, and that an unlimited [in either number or measure] substance became intermixed with another unlimited substance. What would you say [to be the ruling] in regard to a portion of that [intermixed] substance on which there is no particular evidence [to indicate whether it was lawful or unlawful]?

My answer is that the most prudent thing to do in my opinion would be to leave it alone, even though to partake of it would not be unlawful. This is because the legal presumption is that all things are lawful unless proven otherwise, as [already mentioned] in the case of the dirt in the streets and so on. Rather, I will go even further and say that if the unlawful were to overspread the entire world, such that it could be known for a certainty that nothing lawful remained on the face of the earth, I would say that we should begin over again from that moment onward, and all that happened beforehand should be forgiven. In this case we could say that whatever has passed beyond its limit will be transformed into its opposite; or that when everything becomes unlawful everything becomes lawful.[A]

The proof [of the matter] is that if this were ever to happen, there would be five possibilities:

The First: To have it said that people should give up eating until every last one of them perishes.

The Second: To limit themselves to no more than what is essential in order to stave off hunger, and to continue in this manner for as long as they live.

The Third: To partake of only as much as is necessary, in any way they please, by theft, by fraud, or by mutual agreement,

[A] Here the author uses a rhetorical device in which taking matters to their logical or illogical extremes shows them to be absurd and untenable. No one should suppose that the author is advocating for *ibāḥa* or the legitimization of everything illegitimate. By reading what follows, this shall become clear to the reader.

without discriminating between one kind of wealth or another, or between one source or another.

The Fourth: To follow the stipulations of the *Sharīʿa*, beginning again with its principles and not limiting themselves to what will merely stave off hunger.

The Fifth: To limit themselves, while abiding by the stipulations of the *Sharīʿa*, to only what is necessary.

Obviously, the first of these possibilities is unacceptable. The second is also decidedly untenable for the reason that if people were to limit themselves to partaking of only as much as would stave off hunger, they would soon weaken and disease would kill them off. Then all deeds would become invalid, all industry would come to a halt, and the whole world would be ruined. Certainly, the ruin of the world would mean the ruin of religion because the world is the seedbed of the Afterlife. Indeed the precepts of the caliphate, of the judiciary, of public policy, and most of the precepts of the law (*fiqh*) as well, have as their objective the maintenance of worldly interests thereby to ensure the interests of the next world.

The third possibility is to partake of only as much as is necessary and no more, treating one kind of wealth the same as another, whether it is obtained by theft, by fraud, by mutual agreement, or by whatever means. This is to lift the protective shield of the *Sharīʿa* that guards against the doers of wrong and all manner of corruption. Otherwise, thieving and usurping hands would be outstretched, and all manner of injustice would occur.

Under such circumstances it would be impossible to rebuke anyone because they would simply reply that there is no way to distinguish between who is truly entitled to something, the possessor or themselves! 'What is unlawful to us,' they might then object, 'is unlawful to him as well! And, anyway, the possessor is entitled to only as much as he needs. Then who is to say that he is more deserving of it than we are? Finally, if what I have stolen is more than I need, then it was likewise more than what was needed by the one I stole it from!' How, then, should we consider our needs? On a day to day basis? Or for the whole year? Obviously, this is a situation that would lead to nullification of the policies of the *Sharīʿa*; it would also encourage the corrupt to spread even more corruption.

This leaves only the fourth possibility. This would be to say that everything in the hands of the possessors is best considered their property; and that it will not be lawful to take it away from them by theft or usurpation. Rather, it may only be taken by mutual agreement because mutual agreement is the means approved by the *Sharīʿa*. If nothing other than mutual agreement is permitted, then mutual agreement has its methods in the *Sharīʿa*, and these are connected to the public interest. If these interests are not given consideration, the principle of mutual agreement will not have been realized, and its particulars will be invalid.

The fifth possibility, the one that specifies limiting oneself to no more than what is necessary while adhering to the *Sharīʿa* in the way one earns one's living is the possibility that I consider suitable, in terms of prudence, for those who would tread the path to the Afterlife. Still, there is no way to compel people to adopt it, or to issue a legal edict (*fatwā*) to be followed by one and all, because the hands of the unjust will always stretch out to take from others more than what they need. The same is true of thieves. Anyone who comes to power will plunder, and anyone who has the opportunity will steal. In this they will excuse themselves by saying that the other had a right only to as much as he needed, and that they were in need as well.

Thus, the only recourse remaining would be for it to become the responsibility of the ruler to take whatever is in excess from the landowners and, with it, to fulfil the requirements of the needy, distributing wealth among all the people from day to day, or week by week, or on a yearly basis. This, however, would entail great difficulty, and would moreover be a waste of wealth. The great difficulty would be that the ruler could not possibly see to the interests of so many people. This is inconceivable.[A] The waste would occur when there is more fruit, seed and meat than is needed, and it has to be thrown into the sea or otherwise disposed of until it rots. For certainly the fruit and seed created by God is greater in quantity than the amounts consumed by mankind, even in extravagance! So what, then, of the amount that they actually need?

Finally, all of this would amount to the collapse of the pilgrimage (*ḥajj*), the *zakāt*, all forms of expiation (*kaffāra*) involving payment, and every act of devotion associated with wealth. This is why it is repulsive to imagine a situation where people possess only as much as they require.

In fact, I will say that if a prophet were to come to people in such a day and age as our own, he would have to begin the matter over again by providing anew the means for private ownership on the basis of mutual agreement, and all the other [legitimate] ways. He would have to do exactly what would be required of him if every form of wealth were found to be unlawful.[51]

When I say that he would 'have to' do this, I mean that the prophets were sent in the interests of humankind in both this

[A] It is interesting to contrast the comments on the text made by the classical commentator, Zabīdī with those of the modern editor of the Dār al-Arqam edition, ʿAbd Allāh al-Khālidī in 1998. Zabīdī says, 'It may be said that the "great difficulty" mentioned here is rather something required (*mutaʿayyan*), and that the claim that to do so would be inconceivable is unacceptable. For, indeed, the ruler may negotiate, as a matter of custom and in the interests of all concerned, with the tribal leadership and, indeed, with the leadership of every neighbourhood in every city. Then, they could distribute to all [the people in their jurisdictions] as much as, in the estimation of the leaders, the people require. This could be done once a month, or even more often. Indeed, this is not impossible for the rulers [to accomplish]. Think about it!' Z.vi.50. Al-Khālidī writes, 'How excellent an achievement has God granted al-Ghazālī! He foresaw, seven hundred years before the fact, the futility of the Marxist system because it led to great difficulty and was essentially unreasonable. He also alluded to the excesses of the capitalist system and its intentional destruction of crops, as happens in the West.' D.ii.132.

world and the next. Clearly, these interests will not be seen to if people are returned to existing on merely as much as is absolutely necessary. If a prophet were not sent in the interests of humankind, he would not have to do this.

Of course, I admit the possibility of God creating something that would destroy all of creation, so that they lose their world and their religion. After all, He guides whomsoever He wills, and He leads astray whomsoever He wills, and He brings death to whomsoever He wills, and He gives life to whomsoever He wills. But I am assuming the matter to continue in the way we know as it is the divine precedent (*sunna*), or His sending prophets for the betterment of religion and the world.

Why should I [not] suppose this to be the case when what I suppose has actually happened? Our own Messenger (may God bless him and grant him peace) was sent at a time of hiatus between prophets. Nearly six hundred years had passed since Jesus (may God bless him and grant him peace), during which time people were divided among those who belied him, like the Jews and unbelievers [lit., those who worshipped idols], and those who believed him.

Moreover, wrongdoing had spread among them in the same way that it has spread among us in our own times. While the detailed injunctions of religious law were binding even on the disbelievers,[A] wealth was in the hands of both those who believed and and those who did not believe in him [Jesus]. The disbelievers, for their part, used to conduct their transactions in accordance with other than the religious law of Jesus (upon him be peace), while the believers, much like the believers of our own times, used to take liberties with the law even though they believed in their Messenger. The only difference is that we are closer in time to the era of our Messenger (may God bless him and grant him

[A] See Qurṭubī, *al-Jāmiʿ li-aḥkām al-Qur'ān* (Beirut, 1427/2006), iv in commentary of iii.96–97; and viii in commentary of ix.34; and Sharbīnī, *Mughnī al-muḥtāj*, iii.132 for more detailed discussions on this point.

peace). Thus, all of the wealth, or most of the wealth, or a great deal of the wealth was unlawful.

But then he (may God bless him and grant him peace) forgave everything that went before, and did not press the matter. Rather, he maintained for those in possession all that they possessed, and thus prepared the way for the religious law. Moreover, whatever is unlawful in one body of religious law does not automatically become lawful when another Messenger is sent, or when someone in possession of the unlawful converts to Islam, because we do not accept as payment of the protected minority tax (*jizya*) monies that we know to have been the price of wine or earnings from interest. So their wealth in those times was like our wealth today. In fact, the situation of the Arabs was even worse, owing to the widespread occurrence of raiding and plundering among them.

Therefore, it is clear that the fourth possibility is the one on which the legal edict (*fatwā*) must be given; while the fifth possibility is the one that is dictated by prudence. Rather, the completely prudent position would be to limit oneself to what is permitted, and only to as much as is necessary, while foregoing any sort of increase. This is the sure way to the Afterlife. At the moment, however, we are speaking of laws connected to the beneficial interests of creation. A *fatwā* addressing externals will have a ruling and a rationale that accord with the dictates of these interests. The way of true religion, however, may only be tread by those few who are capable of it. If all of humankind were to involve themselves with it [exclusively], all order would fail and the world would be destroyed. This would be to seek the great domain of the next world. Likewise, if all people were to seek the domain of the present life and forsake all the humble professions and lowly industries, the world-order would fail. Then, with the failure of order, the domain will fail also.

Thus, the peoples of the professions have been reconciled to their professions so that the domain [of the present life] may fall into order for the rulers. Likewise, those who seek the world have been reconciled to their quest so that the way of religion remains open to the people of religion; religion being the domain of the Afterlife. Were it not for this kind of reconciliation there would be no religion for the people of religion. Thus, the condition for the well being of their religion is that the rest of the people neglect it and concern themselves instead with worldly matters.

All of this, of course, is an allocation (*qisma*) that has been determined by the divine will. This is what is alluded to in the verse, *We have divided among them their livelihood in the life of this world, and we have elevated some of them over others in degrees*.[52]

It may be objected that there is no need to speculate about the unlawful becoming so prevalent that nothing of the lawful remains because the actual situation is known to be otherwise. Furthermore, there is no doubt that some of it is unlawful; but the question is whether it is a lesser part of it or a greater part? Likewise, what you mentioned about the unlawful's being the lesser part in relation to the whole is clear. But there is still a need to give evidence based on other than the notion of benefit [as a legal indicator],[A] as all of the [five] possibilities were based on that [approach], and not all of the scholars accept it as evidence.

My answer to these objections is that if it is accepted that the unlawful is the lesser part, then the era of the Messenger of God (may God bless him and grant him peace) and the Companions, in which there was usury, theft, and misappropriated spoils and plunder, should suffice as proof.[B] If we were to suppose a time

[A] The legal debate among the classical jurists was whether or not law may be formulated on the basis of objectives, or the objectives of the Almighty Legislator, even when these are undefined (*mursal*) in the relevant texts of the Qur'an or the *Sunna*. The argument in favour of doing so would be that objectives, like benefit or the greater good, might be considered indicators (*adilla*) in their own right and, by extension, the basis for formulating a ruling on a case for which there is no definitive textual evidence. See Weiss, *The Search for God's Law* (Utah, 1992) pp. 676–679. See also Ghazālī's discussion of the issue in *Mustaṣfā*, 1.284–315.

[B] i.e., that in spite of the presence of the unlawful, it is lawful to partake and to transact.

when the greater part of all wealth were to be unlawful, even then it would be permitted to partake of it. Three factors argue in favour of this position:

The first proof is the division that I mentioned [above] in which four possibilities were eliminated while a fifth was retained. If this were to be applied when all wealth was unlawful, it would be even more suitably applied when the unlawful constitutes either a lesser or a greater part of all wealth.

Moreover, the assertion that this is based on the notion of benefit [as a legal indicator] is nonsense. This is because those who supposed this to be the case did so in relation to mere possibilities. On the other hand, what we have mentioned is a certainty because there can be no doubt that the best interests of this world and the next are what the law (*sharʿ*) intended. This is a known fact and not a possibility. Moreover, there can be no doubt that sending people back to living on only as much as is essential, or enough to care for their needs, or to eating only what they can gather or hunt, would lead to the ruination of the world to start with, and then by means of it to the ruination of religion. Secondly, if there is no doubt about something, there is no reason to seek a proof for it either. Proof is sought only for theories and hypotheses that are put forward by individuals.

The second proof is to provide an occasioning factor (*sabab*) by means of determined analogy that may be traced to a principle that can be agreed upon by the jurists who are accustomed to dealing with analogies on legal particulars. Of course, legal particulars are considered by the great jurists to be insignificant in relation to the kind of general principle we illustrated; about how the world would fall into ruin if a prophet, sent at a time when everything is unlawful, ruled in any way other than the way we indicated.

The particular analogy, however, is that when legal presumption conflicts with what is probable in cases of unlimited substances where there is no specific evidence, the ruling will be based on legal presumption and not on probability. The analogy here is drawn on the [cases discussed earlier regarding purity and the] dirt of the street, the vessels of Christians, and the vessels of unbelievers. All of this I mentioned previously as having been established through the practice of the Companions. The reason I specify cases in which 'there is no specific evidence' is because I mean to rule out the sort of vessels on which legal reasoning (*ijtihād*) might be used [to determine if the contents were lawful or not]. Likewise, the reason I say 'unlimited' is to rule out confusion with cases like those [mentioned earlier regarding intermixture] of slaughtered animals [with carrion] and nursed sisters [with unrelated women].

It might be objected that while the water's purity is a certainty, and that its purity is a legal presumption, it is not agreed that the legal presumption in regard to wealth is that it is lawful. On the contrary, it is unlawful.

My reply is that the forms of wealth that are not unlawful owing to a characteristic in their substance, like [is the case with] wine or pork,[A] were created with the characteristic of being acceptable for transactions undertaken by mutual consent, in the same way that water is created with the characteristic of being acceptable for ablutions. When, however, there is doubt about their being acceptable, there is no difference between the two matters. This is because wealth will lose its acceptability for mutual consent when the element of injustice is introduced, in the same way that water will lose its acceptability for ablutions when impurities are introduced. So there is no real difference between the two.

The second reply I will make is that possession is clear evidence of ownership and is to be considered analogous to a presumption of continuing existence, and even more forceful.[B] The reason for this is that the *Sharīʿa* connected the two[C] because one

[A] Both pork and wine are *ḥarām* owing to something in their substance.

[B] What the author is arguing is that the legal presumption is that things are lawful until proven unlawful. Otherwise, the ruling in this case would be that possession alone would not suffice to establish ownership.

[C] i.e., possession and ownership.

against whom a claim of debt is made will have his word [that he owes no such debt] legally accepted. This is because the legal presumption here is freedom from responsibility, which is a presumption of continuing existence.[A] Likewise, one against whom a claim is made, that what he possesses is the property of another, will have his word legally accepted, because the fact of possession acts as a presumption of continuing existence. Thus, anything found in a person's possession will be assumed to be his property because the legal presumption is that it will belong to him unless definitive evidence indicates the contrary.

The third proof is that whatever is indicative of a class that is unlimited, but yet is not indicative of anything in particular, may not be considered, even if it is incontrovertible as evidence. When such evidence is presented as opinion, then with even greater reason it may not be given consideration. By way of explanation, if something is known to be the property of Zayd, for example, it will be Zayd's right to prevent another from disposing of that something without his permission. If it is known that an item has an owner somewhere in the world, but hope is abandoned of ever finding the owner, or his heirs, then the item will become wealth that is set aside for the benefit of Muslims, and it will be lawful to dispose of it because to do so will be in the interests of the general welfare (*maṣlaḥa*). If it is known, however, that it is owned by one person among a group of ten, for example, or twenty, it will not be lawful to dispose of that item [for the general welfare].

Something, then, about which there is doubt in regard to its owner, whether or not the one who possesses it actually owns it, and something about which there is certainty that it has an owner, though it is not known exactly who the owner is, will legally be the same. The one will not be any more [the property of the owner] than the other. The legal ruling in this case is *maṣlaḥa*, [that to do so is beneficial and in the best interests of society. This is the same principle] mentioned earlier in regard to the five

[A] As if from birth, or minority, when one has no financial responsibilities.

possibilities. Here, the same principle may be cited as evidence.

And why not? Anything of value whose owner is unknown may be disposed of by the sultan in whatever serves the interests of society, like [feeding] the poor and the like. Thus, whatever wealth is given to a poor person becomes the property of that [poor] person, and he will have the right of disposal in relation to it. Therefore, if a thief were to steal that wealth from the poor person, the thief's hand could be cut off.[A] See, then, how the poor person's right of disposal was established in regard to another's wealth [when the same was gifted to the poor person].

The only reason for all of this is our decision that the juristic principle of allowing what is in the best interests of society requires that ownership be transferred to him, so that it becomes lawful to him. Thus, we have decided on the basis of what is required in the best interests of society.

If it were then to be objected that this applies only to the sultan, I would reply that the sultan may not lawfully dispose of the wealth of another unless that person allows him to do so. So there is no legal reason here other than the best interests of society. This principle takes note of the fact that if wealth is neglected it will go to waste. In such cases [the sultan will have to choose] between wasting it or spending it on something of significance. Obviously, spending it on something of significance will serve the interests of society better than allowing it to go to waste; and this is why preference is given to that option.

Moreover, in regard to something about which there is doubt, but which is not known to be unlawful, consideration for what is in the best interests of society (*maṣlaḥa*) dictates that the ruling be given on the basis of possession. Such things are best left in the hands of those who possess them because to confiscate anything on the basis of doubt alone, and to insist that people confine

[A] This is further proof that the poor person becomes a true owner, because the punishment of cutting the hand of a thief may only be applied when the thief steals from one who has complete ownership.

themselves to only what is necessary, will undoubtedly lead to the detriment I spoke of earlier.

There may be differences of opinion with regard to what is in the best interests of society. The sultan, for example, may consider it in the best interests of society to spend money on the construction of a bridge. At another time, he may consider expenditures on the military of Islam [to be in the interests of society]. While at still another time, he may consider [the distribution of funds] to the poor [to be in the best interests of society]. In this manner, his decision will follow wherever the interests of society lead. Likewise, in matters of this nature, the *fatwā* will follow the lead of whatever is in the best interests of society.

The result of all this is that people will not be held responsible with regard to substantial wealth [in their possession] on the basis of suspicion, when no particular evidence is present in the substance itself. In the same way, the sultan and the poor will not be held responsible for taking that wealth even when they know that it may have an owner. This is because their knowledge does not go so far as to tell them exactly who the owner is. In this respect, there is no difference[A] between the wealth possessed and the person of the possessor.

This, then, has been an explanation of the doubt of intermixture. It remains now to consider the mixing of liquids, dirhams, and goods in the hand of a single owner. The explanation of this matter will come in our detailed discussion on 'Extricating the Repentant from Financial Iniquity.'[B]

The Third Reason for Doubt: When a Legitimising Factor is Compromised by Sin

This may occur in conjunction with a legitimising factor, or as an adjunct to it, or an antecedent, or through compensation; when

[A] i.e., the same legal ruling will apply to both.

[B] Chapter Four of this volume.

the sin is of the sort that does not require either vitiation of the contract or nullification of the legitimising factor.

Among the examples of sin in conjunction with a legitimising factor are buying and selling (*bayʿ*) at the time prayer is called on Friday (*jumuʿa*),[A] ritual slaughter with a stolen blade, chopping wood with a stolen hatchet, selling while another seller is still negotiating, and bargaining while another is still bargaining.[B] Thus, prudence dictates abstaining from any transaction concerning which there is a prohibition, even though that prohibition does not indicate that the transaction will actually be vitiated. This will hold true even when the results of these legal factors may not be characterised as unlawful.

There is a certain amount of levity in using the term 'doubt' for this sort of thing. This is because in most cases doubt is used to mean confusion or ignorance. There is no confusion here, however. Rather, the sin in using a stolen blade to perform the ritual sacrifice is well known. Likewise, that the flesh[C] will be lawful is also well known. The word for doubt, however, may be understood as having been derived from the root meaning to resemble. Partaking of whatever results from[53] these acts is disapproved, and the legal categorisation of 'disapproved' resembles 'prohibited.' Therefore, if this is the intended meaning of doubt, then there is at least a reason for the term. Otherwise, it should be termed 'disapproval' rather than doubt. Even so, if the meaning is clear, there is no harm in using any term. Indeed, the jurists are customarily lenient in their use of terminology.

Know, also, that there are three degrees of disapproval. The first degree closely resembles prohibition and therefore it is important

[A] The prohibition is mentioned in the text of the Qur'ān at LXII.9. See also Ghazālī, *Mustaṣfā*, I.79; Zarkashī, *al-Baḥr al-muḥīṭ* (Kuwait, 1992), V.399; ʿAṭṭār, *Ḥāshiyyat al-ʿAṭṭār ʿalā sharḥ Jamʿ al-jawāmiʿ* (Egypt, n.d.), I.263.

[B] See the commentaries of Nawawī (*Majmūʿ*) on Muslim; and Mubārakpūrī, *Tuḥfat al-aḥwadhī* (India, 1359/1940) on Tirmidhī for discussions of these last two rulings, each of which has its basis in the *Sunna*.

[C] i.e., of an animal slaughtered with such a knife.

to practise prudence in regard to things so categorised. The last, or third degree, borders on exaggeration [unfounded suspicion] so that it closely resembles the caution of the overly suspicious. Between these two is a degree that may lean in either direction.

[THE FIRST DEGREE OF DISAPPROVAL] The degree of disapproval is greater in game taken with a stolen hunting dog than in flesh slaughtered with a stolen knife or game killed with a stolen spear. This is because a dog can make choices. There is a difference of opinion, however, as to whether the game will belong to the owner of the dog or to the hunter.

This [degree of disapproval] is followed for seeds planted in usurped farmland, in which case the produce will belong to the owner of the seeds. Even so, the matter is dubious because if we establish the right of possession for the owner of the farmland, it will be like using something unlawful as payment [for the land's usufruct]. So, the most accurate analogy [will result in the opinion] that such a right will not be established, like flour from a stolen mill, or game from a stolen trap. This is because the right of the owner of the trap has nothing to do with the right to benefit from the game. This [degree] is followed by the use of a stolen hatchet to gather wood, and then by the use of a stolen knife to slaughter an animal one owns, because none of our scholars was of the opinion that such meat is unlawful.

This is followed by buying and selling after the call to prayer has been made [on Fridays]. This is because its connection to the purpose of the contract is tenuous; though some scholars have held the contract vitiated because there is no more to the matter than that the parties to the sale become preoccupied and so neglect another duty requiring discharge. Still, if something like this were to void a sale, then the sale of one owing a single dirham of *zakāt* would be void, and the [presently due] prayer of one who owed a single missed prayer would be void because preoccupation with sale would prevent that person from performing his duties. So, on Fridays after the call to prayer has been made, there is only that duty [to be discharged].

The same principle may lead to the conclusion that it is unlawful to wed the children of tyrants, or anyone owing even a single dirham, because to do so would cause one to neglect a duty. Even so, since the prohibition in the text was revealed specifically in regard to Fridays, one might naturally assume that specificity. This is why its disapproval is greater, and this is why it is better to avoid it. Even so, it might just lead to unfounded suspicion so that people begin to avoid marriage to the daughters of tyrants and every other form of dealing with them.

A story is related about someone who purchased an item from another. Later, he heard that the seller had [originally] bought that item on a Friday, so he returned the item because he feared that it might have been purchased after the call to prayer. This is the height of exaggeration, because[54] he returned the item on the basis of doubt alone. Such suspicion, moreover, with regard to what is prohibited or dubious will not end with Saturday, or with any other day of the week. Prudence is surely a good thing. And heightened prudence is even better; but only within limits.

He (may God grant him peace and blessings) said, 'Extremists will come to ruin.'[55]

Beware, then, of such exaggeration because while it may not be harmful to you, it may give others the impression that it is important.[A] Indeed, when others find themselves incapable of such prudence, they may abandon prudence altogether. In our own times, this is the way of most people. If they find something to be difficult, they simply abandon it. In the same way, people with unfounded suspicions regarding purity (*ṭahāra*) will often neglect it entirely. The same thing is true of people with unfounded suspicions regarding what is lawful. They suppose that all the wealth in the world is unlawful, and so they extend their involvement without even trying to distinguish [between lawful and unlawful]. Obviously, this is precisely what delusion is.

[A] i.e., for them to do likewise, in emulation of your example of prudence.

The example of sin adjunct [to a legitimising factor] is the disposition [of wealth] that leads by means of its context to the commission of sin. The worst [examples] of such sin are the sale of grapes to winemakers, the sale of youths to known pederasts,[56] and the sale of swords to highway robbers. The jurists have differed over the whether or not such sales are lawful, and whether or not the money taken in return for the goods in such sales is lawful.

The ruling that accords best with legal reasoning is that the sale is lawful, the money taken in return is lawful, and the person who enters into such a contract is a sinner; in much the same way that one who slaughters an animal with a stolen blade is a sinner, even though the meat [of the slaughtered animal] will be lawful. In such cases the sin is the sin of assisting in sin. Even so, this does not attach to the actual contract. Money taken in return for such sales is disapproved in the strongest sense of disapproval. Therefore, to eschew such money will be prudent even though it is not forbidden.

The next degree [of disapproval on these grounds] is the sale of [wine] grapes to a drinker of wine who is not, however, a maker of wine; or the sale of a sword to someone who sometimes fights for right and sometimes commits injustices. In such cases there is clearly a conflict of possibilities. Moreover, our Predecessors disapproved of the sale of swords during times of unrest out of fear that the swords might fall into the hands of tyrants. So this sort of prudence is even greater than the sort mentioned previously, while the degree of disapproval is less.

This [degree of disapproval] is followed by that in which there is exaggeration to the degree that it approaches unfounded suspicion. This is like the opinion of certain people that it is not lawful to transact with farmers for planting implements because they will use these to plow the earth and plant seeds; and thereafter they will sell their produce to tyrants. Therefore, these jurists opine, neither oxen nor plows may be sold to them. This, however, is [another example of] the prudence of unfounded suspicion. The logical extension of this would be to say that food must not be sold to farmers, nor must they be allowed access to public water, because these sustain them in their efforts to plant!

All of this leads to extremism of the sort that is forbidden. Moreover, anyone who intends to do good will undoubtedly commit excesses unless he is guided by true scholarship. Such a person may [with the best of intentions] actually commit blameful innovation in religion, such that those who follow after will be harmed by that innovation. All the while, however, the person will suppose himself to be doing good.

It was for this reason that [the Messenger of God] (may God bless him and grant him peace) said, 'The virtue of a scholar over an ascetic is like my own virtue over that of the least of my Companions.'[57] It is to be feared that those who go to extremes are the ones concerning whom the Qur'ān stated, *It is they whose efforts have gone astray in this world, and who nonetheless suppose themselves to be doing good!*[58]

Generally speaking, then, people should not delve into the subtleties of prudence unless they do so under the guidance of an accomplished scholar. Once a person has gone beyond his limitations, and relies solely on his own reason without listening [to the advice of one who is learned], the harm he does will undoubtedly exceed the good.

It is related concerning Saʿd b. Abī Waqqāṣ (may God be pleased with him) that he burned his grapevines out of fear that its grapes might be sold and then put to use by a winemaker. I can find no reason for this action unless he, Saʿd, knew of a particular reason to do so. Certainly, none of those greater than he in rank from among the Companions ever burned their vines or date palms.[A] Moreover, if this were allowed, it would be lawful to cut off the penis for fear of adultery, it would be lawful to cut off the tongue for fear of falsehood, and there would be no end to calamities!

[A] In Arabia, dates were also used for making wine.

Antecedents [that compromise a legitimising factor] are also of three degrees:

THE DEGREE OF GREATEST DISAPPROVAL is for [sin in an antecedent when] traces remain in the substance partaken of, like eating a goat that had been fed with stolen grain, or grazed on usurped land. These are sinful things, and they are the reason for the survival [of the animal]. Moreover, the flesh, blood, and other parts of the animal are likely to have come about because of them. It is very important, then, to be prudent in regard to these things; though it is not strictly obligatory (*wājib*), to do so.

In fact, some of our Predecessors practised this sort of prudence. Abū ʿAbd Allāh al-Ṭūsī al-Turūghundī,[59] for example, had a goat which he would carry each day on his shoulders into the desert[A] to graze. Abū ʿAbd Allāh would say his prayers there and drink from the milk of the goat. One day, however, he neglected the goat for an hour and it ate a leaf from a grapevine in a garden by the road. So he abandoned the goat there in the garden, as he no longer considered it acceptable.[60]

Someone might object by citing what was related concerning ʿAbd Allāh and ʿUbayd Allah, the two sons of ʿUmar who together bought a camel and then grazed it on land set aside for camels given in charity. In time, the camel grew fat, and ʿUmar questioned the boys, 'Did you graze the camel on the land reserved for camels given as charity?' [When they answered, 'Yes,'] ʿUmar had them sell the camel and return half of its price [to the public treasury]. What this shows is that he, ʿUmar, considered the fat on the camel to have come about as a result of its grazing on the reserve. This, then, should mean that it is unlawful.

My answer to this objection is to say that this is not so. The grass the camel consumed on the reserve was processed when it was eaten. The fat on the camel is a separate creation, and not the actual substance of the grass. Thus, the owner of the grass is in no

[A] The meaning here is that he took the goat to graze on land that did not belong to anyone. Evidently, Abū ʿAbd Allāh did not have property of his own.

legal way a partner to the camel's growth. Rather, ᶜUmar fined the boys the price of the grass consumed by the camel while it grazed on the reserve. As he considered the price of the grass equal to half the price of the camel, he reasoned that it was right to take that amount. Similarly, when Saᶜd b. Abī Waqqāṣ returned from [his assignment as governor in] Kufa, and when Abū Hurayra (may God be pleased with him) returned from [his assignment as governor in Bahrain], he [ᶜUmar] took a half [of their earnings] from each of them because his view was that his governors did not deserve the entire amount. Rather, he reasoned that a half was sufficient as recompense for their duties.[61]

THE MEDIAN DEGREE [OF DISAPPROVAL] is what was related[62] concerning the refusal of Bishr b. al-Ḥārith [al-Ḥāfī] to drink water from a canal that had been constructed by an unjust ruler because the canal brought the water to him and the ruler had sinned against God in digging the canal.[A] Another refused to eat a grape from a vine watered by a canal constructed by tyranny. This [refusal] is subtler and more prudent than the [refusal in the] previous example. Another refused to drink from the roadside wells[B] constructed by rulers. An even greater degree of prudence was exhibited by Dhū'l-Nūn when he refused to eat food that was perfectly lawful because it had been delivered to him by prison guards, saying that, 'It came to me on a platter of an oppressor.'[63] Indeed, there is no end to the degrees of this sort of prudence.

THE THIRD DEGREE [OF DISAPPROVAL] resembles unfounded suspicion and exaggeration. This is like someone's refusing something perfectly lawful because it comes from the hand of someone unjust who sinned against God by committing adultery or by falsely accusing another. This is not the same as

[A] The sin may have been that the ruler usurped the land on which the canal was built, or it may have been that the ruler used wealth acquired in an unlawful manner to pay for the construction.

[B] These were built for the pilgrims to drink from as they made their way to Mecca.

[refusing something perfectly lawful because it comes from the hand of someone who is] a consumer of unlawful substances. This is because the ability to deliver comes directly from consuming what is unlawful; whereas adultery and false accusation endow no such ability. Rather, the refusal to eat something delivered by the hand of a disbeliever is unfounded suspicion. The matter is different with regard to a consumer of unlawful substances. This is because disbelief has nothing to do with [the ability or strength required for] delivering food. Taken to its logical conclusion, this would mean refusal to take from the hand of a person who [once] spoke behind another's back, or told a lie. This is clearly the limit of extremism and excess.

Then, take as your rule the prudence of Bishr or Dhū'l-Nūn regarding sin in the occasioning or delivering factor, like the canal or the strength derived from consuming unlawful substances. If someone were to abstain from drinking from a vessel because the potter who fashioned the vessel had once sinned against God by beating another person or cursing him then that would be unfounded suspicion. If one were to abstain from eating the meat of a goat shepherded to market by a consumer of unlawful substances that would be even more excessive than abstaining from what is brought by a prison guard because at least the food would be delivered by means of the guard's strength, whereas the goat walks [to market] on its own while the shepherd merely keeps it from straying off the road. So this is very nearly unfounded suspicion.

See, then, how I have gradually explained the issues summoned by these matters. At the same time, you must know that all of this is beyond the scope of the rulings given by conventional (*ẓāhir*) scholars. This is because the rulings issued by those scholars will apply only to the first degree [of disapproval], or the one for which people can be held responsible. If everyone were to do these things, the natural order of the world would not be undermined. This would not be the case, however, with regard to the caution of the prudent and the pious. The ruling in such cases will be based on the saying of [the Messenger of God] (may God bless him and grant him peace) to Wābiṣa, 'Inquire of your heart; even though others may answer you with *fatwā* after *fatwā*.'[64] He (may God bless him and grant him peace) explained this by saying, 'Surely, wrongdoing pricks the heart.' Thus, if the seeker of truth ignores what troubles his conscience, he will have to suffer the consequences. This is because, the extent to which he feels the prick will be the same extent to which he will have done injustice to his heart.

If that person commits something forbidden by God, supposing it to be lawful, this will not contribute to the hardening of his heart. However, if that person commits something the conventional scholars consider lawful, but which is disconcerting to that person's conscience, then this will be harmful.

When I mentioned the prohibition against exaggeration, I meant that a pure and temperate heart would not be troubled by such things. If the heart of an overly suspicious person were to become intemperate and feel distressed, such that the person committed something even while feeling that way, then that would also be harmful. This is because between God and himself that person will be held responsible, with regard to himself only, for the *fatwā* of his heart.

This is why the matter of ritual purity is often so difficult for the overly suspicious. The same is true in regard to the intention for prayer.[A] If, in his heart, he is of the opinion that the water [for ablutions] has not reached all of the surfaces of his body [required

[A] One of the pillars of *ṣalāt* is the *niyya* or intention. Oftentimes, the overly suspicious will begin their prayers and then be assailed by doubts about whether or not they began their prayer with the formal recitation of intention. In fact, all that is required is that one intend to perform *ṣalāt*. Whether or not one actually articulates that intention is unimportant. Nonetheless, many people are confused on this matter and mistakenly suppose the formal recitation of a stylised intention to be a part of their *ṣalāt*. The reference here is to their doubts, after they have begun their prayers, as to whether or not they began their prayer by reciting the stylised intention.

to be wet] the requisite three times, owing to his overly suspicious nature, then such a person will have to [wet those surfaces] a fourth time. In relation to that person, in particular, this will be the applicable ruling; even if the person is, in fact, mistaken [on the matter of the count].

These are people who have been unduly severe with themselves, and with whom, in return, God has been severe. It was for this reason that the people of Moses (upon him be peace) were dealt with harshly when they persisted in asking for more and more details about the sort of cow [they were commanded to slaughter]. Had they simply interpreted the command in its broadest sense at the outset, and slaughtered any cow, their sacrifice would have been accepted.[A]

You must not neglect the subtleties I have, in both a positive and a negative manner, mentioned here. Indeed, those who fail to appreciate inner meanings are likely to lose their footing on the road to what they seek.

Now, there are degrees, too [and there may be ways in which] a legitimising factor may be compromised by compensation.

[The first degree of compromise by compensation] The first degree, and the one in which the disapproval is greatest, is when someone buys something for which he becomes responsible and [later] pays the price with stolen or [otherwise] unlawful wealth. In such a case, if the seller delivers the food [for example] to the buyer before collecting the price, and does so willingly, then the buyer's consuming the food before the price is paid will be lawful.[B] Nor, by consensus of the jurists, will it be necessary [for the buyer] to relinquish possession, that is, before the price is paid. Nor may [such relinquishing] be categorised as the sort of prudence that is encouraged.

If, after eating, the buyer pays the price with something

[A] Allusion to Q.II.67–71.

[B] At this point in the transaction nothing has occurred to cause it to be anything other than lawful.

unlawful, it will be as if he has not paid the price at all. When he does not pay [for what he buys], the sin that attaches is the neglect of his responsibility to pay. This does not, however, transform [the food or goods sold] into an unlawful substance.

If he pays the price with something unlawful and the seller absolves him of any further responsibility, in the knowledge that the payment was unlawful, then the purchaser is absolved of responsibility and nothing more attaches to him other than [the sin of] spending unlawful dirhams. If, however, the seller absolves him, thinking that the payment was lawful, then the buyer will not be absolved of responsibility. This is because the seller absolves the buyer [of responsibility] on the basis of what the seller takes as absolution through full payment; and what was tendered is not suitable as payment. This is the ruling in regard to the buyer and consuming,[65] and the ruling in regard to the responsibility [to pay].[66]

If the seller does not deliver the food willingly, but the buyer takes it anyway, then the buyer's consumption of the food will be unlawful regardless of whether he consumes it before or after payment is made. This is because the ruling on the subject points to the seller's right to withhold [delivery] because his ownership is established by possession in the same way that the buyer's right is established [by possession].[67] The right to withhold will become void either by means of absolution or full payment and, in this case, neither has taken place. Instead, the buyer is consuming his own property and is committing a sin by doing so. This is like the sin of a pledgee who consumes, without permission from the pledger, produce held as a pledge (*rahn*).

There is a difference, however, between this and consuming another's food.[A] Even so, the prohibition[B] is inclusive of both. Of

[A] The one may be likened to a pledge, *rahn;* while the other is more like a deposit, *wadīʿa.*

[B] The reason why both are unlawful is that they include dealings for which no permission is given.

course, all of this [will apply] when the buyer takes possession [of the food] before paying the price [to the seller], and regardless of whether or not the seller is willing to grant this.

If, however, the unlawful payment is made before taking possession [of the food], then, if the seller knows that the price [tendered] is unlawful and still delivers possession of the food over to the buyer, his right to withhold the food will become void. Even so, the seller will still be owed the price because what he received [in return for what he sold] may not be considered a lawful payment. Moreover, it will not be unlawful [for the buyer] to consume what is bought because [payment of] the price remains [his responsibility].

On the other hand, if the seller does not know that the price tendered is unlawful, such that if he had known he would never have delivered possession over to the buyer, his right to withhold the food will not become void as a result of the buyer's deception. In such a case, the buyer's eating the food will be as unlawful as a pledgee's eating what was pledged, at least until he is either absolved [of the responsibility to pay] or he pays in full with something that is lawful or that the seller agrees to accept, even if it is unlawful. In that case, the seller will absolve the buyer of the responsibility to pay [anything more], and that will be lawful. However, his acceptance of something forbidden is not lawful.[A]

All of this is what is required by practical jurisprudence, and explains the ruling, whether lawful or unlawful, for the first degree.[B] To abstain from this [degree] is prudence itself, because if sin attaches to a legal factor that occasions something, then the disapproval will be severe. Obviously, among the more potent occasioning factors is [payment of a] price. Had the seller not

[A] Therefore, the seller will have to accept the sin as well as the unlawful payment.

[B] The first degree, as explained above, is 'when someone buys something for which he becomes responsible and [later] pays the price with stolen or [otherwise] unlawful wealth.'

agreed to [accept] the unlawful payment, he would not have delivered the goods. Even so, his approval did not alter the legal categorisation of such a transaction as strongly disapproved. At the same time, a party to such a transaction will not lose his legal standing,[A] though he will fall from his spiritual station in terms of prudence and heeding God.

If a sultan were to purchase land, for example, or clothing, on credit, and then, with the approval of the seller, were to take possession before paying the price, then if the sultan gives these to a scholar as a present or an award, and the scholar were to doubt whether or not he [the sultan] intended to pay the price, then that would be a lesser degree.[B] This is because doubt has occurred with regard to whether or not sin attaches to the payment. Moreover, differences in regard to the significance of this degree will be based on how much or how little of the unlawful is present in the sultan's wealth, or is judged to be present. Obviously, the more there is, the greater the disapproval. The ultimate authority in such cases will be the degree to which the heart [of the recipient] is affected.

[THE MEDIAN DEGREE OF COMPROMISE BY COMPENSATION] The median degree is when compensation is not something unlawful or stolen, but a factor [that may occasion] sin. This is like paying with [wine] grapes when the seller is a drinker of wine, or with a sword when the seller is a known highway robber. This will not mean that whatever was purchased (and then became a financial responsibility) will be unlawful. It will, however, result in a categorisation of disapproval, though to a lesser degree than the sort of disapproval accorded compensation with

[A] So here is an example of how legal and ethical considerations, *taqwā* and *fatwā*, may lead in different directions. The legal standing mentioned here is *ʿadāla*, which is not the same as competence, *ahliyya*; but rather more resembles an individual's legal reputation as an honourable person. The difference may be illustrated in the matter of witness. In an Islamic court, a witness must be both competent and honourable if he is to testify. Mere competence is not sufficient. Here, Ghazālī is alluding to an even higher level, a spiritual station.

[B] i.e., than the degree described in the paragraphs above.

stolen[A] wealth. Likewise, differences in regard to the significance of this degree will be based on the extent to which sin is judged present in the one accepting the payment. So, to the extent that something is unlawful, so also will its recompense be unlawful. If there is a possibility that something is unlawful, yet it is allowed on the basis of an opinion [to the contrary], then the recompense for that something will be disapproved.

In my opinion, this is the explanation for the prohibition [by the Messenger of God] (may God grant him peace and blessings) of a phlebotomist's earnings[68] and the categorisation of the same as disapproved. In fact, he prohibited it many times. Later, he ordered[69] that the [blood-letter's] camel be allowed to graze[B] [on the property of his patient].

The thought that immediately comes to mind, that the reason [for such a prohibition] is direct contact with unclean and impure items, is not a valid one. If that were so, it would be necessary to apply the same [ruling] to tanners and cleaners; and no one has ever made that assertion. Even if such a rule were to be applied, it could not carry over to butchers. How can a butcher's earnings be categorised as disapproved when these are given in exchange for meat, and meat is not disapproved? Even so, the contact of a butcher with blood and other impurities is far greater than that of a blood-letter. Indeed, a blood-letter uses a lancet and wipes it on cotton.

[A] Or with other unlawful goods, as explained above in regard to the first degree.

[B] The story here is that Maḥīṣa asked the Messenger of God (upon him be peace) for permission to hire a blood-letter and he refused. When Maḥīṣa continued to ask for permission, the Prophet finally said, 'Let him graze his camel with you so that it feeds on your grain.' According to Z.VI.63, Ibn Munda related, in his *Kitāb al-maʿrifa*, that Maḥīṣa had a slave named Abū Ṭayba who earned a great deal of money [from blood-letting]. When the Prophet, upon him be peace, prohibited the same, Abū Ṭayba conferred with the Messenger (upon him be peace), and still the Messenger prohibited it. Abū Ṭayba, however, continued to speak with him on the subject and explain the need for it. Finally, the Messenger said, 'Then let its earnings go to the stomach of your animal.'

The reason for [a categorisation of disapproval] is that blood-letting damages the constitution of an animal by draining its blood which is the basis of life. The legal presumption in this regard is that it is unlawful. Permission was given, however, on the basis of necessity. Moreover, need and necessity are determined by means of supposition and legal reasoning. Something may be supposed to be beneficial when in reality it is detrimental. Such a thing will be unlawful where God is concerned; but a categorisation of permitted will be given on the basis of legal opinion and supposition. It is for this reason that a blood-letter may not bleed a slave, a child, or an insane person without permission from those responsible for them, in addition to the advice of a doctor.

Still, if blood-letting were not lawful, [the Messenger of God] (may God grant him peace and blessings) would never have paid the fee for blood-letting. And were it not disapproved, he (may God grant him peace and blessings) would never have prohibited it. The only way to reconcile his permission and his prohibition is through the meanings I have deduced above. In fact, I might have mentioned this in [a discussion of] evidence linked to legal factors because the matter is closely related.

[The lowest degree of compromise by compensation] The lowest degree is the degree of unfounded suspicion. An example of this is when a person swears that he will not wear cloth woven by his mother. If that person then sells that cloth [and uses the proceeds from the sale] to buy another garment, nothing in that may be categorised with disapproval. Thus, to avoid such a transaction out of prudence will be no more than unfounded suspicion.

It is related that al-Mughīra said of this case that it is not lawful, citing [a tradition in which] the Prophet (may God grant him peace and blessings) said, 'God cursed Jews when [He revealed to them that] wine was prohibited, and [their response was that they] sold it and consumed its wealth.'[A] This [opinion], however,

[A] According to Z.vi.63–64, ʿIrāqī said that he could not find the tradition

is mistaken because the sale of wine is invalid for the reason that [following its prohibition] it has no legal value. Thus the price in such a sale is unlawful; and that is not the case here.[A] Rather, the [correct] example is when a man owns a female slave who is his nursed sister.[B] If he sells that slave and purchases another [with the proceeds of that sale] there will be nothing for anyone to be prudent about.[C] So, to compare that to the sale of wine is far-fetched.[70]

I have now explained all of the categories and how these are subdivided even though, in fact, the degrees of those divisions may not be covered by the three or four I have mentioned. Nonetheless, my purpose in making those divisions, however limited, is merely to approximate and elucidate.

An objection may be raised here because [the Messenger of God] (may God bless him and grant him peace) said, 'If someone buys a garment for ten dirhams, and one of those dirhams is unlawful, then no prayer performed in it will ever be accepted.' Ibn ᶜUmar, the narrator of this tradition, placed two of his fingers in his ears and said, 'I am deaf if this is not what I heard him say!'[71]

My reply [to such an objection] is to explain it in terms of payment that is handed over immediately, rather than deferred. I have already explained how, in most cases, that is unlawful; so let that be the interpretation [of the tradition cited here]. Moreover, how many possessions are threatened with non-acceptance of

in the way in which it is quoted here. The well-known version of the tradition is about fat, not wine. Both Bukhārī (p. 458) and Muslim related that *ḥadīth* in their authentic collections on the authority of Jābir. 'May God make war on the Jews! When He prohibited their consuming fat, they collected their supplies and sold them. Then they consumed the proceeds.' Zabīdī also states that certain of the copies of this text contain the word fat instead of wine; as if the scribes had corrected it.

[A] The author, then, rejects al-Mughīra's analogy and opinion on the matter.

[B] Owing to this relationship, of having shared the same nurse's milk, the two are prohibited from marrying.

[C] In other words, the owner may have relations with the new slave.

prayer owing to sin that attaches to them by means of a legal factor, even when this does not result in invalidating the contract? This is like [what was discussed earlier in this chapter regarding] a purchase completed after the call to prayer has been made.

The Fourth Reason for Doubt: Contradictory Indicators

This is akin to contradictions in the occasioning factor (*sabab*), because an occasioning factor leads to a categorisation of either lawful or unlawful; and indicators (*adilla* [*pl. of dalīl*]) lead to knowledge of what is lawful and what is unlawful. Indicators are therefore occasioning factors in regard to knowledge; and what cannot be known to another is useless by itself, even if it is known to God.

Differences may occur when indicators conflict with one another, or when signs in the indicators are contradictory, or when appearances are contradictory.

[1: When indicators conflict] The first category, when conflicts arise because different indicators are cited, is like two contradictory general references[A] in the Qur'ān or in the *Sunna*, or like two contradictory analogies, or a contradiction between a general reference and an analogy. All of these give rise to doubt.[B] In such cases, reference must be made to the presumption of continuing existence[C] or to whatever was known beforehand, if preponderance

[A] An example of a general reference or, in the terminology of the early jurisprudents, *al-ʿāmm*, is that a verse in the Qur'ān that establishes the obligation of 'Muslims' to perform *ṣalāt* will apply to slaves as well as to free men because the reference is inclusive or univocally signified in the verse.

[B] The commentator added here, '... and lead to doubt when it is impossible to accord preference to one of the two general references, or to one of the two analogies, or to the general reference over the analogy when these are contradictory.' See Z.vi.65.

[C] This indicator, the presumption of continuing existence, was discussed at the outset of this chapter.

cannot be established [among the contradictory legal indicators]. If it should become apparent that [the evidence for] prohibition is preponderant, it [the prohibition] must be assumed. If, however, it should become apparent that permission [is preponderant], it may be assumed, though it will be prudent to avoid it.

It is important, in regard to prudence exercised by a legal authority (*muftī*), that he avoids [in his own practice] all instances of contradiction. The same is true for those who take the advice of such authorities. It is certainly permissible, however, for such people to follow the authority's ruling, especially if they consider the authority to be the best scholar in the city, or know this to be his reputation. This is like one's knowing, by reputation and other evidence, that certain doctors are proficient, even if one is not a doctor oneself.[A]

Those taking the advice of legal authorities may not pick out the most liberal of all legal opinions; instead they must study the matter until they find the one they consider to be the best. That is the one they must follow. Nor may they deviate from it. Yes, if an imam gives a *fatwā* on a subject, and there are those who differ with the imam on that subject, then it will clearly be prudent to abandon what is contradictory for something on which there is consensus. Likewise, a jurist (*mujtahid*), when confronted with contradictory indicators, if his instinct or personal opinion leans toward the side of permission,[B] it will be prudent for him to avoid doing that.[C] The *muftī*s of old used to rule that certain things were lawful, and yet they would avoid those things themselves out of prudence, so as to avoid all dubious situations.[D]

[A] i.e., even if one is not in a position, or does not possess the qualifications, to judge for oneself.

[B] As indicators, instinct and personal opinion are of little legal value.

[C] In other words, even though the *muftī* may be comfortable with the decision he makes on the matter, it will be prudent if he does not practise it himself.

[D] Abū Ḥanīfa ruled in a *fatwā* that a speck or two of urine on cloth will not be enough to invalidate the performance of prayer in it. One day, as he strolled down a street in Kufa with his student, Abū Yūsuf, the imam's clothing was

This, too, may be divided into three degrees.

The first degree is that in which prudence is clearly to be preferred. This would be a case in which the indicator cited by those who disagree [with a legal opinion that you hold] is a strong one, and the reason for the preponderance of your opinion is so subtle that the opposing opinion seems clearer. For example, it will be prudent to abstain from eating meat taken by a hunting dog, even if the *muftīs* say that it is lawful. This is because the explanation for the preponderance of that legal opinion is recondite. We, however, the jurists of the Shāfiᶜī school, have chosen[72] to say that it is unlawful. This is the opinion that is most likely to have been the Imam's own opinion. Moreover, whenever it is possible to find an opinion from Shāfiᶜī (may God be pleased with him) that accords with the opinion of Abū Ḥanīfa (may God be pleased with him) or any of the other major jurists, it will be prudent to act on that opinion, even if a *muftī* gives another opinion.[A]

dirtied with just such a trivial measure of impurity. From that moment, until he reached his own home, Abū Ḥanīfa walked with that portion of his clothing clenched in his hand. When they arrived at the house, Abū Ḥanīfa immediately went and washed the entire garment. Afterwards, Abū Yūsuf said, 'I thought you told us that that much impurity was insignificant?' Abū Ḥanīfa replied, 'That's the *fatwā*. This is *taqwā*.' See Z.vi.65.

[A] In many instances, the classical jurists or imams expressed more than one opinion. This was not unusual because their opinions were recorded by their students, often years apart. In the interim, the jurist may have collected additional evidence, or moved to another city where legal custom was different, and so on. Later, the jurists of the four classical schools of legal thought in the Sunni tradition attempted to classify the opinions of their imams, so that the most authentic might be known from the least. Obviously, in any such classification, the imam's final word on an issue (if it could be known with any sort of certainty that it was, chronologically, the last opinion voiced by the imam) would enjoy the highest degree of authenticity as the most mature and informed expression of his legal thinking on the matter. In order to ensure greater clarity to the point raised by the author, I have not translated the qualifier to 'opinion from al-Shāfiᶜī', leaving it to read 'an opinion' when it actually reads 'a new opinion'. In the Shāfiᶜī school of jurisprudence, the imam's 'new' opinion refers to his last word on the subject and therefore the most authentic

An example of this degree is prudence in regard to [meat] over which the name of God has not been mentioned, even though Shāfiʿī (may God be pleased with him) did not hold contradictory opinions on the matter.[A] This is because the verse[B] explicitly requires it, and many traditions have been related on the subject. Indeed, [the Messenger of God] (may God grant him peace and blessings) said to everyone who asked him about hunting, 'If you pronounced the name of God when you sent your trained hunting dog [after the game], then eat!'[73] This tradition was related repeatedly. Moreover, it is well known that pronouncing the name of God is a part of slaughtering. All of this strengthens the argument that pronouncing is a condition.

Even so, it is true that [the Messenger of God] (may God bless him and grant him peace) said, 'A believer always slaughters in the name of God, whether he pronounces the name or not.'[C] It is possible that this tradition is an expression of general reference requiring that the verse and all the other traditions be turned away from their literal meaning. It is likewise possible that the tradition is to be understood as referring specifically to one who forgets [to pronounce the name of God], so that the literal meaning is rejected and there is no need for interpretation. Thus, by understanding the tradition to refer specifically to one who forgets, the

of his opinions. The author, as a follower of Shāfiʿī, prefers that his readers follow the most authentic of the imam's positions, even when attempting to reconcile these with those of other imams. To a reader with no particular jurisitic preference, however, the translation given here is clearly more meaningful.

[A] The imam's opinion was that it is lawful to eat meat regardless of whether or not the one who slaughtered it recited the name of God at the time of slaughter, i.e., whether neglecting to do so out of forgetfulness or intentionally. See Ghazālī, *Wasīṭ*, IV.223; Rāfiʿī, *al-ʿAzīz sharḥ al-wajīz*, XII.35–37.

[B] The verse is as follows: *Eat not of that over which Allah's name has not been spoken* Q.VI.121.

[C] According to ʿIrāqī, the tradition is not well known, and not authentic; and Ibn Ḥajar concurred with that opinion. See Z.VI.67 and also Abū Dā'ūd, *Kitāb al-marāsīl*, p. 369.

way is clear to excuse such a person when he fails to pronounce the name of God while slaughtering. Even so, there is a greater possibility that the verse is an expression of general reference, and may therefore be considered preponderant. At the same time, however, the other possibility cannot be denied. Prudence in matters of this nature, of the first degree, is very important.

The second degree is one that borders on unfounded suspicion. This is like someone's refusing to eat a foetus found in the stomach of a properly slaughtered animal—or [refusing to eat] a sand lizard—even though there is an authentic tradition that states that the slaughter of the mother is [the same as] the slaughter of the foetus,[74] and even though another tradition states that sand lizards were eaten at the table of the Messenger of God (may God bless him and grant him peace).

Khālid b. al-Walīd asked about it, enquiring, 'Is it forbidden, O Messenger of God?' The Messenger of God, upon him be peace, replied, 'No. But these are not found in the lands of my tribe, and so I find myself disliking it.'[75] Then Khālid went ahead and ate it while the Messenger of God watched. This is related in both of the two most authentic collections of *ḥadīth*. It is to be believed of Abū Ḥanīfa that these *ḥadīth*s never came to his attention for, if they had, he would have ruled in accordance with them if he was being fair. If someone, however, did not rule fairly, that person's ruling would be a mistake, and would be undeserving of serious attention. Nor should such a ruling give rise to uncertainty because the ruling would be like one's not voicing opposition when something is known by means of a *ḥadīth* with a chain of narrators which, at some point, includes only a single narrator.[A]

[A] The reference by the author here is to a technical aspect of *ḥadīth* narration upon which nearly all scholars are agreed; and that is that the *khabar wāḥid* (the report of a trustworthy individual, explained at footnote B, below) may be accepted as a sound or *ṣaḥīḥ ḥadīth*. What the author is saying here is that, since a *khabar wāḥid* leads to nearly certain knowledge, an opinion in opposition to it (with no other evidence) will be meaningless and, in the words of the author, '...undeserving of serious attention'.

The third degree is when there are no contradictory opinions on a question, but its lawfulness is known[A] only by means of the report of a trustworthy[B] individual. Someone might say that there are differences of opinion in regard to the reports of trustworthy individuals and therefore I shall be prudent. For narrators, even if they are classified as trustworthy, can make mistakes and, for hidden reasons, can even lie.[C] This is because even trustworthy people can tell lies. Such people are also capable of unfounded suspicion. It is also possible that what they hear is not always what

[A] To better understand the discussion that follows, it is important to note that the jurists classified traditions in different ways. The significance of the category mentioned by the author here, the *khabar al-wāḥid*, is in its focus not on whether a tradition is true or false, but with the knowledge of truth and falsehood. In the classical scheme of understanding traditions, certain reports could be known to be true, either from the tradition itself or by means of other evidence. Another category was of traditions that are not known to be either true or false, but which were probably true, or probably false, or somewhere in between. A third classification concerned how a tradition was related; either by a successive collectivity of narrators, or by a succession of individual narrators. The first of these two categories, termed *mutawātir* in Arabic, is assumed to be truthful, as a result of knowledge from the tradition itself. The other category, the *khabar al-wāḥid*, or report of an individual, does not of its own accord necessarily yield the truth. In other words, knowledge occasioned by a *mutawātir* tradition is held necessarily to be true; whereas knowledge arising from a *khabar al-wāḥid* is not necessarily true. See Weiss, *Search for God's Law*, pp. 274–313.

[B] 'The most important subcategories within the larger category of report of the individual are reports that are known to be true by virtue of an extraneous factor such as miraculous attestation and reports that are held to be probably true. Of these two subcategories, it is the latter alone that has relevance for the discussion of the transmission of texts, and it is this subcategory that the Muslim jurisprudents usually have in mind when the report of the individual is under discussion. Since the trustworthiness of the reporter is the basis on which a report is held to be probably (as opposed to certainly) true, "report of the individual" becomes synonymous in most discussions with "report of the trustworthy individual."' Weiss, *Search for God's Law*, pp. 274–313. Following Weiss' clarification, I too will use the latter phrase.

[C] This is at least a logical possibility.

was actually said; or that what they understand is not always what was actually meant [by the speaker]. Even so, the Companions never took their practise of prudence to this degree. If they heard a report from a trustworthy individual they were satisfied with it. If, however, there was a particular reason to doubt the veracity of a narrator, that would clearly be grounds for pause, even if the narrator were known to be trustworthy.

The opinion held by those who contradict [the majority of scholars] in regard to the [veracity] of reports related by trustworthy individuals is not worthy of serious consideration.[A] This is like the opinion of al-Naẓẓām who held that consensus (*ijmāʿ*) was not a valid legal indicator.[B]

Were this sort of prudence justifiable, it would be prudent to refuse an inheritance from a grandfather [if one's father were not alive to inherit from his father], saying that, 'There is no mention of other than sons in the Qur'ān, and the equating of a son of a son with a son was accomplished by means of a consensus[C] of the Companions. Yet, none of them was infallible, and it is possible that they made a mistake. Moreover, al-Naẓẓām disagreed with their opinion.'

All of this, however, is folly and a call to reject every general reference in the Qur'ān. Indeed, among the theologians there are those who hold that general references have no legal significance.

[A] The majority of the scholarly community held that it is unnecessary to stipulate a successive collectivity of trustworthy narrators for a tradition to be considered sound. The Muʿtazila, however, declared a tradition to be like legal testimony and thus in need of corroboration. Abū ʿAlī al-Jubā'ī, for example, wrote: 'A tradition may not be accepted if it is narrated by a [single] trustworthy individual, unless it is substantiated by the report of another trustworthy individual and is supported by evidence from the Qur'ān or the *sunna*.' See Z.VI.73 and also Juwaynī, *al-Burhān fī uṣūl al-fiqh*, (Beirut, 1997), I.217–220.

[B] Those who denied the authority of consensus included the Shīʿa (unless one of their imams was a party to the consensus), the Khawārij, and certain of the Muʿtazila.

[C] The legal ruling that a grandfather may inherit from his grandson if his son has died was also the result of a consensus by the Companions.

Rather, they insist that legal authority [in interpreting the Qur'ān] must be confined to the interpretations arrived at by the Companions by means of evidence and indicators. All of that, of course, is unfounded suspicion. There is no aspect of any disputed issue in which exaggeration and excess are not possible. This point should be understood well.

Whenever there is difficulty in understanding a matter of this nature, recourse should be had to one's heart of hearts. Yet, prudence dictates that what gives rise to doubt should be rejected in favour of what leaves you free of doubt. So, abandon whatever pricks the conscience. All of this, however, will vary from person to person and case to case. Even so, one should protect one's heart from whatever may lead to unfounded suspicion. This is the only way that one may make correct decisions. In instances of unfounded suspicion one's heart should not be troubled, while in instances in which disapproval is involved, one's heart should register some measure of uneasiness. What could be better than this sort of heart? Indeed, this is why he [the Messenger of God] (upon him be peace and blessings), did not direct everyone to consult their heart. Rather, he did so in the case of Wābiṣa because he knew him and his [heart's] condition.[A]

[II: WHEN SIGNS IN THE INDICATORS ARE CONTRADICTORY] The second category of differences is of those that may be attributed to contradictory signs in the indicators.[B] For example, a certain item will be widely known as plunder because it is only rarely available by means other than plunder. Then, if this item is seen in the hands of a pious person, the man's piety will indicate that the item is lawful, whereas the item's nature and its rarity will indicate that it is unlawful.[C] In this manner, the indicators will

[A] The *ḥadīth* about Wābiṣa was mentioned earlier in this chapter. 'Inquire of your heart; even though they may answer you with *fatwā* after *fatwā*.'

[B] One will indicate that something is lawful while another will indicate that it is unlawful.

[C] i.e., under normal circumstances, people would naturally suppose that it was acquired by unlawful means.

be contradictory. The same situation will obtain if a trustworthy person reports that something is lawful, and another trustworthy person reports that it is unlawful; or if two unreliable witnesses give conflicting testimony, or if a boy and an adult do the same. Then, if preponderance should emerge [in regard to either of the two] a ruling must be given in accordance [with the preponderant indicator], though prudence will dictate one's refraining. If there is nothing to indicate preponderance, however, the only course will be to suspend judgement. Details of this matter will be explained in Chapter Three.

[III: WHEN APPEARANCES ARE CONTRADICTORY] The third category is of differences that may be attributed to characteristics on which legal categorisations are based. An example is when money is bequeathed 'to jurists' such that the bequest obviously includes accomplished jurists but not those who have only just begun their legal careers the month or the day before [the bequest is made]. Clearly, between the two [types of jurists] there may be any number of degrees. In such a case, the jurisconsult (*muftī*) will have to decide on the basis of his own opinion; and therefore it will be prudent[A] to avoid [the money that is distributed].

This is perhaps the most abstruse of reasons for doubt, for there are aspects to it that will surely lead the jurisconsult to the sort of confusion from which there is no escaping. This is because what is described is an intermediate degree between two opposites, and there is nothing to suggest an inclination toward one or the other. The same might apply in regard to the distribution of charity to the needy. Obviously, those without money are in need, while those who have money are not. But between the two there are inscrutable issues.[B]

For example, what of someone who has a house and furniture and clothing and books? [If these items are present to the extent

[A] i.e., prudent on the part of those jurists who find themselves between the two obvious types, beginners and accomplished jurists.

[B] i.e., issues to be understood before any determination may be made.

that he still has needs,] the degree of need will not prevent the distribution of charity money to such a person; whereas if they are present in excess of his needs, the charity money may not be distributed to him. Need, in such a case, is not [something that can be] clearly defined, but must be determined by approximation. The jurisconsult will want to look at how big the house is, and how high. He will consider its market value and its location; and whether or not a smaller house might be sufficient. Likewise, he will consider the furnishings; whether brass or earthenware, how many, and what they cost. He will also want to see if daily needs are provided for, or seasonal needs, or annual needs. Such considerations are truly without limit.

In such a case, reference must be made to what he (may God bless him and grant him peace) said, 'Reject what gives rise to doubt in favour of what leaves you free of doubt.'[76] Everything [discussed here] has to do with doubt. If the jurisconsult suspends judgement, there will be no reason for anything other than to suspend judgement. If the jurisconsult, however, rules on the basis of his own opinion, or intuition, it will be prudent [for the potential recipient] to suspend [judgement]. This is one of the more important instances in which prudence is to be exercised.

Similar considerations apply to what may be considered a sufficient measure in regard to expenditures on one's family, or clothing for wives, or the needs of jurists and scholars from the public treasury (*bayt al-māl*). This is because in every instance there are two aspects; one of which indicates insufficiency and the other of which indicates sufficiency, while between the two are degrees that differ from person to person and case to case. The only one who knows what is truly needed is God; humans have not the capacity to comprehend these matters. A Meccan measure of gold (*ratl*) may suffice for the daily needs of one large man, while more than three such measures will surely be in excess of his needs. But there is no way to quantify what lies between the two with certainty. Therefore, be prudent, and reject what gives rise to doubt in favour of what leaves you free of doubt.

This principle will apply to every matter attached to an occasioning factor, which may be known by means of a word that indicates it. This is because the Arabs, and speakers of every other language, do not place limitations on the number of meanings a word may carry, except in the case of words used to designate numbers. The word, 'six', for example, will not admit of any number that is less or greater than itself. This is true of all words that denote numbers or values. It is not true, however, of other words. There is no word in the Book of God, for example, or in the precedent (*Sunna*) of the Messenger of God (may God bless him and grant him peace) that is not subject to a degree of speculation. Indeed, the need for expertise in these matters is great, especially with regard to bequests and trusts (*awqāf* [pl. of *waqf*]). For instance, a bequest to 'Sufis' will be lawful, but it is not an easy matter to specify just who falls under that heading.[A] Indeed, the matter is a subtle one and applies to all words. I will [later] discuss the meaning of the word 'Sufis' in particular so that the way to deal with words may be known [by means of that example]; otherwise, there is no point in discussing every word.

So these are [the sorts of] differences that may be attributed to contradictory signs and which [seem to] pull in opposite directions. Moreover, all of these are dubious issues of the sort which must be avoided if there is no preponderancy of evidence for their lawfulness, either by means of a specific indicator or by means of a presumption of continuing existence. This is the requirement of his (may God bless him and grant him peace) directive, 'Reject what gives rise to doubt in favour of what leaves you free of doubt,' and of all the things we have discussed [in this chapter].

These, then, are the things that give rise to doubt. Some of these are clearly more severe than others. When several of these appear in regard to a single matter, the issue is even more serious. An example of this would be if one were to take food

[A] i.e., who is deserving of the appellation.

concerning which opinions differ[A] in return for grapes sold to a vintner[B] after the call to prayer on Fridays[C] when the seller's wealth is mixed with unlawful elements constituting less than the major share of his wealth, but intermixed with it.[D] Thus, when dubious elements pile up, one's involvement becomes increasingly serious.

I have attempted here to explain how to recognise the degrees of the dubious, in the understanding that it is not in the power of any human being to list all of those degrees. Whatever is clear from this explanation should be put into practice; while whatever is unclear should simply be avoided. Sin, moreover, is what pricks the heart. So, with regard to what I stated about consulting one's heart of hearts, I should explain that I meant this in reference to what a jurisconsult has declared lawful. In reference to what he declares unlawful, however, abstention will be required.[E]

Not every heart is to be trusted. Indeed, many are the overly suspicious who run from every little thing; and many are the ravenous, the lenient who are comfortable with everything. Neither of those sorts of heart is of any legal consequence. Rather, the sort of heart that can be relied on is the heart of certainty that regards attentively the subtleties of one's [spiritual] state and acts as a touchstone that tests what is normally hidden. How precious is such a heart among hearts! Then, those who cannot fully trust their own hearts, let them seek the light from a heart in possession of these attributes. To such a heart they may relate their experiences.

[A] This is one issue that will occasion doubt.

[B] This a second doubt occasioning issue.

[C] This is a third doubt occasioning issue.

[D] This is a fourth issue that gives rise to doubt. Note here that the unlawful elements are not dominant for, if that were the case, the transaction would clearly be unlawful; while the author's purpose here is to give an extreme example of a dubious transaction.

[E] Abstention or avoidance will be required regardless of what your heart of hearts tells you.

Chapter Two

In the Psalms [of David] it is related that the Almighty revealed to David (upon him be peace) and to the Children of Israel, 'I have no regard for your prayer or your fasting. Rather, my regard is for those who have misgivings about something, and then avoid it for My sake. Those are the ones whom I shall regard, support with My succour, and hold up as examples to the angels!'[77]

CHAPTER THREE

On Scrutiny and Inquiry or Silence and Disregard and their Indications[A]

KNOW THAT YOU are not at liberty to question those who present you with food, or a donation, or from whom you would like to purchase something, or from whom you would like to accept a gift. Nor may you say to such a person, 'I am not sure that this is something that is lawful. Therefore, I must not take it before I have examined it.' Likewise, you may not omit scrutiny (*baḥth*) and simply take everything without first making certain whether it is [lawful or] unlawful. Rather, it is sometimes essential that you question (*su'āl*), and sometimes it is prohibited (*ḥarām*); it is sometimes recommended (*mandūb*) that you question, and sometimes it is disapproved (*makrūh*). The matter, then, is in need of detailed explanation.

The unequivocal teaching on the matter comes down to this: Questioning is required when doubt occurs. Moreover, reason for doubt may arise either in regard to wealth or its possessor.

The First Reason: *The Circumstances of the Possessor*

The circumstances of a possessor may be one of three kinds: unknown (*majhūl*), ambiguous (*mashkūk*), or known (*maʿlūm*), at least to the extent that is made possible by evidence.

[A] i.e., in the sense of indicating the circumstances and situations in which each of these approaches may be thought appropriate.

Chapter Three

THE FIRST [KIND OF] CIRCUMSTANCE is of the unknown. The 'unknown' is a person concerning whom there is no visible sign of corruption or injustice, like the uniform of a soldier,[A] or [no visible sign] of piety, like the clothing of the Sufi ascetics, or of traders, or scholars, and other such indicators. If you were to enter a town for the first time and you saw a person concerning whose circumstances you knew nothing, and moreover there was no sign of his being either corrupt or pious, then that would be a person of the unknown category of circumstances. Likewise, if you went into a marketplace as a stranger and you found a baker or a butcher or anyone else with no sign of his being impious or deceitful, and with nothing to indicate the contrary, then such a person is 'unknown' because his circumstances are unknown. Moreover, such a person will not be termed an ambiguous case, because ambiguity is something brought on by two conflicting convictions, each with its own set of justifications.

In fact, most jurists are unable to distinguish between what is ambiguous and what is unknown. You have learned, in what preceded, that true prudence is one's abstinence from whatever is unknown.

Yūsuf b. Asbāṭ once said, 'For thirty years now, nothing troubled my heart but that I refrained from it.'[1]

A group once attempted to determine which of all deeds[B] was the most difficult; 'acting prudently' was their decision. So Ḥassān b. Abī Sinān said to them, 'Nothing could be easier to me than prudence. If ever my heart is troubled by something, I abstain from it.'[2]

That is the condition for prudence. We are speaking here of the legal categorisation based on outward circumstances (*ḥukm*

[A] In the times of the author, mercenaries in the employ of tyrants were commonplace. The uniform here is an indicator of injustice; the soldier being in the employ of the ruler who, most often than not, is considered corrupt.

[B] Some, for example, mentioned *jihād*, while others mentioned fasting, and so on.

al-ẓāhir). Therefore, we say: the legal ruling on such circumstances is that if an unknown person offers you food, or presents you with a gift, or if you wish to purchase something from his shop, you need not question him. Rather, the fact of his having possession, in addition to his being a Muslim, are sufficient to enable you to quietly accept what he offers.

Nor may you object that corruption and injustice have overcome nearly everyone these days, because that would be no more than unfounded suspicion about a particular Muslim; and certainly some kinds of suspicion are sinful.[A] This Muslim, then, deserves by virtue of his Islam, that you not have misgivings about him. If you were to think ill of him, simply on the basis of what you had seen in others, then you will have wronged him, and sinned at the same time for being critical of him when there was no [basis for] doubt. In such a case, were you to take possession of something he offered, its being unlawful would be a matter of doubt.[B]

By way of evidence for the above, we know that the Companions (may God be pleased with them) used to stay the night in different villages, while at war and on journeys, and never did they refuse the hospitality offered them. Likewise, they went into cities, and into the marketplaces, even though the unlawful certainly existed in their times. Not a single question is recorded from them, except in cases where there was doubt.

[The Messenger of God] (may God bless him and grant him peace) did not ask questions about everything that was brought to him [as a gift]. He did, however, when he first arrived in Medina, ask whether certain of the gifts brought to him were charity[C] or

[A] The author alludes here to a verse in the Qur'ān (XLIX.12) that is quoted later in this section.

[B] This is because there would be two equally valid, yet contradictory, reasons for its being either lawful or unlawful. In other words, there would be just as much reason to believe it lawful as there would be to believe it unlawful.

[C] As briefly mentioned above regarding *ṣadaqa*, the reason for the Messenger's asking was that he was prohibited by God from taking *ṣadaqa*. This

outright gifts.[3] This was because the circumstances at the time indicated that what was gifted might indeed be charity, as the Meccan immigrants (*muhājirūn*) to Medina were mostly poor, and thus it seemed likely that whatever was brought to them would have been given as charity. Moreover, the Islam of the giver and the fact of his possession are no guarantee that what is given is other than charity. Still, he (may God bless him and grant him peace) used to be invited to share meals with others. While he always accepted, he never once asked if [the meal] was offered as charity (*ṣadaqa*).[A] This was because there was no custom of hosting on the basis of charity.

This was why Umm Sulaym invited him,[4] and also why the tailor did, as related by Anas b. Mālik (may God be pleased with him) in the tradition, when he served gourds.[5]

A Persian man invited the Messenger of God (may God bless him and grant him peace) to a meal. He (may God bless him and grant him peace) asked, '"ᶜĀ'isha and I?' 'No,' the man replied. 'Then, no,' he said. Later, however, the matter was agreed upon, and he [the Messenger (may God bless him and grant him peace)] and ᶜĀ'isha raced each other[6] to the man's house where, at the meal, he served them melted fat as a delicacy.[7]

In none of these cases is there any mention of him asking [whether or not the food was charity].

Abū Bakr (may God be pleased with him) asked his slave about what he had given him to eat only when he began having doubts about it.[B]

Likewise, ᶜUmar (may God be pleased with him) questioned the one who had given him milk to drink from a camel gifted as

prohibition was restricted to the Messenger and his family (the peace and blessings of God be upon them) and did not extend to the rest of the Muslims.

[A] There are several authentic traditions on the subject. Among them, in particular, is the tradition related by Abū Masᶜūd al-Anṣārī. See Bukhārī, *Ṣaḥīḥ*, p. 432; Ibn Ḥanbal, *Musnad*, XII.112; Tabarani, *Muᶜjam al-Kabīr*, XVII.197.

[B] See Chapter One of this volume for details of both this story and the one about ᶜUmar that follows it.

charity only because the milk had tasted so good to him, and so different from what he had been accustomed to.

These, then, are some of the reasons for doubt.

Anyone who is taken in as a guest by someone they do not know will not be doing wrong if they accept without questioning. If one should then notice that the home of the host is lavishly decorated and obviously expensive, one may not say something to the effect that, 'Lawful money is hard to come by; and this house must have cost a great deal. So, how did you manage to accumulate so much lawful money?'

Surely, it is possible that the host may have inherited that wealth, or earned it lawfully, so that he deserves at least to be thought well of.

To the above, I will add the following: It is not for the guest to ask the host about anything. If the guest is truly prudent, then he will consume only what he is certain of, and knows to be good. And if he must, he should be polite about refusing something offered. Yet, if there seems to be no way out of it, then he should eat what he is offered without questioning. This is because such questioning is offensive, degrading and insulting; and all of that, is undoubtedly unlawful.[A]

If you were to object: 'Maybe the host would not mind being asked?'

I would reply: 'Maybe he would!'

Furthermore, the reason you ask is that you do not want uncertainty. But when you say 'maybe', then maybe the host's wealth is lawful.

Likewise, the sin in one's giving offence to a Muslim is no

[A] On the one hand there may be doubt in the mind of the guest about the food he has been invited to consume, but nothing more than doubt. On the other hand, it is quite clear that to question the host in such a situation is to insult him, and that is clearly prohibited. Then, when weighing the choices, it is clear that the questioning will lead to what is graver than the merely doubtful. Thus, there should be no difficulty in discerning the proper course of action.

less abhorrent than one's consuming the dubious or even the unlawful.[A]

Indeed, most people are offended by questioning of this nature. Moreover, it is not permitted that a guest question another concerning his host, even if the other person might know something, as that is even more offensive. If the guest questions another about his host, and the other knows nothing about the host, then the guest is guilty of harbouring sinful suspicions. What is more, such a course entails both spying and casting aspersions on another, even if not overtly. All of the above is clearly prohibited in a single verse [of the Qur'ān], God (Exalted is He) says, *O you who have faith! Avoid most suspicion; for some suspicion is a sin. Do not spy on one another, nor speak ill of one another.*[8]

Yet how many ignorant Sufis will offend others by questioning them, and by speaking with them in a harsh and insensitive manner! Indeed, it is most pleasing to Satan that they should seek to bring fame to themselves for their circumspection in consuming only what is lawful. If their concern was truly for Islam, their fear of causing discomfort to the heart of a Muslim would be much greater than their fear that something unknown should enter the stomachs of those who are, in fact, not responsible for the unknown if there is nothing to indicate that it is to be avoided.

Know, then, that the way of prudence is by avoiding rather than by questioning. If there is no escaping it, then prudence lies in eating, and in thinking well of another Muslim. This was the way of the Companions (may God be pleased with them). Anyone attempting to outdo them in his practise of prudence is misguided and a bringer of wrongful innovation; such a one is certainly not 'following the example' of the Companions. No one's charitable

[A] The reason that consuming the dubious is less sinful than offending a Muslim by questioning him was mentioned in the previous note. The reason why consuming the unlawful is less sinful, however, is that it is still the less harmful of the two courses, as it involves detriment only to the self; whereas questioning in such circumstances involves detriment both to the self and to another, or others.

acts will ever equal even the smallest measure given in charity [by the Companions], or even a half thereof, even if one were to spend everything on the face of the earth!

The Messenger of God (may God bless him and grant him peace) ate a meal served to him by Barīra. When it was said to him, 'That is charity (*ṣadaqa*),' he replied, 'It may have been charity when it was given to her, but to me it is a gift!'[9] Nor did he [upon him be peace], ask about whoever had given her the charity. Then, notwithstanding the fact that the person was unknown to him, [the Messenger of God (may God bless him and grant him peace)] did not refuse the food.

THE SECOND [KIND OF] CIRCUMSTANCE is that of ambiguity owing to evidence that gives rise to doubt. We shall now mention the forms [giving rise to] doubt and then the legal ruling [for each]. Indeed, it is the form that indicates the lawfulness [or otherwise] of whatever is in a person's possession.[10] Such forms include physical characteristics, clothing, deeds, and words.

Physical Characteristics: Examples include looking like a Turk,[A] or a Bedouin, or those notorious for their iniquity and highway robbery. Having a long moustache or parted hair in the manner of the debauched are also indicative of the same.

Clothing: Long sleeved outer garments, caps, and the clothing worn by the overbearing and corrupt, like soldiers and their ilk.

Word and Deed: This would entail one's witnessing another's doing what is not lawful; for such a person would be lenient to the point of negligence in matters concerning wealth, and would surely think nothing of taking the unlawful.

These are the kinds of things that may give rise to doubt.

Then, if one intended to purchase something from such a person, or to accept a gift from him, or to accept his invitation to dine, and the person was a stranger, unknown except for the signs mentioned above, then it is possible to say that the fact of possession indicates ownership, while these signs and indicators

[A] In the author's times, most mercenaries were Turks.

are essentially weak evidence, and that therefore one may proceed with what one intends. Nonetheless, to avoid doing so would clearly be the more prudent course of action.

Likewise, however, it is possible to say that the fact of possession is essentially weak evidence. Furthermore, it is countered by the kind of indications that give rise to doubt. Therefore, it is not lawful to remain silent under such circumstances. This is the argument that I prefer, and the ruling is the one I give as a *fatwā*, as it complies with what [the Messenger of God] (may God bless him and grant him peace) said, 'Reject what gives rise to doubt in favour of what leaves you free of doubt.'[11]

The implicit sense of the text of this tradition is the imperative,[A] though it admits as well of merely recommending because [the Messenger of God] (may God bless him and grant him peace) said, 'Wrongdoing pricks the hearts.'[12] And there is no denying that such dealings will cause one to feel discomfort in one's heart. Anyway, the Prophet (may God bless him and grant him peace) did ask [his Companions] if [what they brought to him] was charity or outright gifts. Moreover, Abū Bakr (may God be pleased with him) questioned his slave, and so did ʿUmar.[B]

Of course, in each case there was reason to doubt. Thus, while it might be possible to interpret what they did as prudence, that is unlikely because such an interpretation would have to be arrived

[A] The legal implication attached to the imperative is *wujūb*, or that compliance is an essential duty. In some cases, however, the imperative is seen as having been used figuratively, and thus the implication is for recommended action, or *nudub* only. The latter interpretation is resorted to, however, only when there is evidence to indicate that *wujūb* is not intended.

[B] The incidents involving Abū Bakr and ʿUmar were mentioned at the beginning of Chapter One. In the one case, a servant had purchased milk with the proceeds of his soothsaying, and then had given the milk to Abū Bakr to drink. Even so, it may be pointed out that Abū Bakr questioned the servant about the milk only after he had accepted to drink from it because the story clearly mentions Abū Bakr's induced vomiting. The same occurred in the story told concerning ʿUmar. Thus, neither of the two began by questioning; but questioned only after they became suspicious.

at by means of legal analogy,[13] and analogy in this case does not indicate the lawful. Both possession and Islam are contradicted by the other evidence, the kind that gives rise to doubt,[14] with the result that they mutually cancel one another, leaving no basis for categorising the dealings as lawful.

The fact of possession and the presumption of continuing existence may not be rejected on the basis of doubt that is not accompanied by clear evidence. This is like finding water with changed characteristics. The changed state might be due to its having stood for a long time or to impurities. But if we witness a deer urinating in it, the second possibility for the changed state of the water comes to mind; and thereafter we will reject any assumption made on the basis of normal circumstances. This situation is close to the one we are describing here.

Nonetheless, there is a good deal of difference between indicators. For example, lengthy moustaches, wearing a cap, and looking like a soldier may indicate impropriety in regard to wealth. In regard to the word and deed that contradict the *Sharīʿa*, however, if they have to do with impropriety in regard to wealth, then they are clear indicators. This is like one's overhearing another giving an order to usurp property or to commit injustice, or entering into a usurious transaction. If, on the other hand, one were to witness a person cursing another in anger, or following a passing woman with his eyes, then these would be weak indicators. After all, how many people take pains about the way they earn their livings, striving only to take in the lawful! Yet, the same person, when his anger or passion is stirred, will find it difficult to control himself. This is a point deserving of notice, and one that is impossible to determine precisely. In such cases, the best that one can do is to seek the guidance of one's own heart.

Moreover, I will add that if one witnesses this type of thing in a stranger, there will be one ruling. However, if one witnesses it in an acquaintance, someone known for his prudence in matters of cleanliness, prayer and regular recitation of the Qur'ān, there will be another ruling. If the evidence about wealth and the indicators in such cases should be contradictory, all of it will be invalidated, and the person will become as an 'unknown'. This is because none of the evidence is particularly suited to wealth. After all, how many people take pains over wealth, and bother very little with anything else? And how many people are perfectionists in the performance of their prayers, ablutions and recitation of the Qur'ān, yet are least concerned about where their money comes from?

Thus, the ruling in all such cases is with the way the heart inclines. Ultimately, the matter is between the individual and God. Nor is it unlikely that a decision will be based on some subtle factor that will be incomprehensible to anyone other than the individual and his God.[15] This is the kind of ruling that goes with the pricking of the heart.

There is another subtlety to be considered here.[16] The evidence should only be considered if it indicates that the greater portion of the person's wealth is from the unlawful, like if the person were a mercenary, or the sultan's tax collector, or a professional mourner, or a singing girl. If the evidence indicates that only a little of the person's wealth comes from the unlawful, it will not be necessary to question the person; though it may certainly be prudent to do so.

THE THIRD [KIND OF] CIRCUMSTANCE is when a [person's] state is known by means of experience and exposure on the basis of which an assessment may be made as to whether [the person's] wealth is from lawful or unlawful sources. For example, one might know of someone's apparent piety, religiosity and integrity, while admitting that the person's inner state may be quite otherwise. In such a case, it is not necessary to question the person, nor is it permitted; as in the case of the unknown. It is best, simply, to proceed with the matter. In fact, to proceed in such a case is less dubious than to go through with eating the food of an unknown because that is far from prudent, though certainly not unlawful. Partaking of the food offered by people of piety, however, is the way of the prophets (upon all of whom be peace) and the saintly (*awliyā'*).[A]

[The Messenger of God] (may God bless him and grant him peace) said, 'Eat not except the food of the heedful (*taqī*). And feed not from your food except the heedful.'[17]

If, on the other hand, one were to know from personal experience that another is a mercenary, or a singer, or a usurer, and was thus in no need of further evidence as to appearance and clothing, then in such a case it is essential that one question the person, as in cases where there is doubt. Rather, there is all the more reason that one should do so.

The Second Reason: Doubt Caused by the Possession Rather than the Possessor

This happens when the lawful is intermixed with the unlawful. For example, when bundles of usurped produce are put up for sale in the marketplace and bought by the merchants there. Under such circumstances it will not be necessary for buyers in that town, or in that marketplace, to question the merchants about everything they [the buyers] buy from them, unless it were to become evident that the majority of the goods in their [the merchants'] possession were from unlawful sources. Then it will be necessary to ask. If the majority of their goods and wares are not unlawful, it will be prudent to investigate but not necessary (*wājib*). Moreover, the ruling in regard to a large marketplace is the same as in regard to a town.

The proof that inquiry and scrutiny are unnecessary when the majority of goods are not unlawful is that the Companions (may God be pleased with them) never refused to buy goods in the markets, even though dirhams earned in usurious transactions were in circulation there, and illegal plunder and the like. Nor did they question every transaction. Rather, questions were asked rarely

[A] Makkī expresses the same opinion in *Qūt*, II.311-315.

and only when there was doubt concerning a particular person.

Likewise, [the Companions] used to take spoils of war from the disbelievers who fought against Islam when it was possible that those spoils included the possessions of Muslims that had been misappropriated by the disbelievers. It is agreed that taking such things freely is unlawful. According to Shāfiʿī, such articles must be returned to their former Muslim owners. According to Abū Ḥanīfa, the former owner has a greater right to such an article, but he must pay market value for it.[A] Yet, it was never related that [the Companions] investigated any such matter.

ʿUmar (may God be pleased with him) wrote to Azerbaijan, saying, 'You are in a land where carrion is sold. Beware, then, of the difference between what is carrion and what are properly slaughtered animals.' Thus, ʿUmar not only gave permission, but actually commanded [the Muslims] to ask questions. Even so, he issued no orders in regard to questioning about the dirhams because most of their dirhams [in Azerbaijan] were not [derived from] the price of [improperly slaughtered and thus unclean] hides, though these too were sold and, in fact, most hides were like this [i.e., improperly slaughtered and thus unclean].[18]

Ibn Masʿūd (may God be pleased with him) said, 'You are in a country where the majority of butchers are Magians. Look, therefore, to see what is properly slaughtered and what is not.' Thus, he also ordered questioning on the basis of preponderance.

The purpose of this chapter will not be clear without mention of specific issues and frequently occurring questions. We shall, therefore, envision some of these in what follows.

ISSUE: What of a person whose wealth becomes mixed with

[A] For a full discussion of this topic, see Zaylaʿī, *Tabyīn al-ḥaqā'iq* (Cairo, 1313/1895), III.262; Sarakhsī, *Mabsūṭ*, X.52–54. The difference in the ruling of the two great jurists in this case is based on a fundamental difference of opinion on the question of whether or not the disbelievers may become the legitimate owners of property taken forcibly from Muslims in their territory. The position taken by Shāfiʿī is based on the verse: *...and never will God allow the disbelievers a way [to supremacy] over the believers.* Q.IV.141.

the unlawful? Like one who sells usurped produce or stolen goods? Or like a judge, or a director, or a tax collector, or a jurist who finds favour and abundance with a tyrannical ruler, yet who also possesses lands or business through inheritance? Or like a merchant who conducts lawful business, but who sometimes transacts in usury (*ribā*) as well?

If the greater portion of such a person's wealth is unlawful, it is not permissable to accept his hospitality or gifts or charity without investigating. If it then appears that what is offered has come from the lawful portion of his wealth, then that may be accepted. Should it appear otherwise, however, it must be rejected or refused.

Furthermore, if the lesser part of his wealth is unlawful, and the item offered is dubious, there is need to look deeper. This is because the matter will then be on a level between two levels. We have ruled, for example, that if one slaughtered animal is lost among ten dead (improperly slaughtered) ones, it will be necessary to avoid all of them.[A]

This is similar to the case at hand in that the wealth of a single individual is [finite] like something confined, especially if he is not an extraordinarily wealthy person like a sultan. But in another way it differs from the case at hand because the presence of carrion can be known with certainty, whereas the unlawful part of someone's earnings may or may not have left his possession at a given time.

If the person's wealth is limited, and it is known with certainty that the unlawful portion is still in his possession, then this case is the same as the case of the slaughtered animal mixed in with the carrion.

[A] This issue was mentioned in Chapter Two in the *Second Reason for Doubt: Doubt Predicated upon Intermixture*, under the First Category. The legal principle explained there is that when something becomes intermixed with a limited number, the entire lot becomes as one, and the certainty of its being lawful is contradicted by the certainty of its being unlawful.

If his wealth, on the other hand, is great, and it is possible that the unlawful part is not present at the time, then this is a less serious matter as it resembles, in a way, the intermixture of the unlawful with what is unlimited, as in the cases [above] of the marketplace and the town. At the same time, though, the matter is more obscure for the reason that it has to do with the wealth of an individual. So, to go ahead and accept it is undoubtedly far removed from prudence. But the question is whether by doing so one will actually become corrupt in a way that tarnishes one's religious and legal status (*ʿadāla*).

The question from a rational viewpoint is as obscure as it is from the traditional, because whatever has been recorded about the abstinence of both the Companions and the Successors may be interpreted as prudence. There is no textual evidence to suggest it was based on their understanding that something was actually unlawful.

Abū Hurayra (may God be pleased with him), for example, ate food at the table of Muʿāwiya.[A] Yet, even if it were supposed that all of his wealth was unlawful, it is still possible that [Abū Hurayra] ate only after ascertaining that what he consumed had come from lawful sources. Thus, deeds [recorded in the traditions] have little meaning as evidence in this case.[19]

Likewise, the opinions of the later generations of scholars are divided even to the point that one of the scholars [is on record as having] said, 'If (I were desperate and) the sultan[B] offered me something to eat, I'd take it (rather than beg).'[20] At the same time he held it unlawful, if nothing is known about the provenance of

[A] Muʿāwiya b. Abī Sufyān (d. 60/680) was the founder of the Umayyad dynasty. As he opposed ʿAlī b. Abī Ṭālib, and even went to battle against him, at Ṣiffīn, he became widely reviled, even among Sunni Muslims.

[B] This quotation from Yaḥyā b. Maʿīn, the famous scholar of *ḥadīth* criticism, was cited in Chapter One, but with the difference that instead of sultan, the word used there was *shayṭān*. At any rate, as the two words have often been synonymous among Muslims throughout history, there should be no difficulty in following the intended meaning.

what in particular is offered, when the greater part of the host's wealth is unlawful; even though there is a possibility that it is indeed lawful.

The acceptance, by certain of our pious Predecessors, of gifts and rewards given by rulers is sometimes cited as evidence. We shall discuss this later on in the chapter concerning the wealth of rulers.[A]

When the lesser part of [the host's] wealth is unlawful, and it is possible that the unlawful is not present at a certain time, it is not unlawful to consume what is offered. If, however, the unlawful proved to be present at that time, like in the question of the carcass of a slaughtered animal lost among carrion, then I do not know what I can say about that. Indeed, this is one of those ambiguous questions that will bewilder a *muftī* owing to its resemblance to both the case in which [the host's] wealth is limited, and the case in which it is unlimited.

In a case of a nursed sister (*raḍīʿa*)[B] who lives in a village with only ten other women, then abstinence is essential; but if she lives in a town with ten thousand women, it is not. Of course, between the two extremes there are a multitude of possibilities. If I were asked concerning them, I would not know how to answer.

Indeed, there were scholars of Islam who refused to answer questions that were clearer than this one. For example, Aḥmad Ibn Ḥanbal (may God have mercy on him) was asked about a man

[A] Both Chapter Five and Chapter Six deal with issues related to rulers and their wealth.

[B] The case referred to here is that of a proposed marriage in which there is a possibility that both the bride and the groom were weaned by the same wet nurse, now deceased or otherwise unable to testify regarding the identity of the nursed sister. Since those nursed by the same woman are not allowed to marry, and the sister's identity is not known for sure, if there is one chance in ten that the prospective bride is the man's 'nursed' sister, he must abstain from proposing. If there is one chance in ten thousand, however, they may go through with the marriage. The same situation was alluded to in Chapter Two, under *The Second Reason for Doubt*.

who shot some game that ran off and then died on another's property. Does the game belong to the archer or to the owner of the property?[A] [Ibn Ḥanbal] said, 'I do not know.' Then, although he was questioned repeatedly about the matter, he continued to say, 'I do not know.'[21]

I have discussed many of these matters about the Predecessors in the Book of Knowledge.[B] Thus, a *muftī* should curb his desire to reach a decision in every case.

Ibn al-Mubārak's companion from Basra asked him about his transacting business with people who had dealings with rulers. [Ibn al-Mubārak] replied, 'If their dealings are limited to the sultan, then have nothing to do with them. But, if they deal with others as well, you may deal with them.'[22]

That answer indicates that there is license to do so as long as the dealings are limited, and it gives rise to the possibility that the same may be true even when the dealings are conducted on a wider scale.

So, generally speaking, it is not related concerning the Companions that they severed relations with a butcher, baker, or trader for the reason that he had transacted one imperfect transaction, or had once had dealings with a ruler. To define exactly the extent to which such dealings are lawful is impossible; and the question is difficult enough as it is.

Still, someone might object that ʿAlī b. Abī Ṭālib (may God be pleased with him) had given permission for the same, saying, 'Accept whatever the sultan gives you, for certainly he gives you from what is lawful because the lawful he collects [in revenues] is greater than the unlawful.'

Ibn Masʿūd (may God be pleased with him) was asked about a similar matter. The questioner said, 'I have a neighbour of whom

[A] Later jurists of the Ḥanbalī school did offer their opinions. See Bahūtī, *Sharḥ muntahā al-irādāt* (Beirut, 1416/1996), III.432–433; and Raḥībānī, *Maṭālib ūlū al-nuhā* (Damascus, n.d.) VI.353.

[B] The Book I of the forty books of *The Revival of the Religious Sciences*.

I know only evil.[23] But he invites us, and sometimes we are in need and so we borrow from him.' He [Ibn Masʿūd] replied, 'If he gives you an invitation, accept it. And if you are in need, borrow from him. For the benefit of his wealth will go to you, and the detriment to him.' Salmān [al-Fārisī] (may God be pleased with him) gave a similar *fatwā*.[24]

The reason given by ʿAlī (may God be pleased with him) had to do with the abundance of wealth, while the reason indicated in Ibn Masʿūd's (may God be pleased with him) ruling was that the sin would fall upon the neighbour because he was aware of what he did, whereas the questioner was free of sin because he was not aware.

It is related that a man said to Ibn Masʿūd (may God be pleased with him), 'I have a neighbour who consumes usury, and who invites us to have meals with him. Should we dine with him?' He said, 'Yes.'[25] A great number of similar rulings by Ibn Masʿūd (may God be pleased with him) have been related.

Imams Shāfiʿī and Mālik (may God be pleased with them) are both known to have accepted presents and awards from caliphs and sultans, fully knowing that their wealth was intermixed with the unlawful.

To this objection we reply that what was related from ʿAlī (may God be pleased with him) is far outweighed by what has become so well known about him.[A] [ʿAli] used to refuse to take money from the treasury, preferring instead to sell his sword when he was in need.[26] Likewise, he possessed only one shirt and, when he bathed, he could find no other. I do not deny that the permission he gave clearly indicates the lawful, while his own deeds may be attributed to his prudence.[B] However, if that report

[A] ʿAlī's prudence is well documented. For more examples, see Makkī, *Qūt*, I.452; and Z.VI.86.

[B] The author, here, is anticipating a question of theoretical jurisprudence (*uṣūl al-fiqh*) in which the established principle is that the evidence of unambiguous words will be considered preponderant whenever words and deeds are contradictory.

is sound, then it is for the reason that the wealth of a sultan has a different ruling, owing to its abundance, so that it is joined with, in a sense, what is unlimited; and an explanation of what that is will be forthcoming.

Likewise, the practise of Shāfiᶜī and Mālik (may God be pleased with them) was related to the wealth of the sultan, and that will be explained [later in this volume]. What we are discussing here is the wealth of individuals, or wealth that is limited.

As to the ruling of Ibn Masᶜūd (may God be pleased with him), it was narrated by Jawwāb[27] al-Taymī who had a poor memory. Moreover, it is well known that [Ibn Masᶜūd] used always to avoid the doubtful. It is related that he said, 'Never let one of you say, "I hope", or "I fear", because the lawful is self-evident and the unlawful is self-evident, and between the two are doubtful matters. So reject what gives rise to doubt in favour of what leaves you free of doubt.' And he said, 'Avoid what pricks [the heart], for there is sin in that.'[28]

Someone might further object: Why did you say, 'If the greater part of someone's wealth is unlawful, then it is unlawful to accept anything from that person,' when what is accepted has nothing on it to indicate that it, in particular, is unlawful? Moreover, possession indicates ownership, so that anyone who steals money from such a person will have his hand cut off for it. Abundance, furthermore, occasions indefinite probability that is unconnected to anything in particular. So the matter should be like probability in regard to the dust of the road, or probability in regard to something mixed with what is practically unlimited, if the greater part is unlawful.

Moreover, the tradition, 'Reject what gives rise to doubt in favour of what leaves you free of doubt,'[A] may not be cited as proof of what you claim because it is agreed that the tradition pertains especially to situations in which someone has doubts about a

[A] This is a sound *ḥadīth*, and was cited earlier, in this and the preceding chapter, by the author.

particular possession owing to the mixing of a small amount with what is practically unlimited, because that causes doubt. Yet, in view of all this, you have still ruled that these things do not render it unlawful.

The answer to this objection is that possession is weak evidence, like a presumption of continuing existence (*istiṣḥāb al-ḥāl*), and is valid only when not contradicted by stronger evidence. Thus, when we have ascertained that intermixture has occurred; when we have ascertained that the mixture presently contains an unlawful [element], such that the wealth is not free of it; when we have ascertained that the greater portion of the wealth is indeed unlawful; and when this is true in the case of a certain person whose wealth can be accounted for, the reason why it is essential to reject the evidence of possession and its consequences becomes evident.

Furthermore, if the saying of [the Messenger of God] (may God bless him and grant him peace), 'Reject what gives rise to doubt in favour of what leaves you free of doubt,' is not relevant to this case, it is not relevant to anything. This is because it is not possible to be construed as the mixing of a small amount with lawful wealth so great as to be beyond accounting; because that type of thing happened in his [upon him be peace] times, and he did not avoid it. Thus, wherever this tradition is applicable is where this interpretation may be given to it.

Moreover, to construe it [the tradition] as merely a heedful prohibition would be to turn it away, without reasonable justification, from its literal meaning. Indeed, the ruling that it is unlawful [to accept anything from a person the greater part of whose wealth is unlawful] is not far from what analogy or a presumption of continuing existence would lead one to decide in the case.

Furthermore, abundance certainly effects the substantiation of probability, as does limitation. Indeed, the two are combined in this case.

Abū Ḥanīfa (may God be pleased with him) said, 'Do not even attempt to apply legal reasoning (*ijtihād*) in relation to water vessels unless it is evident that the greater part is pure.' Thus, he made it a condition that a combination of several factors be present, including: a presumption of continuing existence, legal reasoning on the basis of evidence, and established abundance.

However, those who opine that any vessel may be picked up and used, even to drink from, simply on the basis of a presumption of continuing existence, and without even a look at other factors, they are the ones who, in this case, must rule, on the basis of no more than possession, that it is lawful to accept or consume something [received] from a person the greater part of whose wealth is unlawful.

The same does not apply, however, in a case where urine is mistaken for water. This is because a presumption of continuing existence in such a case is of no legal relevance. Likewise, the same will not apply in the case of carrion lost among slaughtered animals, as a presumption of continuing existence is not relevant to carrion. And certainly mere possession does nothing to indicate whether it is other than carrion; even though, in regard to lawful food, possession does indicate ownership.

Here, then, are four related factors: a presumption of continuing existence (*istiṣḥāb*), either abundance or scarcity in what is mixed (*al-makhlūṭ*), either limitation or the lack of it in the intermixture with the other (*al-makhlūṭ bih*), and particular indicators (*ʿalāma*) on the substance of the matter that may help in the formulation of a legal opinion. So, anyone who overlooks these four factors is likely to err, by giving the same ruling when certain questions seem to resemble certain others, but in fact do not.

The result of what has been mentioned above is that whenever there is intermixing in an individual's wealth, the unlawful portion will be either greater or lesser, and this will be known either as a certainty or as a probability, which, in turn, will be known either by means of evidence or by mere suspicion.

Thus, questions are required to be asked under two sets of circumstances:

Firstly: When it is a certainty or a probability that the greater portion is unlawful. For example, in the case of an unknown Turk[A] one must question, even though it is possible that all of his [the Turk's] wealth came from his legal share in the spoils of war.[29]

Secondly: When it is a certainty that the lesser portion of wealth is unlawful. This is a situation, however, that requires thought. The way of nearly all the pious Predecessors, and the dictates of circumstances, is to incline toward concession in such cases.[B]

In the three following issues, it goes without saying that it is not essential to ask questions.

Issue: If food is sent by someone concerning whom it is known that unlawful earnings (like a gift from a sultan or any other source) composed a part of his wealth, though it is not known if those earnings still remain a part of his wealth, the food may be consumed and it will not be necessary to question [the man about his earnings]. Even so, it will be prudent to question. If it is learned that something of those earnings remain [as a part of the man's wealth], though it cannot be determined if these form a greater or a lesser part of his wealth, the food may be consumed on the assumption that the unlawful forms the lesser part. I have discussed earlier how the lesser part is always problematic; and this is no different.

Issue: When the administrator of a charity, or a trust (*waqf*), or a bequest has two [different] grants to distribute, and someone deserves to receive one but not the other because he does not fit the description prescribed by the grantor [for the other], may that person accept whatever is given to him by the administrator?

This question requires consideration. If the description is easily discerned by the administrator, and he appears to be trustworthy, the person may accept what he is given without questioning [whether it came from one or the other of the two grants]. This is because the assumption with regard to the administrator is that

[A] As explained earlier, in the author's times, most mercenaries were Turks.

[B] i.e., so that one need not question.

he will not distribute what he distributes save from the wealth to which the recipient is entitled.

If the description is not easily discerned, however, and the administrator is known to be negligent in these matters and to intermix, then the potential recipient must question because neither possession nor a presumption of continuing existence is of any value in this case. This is similar to the questioning by the Messenger of God (may God bless him and grant him peace) concerning charity and gifts when he was unsure of which of the two he had been presented with. Indeed, possession was no indication of whether it was charity or a gift, nor was a presumption of continuing existence of any help in the matter. The only deliverance in this instance is through questioning.

When we dispensed with the need for questioning in regard to an unknown person, we dispensed with it on the basis of possession and a presumption of Islam. If someone does not know if another person is a Muslim, and wants to buy meat that the person has slaughtered, when it is possible that the person is a Magian, it will not be lawful for him to buy the meat. Mere possession in such a case will not indicate anything about the meat, and mere appearance will not indicate anything [definitive] about the man's faith. If, however, the majority of people in the city are Muslims, it will be lawful to presume that someone on whose person there are no signs of disbelief is in fact a Muslim, even though the possibility exists that the presumption is false. It is important, then, not to confuse cases in which possession and a presumption of continuing existence are acceptable as evidence with those cases in which they are not.

ISSUE: One may purchase a house in a city, even if it is common knowledge that some of the houses in that city have been usurped[A] because the intermixing in this case is intermixing with something of unlimited numbers.[B] It will be prudent, however,

[A] Or otherwise appropriated wrongfully.

[B] The matter of intermixing was discussed in detail in Chapter Two. It to inquire. If there are ten houses in a certain neighbourhood, and one is known to have been usurped, or to be the property of a trust, then it will not be lawful to buy any one of those homes until it is ascertained which among them was wrongfully appropriated. Under these circumstances, questioning will be necessary.

Suppose that a person enters a city and finds accommodations for travellers designated, by the trust, only for people associated with specific schools of thought. Then, even though the person is associated with one of those schools, he may not stay in any of the accommodations, or eat there, until he questions. The reason [for questioning] in this case is that there is intermixing with something limited, and it is therefore essential to distinguish [between what is meant for people associated with one school and what is meant for others]. It is not lawful to simply walk in without knowing which accommodation is designated for which group because the number of such accommodations in any city is limited.

ISSUE: When inquiry is only a matter of prudence, one may not question someone who donates food or money if one thinks the donor will be offended [by such questioning]. Rather, questioning only becomes necessary when it is clear that the greater part of the donor's wealth is unlawful. If that is the case, one should not care whether or not the donor would be offended. In fact, such a wrongdoer should be subjected to even more abuse. Usually, a person like that will not mind being questioned anyway.

Moreover, if one is taking from the hand of one's agent, or servant, or student, or family, or anyone else in one's charge, one may certainly ask questions whenever misgivings arise because these [people] will not be offended. In addition, one has a responsibility to question such people because in this manner they may learn what is lawful.

should be noted here that while today it might be possible to number the buildings in a city, at least in most parts of the world, in the times of the author it was unthinkable.

This is why Abū Bakr (may God be pleased with him) questioned his servant, and why ʿUmar (may God be pleased with him) questioned the one who gave him milk from one of the charity camels,[A] and why he questioned Abū Hurayra (may God be pleased with him) when he brought him a great sum of money, saying, 'Mercy on you! Is all of that good?'[30] This is because he was surprised at the amount, and Abū Hurayra was one of his subjects at the time.[B] Moreover, this explains why [ʿUmar] actually used a gentle expression when questioning. ʿAlī (may God be pleased with him) once said, 'Nothing is more beloved to the Almighty than the justice of a ruler and his gentleness; and nothing is more detested by the Almighty than the tyranny of a ruler and his severity.'[31]

ISSUE: Al-Ḥārith al-Muḥāsibī (may God have mercy on him) said, 'If one has a friend or a brother who will not be offended by one's questioning, it will be prudent not to question that person. This is because the person might reveal something that is better hidden, and one's questioning will lead to its exposure which, in turn, may well lead to enmity.' The point he makes is a good one because if questioning is undertaken by way of prudence, not by way of necessity, then prudence in regard to such a matter will be to avoid exposing what is hidden. Indeed, it will be more important to avoid bringing about enmity.

He further stated that if one is assailed by doubt one should still not question such a person, supposing him only to be offering what is lawful. If one's heart is not satisfied, one should gracefully abstain without attempting to expose, by means of one's questioning, whatever is hidden. [Al-Ḥārith al-Muḥāsibī] said, 'This is because I have never seen anyone among the scholars [of Islam] do this.' So, this shows that [al-Muḥāsibī], in spite of his fame as an ascetic, was capable of leniency with regard to the intermixing

[A] These two incidents have been mentioned in Chapters One and Two.

[B] Actually, ʿUmar had appointed Abū Hurayra to be a tax collector in Bahrain.

of wealth with small amounts of the unlawful. This, however, is in regard to doubt, not certainty. Such subtleties must always be kept in mind.

ISSUE: Someone might ask what benefit there is in questioning those whose wealth is partly unlawful, when people who appropriate unlawful wealth might just as well lie about it? In other words, if it is possible to trust them to tell the truth, it should be possible to trust them to have lawful wealth.

My response to this objection is that when you know that someone's wealth is intermixed with the unlawful, and that person has some ulterior motive in having you attend his function, or accept his gift, his word is not to be trusted and there is no point in questioning him. In such a case, you should inquire of another [about him]. The same will be true if the person[A] is trying to sell you something so as to realise a profit. His word is not to be trusted, so there is no point in questioning him [about whether or not what he intends to sell to you is lawful]. Instead, you should question another [about him, or about the product he is offering].[B]

You may question someone if he has not been accused [of being in possession of dubious wealth], in the same way that you may ask a trust (*waqf*) administrator about money he seeks to distribute, or in the same way that the Messenger of God (may God bless him and grant him peace) asked whether something was a gift or charity. This is because such questioning will not offend anyone, and will not be considered an accusation.

Likewise, if someone is accused of not knowing how to obtain lawful earnings, his word may not be rejected if he is able to explain how lawful earnings may be earned. At the same time,

[A] N.B. The author is speaking of the same person, i.e., one whose wealth you know to be intermixed with what is unlawful.

[B] To extrapolate this directive to our own times, when conventional banks open Islamic subsidiaries in order to market *Sharīʿa*-compliant financial products and services, consumers should be sure that these have met with the approval of a reputable *Sharīʿa* supervisory board.

however, his slaves and servants must be questioned as to how he earns his living. So, in such a case, it will be beneficial to question.

However, if the [accused] person in possession has been accused [of possessing unlawful wealth], another must be questioned. If a single trustworthy person answers, his testimony will be accepted. If an untrustworthy person answers, and it may be determined from his circumstances that he is not lying because he has no reason to do so, his testimony may be accepted. This is because [in that case][A] the matter [of what the accused might be doing wrong] is one that is between him and the Almighty. After all, what is sought [by the questioner] in this matter is a degree of self-satisfaction.

Then, in some instances one may find the answers of an untrustworthy person to be more satisfactory than the answers of a trustworthy person. Not every untrustworthy person is a liar, and not every person who appears trustworthy is truthful. Formal testimony, however, has been linked to apparent trustworthiness because this is what is required for a legal ruling. Even so, no one knows what people harbour inside themselves. It is said, in fact, that Abū Ḥanīfa (may God have mercy on him) accepted the testimony of a known wrongdoer. Indeed, how many people do you know, people who are always ready to rush into something sinful. But if that same person were to give you information, you would trust him. Likewise, if a child you knew to be intelligent and circumspect told you something, the information you received could be considered trustworthy, and it would be lawful to depend on it.

On the other hand, if someone unknown to you were to report on the matter, then [it must be borne in mind that] he is among those from whose hand we ruled[B] that it is lawful to accept [food or a gift] because possession is an apparent sign of ownership; and

[A] i.e., when there is no apparent reason for him to tell anything other than the truth.

[B] This was discussed at length in Chapter Two.

it is likewise possible to state that his Islam is a sign of his veracity. That, however, is a matter that deserves further study. Obviously, whatever he says will leave an impression on the heart. If several people say the same thing, one will tend to believe it. But if only one person says it, the matter is certainly less convincing. Even so, one should look to the impression made on one's heart. Indeed, the true *muftī* is the heart in such situations. This is because the heart notices subtleties that defy normal expression. So, consider this matter carefully.

Attention to the impressions of the heart is indicated in the following tradition related by ʿUqba b. al-Ḥārith[32] who said that he went to the Messenger of God (may God bless him and grant him peace) and stated, 'I married a woman. Afterwards, a black slave woman claimed that she had nursed the two of us.[A] But she is a liar!' He (may God bless him and grant him peace) said, 'Leave her.'[33] Then [ʿUqba] replied, 'But she's a black woman!'[B] So [the Messenger of God] (upon him be peace) said, 'But, how [can you continue in this marriage]? The woman claims to have nursed the two of you! There is no good in it for either of you. Leave her.' In another version of the same tradition, he (may God bless him and grant him peace) said, 'How? After what was said!'[34]

As long as an unknown person is not known to tell falsehoods, and he appears to have no particular motive [for saying what he says], what he says will undoubtedly have some impression on the heart. For this reason it is highly recommended that one make a [personal] assessment. If one is thereafter satisfied

[A] The significance of this assertion is that the man and, likewise, the woman he had just married were nursed brother and sister; and nursed brothers and sisters may not marry one another.

[B] Clearly, ʿUqba's intention was to discredit her. But she was, after all, his foster mother. One can only wonder, then, about the meaning of this statement. Perhaps it is best understood as emanating from an angry and frustrated man. On the other hand, of the eleven sources for the narration of this tradition, only one includes this slur. Thus, there is every possibility that a later narrator added this as an embellishment of his own. And God knows best.

with the assessment in one's heart of hearts, one must follow one's heart in the matter.

ISSUE: In instances in which questioning is required, if two trustworthy people give contradictory testimony, the testimony of both will be void. The same will apply to the testimony of two untrustworthy people. It is lawful, however, for the testimony of either one of the two trustworthy people, or the two untrustworthy people, to be preponderant in one's heart. The preponderance of evidence on one side or another, likewise, may be achieved through numbers, or expertise, or specialised knowledge. Obviously, the forms that these may take will vary considerably.

ISSUE: Certain goods are stolen, and then by chance goods of the same sort are found in someone's possession. If someone wants to buy those goods, then if they were actually stolen, and the person selling them is known to be pious, the sale will be lawful. The most prudent course, however, will be not to proceed with the transaction. On the other hand, if the seller is unknown, then if the goods are commonly available in the market, their sale will be lawful. If the goods are not commonly available in the local market, and are only available if they show up as plunder, in that case the only thing indicating lawfulness is possession, but this is negated by special evidence in the form of the sort of the goods [and their rarity]. Thus, it is important in such a case that one exercise prudence and not purchase those goods. To opine, however, that it is obligatory (*wājib*) to abstain from such a transaction is open to debate because the evidence is contradictory.

Nor am I prepared to give an opinion on the matter without reverting it back to the heart of the quesioner himself, so that it may determine which evidence is preponderant in its estimation. Then, if preponderance lies with the perception that the goods are stolen, their purchase must be avoided. Otherwise, [if preponderance lies with the perception that the goods are not stolen] it will be lawful to purchase them. Cases of this nature are often confusing, and fall under the category of ambiguous matters that are not generally understood.[A] Those who manage to avoid these matters, then, will preserve their reputations and their religion; while those who become involved in them will hover around danger and place themselves in jeopardy.

ISSUE: It might be possible for someone to object that the Messenger of God (may God grant him peace and blessings) once questioned milk that had been offered to him. When he was told that it came from a goat, he (upon him be peace) asked where it was. When he was told, he (upon him be peace) asked no more questions.[35] So, is it obligatory to question the source from which wealth is derived, or not? If it is obligatory, then is it obligatory to ask about one source? Or two? Or three? What is the rule?

My response is to state that there is no rule here, and no way to estimate. Rather, the doubt that led to the question must be considered. There is no point to questioning unless it dispels the doubt that led to it; but this will differ with differences in circumstances.

Suppose that the doubt arises because it is suspected that the person in possession [of the goods for sale] does not know how to make lawful earnings. If he answers, 'I bought [the milk],' the matter is ended with a single question. If, however, he answers, 'It came from my goat,' there will be doubt concerning his goat. If he answers, 'I bought [the goat,]' there is no need for further consideration.

If the doubt arises as a result of [suspicion regarding] injustice, since the goat had been in the hands of the bedouin Arabs and they were known to plunder livestock and breed the same, the doubt would not be dispelled by the man's answering, 'It is one of my goats.' Nor would it be dispelled by his answering, 'This goat was born of one of my goats.' If, however, he ascribes the goat to his inheritance from his father, even if his father's character is unknown, there will be no need for further questions. If, on the other hand, it is known that all of the man's father's wealth

[A] This is a reference to the verse in the Qur'an at III.7.

was unlawful, then it is clear that prohibition is indicated. If it is known that most of his father's wealth was unlawful, then even if there was breeding, and a passage of time, and the intervention of inheritance, the ruling on the matter will remain the same. So, all of these matters need to be considered.

ISSUE: I was once asked about a group of Sufis living in a retreat. Their servant, the one who provided them with food, held a trust (*waqf*) for them, in addition to another trust for another group. But the servant mixed [the income from] the trusts together, and spent it on the one group and the other. Is it then lawful, or unlawful, or doubtful, to consume the food he provided?

I replied that the question requires consideration of seven different legal premises.

The First Premise: For the most part, the food he provides is bought by means of mutual exchange in silence.[A] My preference is that mutual exchange in silence is lawful, especially in regard to foodstuffs and smaller items. Thus, the only matter for concern here is the existence of differing opinions [on the subject of mutual exchange in silence].

The Second Premise: It must be ascertained if the servant uses unlawful money[B] to purchase food, or if he buys on account. If he uses unlawful money, then it is clearly unlawful to partake of the food he provides. If it is not known with certainty [that he uses unlawful money], the likelihood is that he buys on account, and it will be lawful to partake of what he provides because the ruling will always be made in light of what is likely. Nor will this give rise to prohibition, but merely to doubt concerning an unlikely possibility, which is purchase by means of unlawful money.

[A] The jurists term this sort of transaction *muʿāṭā*, and it occurs when a buyer takes possession of an item and pays the price to the seller, without either party saying a word, in silent agreement to the sale. See Nazīh Ḥammād, *Muʿjam al-muṣṭalaḥāt al-iqtiṣādiyya fī lughat al-fuqahāʾ* (Virginia, 1995), p. 315.

[B] The unlawful money, in this case, is money generated by, and intended specifically for the use of, the other trust.

The Third Premise: Where does he buy? If he buys from someone the greater part of whose wealth is unlawful, it will not be lawful [to consume what the servant provides]. If the greater part of the seller's wealth is lawful, then the matter is in need of further consideration, as explained earlier. If nothing is known [about the seller's wealth], it will be lawful [to consume what the servant provides from it]. This is because he will be buying from someone whose wealth is lawful or from someone concerning whose wealth the buyer is unable to make any sort of determination with certainty, like an unknown; and we have already discussed how it is lawful to buy from an unknown. Such a circumstance will not give rise to prohibition, but merely to doubt concerning a possibility.

The Fourth Premise: The servant buys either for himself, or for the group. This is because the servant and the trust administrator are like representatives for these people. At the same time, they also have the right to transact for themselves. Then, whatever the case, the determining factor will be the intention (*niyya*) or a clear statement.

Thus, if the sale takes place by means of mutual exchange in silence, there will be no clear statement. The likelihood in such an exchange is therefore that the servant is not buying for the others [but for himself]. In that case, the butcher or the baker or whoever else is transacting will depend on him, and suppose that they are dealing with him and not with people who are not even present. Thus, the transaction will be with him, and possession [of whatever goods are sold] will pass to him. In this premise, then, there is nothing about either prohibition or doubt concerning the possibility of prohibition. Rather, what it establishes is that they [the Sufis in the retreat] eat from what he [the servant or trust administrator] owns.

The Fifth Premise: The servant provides food to them, but [his providing] may not be considered either hospitality or a gift without recompense because [the servant] would not be comfortable with that [description].[A] Rather, he provides whatever he provides in the expectation of reimbursement from the trust. This is not, however, a sale or a loan because if he sought repayment from them (for what he provides), his request would be rejected. Moreover, this is not what is indicated by the circumstantial evidence. Instead, the premise most approximately indicated by these circumstances is that it is a gift that is given in expectation of a reward. In other words, it is a gift given without words by a person whose circumstances indicate that he expects a reward (i.e., recompense). Such a transaction is both lawful and binding. In this case, the servant did not seek any reward for what he provided other than what he was owed by the trust and with which he might pay his debts to the butcher and the baker and the grocer. Thus, there is no doubt here concerning the possibility of prohibition because the spoken word is not a condition in a gift, or in the providing of food, even if it is provided with the expectation of a reward.

Furthermore, there is no reason to be concerned with the opinion that it is not lawful to give a gift in expectation of a reward.

The Sixth Premise: There is a difference of opinion in regard to the reward deserved [by the servant]. According to one opinion, it should be the least amount required [to pay for the food]. Another opinion is that it should be in the amount of the value [of the food]. Another opinion is that it should be however much the donor is pleased to give, to the point that he may give many times the price [of the food]. The correct opinion is that the matter is subject to [the servant's] wishes, so that if he is not pleased with the amount, he may return it.

In this particular case, the servant is satisfied with what he has taken from what is owed by the trust to the residents [of the Sufi retreat]. Therefore, if they receive an amount equal to the amount they consume, the matter is finished. If that amount is less [than what they consume] and the servant is satisfied then,

[A] i.e., because this is not how the servant views the transaction.

in that case too, there is nothing more to the matter. If, however, it is known that the servant is not satisfied [with making up the shortfall], were the other trust not in his possession and available to buy food for the residents, then, it is as if he is satisfied with the reward in an amount of which a portion is lawful and a portion is unlawful. But the unlawful portion never passes to the hands of the residents.[A] This is like something dubious that is attached to the price of an item; and I discussed this matter previously. So when will this give rise to prohibition? And when will it give rise to doubt concerning prohibition? However, in the case I mention here, it does not require prohibition. Nor will the gift become unlawful for the reason that the giver has used it to commit something unlawful.[B]

The Seventh Premise: The servant pays the debts owed to the butcher and the baker and the grocer from the proceeds of the two trusts. Then, if he meets these obligations by taking from the proceeds due [to the residents] in the amount of what he spent on them, the matter will be closed. If, however, the proceeds are insufficient, but the butcher and the baker are satisfied with however much [the servant pays them], whether lawful or unlawful, then that, too, is a shortcoming that is attached to the price of the food.[C]

Therefore, pay attention to what I mentioned above regarding purchasing on credit, to begin with, and then using unlawful money to settle the account. That is in the case that it is known that unlawful money was used to settle the account. So, if a case admits of this possibility, as well as of others, then doubt [concerning its prohibition] will be even more remote.[D]

[A] Instead, the unlawful part is held entirely by the servant because he is the one who takes from the other trust to pay for the food bills of the Sufi retreat.

[B] This is what differentiates it from a bribe, because a bribe is what is used to commit what is unlawful.

[C] In other words, it will not have an effect on the residents because it does not have anything to do with them, at least not directly.

[D] Doubt in that case will be more remote because if lawful money is used

The result of all these considerations is that it is not unlawful to consume what the servant provides. Even so, there are dubious elements in their consumption [in the manner described]. Therefore, it is far from prudent [to do this]. This is because when there are several premises, and each admits of possibilities [that something unlawful is taking place], the possibility that the matter in question is unlawful grows stronger, especially in the heart of hearts. This is like the chain of narrators in a tradition; the longer it becomes,[A] the more likely that untruths and mistakes will find their way into the report.

This, then, is how I categorise this situation by means of a *fatwā*. I mention the matter here only in order to demonstrate how a complicated situation should be dealt with; and how recourse must be had to legal premises and principles. Indeed, this is something that most *muftī*s are incapable of doing.

to pay the bill, there will be nothing unlawful about the transaction.

[A] A chain of narrators grows longer when more people join it. This is why the classical scholars of *ḥadīth* nearly always gave preference to traditions with shorter chains. *Thulāthiyyāt*, for example, was the term used for traditions with only three narrators between the one relating it and the Messenger of God (may God bless him and grant him peace). Among those who collected traditions, like Bukhārī and Muslim, the *thulāthiyyāt* were valued highly.

CHAPTER FOUR

Extricating the Repentant from Financial Iniquity

KNOW THAT ONE who repents while in possession of intermixed wealth must perform one exercise to segregate what is unlawful and to extract it, and another exercise to dispose of what has been set aside. It will therefore be necessary to consider these two exercises.

The First Exercise: Segregating and Extracting What is Unlawful

Know that anyone who repents while in possession of wealth of which a portion is known to have been unlawfully appropriated will be in a simple situation because he will need only to segregate the item[s] in question. If that person's wealth, however, is intermixed with indeterminate unlawful elements, it will consist of either fungibles, like grain, or produce, or oil, or of individually distinct non-fungibles, like slaves, or clothes, or real estate.

Suppose that the wealth consists of fungibles and that the unlawful is thus spread throughout, as in the case of one who earned money through trade by means of sales (*murābaḥa*), in some of which he misrepresented his cost[A] and in some of which he

[A] A *murābaḥa* sale is termed a sale of trust (*bayʿ al-amāna*) because the buyer trusts the seller to quote the exact price that he, the seller, originally paid for the goods, the subject of the sale. As *murābaḥa* is basically a cost-plus sale, if the seller falsifies his original purchase price, he may ensure himself of a greater profit at the expense of the buyer.

represented it correctly; or as in the case of one who misappropriated oil and mixed it with his own supply, or who did the same with grain, or with dirhams, or dinars. In each of these cases, the amount involved will either be known or unknown.

Then, if the amount is known, as if the owner knows that one half of his wealth is unlawful, then he must segregate [and set aside] one half of his wealth.

If that proves difficult, however, he may take one of two courses of action. One is to [segregate the wealth] on the basis of certainty, and the other is to [segregate it] on the basis of a preponderant opinion. In fact, the jurists mentioned both methods in regard to confusion about the number of cycles (*rakaʿa*) that one has completed in prayer.[A] Our position is that one may only rely on certainty in prayer because the legal presumption is that one is responsible [for performing the prescribed number of cycles] and may presume continuing existence (*fa yustaṣḥab*).[B] One may not, however, change one's mind [about the number completed] except on the basis of substantial evidence. And there are certainly no signs in the number of cycles that one may depend upon.

In this case it is not possible to state that the legal presumption is that whatever is in his possession is unlawful. Rather, the matter is problematic. The process of formulating the law (*ijtihād*) dictates that it will be lawful to settle the matter on the basis of a preponderant opinion. At the same time, however, prudence dictates that one act only on the basis of certainty. Therefore, if one seeks to be prudent, one will retain only as much of one's wealth as one may know with certainty to be lawful.

If, however, one prefers to operate on the basis of preponderant

[A] This matter was discussed by the author in some detail in Chapter Two.

[B] When one is unsure whether one has completed three or four cycles, when one is certain of having performed at least one cycle after the first two and assumed the sitting position (*qaʿda*) in between, then the certainty is that one has completed three. The only uncertainty in such a case is whether or not one has performed the fourth and final cycle. The presumption of continuing existence here will apply only to as much as is certain.

opinion, then the way to settle the matter, for example, is as follows. If one is in possession of money earned through trade, a portion of which was conducted improperly, then if it is known that a half of the money is lawful, a third is unlawful, and a sixth is problematic, we will use preponderant opinion to rule on the matter.

The method to be used, which may be applied to all sorts of wealth, will be to segregate from what is lawful and what is unlawful the amounts concerning which there is certainty. Thereafter, with regard to the amounts in which there is uncertainty, if the preponderant opinion[A] is that these are unlawful, then those amounts must be extracted [and set aside for disposal]. However, if the preponderant opinion is that these are lawful, it will be lawful to retain those amounts. Even so, prudence in the matter dictates that the amounts be extracted. If there is doubt about whether the amounts are lawful or unlawful, then it will be lawful to retain them. Again, however, the prudent course will be to extract them; and prudence in this instance is more important than in the previous case.

The reason [for the greater importance of prudence in the latter case] is that there is doubt concerning the wealth, and the only reason for allowing its retention is the circumstance of possession that leads to a preponderant opinion that the wealth is indeed lawful. Even so, this [line of reasoning] is weakened by the certainty that unlawful elements have become intermixed. It is also possible to hold, as a legal presumption, that the wealth is unlawful; then only that wealth for which there is a preponderance of opinion [to the contrary] may be considered lawful. If neither of the two categorisations[B] takes precedence over the other, and there is nothing to suggest[1] a preponderance of opinion either way, then this will constitute a truly difficult question.

OBJECTION: Suppose that one acts on the basis of certainty.

[A] Obviously, such a preponderance will be based on evidence of some sort.

[B] i.e., neither lawful nor unlawful.

There is no way of knowing that whatever wealth is extracted is actually unlawful. After all, it is possible that the unlawful portion will still be in one's possession. That being the case, how can one use it? If this were lawful then the following would also be lawful. If one dead carcass were to be mixed in with nine properly slaughtered [goats], so that it becomes the tenth, then one may simply set aside one of the carcasses, any one of them, and retain the rest on the assumption that they are lawful. Even so, it might then be said that the dead carcass is one of the nine that were retained. In fact, if nine were set aside, and only one was retained, that too would not be lawful because of the possibility that it was the unlawful [carcass].

My response to this objection is to point out that this assessment would be correct were it not for the fact that wealth will become lawful[A] when a substitute value is extracted because that is something that can be offset, whereas carrion is not like that.[B]

We may attempt to shed light[C] on this problem by means of a hypothetical case involving a certain dirham that was confused for another dirham. In this case, a man finds himself in possession of two dirhams, and [he knows that] one of them is unlawful.[D] But he is confused as to which is which. When Aḥmad Ibn Ḥanbal (may God be pleased with him) was asked about such a situation he said, 'Set both of them aside until such a time as the matter may be clarified.'[2]

He [Ibn Ḥanbal] had pledged a water vessel [to a creditor] and when the debt was paid, the pledgee (*murtahin*) brought two water vessels to him and said, 'I don't know which of the two vessels is

[A] This might be read 'purified' instead of lawful, in the context of modern Islamic financial terminology and practice.

[B] Thus, the two cases are different because while trade goods or other assets may be exchanged for items of like value, carrion is not an acceptable substitute for properly slaughtered meat.

[C] Literally, 'to lift the covering'.

[D] He knows it is unlawful for him because he knows that one of the two dirhams does not belong to him.

yours.'[A] So, he [Ibn Ḥanbal] rejected both. Then the pledgee said, 'This one is yours. I was only testing you!' But, even though he had paid his debt, he [Ibn Ḥanbal] refused to take back his pledge. That was prudence. But it was not necessary.[B]

Let us give further consideration to the case of the two dirhams.[C] If the dirham has an owner[D] who is present, we may say that if one of the dirhams was returned to him, and he accepted it in full knowledge of the truth of the situation at hand, then the other dirham would become lawful for the other.[E] This is because either the returned dirham, in the knowledge of God, is the same one that was taken [from the original owner]; in which case that which was sought was accomplished.[F] Or the returned dirham

[A] Thereby giving Ibn Ḥanbal the choice to take either one of the two vessels.

[B] For detailed explanations of the rules regarding pledges, see Rāfiʿī, *al-ʿAzīz sharḥ al-Wajīz*, IV.437–544.

[C] It should be understood at the outset of this discussion that dirhams in the time of the author were not fungible in the way that currency today is fungible. Instead, dirhams and coins in general would be valued on their characteristics and not on their face value. Thus, a newly minted dirham would be worth more than one that had been altered by time or usage or by means of paring off shavings or by means of adulteration with other metals. Gold coins, made of soft metal, were often subject to shaving and paring. For futher details on this practice, see next footnote.

[D] A previous owner. It should be explained here that dirhams, in the time of the author, were not standardized, even if they came from the same mint. Rather, as gold, they were subject to alteration. When a seller did not have change, the buyer might simply take out a knife and pare off some of the coin. Thus, over time, dirhams often grew smaller and smaller. The paring, too, would leave each dirham with its own, distinct appearance (at least for as long as it remained 'unchanged'). That is why someone who had possessed a dirham for a period of time might very well recognise it.

[E] In other words, if the previous owner recognised it as the one he had paid or otherwise transferred, willingly or otherwise, to the one in possession of it, then the dirham remaining in the hand of the other will be lawful.

[F] i.e., because both dirhams are with their rightful owners and both are lawful.

was other than that one, in which case one dirham is in the possession of each of the two parties. Prudence, in that instance, will be for each to verbally express a mutual exchange. If they do not do so, then their debts[A] will cancel one another merely by means of silent mutual exchange.

Furthermore, if the wronged party is one who loses a dirham at the hand of a usurper and finds it difficult to identify that particular dirham,[B] such that he becomes entitled to its value, then whatever he takes [from the usurper] will be set against [the dirham] merely by the circumstance of possession. That, in respect of the wronged party, is clear because one who receives a guarantee will become the owner of the guarantee merely by means of possession, and without a word being said.[3]

The problem here is in respect of the other party because [as a usurper] he never takes actual ownership. Therefore, I will say that this is because when he hands over his own dirham,[C] he is also losing that dirham to the hand of the other, and there is no way for him to get it back. The dirham,[D] then, becomes like something that has been lost. And, in the sight of God, this will take the place of the other, if this is the case. Or this exchange will take place much like mutual cancellation when two men destroy, each one of them, a dirham possessed by the other.

Suppose, in the hypothetical case we are discussing, that each

[A] In this instance, each holds a dirham belonging to the other. If they do not formally agree to an exchange, then the law will consider the one debt to cancel out the other, even if there is no formal representation of the same. Silent mutual exchange, or *muʿāṭā* was discussed above.

[B] i.e., among all the other dirhams the usurper holds in his possession; supposing, of course, that the usurper is cooperating in the process of arriving at the truth in the matter. This will apply equally to the situation in which the usurper is not cooperating because there too identification will be next to impossible.

[C] The author is speaking of the instance in which the dirham returned is not the one that was misappropriated.

[D] i.e., the one that would be the lawful property of the usurper, who has mistakenly handed over his own dirham.

one was to throw what he possessed[4] into the ocean, or into a fire, he will have destroyed it. But, owing to mutual cancellation, neither will be responsible to the other. The same will apply even if nothing is destroyed.

Indeed, this opinion is better than going on to say that whoever takes an unlawful dirham and then places it with a thousand thousand dirhams belonging to another will cause all of that wealth to become prohibited to its owner, and that he will relinquish the right to its disposition. Such an opinion will lead to this result. Consider, then, how impractical that would be.

In the solution I have mentioned there is nothing more [objectionable] than a failure to vocalise [the transaction in a formal manner]. Even so, silent mutual exchange is a valid [mode of] transacting.[A] Moreover, those who do not consider silent mutual exchange a [valid mode of] transacting do so because there is a possibility that [an exchange is not intended] because an action is a weak indicator, while verbal expression is possible.[B] Here, in this case, the delivery and taking delivery are clearly for the purpose of exchange. Even so, it is not possible for this to be a sale because the object of the sale is neither indicated nor even known. It might be something that cannot be sold, as if one's single dry measure of barley were to become intermixed with another's thousand dry measures of barley, or if the same were to happen with molasses, or dates, or with whatever it is not possible to sell a portion of for another portion.

OBJECTION: An objection may be formulated as follows: 'You

[A] Among the scholars of the Shāfiʿī school of jurisprudence, the author was nearly alone in espousing this opinion. See Nawawī, *Majmūʿ*, IX.190; Zarkashī, *Manthūr*, III.185; Anṣārī, *Asnā al-maṭālib*, II.3; Haytamī, *Tuḥfat al-muḥtāj ʿalā al-minhāj* (Cairo, 1315/1938) IV.216; Sharbīnī, *Mughnī al-muḥtāj*, II.326.

[B] In silent exchange, even though the two parties are capable of doing so, they do not use words to indicate that an exchange is what they are doing. This, then, gives rise to suspicion. Or so the argument goes. All of this is based on the idea that a contract must include both an offer and its acceptance to be valid. For details, see the sources cited in the previous footnote.

have legitimised the delivery of the rightful measure in this example, but you have made it a sale.' My answer to the same is that I do not consider it a sale. Rather, it is compensation for what was lost while in someone's possession; so that he becomes its owner in the same way that one whose dates are destroyed [by another] becomes the owner of the dates [offered in compensation]. This, of course, will apply only when the owner is cooperative.

[On the other hand,] he may not be cooperative, insisting instead that he will not take a dirham unless it is the actual dirham that he [earlier] possessed; and that if it is impossible to distinguish he will leave it, but he will not make a gift of it [to the one who holds it], thereby making it impossible for [the holder] to use it. I will reply that in such a case it is the responsibility of the judge[A] to represent [the owner] in taking possession so that he may be content[B] with his money, because [the owner's attitude in this case] is no more than obstinacy and obstruction, and the *Sharīʿa* was not revealed to bring such things about. In the event that a judge cannot be found,[C] a religious man may be called upon to take possession for him. If even that is not possible, the possessor may himself take the place of [the owner], and then separate [one dirham from among the others] with the intention of exchanging that dirham [for the one that is unacceptable], so that the dirham [he chooses to separate from the rest] will [legally] become his to dispose of, and [after setting it aside] he will be content with the rest. In regard to liquids that have become intermixed, [such a solution] is even more obvious and more necessary.

Objection: So, if it should be lawful for him[D] to take it anyway, such that what he is entitled to will become his legal

[A] i.e., the *qāḍī* or judicial authority.

[B] i.e., the owner may rest assured, that when the legal authority steps in and accepts compensation on his behalf, that his wealth has been restored and that it is once again lawful.

[C] i.e., in a jurisdiction in which there is no *qāḍī* or any other Islamic judicial authority.

[D] i.e., according to the solution noted in the preceding answer.

responsibility, then what is the need for segregating before [he may legally] begin disposing of the remainder?

My response is to note that many scholars are of the opinion that it is lawful for him to take possession of as much as [he wants] as long as the measure of the unlawful remains.[A] It will not, however, be lawful to take possession of all of it. If he does so, it will not be lawful. Others, however, hold that it is not lawful to take possession until he has set aside the measure of the unlawful, in repentance, and sought to replace it. Still others are of the opinion that it is lawful for the taker to have the right of disposal, so long as he takes from the dirhams; but he may not give dirhams to another. If he does, he, but not the recipient, will be committing a sin.

None of the jurists,[5] however, is of the opinion that it is lawful to take all of the dirhams. This is because the owner, if he should appear, has the right to take what he is entitled to from among the others, being [then] able to say, 'Perhaps the dirhams given to me will be exactly the same dirhams that are owed to me.' Once the dirhams are identified, and those belonging to the other are segregated as a result of this identification, the possibility[B] will be put aside. Thereafter, having dispensed with this possibility, the wealth may be preferred over other sorts of wealth. Indeed, preference is always to be given to whatever is closer to the truth, in the same way that a replacement will be given preference over compensation for value, and in the same way that an original will be given preference over a replacement. Likewise, that in which the return of a replacement is possible will be given preference over that in which the return of compensation for value is possible; and that in which the return of the original is possible will be given preference over that in which the return of a replacement is possible.

[A] For example, if there are one hundred dirhams, and the measure of the unlawful is four dirhams, then he may spend (or otherwise dispose of) as many as ninety-six dirhams.

[B] i.e., the possibility that any or all of the dirhams in question are unlawful.

Moreover, if [hypothetically] it is lawful for the possessor [of the dirhams] to say this,[A] it will be lawful for the owner of the other dirham to take two dirhams and dispose of them [as he deems appropriate], saying, 'I am responsible for fulfilling your responsibility in another place' because the intermixing has taken place on both sides.

Nor is it any better to consider as lost what belongs to any one of them, except to determine which [of the two] is worth less, and then consider that amount to be lost; or to regard the one who did the intermixing and consider him by his deed to have destroyed a right of the other. Both considerations, however, are far-fetched (*baʿīdān*).

This should be obvious in the case of fungibles because they may be replaced, if they are destroyed, without [the need for recourse to] a new agreement. If a dwelling, however, were to become intermixed among other dwellings, or a slave among slaves, there is no way to [bring about a solution except through] mutual appeasement or satisfaction [among the two parties]. Suppose that one [of the two parties] refuses to take anything but what was his actual property, but it is not possible [to identify anything specifically as his property] and it is the intention of the other to prevent him from using any of his wealth,[6] in such a case, if the values of the property are similar, the way [out] is for a judge to sell all of the dwellings and then distribute the price among them, each in accordance with his percentage of ownership.[B] However, if the values of the property are disparate, the price of the most valuable dwelling [among the dwellings in doubt] will be taken from the party seeking the sale. [From the proceeds] the price of the least valuable dwelling will be given to the refusing party. And

[A] i.e., 'Perhaps the dirhams given to me will be exactly the same dirhams that are owed to me.'

[B] Suppose that ʿAbd Allāh owned one apartment in a block of apartments owned by ʿUmar, and there was ambiguity in the deed such that, before occupancy took place, it became impossible to distinguish which of the ten apartments belonged to ʿAbd Allāh.

the remaining amount will be held [as if in escrow] until clarification[A] or mutual agreement. Obviously, [such a course of action is required because] this is not a simple matter.

If a judge cannot be found, then the one desirous of a solution, and in possession of all [the dubious property] will have to take the matter into his own hands.[B] This is a matter of public welfare (*maṣlaḥa*). Aside from this, the other possibilities[C] are implausible and I do not choose them.

In the preceding there was an explanation of the legal reasoning [for choosing the solution mentioned above]. With regard to [fungibles like] wheat[7] that [reasoning] should be obvious. With regard to currency, it may be less so. In regard to trading goods, however, it may be somewhat exacting because [not all] items may be exchanged for others [of equal value], with the result that a sale is required. In what follows, I shall attempt to illustrate this principle in a series of examples.

EXAMPLE: Suppose that a man inherits land, as one of a group [of heirs], and the sultan had previously usurped the land from the legator. If the sultan returns a particular parcel of land, it will become the property of all of the heirs.[D] If, however, he returns a half of the property, and the share of the man [in the estate] is one half, then he must share it with the other heirs.[E] This is because the half that is to go to the man cannot be distinguished such that he may state that the land returned was actually his and the land that remains usurped was to go to the others. Nor will the land be distinguished by means of the sultan's intention that the land he retains should be the land that is the share of the others.

[A] i.e., until the exact dwelling can be identified, or until one of the two parties makes a legal claim and provides evidence to support it.

[B] And proceed as explained above.

[C] i.e., other possible avenues for legal redress in such a situation.

[D] Thereafter, the land may be distributed to the legatees, each in accordance with his or her rightful share.

[E] In this case the land must be distributed proportionally, each in accordance with his or her share.

EXAMPLE: If one should come to possess wealth taken from an unjust[8] sultan and then repent, when the wealth is in the form of land that has brought in revenue, one should calculate[A] the comparable value of rent on the land for the period that it has been in one's possession. The same will apply to any sort of usurped wealth from which revenues are derived, or that appreciate in value. One's repentance will not be complete until one calculates the revenue from whatever is misappropriated, and calculates the amount of appreciation as well. In the case of slaves [so gifted and then returned to the sultan], utensils, clothing, and the like, things that are not usually rented and for which valuation is difficult except by means of estimation and legal reasoning (*ijtihād*), the prudent course will be to use the highest estimate. Whatever is obtained through credit transactions in which misappropriated wealth is used as payment will remain the property of the one repenting. Even so, there is a certain degree of doubt here because the price was paid with unlawful wealth, as explained earlier. If he had used the [misappropriated] wealth itself to trade with,[9] then those transactions will be vitiated. One opinion, however, is that such transactions will be allowed if the one from whom the wealth was misappropriated should [later] agree. This is a matter of public welfare (*maṣlaḥa*). In that instance, the one from whom the wealth was misappropriated[B] will be considered the one transacting. Legal analogy, however, dictates that the transactions must be nullified, and the goods or their equivalent value be returned. If there were a great many such transactions and the repentant one is unable to do this, the wealth will be unlawful, and the one from whom the wealth was misappropriated will be entitled to the value of his capital. Whatever is in excess [of that amount] will be unlawful and must be set aside for distribution [to charity].

[A] i.e., when returning the land, one must also return the value of rent on the land, as if it had been rented.

[B] i.e., rather than the one who actually entered into the transactions, and profited from them, and then repented.

The excess wealth is not lawful for either the usurper or for the one from whom he usurped. Rather, the wealth will be categorised in the same way as any unlawful wealth that comes into one's possession.

EXAMPLE: If one inherits wealth without knowing how the legator acquired that wealth, and no evidence exists [to indicate whether it was lawful or unlawful], the wealth will be considered lawful. This is the opinion of all the jurists. If one knows that the wealth includes some unlawful elements, but is in doubt as to how much, one must deduct the unlawful portion by means of an estimate. If one does not know [anything about unlawful elements], but knows that the legator had undertaken tasks for sultans, though it is possible that he never received anything for doing so, or that he received something but that nothing of it remained in his possession owing to the passage of time, then this is the sort of case in which one should exercise prudence; though such prudence will not be necessary. If the heir knows that some of the wealth came about as the result of injustice, he must set that amount aside, after determining the amount by means of [his] best estimate (*ijtihād*). Some jurists, however, are of the opinion that this will not be required, and the sin will be the legator's.[10] Such a jurist cites [as evidence for his opinion] the narration concerning a man who had been placed in charge of a sultan's affairs. When he died, one of the Companions said, 'Now, his wealth is good,' meaning for his heirs. This opinion, however, is unconvincing because the name of the Companion was not mentioned.[A] It is possible that the statement was made by someone who was lax about such matters. Indeed, there were those among the Companions who were lax; though we do not name them out of respect for their position

[A] Strictly speaking, the statement of any of the Companions is to be accepted because of the principle which states that all of the Companions were trustworthy (*ʿudūl*). Thus, even if the Companion is not named, the statement should be accepted. On the other hand, if the reason the Companion was not named was that the narrator was attempting to obfuscate the matter, the report may not be accepted.

as Companions.[A] Moreover, how does someone's death legitimise wealth that is certainly unlawful and intermixed? And how can such an utterance[B] be taken [as law]? Certainly, if the heir is not sure [that some of the wealth was earned through injustice], it may be correct to say that he will not be brought to task [by God] for something about which he knows nothing. Thus, it may be for that reason that the wealth was said to be 'good' for the heir, who knows nothing about anything unlawful.

The Second Exercise: Disposing of What has been Set Aside

Once unlawful wealth has been [identified and] segregated, it will have three sets of circumstances:

One: If it has a particular owner, it must be transferred to the owner or to the owner's heirs. If the owner is absent, the wealth must be held until he presents himself, or until it may be sent to him. If the wealth appreciates or earns revenues [while the owner is away] these must be allowed to accumulate until his return.

Two: If it has no particular owner, such that there is no hope of identifying the owner, or knowing if he has died and left heirs or not, then that wealth cannot be returned. Instead, it must be kept until the matter can be clarified. It may be that the wealth belongs to a great number of people, [as might occur] in the theft of the spoils of war.[C] Then, after the army had dispersed, how

[A] Zabīdī, in his commentary, is careful to take exception with this point, making of it a theological issue. He also goes to some lengths to give an explanation, however implausible, of the alleged utterance (Z.vi.99).

[B] i.e., the utterance alleged to have been made by a Companion, 'Now, his wealth is good.'

[C] Generally, such a person, *al-ghāll*, was one who had taken booty in a battle and then, rather than turn it in to the commander for equitable distribution, hid the plunder and kept it for himself. Thus, if such a person were to repent of his deed after the army had disbursed, it would be impossible to dispose of the plunder in the way that was intended.

could so many [soldiers] be gathered together again? And, even if they could be gathered, how would it be possible to divide a single dinar among a thousand? Or two thousand? Such wealth, then, should be spent in charity.

Three: If it comes from tribute[A] or from money kept for the welfare of Muslims it may be spent on bridges, mosques, retreats, or water tanks [used by pilgrims and others] on the way to Mecca, and things of this nature that may be enjoyed by anyone who comes upon them, such that their benefit is shared among all Muslims.

The categorisation of the first set of circumstances is one in which there can be no doubt. With regard to [the second and third sets in which there is] charitable spending and the building of bridges, the matter should be undertaken by a judge, such that the money is entrusted to him. That is in the event that the judge is a righteous man. If he is lax with money, then as soon as the money is handed to him he should be made personally responsible (*ḍāmin*) for it. After all, even if he did not give a guarantee, if he took from it he would be held responsible. So, in this case, when he has given his guarantee, how can he not accept that responsibility?

It will be better [when the judge is not known for his prudence in financial affairs] to appoint a learned and pious person from among the inhabitants of the town. However, if both such a person and a judge are appointed it will be better than leaving the matter to just one person. If such an arrangement is not possible, then let the pious person undertake the matter on his own. After all, the purpose is to disburse the money. Seeking someone specifically to disburse it is a matter that has to do with [better efficiency through experience in] understanding the subtleties of distribution for the public good. Then, just because the more qualified person is not available does not mean that the matter of distribution should be dropped.

OBJECTION: What is the evidence for the lawfulness of charitable spending on something that is unlawful? And how can

[A] *Fay'* is the tribute paid by non-Muslim armies as the price for peace.

something that has no owner be spent as charity? Indeed, a certain group among the classical jurists held that to be unlawful. It is related concerning al-Fuḍayl that two dirhams came into his possession. When he learned that they did not belong to him, he threw them onto a pile of stones and said, 'I will not give in charity other than what is good. Nor will I be satisfied for another except with what satisfies me.'[A]

My response is to say, yes, there is an argument to be made here, and what you say may be possible. I, however, choose to oppose that [argument] on the basis of tradition, narration and legal reasoning.

The Messenger of God (may God bless him and grant him peace) ordered that a grilled lamb be given in charity when the one who presented it to him informed him that it was unlawful.[B] So he (may God bless him and grant him peace) said, 'Feed the prisoners with it.'[II]

[A] The commentator points here to the following verse of the Qur'ān, ...*and choose not for your spending the foul things which you yourselves would not accept without averting your eyes in disdain* (II:267). Z.VI.100.

[B] This incident took place as the Messenger of God (may God bless him and grant him peace) and a group of his Companions were returning from a funeral prayer. In the version related by Muḥammad b. al-Ḥasan al-Shaybānī in *The Kitab al-Athar of Imam Abu Hanifah* (London, 2006) pp. 520-521, on the authority of Abū Ḥanīfa, the following was related, 'A man from among the Companions of the Messenger of God (may God bless him and grant him peace) prepared a meal and invited him. So he (upon him be peace) went and we went with him. When the food was offered to him, he took some, and we began to partake. He took a piece in his hand and licked it, hesitatingly, but was unable to eat from it. Then he dropped it and, when we saw him do that, we stopped eating. The Messenger of God (may God bless him and grant him peace) called for the host and said, 'Tell me about your meat here. Where did it come from?' The man replied, 'O Messenger of God! It's a lamb belonging to one of our neighbours. But he wasn't here, so we couldn't buy it from him. Then, as we were in a hurry, we simply slaughtered the lamb and prepared it for you, thinking that we would pay the man when he returned.' Then the Messenger (upon him be peace) ordered the food lifted and fed to the prisoners' (pp. 520–521).

Moreover, when God (Exalted is He) revealed the verses, *Alif Lām Mīm. Defeated are the Byzantines in a land nearby, though following their defeat they shall be victorious,*[12] the idolaters belied the prophecy and said to the Companions, 'Can you not see what your friend is saying? He claims that the Byzantines will defeat the Persians!' So Abū Bakr made a wager with the idolaters, with permission from the Messenger of God (upon him be peace). When God proved the [prophecy] correct, Abū Bakr brought what he had earned from the wager. So he (may God bless him and grant him peace) said, 'That is filthy lucre! Give it away in charity.'[13] The believers were greatly pleased with the victory given by God. The prohibition against gambling, moreover, was revealed after the Messenger of God (may God bless him and grant him peace) granted permission to Abū Bakr to wager with the idolaters.

The narrations [on the subject include the story about how] Ibn Masᶜūd (may God be pleased with him) bought a slave-girl and could not find her owner in order to pay him for her.[A] He searched for the man a great deal, but still could not find him. Then he gave the price away in charity and said, 'O God! This is for him, if he pleases. Otherwise, I claim the reward for myself.'[B14]

Al-Ḥasan (may God be pleased with him) was once asked about the repentance of one who has stolen from the spoils of war, and what should be taken from him after the army has dispersed. He replied, 'Let him give it away as charity.'[15]

It is likewise narrated that a man allowed himself to be overcome by greed and misappropriated one hundred dinars from the spoils of war [before these were divided and distributed]. When the man repented, he went to his commander in order to give the money back; but the commander refused, saying, 'The army has

[A] The likelihood is that the girl's owner died in one of the wars and that Ibn Masᶜūd, as governor of Kufa during the time of ᶜUthmān, bought her and many other slaves in order to set them free.

[B] N.B. Even though the money did not belong to the owner of the slave, it was given in charity as if it were his property. Moreover, there is nothing to indicate that the owner would have freed the slave for a spiritual reward.

dispersed.' So the man went to Muʿāwiya.[A] But he, too, refused to take it. Then the man saw a certain ascetic and told him his story. He said, 'Give Muʿāwiya his fifth,[B] and give the rest away in charity.' Later, Muʿāwiya heard about the [ascetic's] advice and regretted not having thought of that answer himself.[16] Aḥmad Ibn Ḥanbal, al-Ḥārith al-Muḥāsibī, and other prudent jurists adopted the same opinion.[17]

Legal reasoning [on this issue] is to say that there is uncertainty in regard to such wealth, as to whether it will go to waste or be spent on good, if its owner cannot be located. By necessity, it may be known that it is better to spend it on something good rather than to throw it in the ocean. If we throw it into the ocean we make it unavailable to ourselves, and to the owner, and no benefit may be had from it. If we put it in the hand of a poor person, he will pray for the owner and the blessings of his prayer will accrue to the owner while the poor person will have his needs met.

Moreover, one should not doubt that the owner will receive blessings when he, without his even knowing, gives charity. It is related in a sound tradition that a planter will receive a reward[C] for as much of the harvest as is enjoyed by people and birds.[18] That is clearly not a matter of his own choice.

In answer to the statement, 'I will not give in charity other than what is good,' [I will point out] that it is [correct] when we seek a reward for ourselves. In this case,[D] however, we are seeking deliverance from injustice, not rewards. And we find ourselves [having to choose] between waste and charity. Therefore, we give preponderance to [the choice of] charity over waste.

[A] The man went to Muʿāwiya because, as the first of the Umayyad caliphs, Muʿāwiya was the army's commander in chief.

[B] In dividing the spoils of war, one fifth, *al-khums*, is always given to the ruler.

[C] This text of this tradition reads as follows, 'Any Muslim who plants a seed, or tills the earth, from which a human, or a bird, or an animal later partakes, will have given charity.'

[D] i.e., in purifying tainted or dubious wealth.

In answer to the statement, 'Nor will I be satisfied for another except with what satisfies me,' [I will also agree] that it is [correct, but the point is that it is] unlawful for us but lawful for the poor because there is evidence from the *Sharīʿa* to indicate its lawfulness.[A] Moreover, if there is a legal interest[B] in considering something lawful, it must be considered lawful. So, if something is lawful for [the poor], we will be satisfied for them that it is lawful.

Furthermore, if someone [is poor] it is his prerogative to give charity to himself or to his family. This should be clear with regard to his family because their poverty will not leave them just because they are members of his family. Rather, they are the most deserving of his charity. With regard to [the poor person] himself, however, he may take as much as he needs because he, too, is poor. If he were to give charity to another poor person that, too, would be lawful. So the same will apply to [giving charity to] himself if he is poor.

In what follows, I shall attempt to illustrate this principle in a series of examples.

EXAMPLE: If wealth from a sultan should come into one's possession [what is to be done?] Some jurists opined that it should be returned to the sultan because he knows best to whom it should be given, and he may give it to whomever he pleases. That will be better than spending it in charity. This opinion was the choice of Muḥāsibī, who said, 'How can it be spent in charity when it may have a rightful owner? If that is allowed, then it will also be lawful to steal from the sultan's wealth and give it away as charity.'

Another group of jurists held that it may lawfully be given to charity if it is known that the sultan will not give it back to its rightful owner. That is because [to return it to such a sultan will be] to assist in injustice and to increase the opportunities for more injustice. To return such wealth will be to squander the rights of the owner.

[A] The author has just finished explaining that evidence above.

[B] i.e., like the welfare of the general public.

The favoured opinion is that if it may be known from the habits of the sultan that he will not return it to its rightful owner, then it may be given away as charity on behalf of the rightful owner. This will be better for the owner, if there is a particular owner, than to have it returned to the sultan. Moreover, the wealth may not belong to anyone in particular, but to the Muslims in general. In that case, its return to the sultan will be a waste; and its return to an unjust sultan will be to squander the prayers of the poor. All of this should be obvious. If such wealth comes into one's possession by means of inheritance, and the heir in no way transgresses when receiving the wealth from the sultan, such wealth will resemble abandoned personal property (*luqṭa*) for which there is no hope of finding its owner. Thus, the heir will not be allowed to dispose of it by giving it away in charity on behalf of its owner, though he will have the right of possession, even if he is wealthy, since the wealth was earned by lawful means, abandonment. In the [prior] case, the wealth was not obtained by lawful means, and that has the effect of prohibiting ownership, while not prohibiting charitable giving.

EXAMPLE: If wealth without a rightful owner comes into someone's possession, I have already explained that it is lawful for that person to take as much as he requires if he is poor. The amount he requires is a matter that needs to be considered, and I discussed it in my book, *Kitāb asrār al-zakāt* [*Mysteries of Zakāt*].[A] One group of jurists was of the opinion that one may take however much he and his family require for a year. If he is able to purchase land or a business by means of which he may provide for his family, he should do that. This was the opinion held by Muḥāsibī. Even so, he said that it would be better if the person gives the entire amount to charity if he finds it within himself to place his trust entirely in [the Almighty] so that he may wait for His generosity to become apparent in what is lawful. If he is not able, he may buy the land or use an amount as working capital and live off the earnings from it.

[A] Book v of the *Revival of the Religious Sciences*.

Moreover, any day on which his requirements are met by some other means, he should refrain on that day [from drawing from the wealth without a rightful owner that has come into his possession]. Once [his own] lawful earnings are exhausted, he may return to the other wealth. In addition, whenever he finds [the means to make] a lawful living, he should give charity in the amount that he spent [on himself and his family] before [from the wealth without a rightful owner that came into his possession]. This will remain a debt for which he will be responsible. [When one is in this situation,] one should [learn] not to eat more than bread and shun meat, if one is capable of doing so. Otherwise, one may partake of meat as well, but without excess [in either quality or quantity].

What was mentioned in this regard by [Muḥāsibī] is quite exhaustive. However, I question his opinion that whatever the person spends on himself and his family will become a debt for which he will be responsible. No doubt, prudence dictates that it will become a debt; and if his lawful earnings are sufficient, then he should indeed give that amount[A] to charity. However, if this is to become a debt for that person, then will it become a debt to the poor person to whom he gives charity as well? This will obviously lead to hardship if the wealth [without a rightful owner] comes into one's possession from an inheritance in which there was no transgression through misappropriation or acquisition.

Example: Suppose that someone is in possession of lawful and unlawful wealth, or dubious wealth, and the entire amount is insufficient to meet his needs. If the person has dependents, he should ensure that the lawful portion goes to himself [first] because he is the one,[B] rather than his dependents including his slaves, family and small children, who will be held responsible. The person should encourage his older children [to earn only

[A] i.e., the amount of his debt.

[B] The modern reader will note that the general rule here applies to the earner, regardless of gender.

what is lawful] by protecting them from what is unlawful. This, however, will only apply if his doing so does not result in something more harmful. If it does, he should provide for them [from it] to the extent that they require. In general, whatever is prohibited to others is prohibited to him, and even more so. This is because he partakes of it [when he does have to partake of it] in the knowledge that it is unlawful, whereas his dependents may be excused if they do not know because the matter is not in their hands. So the person should begin with himself [in consuming the lawful] and then his dependents.

He may wonder, with regard to himself, whether he should [use the lawful in his possession] to provide for food and clothing, or for his other needs like [medical care such as] the fee for bloodletting, or the dyer, or the butcher, or [on toiletries like] oil for the hair, or for housing, or for maintaining [a mode of transportation like] a mount, or keeping an oven lit, or paying for firewood, or for oil for a lamp. [In my opinion] the lawful should go first for food and clothing because it is more important that what is related to the needs of the body should be lawful.

If the matter should come to having to decide between food or clothing, it may be possible to say that the lawful should be used to provide food because of its mixing with his flesh and blood when it is well known that 'The Fire is most deserving of flesh nourished by the unlawful.'[A] The benefit of clothing is that it covers nakedness and keeps heat, cold and the eyes of others from one's skin. This [prioritisation] is the one I consider the clearest.

According to al-Ḥārith al-Muḥāsabī, clothing should be given preference because it remains with people whereas food does not. Also, it is related that God will not accept prayers offered in a garment costing ten dirhams if even one of them is unlawful.[19] This

[A] This is an allusion to a tradition related by Tirmidhī in his *Sunan* on the authority of Kaʿb b. ʿAjra. According to Tirmidhī (*Sunan*, II.512,) it was a good (*ḥasan*) *ḥadīth*. Similar traditions were related by Abū Nuʿaym in *Ḥilyat al-awliyā' wa-ṭabaqāt al-aṣfiyā'* (Cairo, 1351–7/1932–8), from Jābir, VIII.247.

is a plausible opinion. Even so, this is something that applies to those who consume what is unlawful, and who are nourished by it. Therefore, it is more important to take care that one's flesh and bones are nourished by what is lawful. It was for this reason that [Abū Bakr] al-Ṣiddīq (may God be pleased with him) regurgitated what he drank unknowingly, so that his flesh and bones would not be nourished by, and grow because of, something that was unlawful.[A]

OBJECTION: If all of it is spent on his things, then what is the difference between him and anyone else? Between one party and another? And how is this difference to be known?

My reply is that this may be known from a tradition related about the death of Rāfiᶜ b. Khudayj[B] (may God have mercy on him) who left [his heirs with] a water-drawing camel and a slave who was a blood-letter. When the Messenger of God (may God bless him and grant him peace) was asked about it, he prohibited all earnings from blood-letting.[C] When he was asked repeatedly

[A] The event to which the author refers was also mentioned in Chapter One of this book. Abū Bakr (may God be pleased with him) drank milk that his servant had earned, and then asked the servant how he had earned it. The servant replied, 'I did some soothsaying for a tribe, and this is what they gave me in return.' Thereupon, Abū Bakr put his fingers in his throat and forced himself to vomit until the narrator, ᶜĀ'isha, thought his life would go out of him. Afterwards he said, 'O Lord! I apologise to You for what was carried by the veins and was mixed in the stomach.'

[B] Actually, this story is about Rāfiᶜ's grandfather who died in the lifetime of the Messenger of God (may God bless him and grant him peace). Otherwise, Rāfiᶜ himself passed away in the days of ᶜUthmān, according to some historians, in the year 73 or 74 AH at the age of 86.

[C] The issue of the blood-letter's fee was discussed in Chapter Two of this book. Ibn Munda related, in his *Kitāb al-maᶜrifa*, that Maḥīṣa had a slave named Abū Ṭayba who earned a great deal of money from blood-letting. When the Messenger of God (may God bless him and grant him peace) prohibited the same, Abū Ṭayba conferred with the Messenger (upon him be peace) and still the Messenger prohibited it. Abū Ṭayba, however, continued to speak with him on the subject and explain the need for it. Finally, the Messenger of God (may God bless him and grant him peace) said, 'Then let its earnings go to the

about the same matter, and was told that the heir had orphans to support, he replied, 'Let the earnings feed your water-drawing camel.'[20] This demonstrates the difference between what a person may consume and what his animal may consume.[A] If the difference is clear, then you may judge by analogy the details I mentioned above.

EXAMPLE: If someone in possession of unlawful wealth should spend it in charity on the poor, he may be generous with it to them. If he spends it on himself, he must be sparing. If he spends it on his dependents, he must be economical to a point somewhere between generous and sparing. Thus, the matter may be divided into three degrees. If a poor guest should visit him, he should be generous to him [in giving charity from the unlawful wealth]. If a wealthy guest should visit, he should not feed him unless he lives in a remote place or the guest arrives at night.[B] If the poor guest who visits is a religious and a pious person, such that he might avoid consuming charity, the host must inform him when serving him, so as to both satisfy the demands of hospitality and the principle that deception is to be avoided.

Thus, one should never feed a brother what may be offensive to him. Nor should one depend on his [guest's] ignorance to spare him from harm. This is because once the unlawful has found its way to the stomach it will cause hardening of the heart, even if the one who consumed it did so without knowing. It was for this reason that Abū Bakr and ʿUmar (may God be pleased with them) caused themselves to vomit, even though they drank without knowing [that what they were drinking was unlawful].[C]

stomach of your animal.' See Z.IV.106–107.

[A] The point here is that the tainted earnings will feed the animal; and the animal will do honest work to provide its owner with lawful earnings.

[B] In both cases, as food will not be readily available elsewhere, the wealthy guest will be legally categorised as a needy person, and will thus be deserving of charity.

[C] This is still another reference to the two stories related by the author in Chapter One of this volume.

All of this, though I issued a *fatwā* to the effect that it is lawful for a poor person, I have opined on the basis of necessity, as in the cases of pork and wine when we allow these [to be consumed] on the basis of necessity. Thus, none of this is to be subjoined [as a permanent categorisation] with the 'good and pure things.'

EXAMPLE: If unlawful or dubious wealth is in the hands of one's parents, one should abstain [to the extent possible] from eating with them. Even if one's doing so causes them to take offence, one must never obey them in regard to what is clearly unlawful. Instead, one should attempt to prohibit them from partaking of it. This is because 'No obedience may be accorded the created in what the Creator has prohibited.'[21] However, if the wealth is dubious, then whether one abstains from it or not is a matter of prudence. On the other hand, one's seeking to please one's parents is a duty. Therefore, if one does decide to abstain, one should do so gently. If one is not able to do so [in that manner], then one should partake. In doing so, however, one should eat sparingly, by taking small bites and chewing longer than normal, without consuming much. The same will apply to one's brother and sister [if they offer one food] because their rights are also emphasised.

Likewise, if one's mother gives one clothes to wear from dubious wealth, and would take offence if one were to refuse to wear them. One should accept the clothing and wear them for her in her presence. Once out of her presence, however, one should remove them and try not to perform prayer in them except when in her presence. In that case, one may perform the prayer of necessity. Whenever circumstances of this nature occasion conflict with regard to the dictates of prudence, one should consider the sort of subtleties mentioned here.

It is related that the mother of Bishr (may God have mercy on him) gave him a date to eat and said, 'By the rights I have over you, eat it!'[22] But Bishr [al-Ḥāfī] disliked eating it.[A] Even so, he ate it

[A] According to Makkī (*Qūt al-qulūb*), the reason for his reticence was related to prudence because even though the dates were his, they were to

and then went to the roof. His mother followed right behind him and saw him regurgitating it. Now, the reason he did this was that he intended to both appease his mother and protect his stomach.

It was said to Aḥmad Ibn Ḥanbal (may God have mercy on him), 'Bishr was asked if one should obey one's parents in regard to something dubious, and he replied, "No."' So Imām Aḥmad said, 'That is severe.' Then he was told that when Muḥammad b. Muqātil al-Abbādānī was asked the same question, he replied, 'Be good to your parents!' Finally, when the questioner asked [Imām Aḥmad], 'What is your opinion?' he replied, 'I hope that you will excuse me, for you have already heard what the two of them had to say about it.' When the questioner persisted, he answered, 'The best thing is to accommodate[A] both.'[23]

EXAMPLE: One who possesses only unlawful wealth will not be required to perform the pilgrimage (*ḥajj*), nor will he have to offer expiation [for non-performance of the pilgrimage] because he is bankrupt.[B] Such a person will likewise not be required to pay the *zakāt*. This is because the *zakāt* requires deduction of a fortieth share, whereas this person must deduct everything. If he knows the rightful owner [of what he possesses unlawfully] he must return the wealth to him; and if he does not know whom the rightful owner is, he must spend the wealth on the poor.

If what such a person possesses is dubious, and only possibly lawful, if he has not segregated [and returned or distributed] the wealth, he will be required to perform the pilgrimage (*ḥajj*). This is because there is a possibility that the wealth is lawful and, while only poverty may be accepted as an excuse for non-performance of the pilgrimage, poverty in this case has not been proved. God

have been distributed in charity to others; and his mother had retained a few for use at home.

[A] i.e., it is best to abstain from what is dubious and to do good to one's parents.

[B] Thus, even though the man may be in possession of the funds required to perform the *ḥajj*, those funds are not lawful and are not legally recognised. Then, from the perspective of the *Sharīʿa*, the man has no funds at all.

(Exalted is He) declared, *Pilgrimage is a duty owed to God by people who are able to undertake it.*[24]

Moreover, if it is necessary for a person who believes his wealth to be unlawful to give in charity whatever is in excess of his needs, then his giving the *zakāt* is even more necessary. If such a person is required to give expiation (*kaffāra*), he must do so by combining fasting and manumission so as to be certain of his clearing his responsibility. One group of jurists, however, was of the opinion that it will suffice if he fasts instead of feeding the poor if he is not wealthy. The opinion of Muḥāsibī was that fasting will suffice. My own opinion is that anyone in possession of dubious items we judge it necessary to abstain from, and require their deduction so that they no longer remain in one's possession owing to the possibility that they are unlawful, will have to both fast and feed others [as expiation]. He will have to fast because he is legally a pauper. Moreover, he will have to feed others because he is required to extract [and spend in charity] everything he possesses though, as it is possible that the wealth is actually his, the requirement will stand only in regard to [the amount required by] expiation.

EXAMPLE: Someone in possession of unlawful wealth who has kept it for his needs proposes to perform pilgrimage (*ḥajj*) as a supererogatory act of devotion. If he travels by foot, then there will be no legal impediment [to what he proposes] because [if he does not go] he will consume the wealth [by spending it] on things other than worship, and consuming it in worship is clearly better. If he is unable to go on foot, but requires more for a mount, it will not be lawful to spend on such a need along the way, nor will it be lawful to purchase a mount in the city [before setting out]. If he expects to be able to earn what is lawful if he remains [at home], such that it will enable him to do without the unlawful in his possession, then to remain at home in anticipation of the lawful will be better for such a person than setting out on foot for a pilgrimage with unlawful provisions.

EXAMPLE: One who sets out on a required pilgrimage with

dubious wealth should try and ensure that his food is paid for with lawful money. If he is not able to do this [throughout the pilgrimage], then [he should do it] from the time he puts on the *iḥrām* garment to the time he takes it off. If he is not able to do even this much, then he should attempt, on the Day of ʿArafa, to ensure that his standing before God in supplication should be a time when his food and clothing are lawful. He should thus attempt to ensure that nothing unlawful is [still] in his stomach at that time, and that nothing he wears is unlawful either. Even though we have given permission for this, we do so out of necessity and not because this may be subjoined [as a permanent categorisation] with the 'good and pure things'. If he is not able to do even this, then he must maintain the fear [of God] in his heart, and remorse for his having no recourse other than to partake of what is not good and pure. Perhaps, if he does this, He will look on him with mercy, and forgive him owing to his remorse, fear and dislike [of the unlawful].

EXAMPLE: Aḥmad Ibn Ḥanbal (may God have mercy on him) was asked about someone whose father had died and left him money, when the father was known to have had dealings with those whose dealings are disapproved [or worse]. He replied, 'Extract as much of his wealth as he earned as profit.' The man said, 'He was owed debts, and he owed debts.' [Imām Aḥmad] replied, 'Pay them, and collect them.' The man asked, 'So this is your opinion?' He replied, 'Do you want to abandon him, shackled by his debts?'[25]

What was mentioned by [Imām Aḥmad] is correct. His saying, 'Extract as much of his wealth as he earned as profit' indicates that he considered it correct to extract an amount of unlawful money, and that he considered the principal of his wealth to be the heir's rightful property; whereas what was spent in void and unlawful transactions would be segregated or set off, regardless of the amount, or of how difficult it might be to return. Finally, in the matter of paying off debts, the heir must assume that these are legitimate. He may not ignore these just because he suspects otherwise.

CHAPTER FIVE

Grants and Gifts made by Rulers and which of these may be Considered Lawful and which Unlawful

ANYONE WHO ACCEPTS something of value from a ruler must consider three things. [Firstly, he must consider] how that gift came to be in the possession of the ruler in the first place. [Secondly, he must consider] the attributes that make him a deserving recipient [of the ruler's largesse]. [Thirdly, he must consider] the amount he is to receive; is he truly deserving of the amount granted if his own circumstances and those of others with similar circumstances are taken into consideration?

The First Consideration: The Sources of a Ruler's Income

Aside from tillable land left by those without heirs, the only wealth that is lawful to a ruler may be divided into two categories:

The First Category: [This is wealth which is] forcibly[1] taken from the disbelievers as the spoils of war[2] (*ghanīma*), and tribute (*fay'*) which is wealth appropriated from them in lieu of fighting, and the minority tax (*jizya*), and arbitration settlements (*ṣulḥ*) taken in accordance with conditions and negotiations.[A]

The Second Category: This is wealth taken [by the ruler] from

[A] For the rules in respect of distribution of these categories, see Ghazālī, *Wasīṭ*, IV.89–95.

Muslims. In this category, only two kinds are lawful. The first is wealth left by those with no heirs; and [conjoined to this is] lost wealth or that for which no rightful owners can be located. The second kind is wealth left as endowments (*awqāf*), but without a trustee [or trustees to administer it]. The sort of endowment known as *ṣadaqāt* [in the early days of Islam] is not to be found in our times [and therefore there is no point in discussing it]. Aside from these categories, all other forms of wealth taken from Muslims in the form of taxes,[A] or duties, or bribes are clearly unlawful.

Therefore when a grant, or a gift, or a fine cloak[3] is decreed for a jurist, or anyone else, there are eight possibilities: [1] the grant will have come from the minority tax revenues (*jizya*), [2] or from the estate of one who died without leaving an heir, [3] or from endowments, [4] or from the reclaimed agricultural lands of the ruler himself, [5] or from the private possessions of the ruler, [6] or from one of the ruler's tax collectors, [7] or from a dealer[B] among the traders, [8] or from the ruler's personal treasury. An explanation of each of these possibilities will follow.

THE FIRST [IS] THE MINORITY TAX: Four-fifths of all revenues from the minority tax are to be used for the public welfare, while one-fifth (*khums*) may be used for specific purposes only.[C] So whatever grant is decreed from the fifth for the purposes designated, or from the four-fifths for the public welfare, when prudence is exercised in regard to the amount [of disbursements], will be lawful. This, however, will be on condition that

[A] N.B. the author is speaking here of the sort of taxes levied by tyrants in his own times. Otherwise, there is nothing in the *Sharīʿa* to prevent legitimate taxation.

[B] The term used by the author here is *bayyāʿ* which, in the classical lexicons, indicates someone who is good at buying and selling or who frequently engages in buying and selling. In modern parlance, this would equate to an investment manager.

[C] These are detailed in the manuals of *fiqh*, in the chapters about the *zakāt*.

the minority tax has been collected in conformance with the *Sharīʿa* injunction to take only one dinar or four dinars per person, no more than once a year. This is because the exact amount of *jizya* is a matter of legal opinion (*ijtihād*), and the ruler has the right in such matters to act on whichever opinion he may favour. Another condition here is that the non-Muslim subject, *dhimmī*, from whom the *jizya* is collected must earn his living in a way that is clearly known not to be unlawful. Thus, he may not be a tax collector for a tyrant, or a seller of liquor, or either a youth or a woman, because the minority tax need not be paid by them,[A] only by [non-Muslim] male subjects. All of these are matters that must be considered in regard to how the tax is collected, how much is collected, the attributes of those to whom it is given, and the amount. All of these points must be considered.[B]

SECONDLY, ESTATES AND OTHER WEALTH WITHOUT OWNERS: If the gift is allotted from the wealth left behind by those without legal heirs, wealth which is also to be used for the welfare of Muslims in general, it must first be determined if all of that wealth was acquired by means of the unlawful, or if most of it was, or less than half, in accordance with what was explained earlier.[C] If it is established that it is not unlawful, it must be determined whether or not granting that wealth to the person proposed is actually in the interests of Muslims, and whether or not the amount proposed is commensurate with those interests.

THIRDLY, ENDOWMENTS: The matters in need of consideration in the previous category also need to be considered when

[A] The minority tax is owed to the state by legally competent, non-Muslim males who are capable of military service but who, by paying this tax, are excused from serving. Thus, women, children, slaves, the insane, the elderly, the blind, and the clergy are all exempted from payment. See Z.VI.110. See also Ibn Sallām, *Kitāb al-amwāl* (Beirut, 1408/1988), pp. 45–61.

[B] i.e., by anyone contemplating acceptance of a ruler's gift that comes from the minority tax revenues.

[C] i.e., in Chapter Two of this volume.

the grant comes from endowment (*waqf*) monies. A further matter for consideration here, however, is the instructions (*shurūṭ*) of the one who financed the endowment.[A] Thus, whatever is taken from the endowment must be in agreement with all of the endowment's stipulations.

FOURTHLY, RECLAIMED LAND: No conditions apply to the category of the ruler's own reclaimed land because this is his personal property and he is free to dispose of it as he wishes; by giving whatever he wants to whomever and in whatever amount. What needs to be considered, however, is [whether or not the ruler] reclaimed the land with forced labour, or paid the workers' wages with the unlawful. The ruler did not himself reclaim the land but, in all probability, had it cleared, levelled, irrigated, tilled, walled, and so on by labourers. Then, if the labourers were forced (without recompense) to prepare the land, the ruler will not be the true owner of the land, and the land will be unlawful to him. On the other hand, if the ruler gave the labourers their wages, but from unlawful funds, then that will give rise to doubt. We have already discussed the matter of how, when a disapproved element enters into a payment, the legitimacy of the article purchased comes into question.

FIFTHLY, PRIVATE POSSESSIONS: Whatever is purchased on credit by the ruler, land, cloaks, horses,[4] and so on is his property and he may dispose of it as he pleases. If, however, these were purchased with unlawful or doubtful funds, then in certain cases these too will be unlawful, or doubtful, all of which has been explained in detail earlier.

SIXTHLY, TAXES: If the grant is decreed from wealth held by tax collectors, or agents, or those in charge of distribution[5] or confiscation then, as filthy lucre, it will most certainly be unlawful. Nowadays,[B] most land grants are of this category. The lands

[A] In using *waqf* funds for a gift, the ruler must not in any way contravene the conditions set by the one who financed the *waqf*.

[B] This is the end of the fifth *hijra* century that the author is writing about.

of Iraq, however, are otherwise because they, according to Shāfiʿī, are to be considered an endowment (*waqf*) for the betterment of all Muslims.[A]

Seventhly, traders: If the ruler makes the grant through a trader who deals exclusively on his behalf, then this category will be the same as that of the ruler's personal possessions. However, if the trader transacts more for others [than for the ruler], then the amount granted through him will be credited against the ruler's account. If this is paid off by means of prohibited funds, then in this case too a disapproved element will have entered into the payment, and the purchased article [or in this case, the gift or the amount gifted] will be rendered dubious. The legal categorisation (*ḥukm*) of an unlawful price was discussed earlier.

Eighth, if a grant is made from a treasury [in which], or through an expert[6] with whom,[B] both lawful and unlawful monies are kept; then if the ruler's income [in those accounts] is known to have come only from the unlawful, then that is filthy lucre.[C] Suppose, on the other hand, it can be established that the account contains both lawful and unlawful money. Then, [further suppose] that it is likely that whatever is granted comes from the lawful, even to the extent that one is nearly convinced of that possibility, the possibility remains that the money is unlawful. This is because these days most of the wealth in the possession of rulers is unlawful, while the lawful wealth in their possession is either rare or non-existent. This is why people dispute this point. Some jurists say that as long as I am[7] unable to determine with certainty that something is unlawful, I will retain the right to take

[A] In accordance with this view, the lands held by those living in Iraq are not actually owned by them. Instead, those people are to be considered tenants of the *waqf*. Abū Ḥanīfa's opinion on the matter is that the land of Iraq is not a *waqf* and belongs to the people who hold legal title to it. See Zaylaʿī, *Tabyīn al-ḥaqā'iq*, III.271 and Makkī, *Qūt*, II.462–463.

[B] i.e., the assumption here is that the expertise alluded to would be in the management of money or finance.

[C] i.e., the gift will undoubtedly be unlawful.

it. Others, however, say that until one is able to determine with certainty that something is lawful, it will remain unlawful because the doubtful is never presumed to be lawful. Both of these opinions, however, are extreme.

The balanced opinion in the matter is the one we mentioned earlier; that if the greater part can be determined to be unlawful, then the whole will be unlawful. But if it is determined that the greater part is lawful, and it is also determined with certainty that a part is unlawful, then this is a matter for pause (*tawaqquf*),[8] as was explained earlier.

Those who allow the acceptance of gifts from the wealth of rulers when these are composed of both the lawful and the unlawful—and when it is known that the gift itself is not unlawful—do so on the basis that it is impossible to establish whether the gift came from lawful or unlawful funds. In support of their opinion they cite as evidence the record of those Companions who lived under the rule of known tyrants, and who nevertheless accepted gifts from them. Among these were Abū Hurayra, Abū Saʿīd al-Khudarī, Zayd b. Thābit, Abū Ayyūb al-Anṣārī, Jarīr b. ʿAbd Allāh, Jābir [b. ʿAbd Allāh al-Anṣārī], Anas b. Mālik, Miswar b. Makhrama, Ibn ʿUmar, Ibn ʿAbbās, and others. For example, Abū Hurayra and Abū Saʿīd are known to have accepted money from Marwān [b. Ḥakam] and Yazīd, and ʿAbd al-Malik.[9] Likewise, Ibn ʿUmar and Ibn ʿAbbās took sums from Ḥajjāj [b. Yūsuf], as did many of the Successors like Shaʿbī, Ibrāhīm [al-Nakhaʿī], Ḥasan [al-Baṣrī], and Ibn Abī Laylā. Shāfiʿī once accepted a sum of one thousand dinars from Hārūn al-Rashīd, and Mālik is known to have accepted a great deal of money from several different rulers.

ʿAlī [b. Abī Ṭālib] (may God be pleased with him) once said, 'Accept whatever is given to you by the ruler because whatever he gives you comes from the lawful, for the greater part of the wealth he accumulates comes from the lawful.'

On the other hand, those who refused to accept sums from rulers did so on the basis of prudence (*tawarruʿan*), as they feared having anything in their possession that might even possibly be unlawful and thus cause their practice of religion to become tainted.

Consider what Abū Dharr said to al-Aḥnaf b. Qays, 'Accept a gift only when you feel comfortable doing so. But when you feel that your religion will suffer as a result, refuse it.'[10]

Abū Hurayra (may God be pleased with him) said,[11] 'Whenever anyone gives us anything we accept it. But if they don't give us anything, we won't ask either.'[12]

Saᶜīd b. al-Musayyab reported concerning Abū Hurayra (may God be pleased with him) that whenever Muᶜāwiya granted anything to him, he remained silent. But if Muᶜāwiya failed to grant him anything at all, he would complain.[13]

Shaᶜbī reported that Masrūq said, 'A gift will remain with its recipient until it lands him in the Fire.'[14] So, even if the gift itself is lawful, it may prompt him to commit the unlawful.

Nāfiᶜ related that al-Mukhtār used to send money to Ibn ᶜUmar (may God be pleased with them both) and that Ibn ᶜUmar used to accept it, saying, 'I ask no one for anything. But I will not refuse the things that God sends my way.'[15]

Once, al-Mukhtār sent Ibn ᶜUmar a riding camel, and he accepted it. The animal was thereafter widely known as al-Mukhtār's riding camel.

These reports, however, are contradicted by another report which said that Ibn ᶜUmar (may God be pleased with them both) never refused a gift from anyone except al-Mukhtār.[A] Of the two reports, moreover, the latter is the more authentic.

Nāfiᶜ also related that Ibn Maᶜmar sent seven thousand dirhams to Ibn ᶜUmar who immediately distributed them. When

[A] The explanation put forward by Zabīdī in his commentary is perhaps the most plausible explanation for the conflicting reports. In the early days of his rule, al-Mukhtār was careful not to overstep the boundaries of his authority. At that time, several of the pious Companions accepted his largesse. Later, however, when he resorted to unjust means to preserve his rule, those same Companions refused to have anything to do with him.

someone arrived late and asked Ibn ʿUmar for some of it, Ibn ʿUmar went to some of those to whom he had distributed the money and asked them for a loan.

When al-Ḥasan b. ʿAlī (may God be pleased with them both) went to Muʿāwiya (may God be pleased with him), Muʿāwiya said to him, 'I will make you a gift the likes of which I never have before, nor ever will again, grant to another Arab.' When he made him a gift of four hundred thousand dirhams, al-Ḥasan accepted the gift.[16]

Ḥabīb b. Abī Thābit related that he saw the gifts al-Mukhtār had readied for both Ibn ʿUmar and Ibn ʿAbbās, and that both had accepted them. When people asked him [Ḥabīb] what the gifts consisted of, he replied that they were cash money and garments.[17]

Zubayr b. ʿAdī reported that Salmān [al-Fārisī] said, 'If you have a tax collector or money lender friend who enters into usurious transactions, and he invites you to eat with him, or gives you a present, do not refuse him because these will be lawful to you, while the responsibility for the wrong will be on your friend.' By analogy, if it is all right to accept gifts from a usurer, it should be all right to accept them from a tyrant as well.[18]

Jaʿfar [al-Ṣādiq] related from his father[A] that both al-Ḥasan and al-Ḥusayn (may God be pleased with them both) used to accept gifts from Muʿāwiya.[19]

Ḥakīm b. Jubayr related that he went to Saʿīd b. Jubayr after he had become the collector of the *zakāt* on agriculture (*ʿushr*) for the lower Tigris river. 'Saʿīd sent notice to all of his deputy tax collectors, asking that they feed him [and those in his jurisdiction] with something from the produce in their possession. When they sent it, he ate it and we ate it with him.'[B]

[A] Muḥammad b. ʿAlī b. al-Ḥusayn Zayn al-ʿĀbidīn al-Bāqir (d. 117/735).

[B] There are obvious difficulties in establishing the relevance of this story to the subject at hand. Zabīdī suggests that the collectors had provisions of their own or from the treasury that were lawful for their own use; and what was lawful for them was lawful for others. Another possibility is that there was famine, or at least shortages, in Saʿīd's jurisdiction and he requested relief from the

Al-ʿAlā b. Zuhayr al-Azdī related that when his father[A] was a tax collector in Ḥilwān he gifted something to Ibrāhīm [al-Nakhaʿī], and Ibrāhīm accepted it. Ibrāhīm said, 'There is nothing wrong in accepting gifts from tax collectors because they earn their living by working. The public treasuries contain both lawful and unlawful wealth. What they give to you will come from the lawful.'[20]

Evidently, then, all of these people accepted gifts from tyrants, even though all of them were vocal in faulting those who give allegiance to a ruler who sins against God. Basically, the position of those of our Predecessors (Salaf) who refused such gifts was not that they supposed acceptance unlawful, but rather that they refused out of prudence. This was the reason for the refusal of the Rightly-Guided Caliphs,[B] and of Abū Dharr, and others, including ascetics who abstained from much of what was absolutely lawful in order to discipline themselves (*zuhdan*), and who abstained from otherwise lawful things that might lead to sin out of prudence and *taqwā*. From the practice of the Predecessors then it is clear that it is lawful to accept gifts from rulers. It is equally clear that the abstinence or refusal on the part of the likes of Saʿīd b. al-Musayyab, who refused grants amounting to over thirty thousand dinars,[21] and Ḥasan al-Baṣrī, who said he would not take water for ablutions from a money-changer even if the time for prayer was about to end, were based on prudence. Certainly, it is better to follow the example of their prudence in abstaining than to follow the example of their open acceptance. At the same time, we may not hold such acceptance to be unlawful.

collectors in other regions. Under those circumstances, he may have partaken of what was sent in order to show others that there was nothing wrong with consuming food from the *ʿushr* (Z.VI.114).

[A] His father, Zuhayr b. ʿAbd Allāh al-Azdī also served as the governor of Ḥilwān.

[B] These are generally understood to be Abū Bakr, ʿUmar, ʿUthmān, and ʿAlī. ʿUmar b. ʿAbd al-ʿAzīz, though he followed much later, is also considered one of their number.

These, in brief, are the doubts[A] (*shubha*) put forward by those who allow the acceptance of gifts from tyrannical rulers.

The answer to these is that the number of people [from the Companions and the Successors] reported to have accepted such gifts is very insignificant in comparison with the number of those known to have refused or returned such gifts. Moreover, if the only possible reason for refusing is prudence, then you should know that in the acceptance of those who accepted there are three possible levels that equate to differences in the degrees of their personal prudence. Altogether, there are four degrees of prudence in relation to rulers.

The first degree [of prudence in relation to rulers] is that of those who accepted nothing from the wealth of rulers, just like the first caliphs. The Caliph Abū Bakr (may God be pleased with him) kept a close account of all the money spent on himself from the public treasury (*bayt al-māl*). Finally, when it was determined that the total came to six thousand dinars, he repaid six thousand of his own dinars to the public treasury.[22] Once, when the Caliph ʿUmar (may God be pleased with him) was distributing money from the public treasury among orphans, one of his own daughters came and took a dirham. ʿUmar immediately stood up and tried to wrench the dirham from her grasp. He did this with such violence that his cloak fell off and left one of his shoulders bare. In tears, the girl put the dirham in her mouth and ran home. But ʿUmar followed her and, when he caught up with her, extracted the dirham by putting his finger into her throat. Then he returned the dirham to the treasury and said to the people who had gathered about, 'People! Neither ʿUmar nor any of his family is entitled to more than what any Muslim, from near or far, is entitled to!'[23]

Abū Mūsā al-Ashʿarī gave a dirham he had earned from

[A] It is interesting to note that the author refers to these as 'doubts', in the sense that they represent a lack of certainty, and not 'arguments' in the sense of facts that give logical support to their assertion.

sweeping the public treasury to one of ʿUmar's young sons who was playing nearby. When ʿUmar saw the dirham in the child's hand he asked where it came from. 'Abu Musa gave it to me,' replied the boy. Then ʿUmar [went to] Abū Mūsā and said, 'To your way of thinking, is no house in all of Medina more wretched than the house of ʿUmar? Is it your intention that the entire community of Muḥammad should petition me for the redress of this injustice?' Having said this, ʿUmar ordered the dirham restored to the public treasury.[24]

So even though the dirham in that case was clearly obtained by means of the lawful, ʿUmar still feared having even that much held against him. In other words, in order to preserve his religion and reputation, ʿUmar was willing to do with less than his rightful share. Such an attitude stems from the teachings of [the Messenger of God] (may God bless him and grant him peace), 'Reject what gives rise to doubt in favour of what leaves you free of doubt,'[25] and 'Those who avoid the dubious will protect their honour and their religion.'[26]

ʿUmar was also familiar with what the Messenger of God [may God bless him and grant him peace] had said to ʿUbāda b. al-Ṣāmit when he sent him to collect the *zakāt*, 'O Abū al-Walīd! Fear God! And let it not happen that on the Day of Judgement a crying camel should come and put its neck on yours (indicating that it holds you responsible for its state of discomfit), or a bellowing cow, or a bleating goat!' ʿUbāda asked the Messenger of God (may God bless him and grant him peace), 'Will it really be like that?' He (may God bless him and grant him peace), replied, 'Yes! I swear by the One who holds my life in His hand! That is how it will be...except for those towards whom God shows mercy.' Finally, [ʿUbāda] replied, 'I swear by the One who sent you with the truth! I will never try to collect anything from anyone.'[27]

He (may God bless him and grant him peace) also said, 'I do not fear that you will revert to idolatry after I am gone as much as I fear that you will compete with one another in amassing wealth.'[28]

In a lengthy narration it is reported that ʿUmar (may God be pleased with him) stood at the door of the public treasury and said, 'I find myself at this door like the guardian of an orphan and a trustee of his inheritance. If I have no need of it, I stay clear of it. But if I have need, I spend from it only as much as is absolutely necessary.'[29]

It is related that one of Ṭāwūs' sons sent a letter to the Caliph ʿUmar b. ʿAbd al-ʿAziz in his father's name and received in reply three hundred dinars. When Ṭāwūs discovered what had occurred, he sold his land so that he could repay the money his son had received from the caliph.[A] This is what happened when the ruler was[30] of the calibre of ʿUmar b. ʿAbd al-ʿAziz! And this is the highest degree of prudence.

THE SECOND DEGREE [OF PRUDENCE IN RELATION TO RULERS] is to accept the ruler's gift, but only after ascertaining that it has come from a lawful source. Then, even if the ruler does possess unlawful wealth, at least the gift has been determined to be lawful. Most of the narrations concerning the practices of the Companions in this regard should be understood as having been based on this level of prudence.

This explains how Ibn ʿUmar, so well known for his prudence, could have accepted sums from the same rulers he is known to have publicly criticised. For example, when Ibn ʿĀmir was on his death bed and people had gathered around him, Ibn ʿĀmir revealed to them his fear of meeting God after having been a collector of revenues for royalty. So those gathered began to console him by saying that they expected the best for him in the next world because of the wells he had caused to be dug for the pilgrimage caravans and for similar deeds. Seeing that Ibn ʿUmar was present, but silent, Ibn ʿĀmir asked him what he thought. Ibn ʿUmar replied, 'I say that the deeds they have mentioned will

[A] Evidently, the family found itself in straightened circumstances, so the son wrote to the caliph for relief. Then, despite the legitimacy of the request, the father felt it necessary to repay the money.

only be of benefit when they are paid for from lawful funds, and very soon you will find out for yourself!' In another version of this narration it is related that Ibn ᶜUmar answered him by saying, 'The tainted will never erase the sinful![31] My estimation is that while you were the governor of Basra you earned nothing but evil for yourself.' Then Ibn ᶜĀmir replied by asking Ibn ᶜUmar to say a prayer of supplication for him. So Ibn ᶜUmar said, 'I once heard the Messenger of God (may God bless him and grant him peace) say, "Just as God will never accept prayer performed without ablutions, He will never accept charity paid out of funds obtained unjustly." And you were the governor of Basra.'[32] This is what Ibn ᶜUmar had to say about what [Ibn ᶜĀmir] had spent in charity.

It is also related that in the days of al-Ḥajjāj b. Yūsuf, Ibn ᶜUmar (may God be pleased with them) said, 'Since the seat of the caliphate (Medina) was laid waste,[A] I have never eaten[B] my fill.'[33]

Of the Caliph ᶜAlī (may God be pleased with him both) it is related that he kept a sealed vessel of barley which he would pour into water and drink. When he went to Iraq someone asked him why, when there was such plenty in Iraq, he kept his barley in a sealed vessel. ᶜAlī replied, 'I do not keep this vessel sealed in order to deprive others of its contents. What troubles me is that something should become intermixed with it, something that is not of the same [lawful] nature. My real concern is that a tainted substance should ever find its way into my stomach.'[34]

[A] The expression used here is ambiguous and may also be understood as a reference to the murder of ᶜUthmān in Medina. In this manner, Ibn ᶜUmar was able to speak his mind without directly criticising the tyrants who ruled at the time. However, it is clear that Ibn ᶜUmar meant this as criticism of the Umayyad caliphs who employed al-Ḥajjāj. See the following footnote.

[B] Though al-Ḥajjāj was governor of Iraq, he was appointed by ᶜAbd al-Malik b. Marwān who was the Umayyad ruler responsible for laying siege to Medina and for spilling the blood of many Companions and Successors. This event also led to looting, and the plunder from the siege was sold in the marketplace. These events and the reaction of Ibn ᶜUmar were mentioned in Chapter Two.

Indeed, this is what their custom was.

It was the practise of Ibn ᶜUmar, whenever he found one of his possessions becoming dear to him, that he would give it away. For example, once Ibn ᶜĀmir offered him thirty thousand dirhams for his slave, Nāfiᶜ. So, rather than merely refuse to sell Nāfiᶜ to him at a gain to himself, Ibn ᶜUmar called Nāfiᶜ and said to him, 'O Nāfiᶜ! I am afraid that I will be tested by these dirhams of Ibn ᶜĀmir's. So go, you're free.'[A]

Abū Saᶜīd al-Khudarī is reported to have said, 'There is no one among us who has not been affected by worldly interests, except Ibn ᶜUmar...for nothing could interest him in the life of this world.'[35]

Obviously, then, it should be clear that it must not be supposed regarding him, or regarding anyone who had attained as high a spiritual station as Ibn ᶜUmar, that he could possibly have accepted anything without knowing that it was indeed lawful.

THE THIRD DEGREE [OF PRUDENCE IN RELATION TO RULERS] is to accept gifts from rulers but then to distribute them among the poor and needy. The ruling of the *Sharīᶜa* is that this is lawful if the true owner of the wealth to be distributed cannot be determined, and if the ruler is such that if the wealth were to remain in his possession he would not otherwise distribute it and it would be used to perpetuate his tyranny. So, in the opinion of many jurists it is better that the gift be accepted and distributed rather than remain in the hands of a tyrant. In what follows this matter will be elaborated upon further. In any case, the acceptance of gifts by the great majority of our Predecessors was based on this understanding.

Ibn al-Mubārak wrote, for just this reason, 'Nowadays people who accept gifts from rulers and then cite the examples of

[A] It is interesting to note that Nāfiᶜ chose to remain with Ibn ᶜUmar as his student and his servant for as long as he lived. The conversation is recorded by Iṣfahānī in his *Ḥilyat*, 1.295. In the version recorded by Dimyarī, it says that Ibn ᶜUmar freed a thousand slaves before he died.

Ibn ʿUmar and ʿĀ'isha, are in no wise following their examples because whatever Ibn ʿUmar accepted, he immediately distributed. He once even borrowed sixty thousand at the same sitting in which he had distributed.[A] ʿĀ'isha used to do the same.'[36]

After Jābir b. Zayd[37] had accepted a gift and distributed it, he said, 'It seems better to me that I should take this money and distribute it rather than allow it to remain in his [the ruler's] hands.'

Likewise, the gift accepted by Shāfiʿī (may God have mercy on him) from Hārūn al-Rashīd was distributed within a day's time. On the second day not a single grain remained.[38]

THE FOURTH DEGREE [OF PRUDENCE IN RELATION TO RULERS] is that at which it cannot be established that the gifted sum was [obtained by] lawful [means]; and when the sum is not to be distributed, but accepted with the intention of keeping it; and only from a ruler whose wealth is known to consist mainly of the lawful. The wealth in the treasuries of the Rightly-Guided Caliphs and those who followed them in the times of the Companions (may God be pleased with them) and Successors was certainly composed, in the main, of the lawful. In verification of this fact, ʿAlī (may God be pleased with him) once said, 'The wealth collected by the ruler is obtained mostly by lawful means.' For this reason, one group of jurists holds that one may base one's decision about acceptance or refusal on what one supposes to be the nature of the major portion of a ruler's wealth. We uphold this opinion only as far as it relates to the rights of the individual.

But when a ruler's wealth is so great as to be beyond counting, it is not surprising that some of our jurists reached the conclusion, by means of their juristic exertions (*ijtihād*), that it is lawful to accept something (from such a ruler) which cannot be determined to have come from unlawful sources, [or earned or collected by unlawful means].[B]

[A] This was done so that he could distribute money to latecomers.

[B] Their reasoning on the matter is that the legal presumption about the nature of a ruler's wealth is that it consists mainly of the lawful: The reason for

Now that you have understood something of these degrees, you should have come to the realisation that the gifts and grants given by tyrants in the present day are nothing like those given in earlier times. Indeed, there are two unmistakable differences between then and now.

The first difference is that at the present time, the wealth of rulers is composed, either entirely or in the main, of the unlawful. Of the lawful categories of income,[39] tribute, the spoils of war, and *ṣadaqāt* are no more.[A] So none of this contributes to the revenues in the hands of rulers today. This leaves only the minority tax (*jizya*). But the way it is collected is so oppressive that the monies collected are tainted, and are thus not lawful. Muslim rulers show no regard either for the proper amount prescribed for collection by the *Sharīʿa*, or for those from whom this tax is to be collected,[B] or for the various conditions and stipulations related to the tax. What is worse than all of this is that in comparison to the monies taken in unjust taxes, impounded property, and bribes, the minority tax revenues amount to less than one percent[40] of the wealth of our rulers.[C]

The second difference is that the tyrants of earlier times, since they ruled not long after the Rightly-Guided Caliphs, were at least conscious of their tyranny. For this reason they were anxious to win the favour of the Companions and Successors, and urged

ruling in favour of prohibition is that the unlawful can be determined with a fair degree of certainty to be predominant. When this is impossible, the ruling may be based upon the presumption of legitimacy.

[A] Each of these categories or sources is explained at the beginning of this chapter. Note that the term *ṣadaqāt* meant a specific sort of endowment. The word is not to be understood as it is today as referring to charity in general.

[B] History has recorded cases in which Muslim rulers discouraged conversion to Islam for the reason that it would lead to decreased revenues.

[C] Abū Zubayr al-Jubā'ī used similar arguments to shame Abū al-Ḥasan al-Karkhī, head of the Ḥanafī school of jurisprudence in the first part of the fourth century, into refusing support offered by the ruler of Baghdad. See Tanūkhī, *Nishwār al-muḥāḍara* (N.p., 1397/1977) p. 391.

them to accept their gifts. Thus, rather than allow the Companions or Successors to suffer the indignity of going to the rulers' courts and asking them for grants, the rulers used to send gifts to them, and do everything in their power to persuade them to accept those gifts. Indeed, the rulers were greatly pleased when they did accept. Thus, the Companions and Successors accepted those gifts, even if they then distributed them. This does not mean, however, that they cooperated with those rulers, or that they attended their courts, or that they promoted them, or wished their rule to continue. On the contrary, they prayed for the downfall of those tyrants, and publicly denounced them, and condemned them for their unseemly deeds (*munkarāt*). The Companions and Successors never feared that the elevation of their worldly status by such rulers would lead to the decline of their spiritual states. Nor certainly did they ever[41] fear those rulers.

In our own times, however, rulers are interested only in those people from whom they desire services, or by means of whom they hope to increase their spheres of influence, or from whom they seek help in achieving their purposes, or who they suppose will benefit them by impressing others, or by saying prayers for their health and continued reign, or by praising them in their presence and their absence.

If one were to refuse, first, to demean oneself in order to ask for the ruler's favour; and second, to do his bidding; and third, to praise him and supplicate for him; and fourth, to assist him in his affairs whenever assistance is sought; and fifth, to enhance the number of sycophants at his court and in his public appearances; and sixth, to proclaim admiration for and loyalty to him, and support for him against his enemies; and seventh, to cover up his tyranny, oppression and excesses, then certainly today's rulers would never grant such a person, even if he were to be the Shāfiʿī (may God be pleased with him) of his day, a single dirham!

Having considered every aspect of the matter, even if it were to be ascertained that a ruler's wealth was lawful, to accept gifts from that wealth would certainly not be lawful as to do so would lead to these excesses.[A] So, in cases in which wealth is determined to be either prohibited or doubtful, the prohibition against acceptance should be even more obvious. Thus, anyone nowadays presumptuous enough to accept such gifts by comparing themselves, by means of legal analogy, to the Companions and Successors should know that they are really comparing blacksmiths to angels! Furthermore, the acceptance of gifts entails a number of other things, all of which are sinful; like meeting with rulers, spending time in their presence, doing the bidding of their advisors, allowing oneself to be degraded by them, praising them, and repeatedly knocking on their doors. All of these matters will be discussed in the chapter that follows.

Now that the matter of the income and wealth of rulers has been explained, how some is lawful and some is unlawful, if we suppose that someone were to be granted by a ruler something commensurate with what that person deserved, and without that person's having to ask for it, or in any way serve, support, or praise the gifting ruler, then acceptance of that gift or grant will not be unlawful. It will, however, still be legally disapproved (*makrūh*) for several reasons, all of which will be explained in the chapter that follows.

The Second and Third Considerations: The Quantity of What is Accepted and the Attributes of Those who Accept It

Let us suppose that the wealth[B] is wealth that is to be used for the public welfare, like the four-fifths of [wealth received as] tribute, or estates without heirs. Other categories of wealth are such that those entitled to them are specified, like endowment monies, or monies collected as *zakāt*, or the fifth portion of either tribute or the spoils of war. However, the personal possessions of the ruler,

[A] i.e., the seven demeaning sins listed in the preceding paragraph.
[B] i.e., the wealth that is to be granted by the ruler.

like agricultural lands that he has reclaimed or purchased with his own money, are his to dispose of as he may wish. He may give such wealth to whomever,[42] and in whatever quantity, he wishes. The categories of wealth with which we shall concern ourselves in this discussion, however, are wealth without owners and wealth that is to be used for the public welfare.[A]

Such wealth should only be gifted to people through whom the Muslim public will benefit, and to those who are truly in need of financial help owing to their inability to earn for themselves. Those who are capable of earning and whose receipt of such grants will be of no particular value to the Muslim community at large must never be given money from the public treasury.[B] While it is true that there is some disagreement among the jurists on this point, it is clear that the most correct opinion is that which dictates not giving public money to such persons.[C]

From the words of the [Caliph] ʿUmar (may God be pleased with him) it is evident that every Muslim has a right to the money in the public treasury, because every Muslim adds to the numbers of Islam.[43] Yet, in spite of this, ʿUmar did not distribute money from the public treasury among all Muslims. Rather, he used to distribute it only among those who possessed certain kinds of attributes. This being the case, anyone responsible for matters that affect the welfare of Muslims, who would have to abandon his activities on behalf of the Muslims if he were required to earn [his living], was entitled to support[D] from the public treasury.

According to this principle, then, all scholars have a right to

[A] These categories, as explained in the opening sentence of this paragraph, include four-fifths of the monies collected as tribute [*fay'*] and the estates claimed by the state when their owners die without leaving heirs.

[B] While the sentence is rendered 'must never be given money' the literal translation is 'it is not lawful to give them money'.

[C] While the commentator has summarised this subject, Z.vi.119–120, a more classical source may be found in Ibn Sallām, *Kitāb al-amwāl*, pp. 271–312.

[D] In other words, such a person has a right to have his needs met (*lahu ḥaqq al-kifāya*) by the treasury.

money from the public treasury. This, however, is on the condition that they be scholars of the sciences that are of benefit to religion; disciplines like Law (*fiqh*), or Traditions (*ḥadīth*), or Exegesis (*tafsīr*), or Qur'ānic Recitation. Even teachers and those who give the calls to prayer are included in this category. Likewise, students who study these disciplines may also receive such grants, for if they are not supported they will not have the opportunity to acquire this knowledge.

Among those deserving of such support are those on whose work the affairs of the world depend; like salaried soldiers who, by means of the sword, protect the kingdom from invaders, rebels, and the enemies of Islam; or like those who keep the public records and accounts and administer the finances of the state, and everyone whose services are required to collect taxes. And I mean the lawful taxes not the unlawful, for only the lawful may contribute to the welfare of the state.

Moreover, welfare is connected either to religious or to temporal affairs. So by means of the scholars, religion may be preserved, and by means of the military the state may be preserved. Thus the religion and the state are like twins, neither is such that it is not in need of the other.

Furthermore, while there is no religious matter that depends on the knowledge of a doctor, physical health does, and religion follows the body.[A] Therefore, it is clearly in the interests of the Muslim public that the treasury should also support medical practitioners and all those whose professions are similarly required for the maintenance of health and society.[B] In this way, those in need of medical attention may receive it without having to pay for it. Moreover, this support will not be conditional upon need. Rather, support may be given regardless of the recipient's financial situation because the Rightly-Guided Caliphs used to

[A] i.e., there can be no religion without physical health.

[B] Literally, 'required for the welfare of bodies and cities.'

make gifts to the Emigrants and Helpers,[A] and none of them were known to be needy.

Nor were the amounts granted determined by a formula. Rather, the matter is left to the ruler's discretion (*ijtihād*). He may give generously and make the person rich,[44] or he may grant only as much as is required for a person's needs, depending on the circumstances and the state of the treasury. Al-Ḥasan (may God be pleased with him), for example, once received a single payment of four hundred thousand dirhams from Muʿāwiya.[45] Likewise, ʿUmar b. al-Khaṭṭāb (may God be pleased with him) gave a yearly stipend of twelve thousand dirhams in smelted silver to a certain group, and he established the same arrangement for ʿĀ'isha (may God be pleased with her), while he granted others amounts of six and ten thousand [dirhams]. In short, then, these categories of people have a right to the public treasury, while there is nothing to prevent even large amounts being given at the ruler's discretion. The ruler, likewise, has the right to reward distinguished people with cloaks and other special gifts, because this was done in the times of our Predecessors. Still, the welfare of the public should always remain a consideration in these matters. Awards given to scholars or heroes should serve as encouragement for others to follow their examples, and to excel in whatever they do. This is the real benefit of cloaks and gifts and all such rewards. All of these matters, however, remain at the discretion of the ruler.

In relation to unjust rulers, however, there are two matters for consideration.

Firstly, an unjust ruler must renounce his authority. This is because a tyrant is either dethroned (*maʿzūl*)[B] or subject to dethronement (*wājib al-ʿazl*). How is it lawful to accept money from him when he is certainly not a legitimate ruler?

Secondly, if a tyrannical ruler is not giving grants to all those

[A] i.e., the people of Mecca who emigrated to Medina and the people of Medina who assisted them when they arrived.

[B] If he has not already been dethroned, then he is deserving of dethronement.

who deserve them, then for those few he favours, how will it be right to accept his gifts? Furthermore, would it be lawful for those few to accept their grants if they were given in the amount of the shares they deserved? Or is it unlawful for them to accept anything at all? Or is it lawful for each to accept whatever is offered?

In the first instance described, my opinion is that there is nothing to prevent the recipient from taking his due. This is because an ignorant and unjust ruler, as long as he is supported by power, as long as it remains difficult to overthrow him, and as long as the attempt to do so will result in intolerable civil strife, must be left in place, and must be obeyed in the same way that all those in command (*umarā'*) must be obeyed.[A] In regard to the need to obey the authorities and to lend them a helping hand[46] there are many commandments and admonishments.[B]

In my opinion, the caliphate may be considered legitimate for those of the descendants of al-ᶜAbbās (may God be pleased with him) who perform its responsibilities. The authority (*wilāya*) of those who rule over the regions of the empire, and who follow the caliph, has legal force (*nāfidha*). I have explained, in my book entitled *al-Mustaẓharī*,[C] which is derived from *Kashf al-asrār wa-hatk al-astār* by al-Qāḍī Abū al-Ṭayyib in refutation of the different sects among the Shīᶜa known as al-Bāṭiniyya,[47] how this

[A] The author deals with the subject of rebellion in his legal manuals, *Wasīṭ* (iv.113–115) and *al-Wajīz fī fiqh al-Imām al-Shāfiᶜī* (Egypt, 1317/1900) ii.164.

[B] The commentator cites several traditions here. See Z.vi.121–122. For an exhaustive study of the subject see Abou El Fadl, *Rebellion and Violence in Islamic Law* (Cambridge, 2001).

[C] This work is named after the ᶜAbbāsid caliph of those times, al-Mustaẓhar bi-Llāh, and is a polemical dealing with the teachings of the Ismāᶜīlī sect of Shīᶜa Islam. It is published under the title, *Faḍā'iḥ al-bāṭiniyya* (Cairo, n.d.) pp. 169-170. 'Ultimately, despite all the polemics in favour of the ᶜAbbāsid caliph, Ghazālī's argument, like those of his teacher, al-Juwaynī, reduces itself to a balancing act between the pros and cons of attempting to overthrow the ruler. Hence, the possibility of disobeying an illegal order or rebellion is not rejected out of hand.' Abou El Fadl, *Rebellion*, p. 184.

matter is related to the public welfare. Briefly, however, the matter is as follows.

The conditions to be satisfied and the attributes to be possessed by a ruler lead to the expectation that he will rule in the interests of the public. If we judge today that his authority is illegitimate, the interests of the public will immediately be compromised. So why squander one's working capital in pursuit of profit? Authority nowadays depends on nothing other than power (*shawka*).[A] Thus, whoever receives the allegiance and support of the powerful becomes the caliph. And whoever is himself powerful and is loyal to the caliph by giving the Friday sermon (*khuṭba*) and minting coins in his name will be deemed a legitimate ruler whose judgement[48] and government will have the force of law throughout the land. I have discussed this matter in detail in a treatise entitled *Aḥkām al-imāma* ('The Requirements of Leadership'), which is included in my book, *al-Iqtiṣād fī'l-iʿtiqād*.[B] Therefore, I shall not dwell at length on the subject here.

In regard to the second question mentioned above, 'If the ruler does not provide for every deserving person, but grants stipends only to a few individuals, is it lawful for an individual to accept such a stipend,' there are four degrees of difference between the opinions of the scholars. Some of them go to the extreme of saying that everything appropriated by the ruler is to be shared by all Muslims. However, as no one knows if their share comes to a *dāniq*[C] or a grain of gold, people must forego all of it. Other scholars hold that such persons may accept only as much as will suffice them for a single day because it is lawful for Muslims to take, in cases of need, whatever will sustain them. Another group said

[A] The commentator adds, 'It was for this reason that Muʿāwiya became the ruler instead of ʿAlī b. Abī Ṭālib. This was also why it was Yazīd who succeeded his father, rather than al-Ḥusayn b. ʿAlī.' Z.vi.122.

[B] Chapter Three of that work is on the subject of political leadership (*al-imāma*).

[C] A *dāniq* was a small coin equivalent in value to one-sixth of a dirham. See Ibn Manẓūr, *Lisān al-ʿArab* (Beirut, 1375/1955), v.39; vi.375; x.105–106.

that they may accept what suffices them for a single year because it is awkward to keep on taking sustenance every day. Since the chosen recipient is entitled to it,[49] how can he be expected to relinquish his right to it?

Still other scholars say that one is entitled to keep however much one receives. If there is injustice, it will have been done to the others.[A] This opinion is the reasonable one. This is because this [particular sort of] wealth is not to be shared by all [members of a class or category of] Muslims, unlike wealth acquired as the spoils of war that is divided among the victors. Nor is it of the nature of an estate, left to heirs, because that has actually become their property. This wealth, if it is not distributed to the deserving before they die, will not then be distributed among the heirs of those people by virtue of the laws of inheritance. Rather, the right to this wealth is an unspecified right that only becomes specific through possession. Therefore, it is like charity (*ṣadaqa*) which becomes the property of the poor only when they actually take possession of it.

Just because the other categories of recipients are wronged does not mean that those who are truly deserving should lose their just shares.[B] This, however, will only hold true if all of the wealth is not distributed to the one class of recipients. Thus, even if the ruler gives to one person, and then gives less to others, it will still be lawful for the one person to accept what he is given. This is because it is lawful to show favour when giving gifts.

When Abū Bakr (may God be pleased with him) gave stipends in equal shares, ʿUmar (may God be pleased with him) asked him

[A] Lit. the ones to whom injustice is done are the rest. In other words, it is not the fault of the recipient that not everyone receives their just share. Rather, the burden of that injustice will be borne by the ruler.

[B] If the ruler should suddenly refuse to give it to needy travellers, or to those in debt, preferring instead to give it to only one category of those eligible to receive charity, like beggars, then just because the ruler is unjust in the way he distributes his charity, this does not mean that the beggars who do receive it will not legally possess it.

to reconsider. He [Abū Bakr] replied, 'How they are favoured is up to God. This world is for nothing more than delivery.'[A][50]

When ʿUmar (may God be pleased with him) became the caliph, he gave a stipend of twelve thousand dirhams to ʿĀ'isha, ten thousand to Zaynab, and six thousand to Juwayriyya and Ṣafiyya.[51] Likewise, he granted exclusive rights to the revenues from a tract of land to ʿAlī (may God be pleased with him).[52] When ʿUthmān (may God be pleased with him) [became caliph] he granted five parcels[53] of regular revenue from agricultural land in Iraq to ʿAlī (may God be pleased with him) rather than keep them for himself. ʿAlī agreed to this, and raised no objection.[B] Thus, all of this is lawful.

In matters in which there are legitimate differences of opinion, the qualified jurist (*mujtahid*) has the right to decide for himself what is right. This is one of those matters in which every qualified jurist earns a reward[C] because there is no definitive text on the issue at hand, or on anything that might be compared to it by way of analogy. The issue of the punishment to be prescribed for one guilty of consuming alcohol is such a matter. This is because the Companions are known to have prescribed both forty and eighty lashes in punishment; and both are consistent with *Sunna* and are correct.[D]

[A] The sense here is that Abū Bakr did not consider it his place to favour anyone over anyone else. However, the author's point in mentioning this incident was to show that it is at least lawful to show favour; otherwise, ʿUmar would not have suggested what he did. See Z.vi.123.

[B] All of these reports indicate that the Companions held it lawful to show favour when giving gifts.

[C] The teaching of the Messenger of God (may God bless him and grant him peace) is that every *mujtahid* earns a reward; a single reward if his effort to discover the right answer (*ijtihād*) does not lead to the correct course of action, and a double reward if it does. This is because, right or wrong, *ijtihād* is itself worthy of reward. See Bukhārī, *Ṣaḥīḥ*, p. 1542.

[D] For details on this issue see, Māwardī, *al-Aḥkām al-sulṭāniyya wa'l-wilāya al-dīniyya* (Cairo, 1386/1966), pp. 284–285; al-Bājī, *al-Muntaqā sharḥ al-Muwaṭṭa'* (Beirut, 1403/1983), iii.142–143; Ibn Ḥajar, *al-Talkhīṣ al-ḥabīr fī takhrīj aḥādīth*

Likewise, both Abū Bakr and ʿUmar (may God be pleased with them both) were correct in their distribution of stipends because the Companions (may God be pleased with them) agreed to both divisions.[A] Those who received more from Abū Bakr and less from ʿUmar did not return the difference in ʿUmar's time. Nor did those who received more from ʿUmar refuse the increase on the basis of the fact that they had received less in Abū Bakr's time. All of the Companions shared in this matter; and all of them believed that each of the two opinions was correct.[B]

Therefore, in matters where there is scope for legitimate differences of opinion, this is the proper approach to take. In issues, however, where definitive texts are to be found, or where a clear analogy may be drawn, if a jurist takes a contrary position, owing either to negligence [of the evidence] or to flawed reasoning, then in such a case we must not suppose that just any jurist is deserving of a reward. Rather, the reward will go only to the one who recognised the text or used the analogy to reach the right decision.

The result of all these considerations is that a person who possess attributes connected to either the worldly or religious welfare of Muslims, and who receives gifts or stipends from a ruler, when those come from property bequeathed to the state,

sharḥ al-rāfiʿī al-kabīr (Delhi, 1307/1890), IV.136; Ṣanʿānī, *Subul al-salām sharḥ bulūgh al-marām* (Cairo, n.d.), II.444; Shawkānī, *Nayl al-awṭār*, VII.165; Zarkashī, *al-Baḥr al-muḥīṭ*, VI.518; ʿAbd al-ʿAzīz al-Bukhārī, *Kashf al-asrār ʿalā uṣūl al-Bazdawī* (Istanbul, 1308/1891), III.293-294.

[A] The significance of having the Companions concur on a decision is that it takes on the legal authority of the *Sunna*. In other words, as those who witnessed the words and the deeds of the Messenger of God (may God bless him and grant him peace), the Companions were expected to comment after he had gone regarding whatever he had done or said. If they said nothing about a common practice, the jurists assume that the practice was one that had the approval of the Messenger (may God bless him and grant him peace), and thus it assumed the same legal standing as something from the *Sunna*.

[B] i.e., that both Abū Bakr and ʿUmar were right in the matter of how they distributed the public wealth.

or from *jizya* properly paid, that person will not become a sinner merely for accepting that gift. Rather, the aspect of sin arises only when such people begin to serve the ruler, or to assist him, or to regularly visit him, or to praise him in his presence, or to do the kinds of things that are usually required of those who expect to receive gifts from rulers. In the next chapter I shall discuss this matter in greater detail.

CHAPTER SIX

What is Lawful in Regard to Socialising with Despotic Rulers and Others; and the Categorisation of Attendance at their Courts, of Calling on them and of Showing them Respect

KNOW THAT THREE relationships are possible to you in regard to despotic rulers and officials:

First, and this is the worst of all possible relationships, that you visit them;

Second, and this is not quite so injurious, that they visit you; and *Third*, and this is the safest, that you avoid them so that you never see them and they never see you.

The First Relationship: Visiting Rulers

This is an extremely blameworthy state from the perspective of *Sharīʿa*. Indeed, there are numerous texts in censure and reproach of such a relationship. Here, in order that[1] you may become acquainted with how reprehensible this is considered by the *Sharīʿa*, I shall quote some of these[2] [texts]. Thereafter, I shall consider what is prohibited, what is lawful, and what is disapproved[3] [in these relationships], according to what is required by a *fatwā* based on clear evidence.

Narrations (*Akhbār*)

When the Messenger of God (may God bless him and grant him peace) described tyrannical rulers, he did so in the following terms, 'Whoever repudiates them will find deliverance, and whoever avoids them will be safe, or almost safe, and whoever falls in with them will be accounted one of them.'[4] Here the meaning is that those who avoid them will be safe in the sense that they will not share in the sin of their [the rulers'] wrongdoing. They might not, however, escape the kind of punishment that envelops all of society if they do not repudiate or actively oppose the unjust.

[The Messenger of God] (may God bless him and grant him peace) also said, 'After me there will come rulers who will lie and oppress. So anyone who upholds the untruths that they speak and assists in the wrong that they do will have no relationship with me, and I will have none with him; nor will that person pass by the pool of paradise.'[5]

Abū Hurayra related that he (may God bless him and grant him peace) said, 'The most detested of all those who recite the Qur'ān are those who visit rulers.'[6]

Another narration states, 'The best of rulers are those who visit scholars; and the worst of scholars are those who visit rulers.'[7]

Still another narration states, 'Scholars are the trustees of God's Messengers over those who worship Him, as long as they do not mix with rulers. If they do that, they will have betrayed the trust of God's Messengers. So be on your guard against them, and stay away from them.'[8] This was related by Anas (may God be pleased with him).[9]

Reports (*Āthār*)

Ḥudhayfa said, 'Beware of the places of trial!' When he was asked what places those were, Ḥudhayfa replied, 'The doors of the rulers. You might visit the *amīr* and find yourself verifying his untruths, and saying things about him that are fictitious.'[10]

Abū Dharr said to Salama, 'O Salama! Do not enter the doors of rulers! You will never take anything from their world except that they will take something better from your religion.'[A]

Sufyān [al-Thawrī] said, 'In the fire of hell (*jahannam*) there is a valley inhabited only by those scholars who used to visit kings.'[11]

Awzāʿī said, 'There is nothing more hated by God than a scholar who visits a governor.'[12]

Sahnūn said, 'What could be less becoming of a scholar than to be sought at his regular place, but not found; and then to have it said to those who seek him, "He is with the *amīr*!" I used to hear it said that if you see a scholar in love with the world, then do not trust him in matters of your religion until you have tested him. I have tested myself and found that whenever I visit a ruler, I incline toward him; regardless of how harshly I speak with him or oppose his desires.'[13]

ʿUbāda b. al-Ṣāmit said, 'An ascetic scholar's love for rulers is hypocrisy (*nifāq*) and his love for the wealthy is dissimulation (*riyā'*).'

Abū Dharr said, 'Whoever frequents a people will become one of them; especially if those frequented are tyrants.'[14]

Ibn Masʿūd (may God be pleased with him) said, 'A person may enter into the presence of a ruler with his religion intact, and then exit without it.' When he [Ibn Masʿūd] was asked why this should be, he replied, 'Because when he pleases the ruler, he angers God.'[15]

When ʿUmar b. ʿAbd al-ʿAzīz appointed someone an official [in his administration] it was pointed out to him that the man had been an official under al-Ḥajjāj. When [ʿUmar b. ʿAbd al-ʿAzīz] ordered him removed from his new office, the man went to ʿUmar and explained that he had done very little while in the service of al-Ḥajjāj. Then ʿUmar replied, 'It is sufficiently evil and iniquitous

[A] i.e., regardless of the opportunities you may find with them for the acquisition of worldly possessions and influence, the price you will have to pay will come from your religion. See Ibn Abi Shayba, *Muṣannaf*, XIV.221-222.

that you spent a single day, or even a part of a day, in that man's service.'[16]

Al-Fuḍayl once said, 'No one ever grew closer to a ruler except that they grew more distant from God.'[17]

Saʿīd b. al-Musayyab used to say of his trading in cooking oil, 'It spares me from having anything to do with rulers.'[A]

Wuhayb once said, 'Those who are constantly in the presence of rulers are worse for this community than gamblers.'

Muḥammad b. Salma said, 'Flies on refuse are more becoming than a scholar at the door of a ruler.'[18]

When Zuhrī began to frequent the company of the ruler, one of his brothers in religion[B] wrote to him saying, 'May God deliver us, you, Abū Bakr and I, from all trials! For your condition at present is such that those who know you should pray to God for you and ask Him to have mercy on you. You have become an old man, and it seems that the bounty bestowed on you by God has become burdensome for you, the bounty of knowledge about the meanings of His Book and the *Sunna* of His Prophet Muḥammad (may God bless him and grant him peace). Yet His covenant with scholars is not like that. God (Exalted is He!) said, *You shall explain these things to people, and you shall not conceal them.*[19] Understand, that the least of the sins you have committed is that you have rendered familiar the injustice of a tyrant and paved his way to wrongful conduct by your proximity. For, when he brought you close, he continued to ignore the rights of others and never ceased to do wrong. They have taken you as a pivot on which the gristmill of their injustice may revolve, as a bridge over which they cross to spread their evil, and as a set of stairs they climb to further their errors. By means of you[C] they cast doubt in the hearts of

[A] Apparently, this was related by al-ʿAjalī because the commentator quotes from him that Saʿīd never accepted their gifts, but had about four thousand dinars in capital with which he carried on a business in olive oil. See Z.vi.128.

[B] The author of the letter was Abū Ḥāzim al-Aʿraj and the ruler was ʿAbd al-Malik ibn Marwān. See Z.vi.128..

[C] i.e., by means of your reputation for learning and piety.

the learned, and win over the hearts of the unlearned. How easy for them to make a life of ease for you in this world while they destroy [your chances for a better life in the next world]! How much more of yours have they destroyed than they have given! Finally, what guarantee do you have that you are not the one intended by the verse, God (Exalted is He) says, *And they left behind them followers who wasted their prayers and followed after base desires.*[20] Of a certainty, you are not dealing with the ignorant! Then treat your religion, for it is ailing. And look to your provisions, for the journey you have ahead of you is a long one! *And nothing in the heavens or on earth is hidden from God.*[21] Peace be upon you.'[22]

All of these narrations explain in general terms the kinds of dangers and temptations with which one's associating with rulers is fraught. In what follows, however, we shall explain the matter in detail from a legal (*fiqh*) perspective so that the prohibited (*maḥẓūr*) may be distinguished from the disapproved (*makrūh*), and the merely permissible (*mubāḥ*). Thus, one who associates with a ruler is in danger of sinning against God (Exalted is He) by means of his deeds, or his silence, or by means of his words, or his convictions.

As for sinful deeds, in the majority of circumstances, one's going into the presence of rulers means that one sets foot on usurped property without the permission of its true owners, and that is unlawful. Nor should one be misled by those who say that to do so is no different from what is customarily lawful without permission, like eating a fallen date or two from a tree, or crumbs from a loaf of bread, because that is lawful only in relation to what has not been wrongfully appropriated. [If the tree] has been wrongfully appropriated, then even that[A] will be unlawful.

It may be objected that one's brief sitting on usurped premises cannot possibly detract from it,[B] and therefore such a sitting, or even a walking through, will be no different from what is

[A] i.e., eating a fallen date or two.

[B] i.e., by causing it to decrease in value.

customarily lawful. But this would apply to people as individuals in the same way that it applies to them collectively, and usurpation (*ghaṣab*) is accomplished by means of a collective deed.

When someone does something the true owner would overlook if he were to know of it, that is lawful. If, however, that deed were to pave the way, by example, for a series of similar infractions, then the ruling of prohibition will be applied in every case. By means of this principle it will be seen why private property may not be taken as a public highway on the grounds that each person who uses it will not, in his individual capacity, detract from that property. Obviously, in such a case, the collectivity will undermine the value.[23] An example of this is that custom allows a teacher to lightly strike a student, on the condition that the teacher alone administer the blow. If, however, a group were to collectively administer blow after blow so that the student died, then blood money (*qiṣāṣ*) would be exacted from each one who participated in the beating, even though each one did no more than to deliver a single blow.[A]

On the other hand, if we suppose the ruler to inhabit a plot of land that was not usurped, like reclaimed[B] land, then if he resides in a simple shelter or in the largest of goat hair tents[C] purchased

[A] In other words, each would be guilty of murder and responsible for restoration through *qiṣāṣ* which, simply stated, amounts to either blood or blood money, at the discretion of the victim's survivors. For details, see the Qur'ān and its commentaries at II.178. See also Ibn Muflih, *Kitāb al-furūᶜ*, (Saudi Arabia, 2003) IX.362; Mardāwī, *al-Inṣāf fī maᶜrifat al-rājiḥ min al-khilāf* (Egypt, 1374/1955), IX.450; Dāmād, *Majmaᶜ al-anhur sharḥ multaqā al-abḥur* (Egypt, 1316/1899), II.627.

[B] The legal ruling on reclaimed land is generally that the one who reclaims it, by improving it, will own it. See Shāfiᶜī, *Kitāb al-umm*, IV.47 and Sarakhsī, *Mabsūṭ*, XXIII.167.

[C] The desert Arabs used different words to designate the variety of tents and shelters that they commonly used. The intent of the author here would appear to represent the entire range of such dwellings, from the most humble to the most elaborate. See Z.VI.131, and Lane, *Lexicon* (Cambridge, 1984), II.1917.

with funds at his disposal, that will be unlawful, and entrance will also be unlawful because one would then be taking benefit and shade from the unlawful. If, however, all of these circumstances are seen to be legitimate, one will not be considered a sinner merely by one's entrance, nor by offering the greeting, 'Peace be upon you.' However, if one were then to prostrate oneself before the ruler, or bow to him, or come stiffly to attention while offering the greeting, then one would be guilty of showing respect to a tyrant owing to his office which he uses as the instrument of his tyranny; and humility before a tyrant is sinful. Indeed, one who is humble before the wealthy, for no other reason than that they are wealthy, destroys two-thirds of his religion. What, then, of humility before a tyrant? Thus, no more than the prescribed greeting of peace is lawful.

Likewise, the kissing of the hand, or otherwise groveling in the service of rulers is clearly sinful, except in the presence of fear [for one's life, or family, or property]; though it is lawful to kiss the hand of a just leader, or a scholar, or one who deserves respect for religious reasons.[A] Abū ʿUbayda b. al-Jarrāḥ kissed the hand of ʿUmar[24] when he met him in Syria. Nor did ʿUmar fault him for having done so.[25]

Still, certain of the Predecessors have taken extreme positions, supposing it unlawful to return the greetings of a tyrant, and supposing it essential to ignore them in such a way as to belittle them. Still, the failure to return the greeting of peace is problematic, because it is a religious responsibility (*wājib*) and should not be abandoned owing to the presence of tyranny. Even so, if the one entering into the presence of a tyrant were to do nothing more than offer greetings in the proper Islamic manner, he will still have to sit on the tyrant's carpet; and if the greater portion of the ruler's wealth comes from the unlawful, then to sit will be unlawful.

[A] This might include one's father or mother, or a teacher, or an elder, and the like.

These are [examples of] sinning by means of deeds.

As for sinning by silence, among the wrongs of omission are that one who enters the court of a ruler will witness the splendour of silken carpets, silver utensils, and fine silk garments on [the ruler's and on his servants' bodies], all of which is unlawful; when the rule is that anyone who sees a wrong and does not speak out against it becomes a party to that wrong. Indeed, to listen to rulers speaking shamelessly, or falsely, or abusively, and not to object to their speech is also unlawful. Thus, to see them wearing unlawful clothing, eating unlawful food, and possessing nothing but unlawful possessions, and then to remain silent about these matters is unlawful. Rather, one who sees such wrongs must enjoin what is good and forbid what is wrong, at least with his tongue if he is unable to do so with his hand.

Objection: Since such a person fears for his life he is legally excused from the responsibility [to enjoin or forbid]. In reply it must be admitted that this is true. But the fact remains that he was in no need of [going to visit the sultan and thus] placing himself in a situation where he commits what is only permitted by means of an excuse. Obviously, if he does not visit the ruler, he will not witness the wrongs there. And if he does not witness them, he will not be held responsible for rectifying them. It is for this reason that I say that if anyone knows of corruption at a certain place and is unable to eradicate it, that person must not ever go to that place and have to witness that corruption without being able to put an end to it. Rather, it is better that he avoid witnessing it.

As for sinning by word, these sins include one's praying for a tyrant, or praising him, or verifying what he says, even though it be false, by nodding in agreement, or by smiling in his face, or by showing affection or loyalty to him, or by displaying a desire to meet him again, or by manifesting the wish that he have a long life. In most cases one will not limit oneself to offering a greeting [of peace] but will, in addition, speak to him; and thereby commit one of the wrongs mentioned here.

One's praying for a tyrant is lawful only when it is of the

nature of the following, 'May God rectify you!' or 'May He guide you to do what is right!' or 'May He give you a life long in obedience to Him!' and so on. One may not, however, simply pray for the tyrant to have a long life, or for God to shower him with His bounty. Likewise, one may not refer to a tyrant in one's prayer as a 'master' or use words to that effect, as this is clearly unlawful.

[The Messenger of God] (may God bless him and grant him peace) said,[26] 'Whoever prays for the longevity of a tyrant loves to disobey God on His own territory.'[27]

One who goes beyond this in his prayer to praise a tyrant by mentioning traits he does not possess will not only be a liar, but a hypocrite and an venerator of tyranny as well. All three of these are sins. He (may God bless him and grant him peace)[28] said, 'When a wrongdoer is praised, God is angered.'[29] In another narrative attributed to him, he said, 'Whoever venerates a tyrant helps to destroy Islam.'[30]

Then, one who goes beyond this to verifying what a tyrant has to say, or to justifying and commending what he does, is a sinner by virtue of his verification and assistance. This is because praise and commendation assist in [the commission of] injustice and sin and encourage these things. In like manner, exposing untruths, condemnation, and denunciation as unbecoming discourage these things and attenuate their appeal.

Sufyān [al-Thawrī] (may God be pleased with him) was once asked about a tyrant who was near death in the desert, 'Should he be given water?' He replied, 'No. Leave him to die. That will be better for him because to let him drink is the same as helping him[31] to commit more injustice.' Another [Sufi] said, 'Let him drink until he revives. Then turn away from him.'[A]

[A] According to the commentator, Sufyān's opinion in this matter was a harsh one (Z.vi.135). For a sampling of opinions on issues in which moral aspects are mingled with legal ones, see the following: Ibn ʿAbd al-Salām, *Qawā'id al-aḥkām*, i.113; Nawawī, *Majmūʿ*, iv.12; Anṣārī, *Ghurar*, v.10; Ibn Taymiyya, *al-Siyāsa al-sharʿiyya* (Beirut, 1988), 74, 126.

If, however, the person [giving him the water] goes beyond that, and begins to show him affection and the desire to meet him [again], while wishing him a long life; then, if he is insincere, he will sin because insincerity and hypocrisy are sins. And if he is sincere, he will sin because he earnestly desires the survival of a tyrant when he should detest him for the sake of God and loathe [what he does].

It is a duty to detest for the sake of God. One who loves sin, or who is pleased by it, is a sinner. Moreover, if someone loves a tyrant, then if he loves the tyrant for his injustice, he is a sinner for loving him. If he loves him for another reason, then he is a sinner because he does not detest him when it is his duty to detest him. If both good and evil are joined in a person, he must be loved for the good that resides within him and hated for the evil. Details of this situation will be explained in the *Book of Brotherhood*.[A]

Even if one is assisted by divine guidance and avoids all of these [pitfalls], one will hardly be able to avoid the corruption that assails the heart as one witnesses his abundance [the ruler's prosperity], and disparages one's own allotment of God's bounty. Such a person is [in danger of] transgressing against the prohibition articulated by the Messenger of God (may God bless him and grant him peace) as follows, 'O Community of Emigrants![32] Do not call on[33] worldly people, for to do so is to bring on discontent with [your own] sustenance.'[34] Add to this that others will emulate the example [and visit the worldly themselves], thereby increasing the numbers of people [at the courts of] the unjust and making [such visits] more appealing to others! All of this is clearly either disapproved or prohibited.

When Saʿīd b. al-Musayyab was invited to pledge his allegiance to al-Walīd and to Sulaymān, the two sons of ʿAbd al-Mālik b. Marwān he said, 'As day follows night, I will not pledge to two

[A] This is Book xv of the *Revival of the Religious Sciences*, in the Quarter of Norms of Daily Life, which follows this volume. An abridged translation by Muhtar Holland was published as *The Duties of Brotherhood* (London, 1975).

[at the same time]! The Prophet (may God bless him and grant him peace) prohibited[A] two pledges.'[35] People said to him, 'Just go in one door and go out the other.'[B] He [Saᶜīd] responded by saying, 'By God! [If I do that] no one will ever follow me[36] again.' [C] Then Saᶜīd was whipped one hundred lashes and forced to wear a rough woolen garment.[37]

It is therefore prohibited to call on such people, except in two [instances which will be] excused.

The first is that the invitation to visit be a binding invitation rather than a courtesy invitation. If one knows that by refusing to attend one will be punished, or that one's non-attendance may lead to civil unrest or political instability, then one must [accept the invitation and] attend, not out of obedience but in consideration for the welfare of the populace and so that no disruption occurs in the state.

The second is when the visit is for the purpose of redressing injustice done to a Muslim, or to oneself, either through official channels or by means of an appeal. In such a case an allowance may be made, but only on the condition that one not speak falsely or give praise, or neglect to offer advice that one might expect to be accepted.

This concludes our discussion in regard to one's visiting rulers.

[A] This prohibition is usually viewed as pertaining to sales and transactions (*bayᶜatāni fī-bayᶜa*) rather than a pledge of loyalty or allegiance. Even so, the wording of the narration admits both interpretations.

[B] ᶜAbd al-Mālik b. Marwān was concerned about the matter of succession, especially after he had gone to such extremes in order to consolidate power for his branch of the Umayyad family. Therefore, before his death, he sought to have the allegiance of the public for two of his sons, Sulaymān and al-Walīd. Those concerned with the welfare of Saᶜīd b. al-Musayyab suggested what they supposed to be a solution to the dilemma he faced, and one that perhaps other public figures had used.

[C] i.e., no one will ever listen to me, or give credence to what I say, or emulate my example, again. Obviously, Saᶜīd's concern was not with how many people followed him, but with his credibility as a religious authority.

The Second Relationship: Unjust Rulers who Call on You to Visit

[If a despot visits you,] you must return his greeting of peace. With regard to one's standing up or otherwise honouring him, this will not be prohibited if it is done in return for the honour he has shown. Indeed, if he shows respect for learning and religion then he will be deserving of praise [in one form or another]. In the same way that his doing injustice makes him deserving of dismissal, by showing respect he will deserve respect and a reply to his greeting of peace.

It will be best, however, not to stand up for him if he comes on his own, so as to demonstrate to him the dignity of religion and the ignominy of injustice. This will also show him [your] zeal for religion, and that you can ignore him in the same way that God (Exalted is He) will ignore him. If, however, he enters with a group, then, as it will be necessary to show deference to the officials in his entourage in the presence of other people, one may therefore rise to one's feet for the ruler. On the other hand, if one is certain that this will not lead to disturbances among the people, or to punishment for provoking the ruler's wrath, it will be better not to honour the ruler by standing up for him.[A]

Thereafter, once the initial meeting is over, it will be necessary to offer him advice. Moreover, if the ruler commits deeds that he perhaps does not know to be unlawful, and it might reasonably be expected that if he knew [they were unlawful] he would abandon them, then he should be informed; and this will be necessary (*wājib*). On the other hand, there is no point in reminding him of the ruling concerning the things that even he knows to be unlawful, like adultery[38] and injustice. Rather, one should put fear into him with regard to the injustices[39] he commits and the sins, if one thinks that this will be effective. One should also point out the way to the greatest good if one knows of a *Sharīʿa*-compliant

[A] According to the commentator, Nawawī authored a book on the subject called *al-Tarkhīṣ bi'l-qiyām* ('License to Stand'). See Z.vi.135.

solution that will allow the despot to attain his objective without sin. In this manner, one will prevent the tyrant from achieving his goals by means of injustice.

Thus, it is necessary to inform [him] when he, [the tyrant] is ignorant [in regard to the *Sharīʿa* ruling on something that he does or contemplates doing]. Likewise, it will be necessary to put fear into him with regard to the things he has had the nerve to commit. Finally, he must be given guidance with regard to what he might have overlooked, so that he may thereby avoid the commission of injustice. These, then, are three matters that must be considered whenever one expects that what one has to say will actually have an effect [on the visiting tyrant]. The same will become binding on anyone who has the opportunity to visit a ruler, either with or without an excuse.

It is related concerning Muḥammad b. Sāliḥ that he said, 'I was with Ḥammād b. Salama, and there was nothing in his home other than the straw mat on which he sat, a Qur'ān from which he read, a case in which he kept his books, and a bowl from which he performed his ablutions. While I was with him thus, there was a knocking at the door. It was [the Amīr] Muḥammad b. Sulaymān, and he was given permission to enter. He did so, and then he sat before him [Ḥammād], and said, 'What is it with me? When I see you I am filled with awe?'

Ḥammād replied, 'That is because [the Messenger of God] (may God bless him and grant him peace) said, "When a scholar seeks by means of his knowledge the countenance of God, then everything will fear him. But when he seeks by means of his knowledge to amass a fortune, then he will fear everything."'

Then Muḥammad offered forty thousand dirhams to [Ḥammād], saying, 'Take these and let them help you.'

[Ḥammād] replied, 'Shall I return them to those you tyrannised in order to gain possession of them?'

[Muḥammad] replied, 'By God! I give you nothing other than what I inherited.'

So [Ḥammād] said to him, 'I have no need for it.'

[The Amīr] said, 'Then take it and distribute it!'

[Ḥammād] replied, 'Even if I am fair in distributing it, I fear that someone who has not had a share in it will say that I have not been just in my distribution, and thereby I would be sinning! So, take it away from me.'[40]

The Third Relationship: To Avoid Them; neither Seeing nor being Seen

This becomes necessary when there is no peace to be had except by means of it. Under such circumstances one must believe it essential to detest them for their injustice and to abhor their continued existence. One must also never praise them, or ask about their affairs, or draw close to those who maintain relationships with them, or lament what might have been had one not avoided them. This, of course, is if one thinks of them at all. If one ignores them entirely, then that will be best.

Moreover, if one thinks of their lives of ease, then recall what Ḥātim al-Aṣamm once said, 'Between me and between royalty there is only a single day. As for yesterday, when it's gone no one can recover its pleasures. And both they and I live in trepidation of what tomorrow [may bring]. So that leaves today; and [who knows] what can happen in a day?'[41]

Or recall what Abū al-Dardā' said, 'Wealthy people eat, and we eat. They drink, and we drink. They wear clothes, and we wear clothes. Then there is the money they have left over. They look at it, and we look at it; but they're responsible for it [to the Almighty], and we are free.'[42]

Anyone who knows of a tyrant's injustice, or of a sinner's sins, should lower his esteem for that person in his heart. In fact, it is required (*wājib*) to do so. This is because if something that is disapproved is committed by a person, it is certain to detract from his standing. So, sin should be disapproved. This is because sin may be ignored, or condoned, or disapproved. Obviously, if there is knowledge of the sin, then it cannot be ignored. And there can be no reason for condoning it. Therefore, it must be disapproved. Anyone's transgression against the rights of God should be the same as a transgression against your rights.

OBJECTION: Disapproval (*karāha*) is not a matter of choice. How, then, can it be required?[43]

My reply is, 'This is not so.' This is because a lover, by nature, will dislike whatever his beloved dislikes and stand opposed to it. Then, anyone who does not dislike sins against God does not love God. Furthermore, only those who do not know God will not love Him. Knowledge [of God] is essential, and [thereafter] love of God is certain to follow. If someone loves Him, he will dislike what He dislikes and love what He loves. A complete explanation of this will be given in the *Book of Love and Contentment*.[A]

OBJECTION: The scholars among our Predecessors used to visit rulers.

My reply is, 'Yes, they did. But first learn how they used to visit, before you go [and do the same].' It is related that Hishām b. ʿAbd al-Malik went to Mecca for the pilgrimage. When he arrived, he said, 'Bring me someone from among the Companions.' When he was told[44] that they had all passed away, he said, 'Then, from among the Successors.' And so Ṭāwūs al-Yamānī was brought to him.

When Ṭāwūs entered, he removed his sandals at the edge of the carpet; and he did not greet him as Commander of the Faithful, saying instead no more than, 'Peace be upon you.'[45] Nor did he use the agnomen.[B] Then he sat by his side and said, 'How are you, O Hishām?' At that, Hishām flew into a towering rage, such that he considered killing him [Ṭāwūs]. But he was reminded, 'You

[A] This is Book XXXVI of the *Revival of the Religious Sciences*. Its complete title is *Kitāb al-maḥabba wa'l-shawq wa'l-uns wa'l-riḍā*, translated by Eric Ormsby as *The Book of Love, Longing, Intimacy, and Contentment*.

[B] To do so would have been another way of showing respect, by saying, for example, O Abū Sulayman! To have neglected to address Hishām either by his title or by his agnomen was to have emphasised the fact that his words were chosen carefully, and that Ṭāwūs had meant to slight the ruler.

are within the sacred precincts of God [Mecca] and the sacred precincts of His Messenger, and that [killing] is not possible!'

So instead he replied, 'O Ṭāwūs! What made you do what you have done?' Ṭāwūs replied, 'What did I do?' Then Hishām grew even more angry and agitated. He said, 'You took your sandals off at the edge of my carpet, but then you failed to kiss my hand. Nor did you greet me as Commander of the Faithful! Nor did you address me by my agnomen! Then you sat down beside me without first taking my permission. Finally, you said, "How are you, O Hishām!"'

[Ṭāwūs] replied, 'As for my removing my sandals by the edge of your carpet, I take them off five times a day when I go [to pray] before the Lord of All the Worlds. He has never punished me for doing so, or grown angry with me. As for your saying that I failed to kiss your hand, I once heard ʿAlī b. Abī Ṭālib, the Commander of the Faithful, (may God be pleased with him), say that it is unlawful for anyone to kiss the hand of another unless it is a man kissing the hand of his wife in a surfeit of passion, or kissing the hand of his child in a surfeit of affection. As for your saying that I failed to greet you as Commander of the Faithful, well, not everyone is happy with your rule; so I disliked having to lie. As for your saying that I did not address you by your agnomen, God called His prophets and saints by their first names, saying, 'O Dā'ūd!' or 'O ʿĪsā!' or 'O Yaḥyā!' and He addressed His enemies, like Abū Lahab, by means of their agnomen.[A] Now, as for your saying that I sat next to you, I heard ʿAlī, the Commander of the Faithful, (may God be pleased with him) say, 'If you want to look at a person from among the inhabitants of the Fire, look at someone who is seated while others remain standing around him.' At that, Hishām said, 'Please, advise me.' [Ṭāwūs] said, 'I heard ʿAlī, the Commander of the Faithful, (may God be pleased with him) say, "Verily in hell there are snakes like the summits of mountains and spiders the size of mules to bite [and sting] any

[A] Instances of all these are to be found in the Qur'ān.

amīr who is not just to his subjects."' Then Ṭāwūs rose and left.[46]

It is related that Sufyān al-Thawrī (may God be pleased with him) said, 'I was brought into the presence of Abū Jaʿfar al-Manṣūr[47] at Mina and he said to me, "Tell us what you need." I replied, "Fear God! For verily the earth is filled with injustice and discrimination!" So he dropped his head [in shame]. But again he raised it and said, "Tell us what you need?" I replied, "You have reached this stage [in the conquest of new territories] by means of the swords of the Emigrants and the Helpers, yet their children are dying of starvation! So fear God, and see that they get their due!" So he dropped his head [in shame]. But again he raised it and said, "Tell us what you need?" So I replied, "When ʿUmar b. al-Khaṭṭāb performed the Pilgrimage, he said to his treasurer, 'How much have I spent?' The treasurer replied, 'Ten and something dirhams.' But here I see more opulence than a camel load of money could pay for!"' Thereafter, Sufyān departed.[48]

So that was how they used to visit rulers, even if they did so under duress.[49] Indeed, they risked[50] their own lives in order to avenge for the Almighty those who had been treated unjustly.

When Ibn Abī Shumayla visited him, ʿAbd al-Malik b. Marwān asked him to speak. Ibn Abī Shumayla responded, 'On the Day of Judgement people will not escape its wrath, or its bitterness, or the sights of destruction, save those who displeased their selves in order to please their Lord.' Tears came to ʿAbd al-Malik and, when [he had composed himself,] he said, 'I will certainly hold these words as a model for the rest of my life.'[51]

When ʿUthmān b. ʿAffān appointed ʿAbd Allāh ibn ʿĀmir an administrative officer [over Basra], the Companions of the Messenger of God (may God bless him and grant him peace) came out to greet him. Abū Dharr, however, tarried.[52] When a friend chided him for his reluctance, Abū Dharr explained, 'I heard the Messenger of God (may God bless him and grant him peace) say, "When a person is given a position of authority, God distances Himself from him."'[53]

Mālik b. Dīnār went to the *amīr* of Basra[A] and said, 'O Amīr! I read in a scripture [that God (Exalted is He) said] 'Who is more foolish than a ruler? Who is more ignorant than one who disobeys Me? And who is more respected than one who shows respect for Me? O evil shepherd! I gave you a fat and healthy sheep. Then you ate its flesh, and wore its wool, and left nothing but whistling bones!'[54] At that, the Amīr of Basra replied, 'Do you know what has allowed you to be bold with us? And what protects you from us?' When [Mālik b. Dīnār] replied that he did not, the Amīr said, 'Your lack of ambition for our office, and your lack of interest in[55] what we possess.'[56]

ʿUmar b. ʿAbd al-ʿAzīz was standing with Sulaymān b. ʿAbd al-Mālik when Sulaymān heard the sound of thunder and shuddered, leaning his chest forward against a pack animal [for protection]. ʿUmar said, 'That is the voice of His mercy.[B] How do you think it will be when you hear the voice of His wrath?' Then Sulaymān looked at the people and said, 'How numerous are the people!' So ʿUmar b. ʿAbd al-ʿAzīz said, 'Every one of them will become your opponent [on the Day of Judgement], O Commander of the Faithful!' At that, Sulaymān replied, 'May God grant that you too be tried through them!'[57]

It is related that Sulaymān b. ʿAbd al-Malik arrived in Medina while on his way to Mecca. So he sent for Abū Ḥāzim and invited him [to visit]. When he arrived, Sulaymān said to him, 'O Abū Ḥāzim, why is it that I fear death?'

Abū Ḥāzim replied, 'That is because you have abandoned your Afterlife and populated your worldly life, and now dislike going from what is populated to what is abandoned.'

[Sulaymān] said, 'O Abū Ḥāzim! How does one approach God?'

[Abū Ḥāzim] replied, 'O Commander of the Faithful! The doer of good will be as one long absent, returning to his family.

[A] The *amīr* at the time was Bilāl b. Abī Burda.

[B] i.e., the mercy of the rain that the thunder announces.

But the doer of evil will be like a runaway slave returned to face his master!'

Then Sulaymān wept [for a while] and said, 'O [Abū Ḥāzim]! If only I knew what it will be like for me when I meet God.'

Abū Ḥāzim replied, 'Place yourself before the Book of God, where He says, *Verily the virtuous will be in luxury. And verily the wicked will be in the Fire.*'[58]

Sulaymān then said, 'And where is the mercy of God?'

Abū Ḥāzim recited, '*Verily the mercy of God is near to the righteous!*'[59]

Sulaymān asked, 'O Abū Ḥāzim! Which of God's servants are more honoured?'

[Abū Ḥāzim] replied, 'Those who are virtuous and prudent.'

[Sulaymān] said, 'Which deeds are the most meritorious?'

[Abū Ḥāzim] replied, 'Performing what is required while avoiding what is prohibited.'

Then [Sulaymān] asked, 'And which words are the best that can be said?'

[Abū Ḥāzim] replied, 'Truth that is told to one who is feared.'

[Sulaymān] asked, 'Which of the believers is the most intelligent?'

[Abū Ḥāzim] replied, 'A person who does something for the sake of God and calls for others to do the same.'

[Sulaymān] asked, 'And which of the believers is the biggest loser?'

[Abū Ḥāzim] replied, 'One who accedes to his unjust brother's wishes, thereby selling his Afterlife for the worldly life of another.'

Sulaymān said, '[O Abū Ḥāzim!] What is your opinion of my present state of affairs?'

[Abū Ḥāzim] said, 'Will you spare me, O Commander of the Faithful?'

[Sulaymān] replied, 'Surely, for it is advice you give to me.'

So [Abū Ḥāzim] said, 'O Commander of the Faithful! Your fathers conquered people with their swords, and took this land by force without ever consulting the Muslims or seeking their approval. They killed great numbers of people, but now they've passed away. Perhaps you should consider what they did, and what was said to them.'

Then someone from the [Sulaymān's] entourage said, 'You have spoken badly, [Abū Ḥāzim]!'

Abū Ḥāzim replied, 'Verily, God has made a covenant with the scholars that they will explain these matters to the people and not seek to hide them.'

Then [Sulaymān] said, '[O Abū Ḥāzim!] And how can we rectify this corruption now?'

[Abū Ḥāzim] replied, 'Take only what you have a right to, and put it to use only where it is deserved.'

Sulaymān said, 'Who is capable of doing that?'

[Abū Ḥāzim] replied, 'Only one who seeks paradise and fears the fire.'

Sulaymān said, '[O Abū Ḥāzim!] Pray to God for me!'

Abū Ḥāzim replied, 'O Lord! If Sulaymān is Your friend, then facilitate for him the good of this world and the next. But if he is Your enemy, then seize him by the forelock and do with him as You please!'

Then Sulaymān said, '[O Abū Ḥāzim!] Advise me!'

[Abū Ḥāzim] replied, 'I will advise you and I will be brief. Glorify your Lord and honour Him such that you never commit what He prohibits and you are never remiss in performing what He commands.'[60]

When ʿUmar b. ʿAbd al-ʿAzīz asked Abū Ḥāzim for advice, he replied, 'Lie down and put death at the side of your pillow.[A] Then think of the virtues you would like to possess at the Hour [when Judgement comes], and hold fast to them from then onwards. Then think of the characteristics you would not like to possess at that Hour, and immediately reject them. For perhaps that Hour is near.'[61]

[A] i.e., to reproduce the state he will be in when in the grave.

A bedouin went to Sulaymān b. ʿAbd al-Malik, so Sulaymān asked him to speak.

[The bedouin] said, 'O Commander of the Faithful! I will speak to you in candour, so please bear with me for, even though you dislike what I have to say, you will appreciate what is behind it.'

Then [Sulaymān] said, 'O Bedouin! My forbearance is so prodigious that I can be patient even with those whose advice we have not solicited and whose honesty we have not established. So, what then of those whose honesty we have established and whose advice we have solicited.'

The bedouin replied, 'O Commander of the Faithful! You are surrounded by men who have made poor choices for themselves; who have sold their Afterlife for the life of this world, and who have purchased your pleasure for the displeasure of their Lord! They have deceived you about God, but they have not deceived God about you! They are at war with the Afterlife, and have sued for peace with the life of this world. Thus, you must not entrust them with what God (Exalted is He) has entrusted you. Verily, they have spared no effort in betraying that trust, and in bringing dishonour and injustice to our community. You are responsible for the wrongs they bring about, but they are not responsible for what you bring about. So do not secure their worldly interests by destroying your interests in the next world. Indeed, the most deluded of all people is a man who sells his own Afterlife for another's worldly life.'

Then Sulaymān said to [the bedouin], 'Well then, bedouin! It appears that you have unsheathed your tongue today! And it has proven sharper than your[62] sword!'

[The bedouin] replied, 'Yes, O Commander of the Faithful! You are right. But I use it for you, not against you!'[63]

It is related that when Abū Bakra went to see Muʿāwiya, he said to him, 'Fear God, O Muʿāwiya! Know that with every day that passes, and with every night that falls, you are moving further from this life and drawing closer to the next. There is a seeker on your trail whom you will not elude, and he has erected a barrier for you that you will not pass. How quickly will you come to that barrier! And how close behind you is that seeker! All that is about us is transitory. But what we are heading for is eternal; if what we do is good, we will be rewarded with good. And if we do evil, we will be rewarded with evil.'

This was how the scholars used to visit rulers, and I refer only to [the sort of] scholars [who might be termed scholars] of the next world. On the other hand, the scholars of this world [are the sort who] visit rulers and attempt to endear themselves to them by offering legal licence and concocting complex legal stratagems, and otherwise suggesting schemes by means of which they may satisfy their own ambitions. Even if they voice the sorts of advice I have mentioned here, their purpose in doing so is not to rectify, but to earn a reputation for themselves and thereby make themselves even more acceptable to the rulers! In this, there are two fallacies to which the foolish are susceptible.

One of these is that [the fool] will portray his purpose for visiting [rulers] as reform by means of advice. In doing so, he may even delude himself into believing this to be the case; but his real motivation is a hidden desire for personal aggrandisement and fame. The sign that a scholar is sincere in seeking reform is if he is pleased, and gives thanks to God (Exalted is He), when another scholar from among his peers proves successful, after undertaking the task of giving advice to the ruler, in actually effecting reform. This would be like one who undertakes the responsibility of caring for a sick person who has no family to care for him; and who then discovers a family member willing to care for that person. Obviously, he would be happy for the sick person and relieved for himself. If, however, he finds in his heart that he prefers his own words to those of the other [scholar], then he is surely deluded.

The second fallacy is that [the fool] will assert that the reason he wants to visit the ruler is so that he may intercede on behalf of a [brother] Muslim in putting aside injustice. This, too, however, is no more than a delusion. The same standard [for assessing sincerity] mentioned above may be applied in this case as well.

Now that the [proper] way to visit rulers has been explained, I shall discuss several issues related to socialising with rulers and dealing with their wealth.

[ISSUE 1:] If a ruler sends you money for distribution among the poor, then if the money has a particular owner,[A] it will not be lawful to accept it. If, however, there is no particular owner, the ruling will be that the wealth must be distributed among the poor, as explained earlier,[B] and you may lawfully accept the money and take responsibility for its distribution. In that case you will not sin by taking the money. Even so, among the scholars there are those who refused to do this. We must therefore consider what is best. In my opinion, you may take the money if you are sure that none of the three following dangers are present:

The first danger is that the sultan will be led to believe, by your acceptance, that his money is good; since if it was not good, you would not have taken it or allowed yourself to become responsible for it. If this is the case, then it will not be lawful to take the money. Rather, this will be unlawful. Nor will the good from distributing the money outweigh the sin of encouraging the ruler to use unlawful money.

The second danger is that scholars and others may look at you and believe that [the money you took from the sultan for distribution] is lawful, so that they seek to follow your example and cite it as proof that it is lawful for them [to take money from the ruler as well]. This is even worse than the first danger. There is a group of scholars that cited the example of Shāfiʿī (may God be pleased with him) [taking a thousand dinars from Hārūn al-Rashīd] as proof that it is lawful to take money from a ruler. What they fail to consider, however, is that Shāfiʿī took that money with the

[A] i.e., from whom the sultan usurped or otherwise misappropriated the money.

[B] This matter was discussed in some detail in Chapter Five.

intention of distributing it among the poor.[A] The followers of that Imam must be careful to avoid this [ignoring that while he took the money, he also distributed it], otherwise what they do may cause many people to be led astray.

Wahb b. Munabbih related that a man was taken before a king in the presence of a crowd and ordered to eat the flesh of swine. When the man refused, he was commanded at the point of a sword to eat lamb. But again the man refused. When he was asked why he had refused, the man explained that the people there knew that he had been ordered to eat pork. 'If I left that place in peace, having eaten, the people might not know for certain what I had eaten, and might have gone astray.'[64]

Another time, Wahb b. Munabbih and Ṭāwūs went to see Muḥammad b. Yūsuf, brother of al-Ḥajjāj [b. Yūsuf], who was an official [in Yemen]. As it was a cold morning, Muḥammad ordered his servant to take a shawl to Ṭāwūs who had seated himself on a chair. When the servant spread the shawl over Ṭāwūs' shoulders, Ṭāwūs began fidgeting until the shawl fell off. At that, Muḥammad grew very angry. When they left, Wahb said to Ṭāwūs, 'I can understand that you are well off and not in need of the shawl. But you can also afford not to anger the ruler! Why didn't you accept the shawl and then give it to the needy?' Ṭāwūs replied, 'True. But I didn't want anyone after me to say that Ṭāwūs took something from the ruler. Were it not for that I might have accepted it.'[65]

The third danger is that your heart will be influenced by the ruler, by his singling you out for attention and his preferring you in whatever he sends your way. If this is the case, then it will not be lawful to take the money. Indeed, that will be as lethal as poison! Or an incurable disease. Anything that makes a tyrant beloved should be understood in this way. Indeed, if you care for

[A] In Chapter Five, the author recorded, 'Likewise, the gift accepted by Shāfiʿī from Hārūn al-Rashīd was distributed within a day's time. On the second day, not a single grain remained.'

someone, you tend to make excuses for them. ʿĀ'isha (may God be pleased with her) said,[66] 'Verily, it is human nature to love those who do good to you.'[67]

[The Messenger of God] (may God bless him and grant him peace) once prayed, 'O God! Never grant someone I know to be a wrongdoer anything that would cause my heart to incline towards him.'[68] In this manner, he (may God bless him and grant him peace) explained that the heart will almost never [be able to] avoid such influences.

It is also related that a certain ruler sent ten thousand dirhams for Mālik b. Dīnār who immediately distributed the money. Then Muḥammad b. Wāsiʿ went to Mālik and said, 'What did you do with what that creature gave you?' [Mālik] replied, 'Ask my companions.' When they told [Muḥammad] that all of the money had been distributed, [Muḥammad] asked Mālik, 'I implore you by God to answer me this! Is there more love in your heart for him now, or before he sent you the money?' [Mālik] answered, 'Now.' So [Muḥammad] replied, 'That's what I was afraid of.'[69]

Indeed, he has spoken truthfully! When one loves a ruler, one will love his survival and hate his removal from office, his reversals, and his death. Likewise, one will love the expansion of his rule and the increase of his wealth. All of this must be considered love for the factors that occasion tyranny, and that is clearly blameworthy. Salmān and Ibn Masʿūd (may God be pleased with them both) said, 'Anyone who is satisfied with authority, even if he is not present [when it is exercised improperly], will be as one who witnessed it.'[70]

God (Exalted is He!) said, *Nor incline toward those who do injustice*[71] *lest the fire caress you.*[72] Certain commentators interpret [this to mean that] if you are in a position of power yourself, such that your affection for the ruler will not increase [as a result of his attention], there will be no impediment to your accepting [the money for distribution].

It is related concerning a certain ascetic of Basra who was known to accept money and distribute it, that he was asked if he feared his developing an affection for the ruler. [The ascetic] replied, 'If someone were to take my hand and lead me into Paradise, and then disobey the Lord, my heart will not love that person because the One who empowered him to take my hand is the One because of whom I will hate the man out of appreciation of His empowering the man [to take my hand]!'

All of this goes to show that accepting money from them, even when it comes from a lawful source, is prohibited and blameworthy because it cannot be separated from these dangers.

[Issue 2:] It might be objected that if it is lawful to accept his money and distribute it, will it then be lawful to steal his money? Or will it be lawful to secret away his deposits and deny knowledge of their whereabouts, and then distribute that among the people?

The answer is that this is not lawful. This is because the wealth may have a specific owner to whom [the ruler] had determined to return the wealth. So this is not the same as the ruler's sending you the wealth. Indeed, it is not likely[73] that a sane person would give wealth away in charity when he knows [the identity of] its [true] owner. Rather, his acceptance of such wealth indicates that he does not know its owner.[A] Moreover, if the donor is one regarding whom such issues have been problematic, it will not be lawful to accept the money from him unless this is known.[B] Moreover, how can this be stolen when it is possible that the wealth was acquired by means of a deferred purchase? Indeed, possession is proof of ownership. Thus, there is no way that this [misappropriation] can be lawful.

If a missing item were to be found, and then it was ascertained that its owner was a soldier,[C] then, since the possibility exists that

[A] i.e., he knows of no owner other than the donor, in this case the ruler who has sent it to him for charitable distribution.

[B] i.e., that the wealth does not have a specific owner from whom it was misappropriated.

[C] The obvious assumption, in the times of the author, would have been that the soldier misappropriated the item.

he purchased the item on credit or otherwise obtained it legally, it must therefore be returned to him.

It is therefore unlawful to steal [a ruler's] wealth, either from them directly or from those who hold it in trust for them. Nor is it lawful to deny [having possession of] their deposits. Indeed, the prescribed penalty (*ḥadd*) must be applied to anyone who steals a ruler's wealth, unless the thief claims that what he took was not the ruler's property. When such a claim is made, the prescribed penalty may be dropped.[A]

[ISSUE 3:] It is unlawful to transact with them [rulers] because the greater portion of their wealth is unlawful.[B] Therefore,

[A] The author's ruling here is based on a question that was debated widely by the jurists. That debate hinged on who had the right to argue for the return of stolen goods. For most jurists, that right resided solely with the owner; with the result that if goods were stolen from a thief by another thief, the first thief would have no right to argue for the return of the goods. In the absence of such a right, the court would have no right to sentence the offender to a *ḥadd* punishment. Likewise, if the rightful owner were to steal the goods from the thief, the thief would have no right to argue for the return of the goods and there would be no *ḥadd* punishment. Furthermore, if the second thief was other than the owner, just another thief, the question that arose in the minds of certain jurists was whether the *ḥadd* could be applied when the protection (*ḥirz*) of the goods was accomplished without the agreement of the owner; when one of the conditions for the application of the *ḥadd* penalty is that the goods be protected (i.e., if they are left out in the open, then no *ḥadd* penalty may be applied). See Ibn al-ʿArabī, *Aḥkām al-Qur'ān* (Beirut, 1987), II.114; Kāsānī, *Badā'iʿ al-ṣanā'iʿ* (Beirut, 1997), VII.73–74; Ibn Qudāma, *Mughnī*, VII.102; Zaylaʿī, *Tabyīn al-ḥaqā'iq*, III.228; Mardāwī, *al-Inṣāf fī maʿrifat al-rājiḥ min al-khilāf* (Egypt, 1374/1955), X.310; Raṣṣāʿ, *Sharḥ ḥudūd ibn ʿArafa*, p. 508; Sharbīnī, *Mughnī al-muḥtāj*, V.398; Ghazālī, *Wasīṭ*, IV.132-139; Rāfiʿī, *al-ʿAzīz sharḥ al-Wajīz*, XI.209. The thief, however, will still be subject to amercement (*taʿzīr*) punishment if the judge decides that punishment is warranted in view of the facts of the case. It is interesting to note that among the jurists whose works the translator consulted in this matter, no one other than Ghazālī took the further step of equating the sultan to a thief.

[B] Z. adds, 'Therefore one may neither deal with them directly nor with those who deal with them' (VI.149).

whatever is received from them in return is unlawful. If the price is paid from a source known to be lawful, then consideration should be given to[74] what is delivered to them. If it can be determined that they will use it to sin against God, like a sale of silk brocade[A] when it is known that they regularly wear it, then that [transaction] will be unlawful. This is like the sale of grapes to a vintner.[B] The only differences [between the jurists] concerning such a sale are in regard to its validity [or voidability].[C] If there is a possibility that the silk is to be worn by women, then this will occasion doubt that renders the transaction merely 'disapproved.' This is in reference to the sort of wealth which may itself become a means to sin. A similar categorisation may be applied to the sale of horses to rulers, especially when these will be ridden into battle against other Muslims, or to plunder their wealth. Obviously, to provide them with horses [with which to carry out such activities] is to assist them; and that is unlawful.

The sale of dirhams and dinars [to rulers], or of whatever [currency] may be used in its place is disapproved,[D] even though these are not, themselves, sinful. This is because these are things that may lead to sin; and the sale of currency to rulers may help them to commit sin because they use money, mounts, and every

[A] It is unlawful for men to wear silk. See Nawawī, *Majmūʿ*, I.11; Shawkānī, *Nayl al-awṭār*, II.81-82; Zaylaʿī, *Tabyīn al-ḥaqā'iq*, VI.14. See also Zaylaʿī, *Naṣb al-rāya* (Cairo, 1357/1938), IV.222–225, for an evaluation of the *ḥadīth* literature on the subject. Even so, the Mālikī jurist, Ibn Sahl quotes Ibn Ghulāb's answer to the question of what he thought about someone engaged in the business of making silk, could he make turbans and the like with it? 'There is no impediment to its sale, even if it is something worn only by men because it might be purchased by someone who will not wear it, but will use it for some other purpose.' See Ḥaṭṭāb, *Mawāhib al-jalīl*, IV.271.

[B] This was discussed by the author in Chapter Two.

[C] As mentioned in the earlier discussion, certain of the jurists held such sales, under certain circumstances, to be lawful.

[D] It should be understood that in the time of the author hard money was not common. Thus, a prerequisite to any major transaction, especially for manufactured or imported items, was the availability of currency.

possible means in the commission of sin. The same legal categorisation, 'disapproved,' will apply to gifts made to rulers, or to work performed for them for no pay, and even to teaching them, or their children, to write, or to correspond, or to do arithmetic. Teaching them the Qur'ān, however, is not disapproved, unless it is done in return for payment.[A] Clearly, that is unlawful unless the source of the payment is known to be lawful.[B]

If someone were to act as their purchase agent in the market for no fee then that will be disliked because it is assistance. If the agent purchases something they are known to use for sin, like a slave[75] boy, or a saddle for a horse that may be ridden on criminal and murderous raids, then that will be unlawful. Thus, whenever it appears that an item to be purchased will be used for the purpose of sin, the purchase will be unlawful. And whenever it appears otherwise, given the circumstances, the purchase will be disapproved.

[ISSUE 4:] It is unlawful to trade in the markets built by rulers with unlawful funds, or to establish residence in them. Even so, if a merchant lives there and earns in a way that complies with *Sharīʿa*, his earnings will not be unlawful, though he will sin by living there. Likewise, the populace may purchase from such merchants; but if they find other markets, it will be best to buy in

[A] This question was widely debated among the classical jurists. The legal principle often cited in regard to this issue is that required (*wājib*) acts are performed because they are required, while unlawful acts are avoided because they are unlawful. Then, if one were to take a fee for performing an act required of him, the fee would be unlawful. But if one takes a fee for teaching another about his duties, then that is a different matter. See Ibn Ḥazm, *Muḥallā*, VII.20; Ibn Taymiyya, *Majmūʿat al-fatāwā*, III.34; Ibn Qayyim, *Iʿlām al-muwaqqiʿīn an Rabb al-ʿĀlamīn* (Cairo, n.d.), IV.259; Ibn Amīr al-Ḥājj, *al-Taqrīr wa'l-taḥbīr* (Egypt, 1316/1899), II.245; Mullā Khusrū, *Durar al-ḥukkām fī sharḥ majalla al-aḥkām al-ʿadaliyya* (Baghdad, n.d.), I.324; Ṣanʿānī, *Subul al-salām*, II.116; Shawkānī, *Nayl al-awṭār*, V.345.

[B] By the time in which the author wrote this book, the practice of paying teachers was widespread. Here, however, he once again cautions against taking tainted money.

those markets. This is because they will be assisting the residents of those [other] markets by increasing the leases for their shops.[A] Likewise, it is better that people transact in markets from which the ruler collects no taxes, rather than in markets in which the ruler does collect taxes. A certain group has taken the extreme position that it is not lawful[76] to have dealings with farmers and landlords who pay taxes [to despotic rulers]. This is because they may, in turn, use the proceeds [of their dealings with you] to pay their taxes; and thus assist them. This, however, is religious extremism and a hardship for Muslims. Taxes are now collected on all land, and people cannot survive without [farm] produce.[77] Therefore, such a prohibition is meaningless. If such a notion were accepted, no landowner would till his fields, so as to ensure [that they would yield nothing and] that no taxes would have to be paid. In a matter of time this would lead to the end of all livelihood.

[ISSUE 5:] Dealings with their [the rulers'] judges, their governors and their officials are unlawful in the same way that dealings with them are unlawful, only more so.

The reason for this, in regard to their judges, is that they openly accept the unlawful money of rulers, and bring increase to the number of their followers, and deceive people by means of their dress. This is because they wear the garb of scholars, yet mix freely with rulers and accept their money. Since human nature seeks to emulate the example of people of elevated status and celebrity, they [the judges] become a factor inducing people to become the followers of rulers.

The reason for this, in regard to officials and courtiers, is that the bulk of their wealth comes from undisguised misappropriations. Nor do they ever come into possession of wealth paid to sue for peace, or from inheritance, or from the tax on non-Muslim residents, or from any other lawful source such that it might become mixed with their unlawful earnings and thus [at least]

[A] An increase in their business will result in an increase in the demand for their shops, which will result in higher valuations.

give rise to doubts concerning intermixing of lawful wealth.[78]

It was for this reason that Ṭāwūs said, 'I will not give testimony before them, even if [my testimony] leads to the truth because I fear they will transgress against whomever I name.'[79]

Generally speaking, the subjects are corrupt because their rulers are corrupt; and rulers are corrupt because scholars are corrupt. Were it not for corrupt judges and corrupt scholars, corruption among rulers would be rare for fear of their disapproval.

It was for this reason that [the Messenger of God] (may God bless him and grant him peace) said, 'This community will continue to abide under the hand of God and enjoy His protection as long as its reciters do not make common cause with its rulers.'[80] The reason he mentioned 'reciters' (*qurrā'*) is that in those times the 'reciters' of the Qur'ān were the scholars. This is because their learning was from the Qur'ān, the meanings they derived from it, and from the Precedent (*Sunna*). All the sciences beyond that were developments (*muḥdatha*) that came after them.[81]

Sufyān [al-Thawrī] once said, 'Do not mix with rulers, or even with those who mix with them.' He also said, 'The one holding the pen, the maker of the inkpot, the maker of the paper, the maker of the clay used as a seal, and the maker of the adhesive are all partners.'[A]

Indeed, [Sufyān] spoke the truth, for the Messenger of God (may God bless him and grant him peace) cursed ten different people in regard to wine, from the one who squeezes the grapes to the one who swallows the wine.[82]

Ibn Masᶜūd (may God be pleased with him) said, 'The consumer of interest, its agent, its witnesses, and its recorder were cursed by the tongue of Muḥammad (may God bless him and grant him peace).'[83] The same was related by Jābir [b. ᶜAbd Allāh al-Anṣārī] and ᶜUmar from the Messenger of God (may God bless him and grant him peace).[84]

[A] The sense here is that all of these people will share in the sin of the scribe who writes the orders of a corrupt ruler when these lead to injustice.

Ibn Sīrīn asserted, 'Never carry a letter to a ruler unless you know its contents.' Likewise, Sufyān (may God have mercy on him) refused, while in the presence of the ruler of his times, to hand an inkwell to him, saying, 'Not until I know what you're going to write with it.'

All those around them, their servants and their followers, are tyrants like them; and all of them must be despised for the sake of God. It is related that when ʿUthmān b. Zā'ida was asked by a soldier where the road might be found, he did not answer. Instead, he acted as if he were deaf, for fear that the soldier might be on his way to commit injustices; and that if he answered he might be assisting in the commission of injustice.

Such excess [as practised by the rulers] has never been ascribed in the past to known miscreants among brokers, or weavers, or cuppers, or the bathhouse people, or the dyers, or any of the tradesmen, even though all of these were notorious for their untruths and their corruption. Nor even was such ascribed to the disbelievers who lived among us. Rather, this is something that is particular to rulers, those who devour the wealth of orphans and the destitute, who constantly inflict pain and suffering on the believers, and who support one another in effacing all signs of the *Sharīʿa* and its features.

Now, this is because sin (*maʿṣiya*) may be divided into transitive (*mutaʿaddiya*) and non-transitive sin (*lāzima*). Iniquity (*fisq*) is personal and non-transitive. The same is true of disbelief, though it is a form of transgression against the right of God (Exalted is He), and its recompense is with Him. The sin of rulers when they commit injustice, however, is transitive. This is why the matter is so serious with them. Then, in proportion to how widespread their injustice has become, and in proportion to how widespread their transgression has become, the extent of God's hatred for them may be measured.[85] It is for this reason that it is necessary to exercise greater caution in regard to them, and greater circumspection in dealing with them.

Indeed, [the Messenger of God] (may God bless him and

grant him peace) said, 'The henchman[A] will be told [when he dies],[86] "Drop your whip, and step into the fire."'[87] He (may God bless him and grant him peace) is also reported to have said, 'Among the signs of the Last Hour is that men will carry whips like the tails of cattle.'[88] This is how such people may be categorised. Those who are recognised for these things have gained notoriety; and the sign of those who have not been recognised is that they wear tunics, lengthy moustaches, and all the other signs of infamy.[B] Those seen to fit the description must be avoided.

Nor may such avoidance be accounted suspicion of a fellow Muslim[C] because such a person brings censure upon himself when he appears dressed in the garb of tyrants. Uniformity of appearance indicates uniformity of sentiment. Thus, only a lunatic looks like a lunatic, and only a miscreant will take on the appearance of a miscreant. True, a miscreant may attempt to mislead others by wearing the garb of the pious. But the pious will never appear dressed in the garb of miscreants because that would contribute to the notion that their numbers are substantial. Indeed, the verse of [God] most Exalted, *those taken by the angels of death when they were unjust to themselves*,[89] was revealed in regard to a group of Muslims who added to the apparent numbers of unbelievers by mixing with them [publicly].[90]

[A] The word, *shurṭī,* which I have translated here as 'henchman' is commonly used in modern Arabic to mean police. However, in the author's times, the word was used to designate those who carried out the iron-fisted policies of the sultan and his officials. The word 'police' may or may not have such a connotation in our own times, its denotation is certainly something more positive and noble.

[B] The commentator adds, 'signs that may change from time to time and place to place' (Z.VI.152).

[C] Here the author addresses a possible objection based on the tradition of the Messenger of God (may God bless him and grant him peace) who said, 'One is always to think well of other Muslims.' Such an objection might also be based on a verse in the Qur'an, XLIX.12.

It is related that God (Exalted is He) advised Yūshaʿ b. Nūn[A] that 'I will destroy forty thousand from among the best of your tribe and sixty thousand of the worst.' When [Yūshaʿ] objected, 'Why the best, O Lord?' He replied, 'They were never offended by them, and thus [thought nothing of] eating and drinking in their company.'[91] From this it should be clear that it is a duty to be offended by what offends God, and to detest the unjust.

Ibn Masʿūd related that the Prophet (may God bless him and grant him peace) said, 'Verily, God cursed the learned among the Children of Israel when they began mixing with the unjust in every aspect of their lives.'[92]

[ISSUE 6:] Public works[93] erected by the unjust,[94] like bridges, way stations, mosques and public fountains should be approached with caution and considered carefully. If there is a necessity, such a bridge may be crossed, though prudence dictates otherwise. If an alternate [route] exists, then prudence is clearly indicated. The reason for giving permission to cross over such a bridge, even when an alternative is available, is that when the ownership of [the bridge] [or other facility] is unknown, it may legally be categorised as having been erected for charity; and that is a good thing. However, if it is known that the bricks and rock came from a certain dwelling, or graveyard, or mosque, then it will clearly not be lawful to pass over such a bridge, except in cases of dire need when one may have to resort even to the wealth of others. In such cases, one must later seek permission from the owner, if an owner can be found.

With regard to a mosque, if it is known to have been constructed on misappropriated land, with wood misappropriated from another mosque that has a known owner,[95] then it is not lawful to enter such a mosque, or to go there for the Friday prayer. If an imam is leading prayer inside the mosque, then one should stand outside and offer prayer [as if] behind the imam. This is

[A] This is the Biblical Prophet, Joshua, who followed Moses as the leader of the Israelites.

because prayer performed on land that was usurped will satisfy the obligation [to pray], and because the prayer will have been realized through one's right to follow [the imam inside the mosque. It is for this reason that we give permission to follow behind someone leading prayer on usurped land, even though the imam is sinning by standing there.[A]

If, however, it was built with materials whose owner is unknown, then prudence will indicate one's seeking another mosque. However, if another cannot be found, then one must not leave off the Friday prayer or the [other] congregational prayers because it is possible, even if it is unlikely, that the materials were owned by the one who built the mosque. If the mosque does not have a specific owner, the mosque will be [considered open] for the general welfare of Muslims. But when a large mosque has a section that was built by a tyrannical ruler, those who pray in it will have no excuse, even if the mosque is huge; I mean in terms of prudence.

Aḥmad Ibn Ḥanbal was asked, 'What proof do you have to support not having to attend congregational prayer while we are with the army?' He replied, 'My proof is that al-Ḥasan [al-Baṣrī] and Ibrāhīm al-Taymī both feared that they would be tested by al-Ḥajjāj. And I, too, am afraid of being tested.'[96]

If the mosque is painted, or if its walls have been finished with gypsum, entrance will not be prohibited because no use is made of these things in prayer and they are no more than decoration; though it is best not to pay attention to them. It is unlawful to sit on mats spread over the floor, if they have a known owner [and have been taken]. Otherwise, they will be considered [to have been placed there] for the general welfare of Muslims and are therefore

[A] With regard to prayer performed in a place that has been misappropriated, see: Jaṣṣāṣ, *al-Fuṣūl fi'l-uṣūl* (Kuwait, n.d.), II.180; Sarakhsī, *Mabsūṭ*, V.76; Nawawī, *Majmū*ᶜ, III.170; Bukhārī, *Kashf al-asrār*, I.280; Ibn Taymiyya, *Majmū*ᶜ*at al-fatāwā*, II.78; Zaylaᶜī, *Naṣb al-rāya*, II.374–377; Zarkashī, *al-Baḥr al-muḥīṭ*, III.400; Shawkānī, *Nayl al-awṭār*, II.163.

lawful to sit upon. Even so, as there may be doubt about them, it will be prudent to avoid them. Likewise, with regard to water fountains, the ruling is as I have mentioned above; and therefore drinking and performing ablutions from them[97] will not be prudent, unless one fears missing the congregational prayer. The same applies to the public works erected on the way to Mecca.

With regard to way stations and schools, if the land [on which they were erected] was usurped, or if the bricks [with which they were constructed] were taken from another place, such that it is possible to return them to their rightful owner, then no permission may be given to enter such buildings. If, however, the owner is unknown, and the building is used for good, prudence will dictate avoiding it; though one will not commit a sin by going there. However, if these [way stations and schools] were erected by the sultan's officials, the matter is even more severe because they have no right to spend treasury money[A] on public works. Moreover, their own wealth is generally unlawful because they have no right to unclaimed wealth. The only ones for whom the collection of such wealth is lawful are the lawful rulers.

[ISSUE 7:] If usurped land is made into a road it is not permitted to travel on it under any circumstances (*al-batta*). If [the land] does not have a specific owner, then travel on it is permitted; though prudence lies in finding an alternate route if possible. If a lawful road is covered by a roof[B] it is permitted to use it, and to sit beneath it, [but only] in a way in which there is no need for a roof, as if one were sitting by a road to do something. If one benefits from the roof, to get out of the heat, or the rain, then that will be unlawful because the roof has no other purpose than that. The same ruling will apply to one who enters a mosque or lawful

[A] Lit. 'lost wealth' (*amwāl ḍā'iʿa*) or wealth that finds its way into the public treasury when its owners die and no heirs or debtors come forward to claim it.

[B] Such as a road between two walls, or two buildings. The apparent meaning here is that the author is speaking of a roof of dubious ownership.

land on which a roof and walls[A] have been erected by means of misappropriation.[98] One does not derive benefit from these things merely by walking through; unless one intends to make use of the roof and walls to avoid the heat, or the cold, or the eyes of others. This is unlawful because it involves one's benefiting from the unlawful. Otherwise, it is not unlawful to sit in a usurped mosque because one is touching it, but because one is benefiting from it. So, when land is sought out for rest, and a roof is sought out for shade, there is no difference between the two.

[A] i.e., from dubious sources.

CHAPTER SEVEN

A Variety of Issues of Such Importance that Questions Concerning them are Asked in the *Fatwā* Literature

[Issue 1][1]

A QUESTION WAS ASKED[2] regarding the servant of Sufis who goes daily to the market with either produce or currency with which to purchase food. Who, it was asked, may lawfully consume what he brings? Is it only the Sufis? Or not?[A] [may] others [lawfully consume it] as well?

My response is to say that there is no doubt regarding the right of the Sufis to consume what he brings, and for others as well, as long as they do so with the servant's approval.

Even so, the issue is not entirely free of ambiguity. The solution,[3] however, is [in understanding] that the servant is given whatever he is given because of the Sufis; even though he, and not the Sufis, is the direct recipient. This is like a man with a family who is given something because of his family. He is the direct recipient because he is the one who cares and provides for the family. Then, whatever he is given becomes his personal property, not that of the family. It is for this reason that he may use it to feed other than his family.

Indeed, to assert that possession has not passed from the giver is problematic (*yubʿad*); nor may the servant be forced to use it for purchases only, or otherwise be told how to dispose of

[A] i.e., Or may others lawfully consume what he brings as well?

it. This is because that would mean that it is not enough to simply give and take,[A] and that is untenable. Indeed, to insist on the same in regard to charity and gifts would be absurd. Nor may it be stated that his [the servant's] possession comes to an end when possession is passed to the Sufis in the retreat at the time the money is solicited,[B] because there is unanimous agreement that the servant may use it to feed any Sufi who comes along[4] at a later time. Likewise, if all the Sufis died, or if even one[5] of them died, it would not be necessary to distribute a share [from what the servant holds in his hand] to the heirs. Nor is it possible to state that this was given to Sufism and therefore no one in particular may claim to possess it. This is because the passing of possession to an ideal does not mean that particular individuals will gain the right of disposal. This is because the number of such individuals may be beyond counting; indeed it may include people to come until the Day of Resurrection. Instead, only those with authority will have the right of disposal, and the servant may not assume such authority on behalf of all Sufism.

Therefore, there is no other way to deal with this matter except to say that the servant becomes the owner of such funds,[6] and that he provides for the Sufis on the basis of their fulfilling the conditions of Sufism and decency (*murū'a*). If he should withhold provisions from them, they may prevent him from representing himself as the one providing for them, in which case he would become as one whose child had died, and could therefore no longer accept anything for that child.

[A] i.e., without the need for contracts and other legalities. This is termed *muʿāṭā*, and it denotes an exchange that is accomplished without the formal articulation of an offer and its acceptance. This was discussed earlier at Chapter Three.

[B] and received on their behalf by the servant.

[Issue 2][7]

An amount of wealth was bequeathed in the name of the Sufis. To whom may such wealth be lawfully distributed?

My response to this question is that Sufism is an esoteric matter. As such, it may neither be witnessed nor may any legal decision be linked[8] to its truth directly. Instead, one must depend on the sort of superficial factors used by people [who] know the customs (*ahl al-ʿurf*) when they employ the word 'Sufi.' The general rule is that anyone may be considered to be one of the Sufis if their appearance is such that when they walk into a Sufi retreat their entrance and their interacting will not be contested.[A]

To be more specific, they must exhibit five characteristics: piety, poverty, Sufi dress, not to be occupied with a profession and a shared life in a Sufi retreat. Some of these characteristics are such that if they no longer apply, then the person will no longer be entitled to the appellation [Sufi]. Others, however, if they are no longer applicable, are of the sort that may be compensated for by other characteristics. Sinfulness, for example, will prevent entitlement because, in general, a Sufi is a person who belongs among the righteous. Thus, a person in whom sinfulness is apparent, even if he appears in the garb of a Sufi, will not be entitled to what is bequeathed to the Sufis. But we will not include minor wrongdoing (*ṣaghā'ir*).[B]

A profession, however, and active involvement in earning will disqualify one from entitlement. Thus, a landowner, a tax collector, a trader, a craftsman who works in a shop or in his home, or an employee who works for wages, all of these will not have entitlement. A scribe,[C] however, or a tailor, or the likes of these,

[A] i.e., will seem natural. In other words they will appear to 'fit in'.

[B] i.e., minor wrongdoing will not be considered something that prevents entitlement.

[C] The word used here (*wirāqa*) includes scribes, stationers, bookbinders and anyone else involved in the production of books or, by extension, the promotion of knowledge.

people whose profession is suitable for a Sufi may be given such a bequest, as long as they do not practise[9] their profession in a shop, or in order to earn a living. This will not prevent their entitlement, especially if the person lives with the Sufis and possesses all the other traits. Likewise, if one is qualified in a profession, but does not practise it, that person will not be disqualified from entitlement [for that reason].

Preaching and teaching, however, do not negate the name Sufi if the rest of the traits are present, like the garb, the residence, and the poverty. It is not contradictory to say 'Sufi Reciter' (*muqri'*), or 'Sufi Preacher' (*wāʿiẓ*), or 'Sufi Scholar' (*ʿālim*) or 'Sufi Teacher' (*mudarris*). It is, however, a contradiction of terms to say 'Sufi Landowner', or 'Sufi Merchant', or 'Sufi Tax Collector'.

With regard to [the characteristic of] poverty, if it is replaced by an excess of wealth, such that this causes the person to appear wealthy, then it will not be lawful for that person, with that wealth, to receive what is bequeathed to the Sufis. If the person has wealth, but his income does not suffice to meet his expenses, his entitlement will not be disqualified. The same will be true if he possesses wealth, but not enough to require payment of the *zakāt*; and even if he does not have expenses. For these matters, there is no proof (*dalīl*) other than custom (*ʿāda*).

With regard to frequenting and living with the Sufis, these do have an effect. However, one who does not live or frequent with Sufis, but keeps to his own home or mosque, while wearing the garb and exhibiting the characteristics of a Sufi, such a person may be given a share of whatever is bequeathed to the Sufis. The wearing of Sufi garb may thus be seen to compensate for frequenting. But if a person does not wear the garb of a Sufi, though all the other traits are present in his person, he will not be considered a Sufi unless he lives with the Sufis in their monasteries or retreats. In this manner, the ruling for them will also apply to him by extension. In this manner, frequenting and wearing Sufi garb may compensate one for the other. The same ruling will apply to a jurist who does not wear[10] their garb. If he lives outside [of their retreats], he will not be considered a Sufi. Yet, if he lives with them, and possesses the rest of their characteristics, it is not unlikely that the ruling for them will apply to him[11] by extension.

With regard to wearing a patched garment gifted by a Sufi master from among the recognised Sufi masters, this is not a condition for entitlement. The lack of the same, moreover, when the other conditions are present, is not disadvantageous. Finally, a person who is [otherwise] qualified, yet who wavers between residence with the Sufis and his own quarters, will not be excluded for that reason from their numbers.[A]

[Issue 3][12]

With regard to whatever is left as a trust (*waqf*) to the retreat of the Sufis and those who inhabit it, the matter is more far-reaching than that of a bequest because the meaning of a trust implies expenditure in their interests.[B] Accordingly, a non-Sufi may indeed partake of their food once or twice at their tables, if they so desire. This is because the matter of food is based on magnanimity. After all, it is lawful for a person on his own to consume food considered the shared spoils of war. Thus, it is lawful for one who recites poetry as a professional (*qawwāl*)[13] to partake, when invited, of food supplied by the trust because this is in the interests [of the Sufis]. It is not lawful, however, to spend money from a bequest on such a professional. A trust is different, though. The same applies to others in their company, whether officials, merchants, judges, or scholars; if it is in the interest of the Sufis to gain their favour, it is lawful for them to partake of the Sufis' food whenever the Sufis wish [to feed them].

[A] By extension, such a circumstance will not disqualify that person from entitlement.

[B] While the bequest is made in the name of the Sufis, and therefore for the Sufis, the trust includes expenditures on the Sufis and on whatever may be considered to be in the interest of the Sufis.

This is because the donor did not expect, when establishing the trust, that the Sufis would do anything other than what is customarily done by Sufis. Such matters, then, depend on custom. Even so, these sorts of things are not to continue on a regular basis. Thus, it is not lawful for a non-Sufi to establish permanent residence with them, and to eat with them regularly, even if they are happy with that person's doing so. This is because they do not have the right to alter the conditions stipulated by the donor in order to accommodate other than their own kind.

With regard to a jurist, if he wears their clothes and possesses their characteristics, then he may join them. Just because someone is a jurist does not mean that he cannot be a Sufi jurist. Indeed, those who truly understand Sufism know that ignorance [of *Sharīʿa* law] is not a condition for being a Sufi. No attention, therefore, should be paid to the statements of certain fools that knowledge is a veil. On the contrary, it is ignorance that is a veil![14] Even so, I have already discussed how this statement may be interpreted in the *Book of Knowledge*. In fact it is blameworthy knowledge that is a veil, not praiseworthy knowledge; and I have previously defined and explained the meaning of both praiseworthy and blameworthy knowledge.[A] Returning to the jurist, if he does not wear their clothes and does not possess their characteristics, they may prohibit him from joining them. If, however, they are satisfied with his joining them, he may partake of their food. But this will be only by extension, [not as one who is himself entitled to partake]. If he does not wear their clothes, that [circumstance] can be offset by his living with them; but only at their pleasure.

All of these are matters to which custom gives witness. Some of these are comparable matters in which extreme cases, whether positive or negative, are not difficult to discern; while moderate cases may appear similar. Then, those who avoid the

[A] The Book of Knowledge is book 1 of the *Revival of the Religious Sciences*.

doubtful will have protected their religion, as I pointed out in the Chapter concerning the dubious.[A]

[Issue 4]

A question was asked concerning the difference between a bribe and a gift, when both occur by consent and neither is free of ulterior motives (*lā takhlū ʿan gharaḍ*), and when one has been declared unlawful but not the other.

My reply is that anyone who spends money does so for a purpose. That purpose,[15] however, may be delayed, as in the case of reward in the next world, or immediate. An immediate purpose, moreover, may be wealth, or a deed, or assistance in achieving a certain goal, or drawing closer to someone in order to bring about affection, either for itself or as a means to an end.

These purposes may be divided into five categories:

THE FIRST CATEGORY: This is [spending] which has as its purpose reward in the world to come. In this category the recipient will be a needy person, or a learned one, or a relation[16] of a religious family [or group], or a pious and religious person in his own right. If the recipient knows, for example, that he has been given something on the assumption that he is needy; then he may not lawfully accept it unless he is truly in need. Likewise, one who is given something owing to his family heritage may not accept if he has misrepresented[17] his claim to be a relation. And if one is given something owing to his knowledge, he may not accept unless he is indeed as learned as the giver supposes him to be. So, if someone is given something by a person who supposes him to be a master [in an academic discipline], when he is not actually a master, he may not accept the gift. One who is given something on the basis of his religion and outward piety may not accept if he is a sinner on the inside such that if the giver knew of his condition he would never have given a gift in the first place. It sometimes happens that

[A] Chapter Two of this book, 'The Degrees of the Dubious'.

a person will appear pious; but if his inner being were revealed, no one would be attracted to him. Instead, it is God's covering [of his inner being] for him that makes him attractive to people. Indeed, fearing that someone might make special allowances for them, truly prudent people have been known to appoint others their agents, without publicising the fact, for the purpose of buying and selling. In this manner they avoid using their religion as a means of consuming. So, this is a dangerous matter as it is hidden: unlike one's need, or family ties, or knowledge. Moreover, to the extent possible, one should always avoid using one's religion as a means of earning.

THE SECOND CATEGORY: This is [spending] that has an immediate and specific purpose. This is like a mendicant's gifting something [relatively insignificant] to a rich man in anticipation of [the rich man's granting him in return] a valuable gift.[A] As such, this is a gift that has been made conditional to the receipt of a reward; and the ruling in regard to such a gift is not difficult to discern. This will be lawful when the desired reward is actually produced, and when all the elements of a valid contract are present.[B]

[A] The word used here is *khalʿa* which was a robe of honour conferred by nobles on the most noteworthy of their subjects, including the learned and pious.

[B] The commentator is careful to point out here that while such a 'gift' may appear to take the form of a bribe, in fact it is not. Thus, he quotes from *Faṣl al-maqāl* by Taqī al-Dīn al-Subkī as follows: 'If you say that the giver may be a beggar who intends to be recompensed for his gift by the recipient, having no other motive, then I will reply that this is a sale carried out in the form of a gift. In fact, if we accept it as a sale, we reject it as a gift; and in this manner we refute the argument [that it is a bribe]. If we accept it as a gift, such that we establish that blessings are attached [to the act of charitable giving], then we will call it a gift in view of its form, not its meaning. Of course, we are speaking here of both its form and its meaning. To call the form mentioned here a 'gift' is the same as calling a painted picture a person. Even so, it may be said that the beggar intended to turn the heart of the recipient so that he feels compassion and gives him something, but not as recompense. When this is the case, the intention is no more than affection, and so the gift may truly be called

THE THIRD CATEGORY: This is when the intention [of one's spending] is [to gain] assistance with a particular matter; like a needy person's giving a gift to the agent of the sultan, or to members of his entourage, or to those he holds in respect. So this is a gift on condition of a reward that is discerned by means of circumstantial evidence. In such a case it is necessary that we look to the reward [that is sought].

If it is something unlawful, like an attempt to secure unlawful riches, or to do injustice to another, then it is unlawful to accept such a gift.

If it is something that is a duty, like the prevention of a specific injustice by someone in a position to do so, or like bearing witness about a specific event,[A] then whatever is accepted will be unlawful because this is undoubtedly a bribe and there can be no doubt about its prohibition.

If it is something that is permitted rather than something that is a duty, or unlawful, and also requires effort such that one might otherwise be hired to undertake it, then one may lawfully accept the gift if one achieves the objective. Such a gift will be treated as a contract of reward (*jiʿāla*),[B] which is like someone saying, 'Tell this story in person to the sultan,[18] and a dinar will be yours' when this requires effort and measurable exertion. Or it might be like someone saying, 'Suggest to such and such

a gift. This is how people commonly understand the matter. Do you not see that the compensation is not specified, or even known [to the beggar beforehand]? Instead, the beggar/giver intends that the wealthy recipient will become favourably disposed towards him, and perhaps show him compassion in return. Thus, we return to the meaning I explained above. Moreover, the beggar does not seek anything in particular, which is most unlike a bribe. It is for this reason that such a gift is not prohibited.' See Z.VI.158.

[A] i.e., when it is their duty to testify anyway.

[B] An arrangement in which a known amount of compensation is given in return for work that is specified and known, unless its nature is such that it is difficult to know [at the time of agreement]. In such an agreement, unless the work is completed, the compensation will not be given. See Ḥammād, *Muʿjam al-muṣṭalaḥāt*, p. 137.

a person that he should help me to do this or that, or that he should give me this or that,' and then the person is required to speak at length in order to bring about the desired result. This, then, is a contract of reward, like what an agent (*wakīl*) takes for arguing a case in front of a judge,[A] and is thus not unlawful as long as the effort expended is not for an unlawful purpose.[19]

If the objective is achieved by means of speech requiring no effort,[20] but the speech is delivered by an influential person, or if a useful action is performed by an influential person, like his saying to the guard, 'Do not close the sultan's door to this man,' or like his narrating a story directly to the sultan, then in that case it will be unlawful [for the influential person] to accept the gift because he will do so in return for his influence only; and there is nothing in the *Sharīʿa* that allows that. On the contrary, the *Sharīʿa* prohibits it, as has been explained in the section about gifts given by royalty.

If it is not lawful to accept compensation for relinquishing the right of pre-emption (*shufʿa*), or for exercising an option to return damaged goods, or for [rent on] overhanging branches when these occupy space [over land] that one owns, or for a variety of other things that are intended [by the law], then how can one take recompense for influence? This approximates a doctor's taking a fee for a single word used to indicate a medicine that only he knows about, like one who has exclusive knowledge of a plant that cures piles or another malady, and who will only mention it if he is compensated for it. Indeed, his effort in articulating the word is too insignificant to calculate, like a single sesame seed. Therefore, it is not lawful to accept compensation for the same, or even for the knowledge of it. This is because the knowledge will not pass from the one to the other; instead, the

[A] For a similar comparison, see *al-Mawsūʿa al-fiqhiyya*, XI.324. Evidently, in the days of the author, lawyers were entitled to compensation only if they won their cases. It is possible, however, that they also worked on the basis of fees, as both *ijāra* and *jiʿāla* are lawful methods of compensation.

student will learn it in the same manner that the teacher learned it; and the teacher will retain the knowledge [even after the student learns]. A master in a trade, however, is different. This is like sharpening, for example, that removes curves from swords or mirrors by a single stroke, owing to the expertise of the sharpener in determining where the curves originate. Indeed, by means of a single stroke, he may greatly increase the value of a sword or a mirror. In such a case, I see no impediment to his accepting compensation because it takes a great deal of effort to master such industries and then to be able to earn from them.[A]

THE FOURTH CATEGORY: This is spending that has affection as its purpose, and attracting it from the heart[21] of the recipient, not for any particular purpose,[22] but out of a desire for friendship, and in order to emphasise [the importance of one's] company, and to bring love into peoples' hearts. This is what is sought by the wise and encouraged by the *Sharīʿa*. For, indeed, [the Messenger of God] (may God bless him and grant him peace) said, 'Give gifts to one another, and bring love to one another.'[23] Generally speaking, people do not usually seek the love of others unless there is some benefit in doing so. However, if the benefit is not specific, and if the giver has no particular reason [for

[A] It may be possible to explain the difference between the prohibition in the first instance, and the permission in the second, that the doctor possessed knowledge that had been imparted to him, rather than knowledge that he had developed or discovered on his own; whereas the master tradesman had spent years developing his craft. Even so, that is hardly a satisfactory explanation from a modern perspective. It is clear that the notion of intellectual property is one that was not yet understood at the time of the author who, to his credit, is somewhat more understanding of the medical profession in Chapter Five. Personally, I would attribute the difficulty on the part of the author, and the classical jurists in general, with the concept of intellectual property to the prohibition of ambiguity in contracts (*gharar*), and the insistence on substance in the countervalues exchanged in transactions. Finally, to return to the text and its implications, one might postulate here that had the master tradesman learned from another of a plant that cured arthritis, it is likely that the author would have considered it unlawful for him to accept a fee for sharing that information.

giving] either at present or in the future, then this will be[24] a gift, and it will be lawful to accept it.

THE FIFTH CATEGORY: This is to seek [by means of spending] to be near to someone's heart and to gain his affection; not for his affection or his friendship per se, but in order to attain by means of the other's status one's own general objectives, even if these are not specified.[25] Were it not for the other's status and position, no gift would be given.[26] If the person's status is due to his learning or his family, then the matter is less serious, and it will be lawful, though diapproved, for him to accept such a gift. This is because there is a clear resemblance[27] to a bribe, even though [what is given] is ostensibly a gift. If the person's status is due to his holding a certain position, like a judgeship, or a governorship, or the office of revenue collector, or a similar official position, even a director of trusts, such that if he did not hold the position he would not receive the gift, then that is a bribe offered in the form of a gift. This is because the purpose of the gift may initially be to seek and earn the other's affection; but for a specific reason because it is obvious that it is possible to attain things by means of the person's position.[28] The proof that it is not affection that is being sought[29] here is that if another were to take that person's position, the gift would go to the new office holder. In such a case, there is agreement [among jurists] that the disapproval is extreme; though they disagree as to whether this is actually unlawful. The meaning here is in conflict, revolving, as it does, between a simple gift and a bribe spent in return for influence in regard to a specific purpose. When there is a conflict between two apparently logical deductions, and one of the two is supported by textual evidence, then that is the one towards which [the ruling] must incline. In fact, the texts are quite strict on the matter.

[The Messenger of God][30] (may God's peace and blessings be upon him) said, 'A time will come over people when gifts will make filthy things lawful, and innocents will be killed as examples to the general populace.'[31]

When Ibn Masʿūd (may God be pleased with him) was asked the meaning of 'filthy things' (*suḥt*), he replied, 'When a man does the needful and is then presented with a gift for the same.'[32] Perhaps the meaning here is that he did the needful by means of a word, such that no effort was expended; or perhaps he did so on his own, without expecting anything in return, so that it is unlawful for him to accept anything later on by way of compensation.

Masrūq once interceded[33] on behalf of another, and then that other gifted him a slave girl.[A] So [Masrūq] returned the girl and said, 'If I knew what was in your heart, I would never have spoken on your behalf. Nor will I say anything more on your behalf [now that I know].'[34]

Ṭāwūs was once asked about gifts from rulers. He replied, 'Unlawful.'[35]

ʿUmar (may God be pleased with him) took the profits earned by his two sons in a partnership based on capital from the treasury, saying to them, 'He[B] gave you this owing to your relationship to me,' knowing that the two had been given the capital because of the status of his [their father, Umar's] office.[36]

The wife of Abū ʿUbayda b. al-Jarrāḥ gifted a bottle of perfume to the wife[37] of the Roman governor who, in return, sent her a jewel. So ʿUmar (may God be pleased with him) took the jewel and sold it. Then he repaid the wife of Abū ʿUbayda the value of the perfume and deposited whatever money remained in the public treasury.[38]

Both Jābir [b. ʿAbd Allāh] and Abū Hurayra (may God be pleased with them) termed the gifts of rulers 'misappropriated plunder'.[39]

[A] Abū Dā'ūd, *Sunan* III.519 and Aḥmad, *Musnad* XVI.248 related on the authority of Abū Umāma that the Prophet (upon him be peace), said, 'One who intercedes on behalf of another and then accepts a gift in return will have entered an ominous door to interest (*ribā*).'

[B] This was Abū Mūsā al-Ashʿarī.

When ᶜUmar b. ᶜAbd al-ᶜAzīz returned a gift, he was reminded that the Messenger of God (may God bless him and grant him peace) was known to have accepted gifts. So ᶜUmar replied, 'For him they were gifts. But for us they are bribes.'[40] In other words, nearness was sought owing to his prophethood, not because of his office; whereas we are given gifts owing to our offices.

Even greater than all this is what was related by Abū Ḥumayd al-Sāᶜidī, that the Messenger of God (may God bless him and grant him peace) appointed an official over the charity (*ṣadaqa*) of the Azd tribe. When he reached the Messenger of God (may God bless him and grant him peace) the man kept for himself some of the money that was with him, saying, 'This is yours, and this is what was gifted to me.' So [the Messenger of God] (may God bless him and grant him peace) said, 'Why do you not sit in the home of your father and mother and wait for your gifts there? If you are indeed truthful!' Then he said, 'Why should I appoint someone among you who tells me that "this is yours and this is a gift for me?" If he sits in his mother's house would he receive those gifts? By the One in whose hands is my life! No one among you may take something to which he has no right except that he meet God carrying it! Be warned that you do not come on the Day of Judgement carrying a foamy-mouthed camel, or a mooing cow, or a bleating goat!' Then he (may God bless him and grant him peace) raised his two hands so that I could see the white of his two armpits, and said, 'O my Lord! Have I delivered the message?'[41]

In view of the severity of these texts, a judge or an official should imagine himself in the home of his mother and father. Then, whatever is given to him after he leaves office, and when he is living in his mother's house, he may also accept while still holding his position. But whatever he knows is gifted to him because of his office will be unlawful for him to accept. Those things, however, which are difficult to determine in relation to gifts from personal friends, like whether they would be giving him those things if he were no longer in office, are dubious and should therefore be avoided.

The Book of the Lawful and the Unlawful is now complete, with thanks to God, and by His largesse, and by the goodness of His direction.

And God knows best.

NOTES

Prologue

1 This *ḥadīth* was previously quoted by the author in Book v of the *Revival of the Religious Sciences*, 'The Mysteries of *Zakāt*'. According to ʿIrāqī, the *ḥadīth* was related by Ṭabarānī, *Kabīr*, x.74 and by Bayhaqī in *Shuʿab al-īmān*, xi.175, by means of a weak *isnād* and without the final words 'of every Muslim' (Z.vi.4). The reason for the infirmity, according to Haythamī, *Majmaʿ al-zawā'id* was that the narrator, ʿIbād b. Kathīr al-Thaqafī was 'rejected' (*matrūk*). The narration was also characterised as 'weak' by Suyūṭī in *al-Jāmiʿ al-ṣaghīr*. See also, Dhahabī, *Mīzān*, ii.370.

2 In A. '...Excellence of the Possessor of the Lawful.'

3 In Z. '...and Related Matters.'

4 In Z. '...of Such Importance and Common Occurrence that they Require Consideration.'

Chapter 1

1 Q.xxiii.51.

2 Q.ii.188.

3 Q.iv.10.

4 Q.ii.278.

5 Q.ii.279.

6 Q.ii.279.

7 Q.ii.275.

8 Ṭabarānī, *Kabīr*, x.74; Haythamī, *Majmaʿ*, x.41 and x.520; Makkī, *Qūt*, ii.287.

9 Ibn Māja, *Sunan*, in *Ihda' al-dibaja*, i.140; Tabarānī, *Kabīr*, x.195; Tabarānī, *Awsaṭ*, ii.296; Haythami, *Majmaʿ*, i.473-475; Makkī, *Qūt*, ii.287.

10 al-Khaṭīb al-Baghdādī, *Tārīkh Baghdād*, viii.168; also, Ṭabarānī, *Awsaṭ*, iv.284; Daylamī, *Firdaws* (Z.vi.6).

11 Iṣfahānī, *Ḥilya*, v.189; Ibn al-Jawzī included this narration in his collection of spurious *ḥadīth*, *Mawḍūʿāt*, iii.144. Suyūṭī, however, opined that there is no more to the matter than that the *sanad* of the *ḥadīth* is weak. Ibn ʿAbd al-Ḥaqq, in his *Sharḥ al-aḥkām*, wrote that though the *sanad* may be weak for technical reasons, the meaning is surely correct. ʿAbd Allāh ibn Mubārak related the *ḥadīth* as a *mursal* narration in his *al-Zuhd* i.359. Another version of the *ḥadīth* was related by Ibn ʿAbbās and is included in the *Musnad al-quḍa'ī*, the *Zawā'id al-zuhd* by Abū Bakr al-Marwazī, and the *Muṣannaf* of Ibn Abī Shayba. See Z.vi.6.

12 This is actually another *ḥadīth*, and not a version of the *ḥadīth* that preceded it. Z.vi.7; Makkī, *Qūt*, ii.287.

13 Ṭabarānī, *Awsaṭ*, vi.310 on the authority of Ibn ʿAbbās. ʿIrāqī commented that the *sanad* of the *ḥadīth* contained a narrator he did not know. This means only that the narration is technically weak, an opinion shared by Ibn al-Jawzī (Z.vi.8).

14 Muslim, *Ṣaḥīḥ*, iii.85-86; Tirmidhī, *Sunan*, v.95; Dārimī, *Sunan*, iii.1786.

15 ʿIrāqī was unable to find this *ḥadīth*, though he did mention a somewhat similar narration related by Ibn Masʿūd in Daylamī's *Firdaws*, iii.591. That version, however, was termed *munkar*. Thus, the authenticity of this *ḥadīth* is nowhere established (Z.vi.8).

16 Ibn Ḥanbal, *Musnad*, v.219; Bayhaqī, *Shuʿab*, viii.210.

17 Tirmidhī, *Sunan*, i.602; Iṣfahānī, *Ḥilya*, viii.247; Ibn Ḥanbal, *Musnad*, xii.118; Bayhaqī, *Shuʿab*, xii.25 (Z.vi.8).

18 Iṣfahānī, *Tārīkh Iṣbahān*, i.399; Daylamī related this *ḥadīth* in his *Musnad al-firdaws*, but Ibn al-ʿArabī, in his commentary on the *Sunan* of Tirmidhī said that the *ḥadīth* was not an authentic one (Z.vi.9).

19 Daylamī, *Firdaws*, iii.79.

20 Tabarānī, *Awsaṭ*, vii.289.

21 This *ḥadīth* was related by Abū Dā'ūd in his *Kitāb al-marāsīl* p. 142 on the authority of al-Qāsim b. al-Mukhaymara. A similar version was related by Ibn al-Mubārak in his *Kitāb al-zuhd*, i.221 (Z.vi.9).

22 This is a part of a *ḥadīth* related by Hakim, al-Mustadrak, i.92; Tabarānī, *Awsaṭ*, iv.196; and Bayhaqī, *Shuʿab*, iii.226.

23 ʿIrāqī commented that he was unable to find any basis for this *ḥadīth*. As the commentator made no further comment, after quoting ʿIrāqī, it is likely that the *ḥadīth* is a spurious one (Z.vi.9).

24 This narration was related by al-Ḥakīm al-Tirmidhī (*Nawādir*, iii.56) on the authority of Ibn ʿAbbās who ascribed it to the Messenger of God (Z.vi.9). See also Ṭabarānī, *Kabīr*, xii.120, Ibn ʿAsākir, *Tārīkh Dimashq*, lvi.113.

25 Ibn Ḥanbal, *Musnad*, xvi.149; Bayhaqī, *al-Sunan al-Kubrā*, iii.16.

26 Suyūṭī, *al-La'ālī*, ii.208; Ḥalabī, *Mawsūʿa*, x.444.

27 Q.ix.109.

28 Ibn Ḥanbal, *al-Musnad*, iii.539; Ḥākim, *Mustadrak*, ii.4.

29 Iṣfahānī, *Ḥilya*, i.130; Makkī, *Qūt*, ii.478; Suyūṭī, *Tārīkh al-khulafā'*, p. 79.

30. Bukhārī, *Ṣaḥīḥ*, p. 803.

31 In this case, the Caliph ʿUmar had not consumed anything unlawful, but rather something dubious. Mālik included a narration in the *Muwaṭṭa'* in which ʿAbd Allāh b. al-Arqam said: 'Would you like it if a fat man on a hot day washed what was under the folds of his

lower garment and then gave you that water to drink? *Ṣadaqa* is like the impurities that people wash away.' Mālik, *al-Muwaṭṭā'*, v.1457.

32 Mālik, *al-Muwaṭṭā'*, ii.379.

33 In Z. '...the principle (underlying) worship'.

34 Iṣfahānī, *Ḥilya*, ii.47; Bayhaqī, *Shu*ᶜ*ab*, x.460.

35 See Z.vi.11.

36 Makkī, *Qūt*, ii.477.

37 Iṣfahānī, *Ḥilya*, viii.103.

38 Ibrāhīm's fear of consuming something unlawful was so great that he even avoided drinking the blessed water of Zamzam if he did not know what kind of bucket had been used to draw it out of the well. Qushayrī related this in his *Risāla*. Z.vi.11.

39 A similar version of this narration was discussed above at endnote 15.

40 Makkī, *Qūt*, ii.477-478; Similar versions were related by Fuḍayl, Iṣfahānī, *Ḥilya*, viii.94.

41 Makkī, *Qūt*, ii.478.

42 Q.lxxxiii.14.

43 This was related by Ibn Abī Dunyā in his *Kitāb al-wara*ᶜ, p. 204.

44 Makkī, *Qūt*, ii.478.

45 Makkī, *Qūt*, ii.480.

46 Makkī, *Qūt*, ii.323.

47 Makkī, *Qūt*, ii.478.

48 Makkī, *Qūt*, ii.479; Bayhaqī, *Shu*ᶜ*ab*, xiii.177.

49 In A. and B. '...a certain pious person'.

50 The version of this story related in *Qūt al-qulūb*, has it that the questioner was a traveller. Other versions, however, make him to be one of the pious. As the original version is the one closest to our understanding, it has been retained in the text of the translation (Makkī, *Qūt*, ii.480). See also Z.ii.12. The reference to the milk of a wild goat is to emphasise the element of unadulterated purity.

51 Makkī, *Qūt a*, ii.480-481.

52 Q.xxiii.51.

53 Makkī, *Qūt*, ii.481.

54 Makkī, *Qūt*, ii.489.

55 Makkī, *Qūt*, ii.491.

56 In A. and B. '...his mother'.

57 Makkī, *Qūt*, ii.491.

58 Makkī, *Qūt*, ii.324.

59 'and the Unlawful' missing in A. and B.

60 'vinegar' missing in Z.

61 The last two sentences in this paragraph, and then the following three paragraphs are missing in D.

62 Bukhārī, *Ṣaḥīḥ*, p. 697, p. 1253; Ibn Hanbal, *Musnad*, vi.552-556; Abū Dā'ūd, *Sunan*, iv. 117-118; Ibn Māja, in *Ihda' al-dibāja*, v.541; Nasā'ī, *Sunan*, vii.202; Dārimī, *Sunan*, ii.1297.

63 This sentence and the one before it are missing in D.

64 In Z., D. and A. '... *Campaigns* in the Book of *Wealth*...'

65 Ibn Māja, *Sunan*, v.541 and Tirmidhī, *Sunan*, iv.643 related this *ḥadīth* on the authority of ᶜAṭiyya b. ᶜUrwa.

66 In D., B., and A., 'causes characterisation as a wrongdoer.'

67 In B. 'the afflictor.'

68 In A. 'of Prudence' is omitted; while in D. and B. 'and their Legal Parallels' is added.

69 Tirmidhī, *Sunan*, iv.668; Nasā'ī, *Sunan*, iv.732; Ibn Ḥanbal, *Musnad*, x.495; Dārimī, *Sunan*, iii.1648 on the authority of Ḥasan b. ʿAlī. Other versions of the same *ḥadīth* were related by Bukhārī in his *Ṣaḥīḥ* on the authority of Ḥassān b. Abī Sinān; Ibn Ḥanbal, *Musnad*, ii.345 and x.495; Ḥākim, *al-Mustadrak*, ii.19 and iv.32; and Darwīsh, *Bughya*, iv.38.

70 Suyūṭī, *al-Jāmiʿ al-ṣaghīr*, v.41-42; Hindī, *Kanz al-ʿummāl*, vii.237; Darwīsh, *Bughya*, iv.38; Tabaranī, *Kabīr*, xii.222; Bayhaqī, *al-Sunan al-Kubrā*, ix.241.

71 Abū Dā'ūd, *Sunan*, iv.183. Another version of the hadith was related by Bukhārī, *Ṣaḥīḥ*, p. 1200.

72 Bukhārī, *Ṣaḥīḥ*, p. 55; Muslim, *Ṣaḥīḥ*, vi.58; Abū Dā'ūd, *Sunan*, ii.182-183; Dārimī, *Sunan*, ii.1273; Ibn Ḥanbal, *Musnad*, xiv.121; Nasā'ī, *Sunan*, vii.203.

73 Bukhārī, *Ṣaḥīḥ*, p. 1198; Abū Dā'ūd, *Sunan*, iii.184; Tirmidhī, *Sunan*, iv.64.

74 Iṣfahānī, *Ḥilya*, v.267. The amount mentioned in Makkī's narration is forty thousand. See Makkī, *Qūt*, ii.445.

75 Tirmidhī, *Sunan*, iv.634; Ibn Māja, in *Dibāja*, v.541; Makkī, *Qūt*, ii.459.

76 ʿAbd al-Razzāq, *Muṣannaf*, viii.152; Makkī, *Qūt*, ii.459, 493.

77 Makkī, *Qūt*, ii.493.

78 Makkī, *Qūt*, ii.163.

79 Makkī, *Qūt*, ii.467.

80 Makkī, *Qūt*, ii.467.

81 Bukhārī, *Ṣaḥīḥ*, p. 316; Muslim, *Ṣaḥīḥ*, iii.117; Dārimī, *Sunan*, iii.1023; Ibn Ḥanbal, *Musnad*, vii.294 and ix.408.

82 Makkī, *Qūt*, ii.467.

83 In B. and A., Nuʿayma al-ʿAṭṭāra. In Makkī's *Qūt*, Nuʿaym related from ʿAṭṭāra.

84 Ibn Ḥanbal, *Waraʿ*, p.37; Makkī, *Qūt*, ii.467.

85 This story and the stories in the two preceding paragraphs are missing from D.

86 Makkī, *Qūt*, ii.467.

87 Makkī, *Qūt*, ii.285.

88 This paragraph is missing from D.

89 This paragraph and three that preceded it are missing from D.

90 Makkī, *Qūt*, ii.467, 469.

91 From this point to the end of the following paragraph is missing from D.

92 According to ʿIrāqī, this *ḥadīth* was related by Dārquṭunī in *al-Afrād*, and he called it weak for the reason that at one point in its *sanad* it was related by only one narrator. The same was related on the authority of Abū al-Dardā' by Mukhlī, Ibn Najjār, and Daylamī. See Z.vi.28.

93 Makkī, *Qūt*, ii.469.

94 Makkī, *Qūt*, i.656.

95 Q.vi.91.

96 In A., Yaḥyā b. Kathīr.

97 This example, and the twelve

that follow it, are missing in D.

98 Makkī, *Qūt*, II.466.

99 Makkī, *Qūt*, II.490.

100 Makkī, *Qūt*, II.323.

101 Makkī, *Qūt*, II.474.

102 Makkī, *Qūt*, II.296.

103 Ibn Ḥanbal, *Wara*ᶜ, p. 59.

104 *Ibid.*, p. 61.

105 ᶜUthmān ibn Za'ida. Ibn Ḥanbal, *Wara*ᶜ, p. 61.

106 ᶜUthmān ibn Za'ida. Ibn Ḥanbal, *Wara*ᶜ, p. 104.

107 Makkī, *Qūt*, II.484.

Chapter 2

1 Bukhārī, *Ṣaḥīḥ*, pp. 26 & 426; Muslim, *Ṣaḥīḥ*, v.50; Nasā'ī, *Sunan*, IV.732; Tirmidhī, *Sunan*, III.502; Ibn Māja, in *Dibāja*, v.334; Ibn Ḥanbal, *Musnad*, XIV.168 and XIV.146.

2 In D. the ten paragraphs that follow are missing; i.e., from 'To attempt to avoid' to 'There are five reasons for such uncertainties.'

3 In B. 'gazelle had an [owner's] tag in its ear' is missing.

4 This paragraph and the three that follow it are missing in D.

5 In B. 'if it is substantiated by.'

6 Bukhārī, *Ṣaḥīḥ*, p. 55; Muslim, *Ṣaḥīḥ*, III.1273; Abū Dā'ūd, *Sunan*, III.182-183; Dārimī, *Sunan*, III.1273; Ibn Ḥanbal, *Musnad*, XIV.121; and Nasā'ī, *Sunan*, VII.203.

7 Bukhārī, *Ṣaḥīḥ*, p. 535; Muslim, *Ṣaḥīḥ*, III.121. Abū Hurayra narrated that whenever food was brought to the Messenger of God he would ask if it was charity or a gift. If it was charity, he would say to his Companions, 'Eat up,' but would not partake himself. If it was a gift, he would clap his hand and eat with them.

8 Ibn Ḥanbal, *Musnad*, VI.266.

9 Nasā'ī, *Sunan*, IV.226; Ibn Māja, in *Dibāja*, IV.404; Ibn Ḥanbal, *Musnad*, XV.149.

10 Muslim, *Ṣaḥīḥ*, XIII.55; Ibn Ḥanbal, *Musnad*, IV.149.

11 Ghazālī, *Wasīṭ*, III.289; Rāfiᶜī, *ᶜAzīz*, IX.39–42.

12 The last two sentences of this paragraph and the following thirteen paragraphs are missing from D.

13 Ibn Abī Shayba, *Muṣannaf*, VI.613.

14 In Z. 'several wives.'

15 In Z. 'preponderant in my opinion.'

16 In B. 'of two persons.'

17 This and the following fourteen paragraphs (to the Fourth Category) are missing from D.

18 Manāwī, *Fayḍ*, v.41; Bayhaqī, *al-Sunan al-Kubrā*, IX.241; Ibn Abī Shayba, *Muṣannaf*, VII.72.

19 Ibn Abī Shayba, *al-Muṣannaf*, VII.89. According to ᶜIrāqī, this *ḥadīth* was not related on the authority of ᶜĀ'isha, but by Mūsā b. Abū ᶜĀ'isha from Abū Razīn. The *ḥadīth* was related by Bayhaqī, *al-Sunan al-Kubrā*, IX.241 and also by Abū Dā'ūd in his *Kitāb al-marāsīl*, p. 281. See Z.VI.37. The same version of the *ḥadīth* was also

related by Ibn Abī Shayba, vii.89.

20 Bukhārī, *Ṣaḥīḥ*, p. 1200; Muslim, *Ṣaḥīḥ*, vi.58; Abū Dā'ūd, *Sunan*, iii.182; Dārimī, *Sunan*, iii.1273; Ibn Ḥanbal, *Musnad*, xiv.121; and Nasā'ī, *Sunan*, vii.203.

21 In B. 'will not act contrary to.'

22 Bukhārī, *Ṣaḥīḥ*, p. 1200; Muslim, *Ṣaḥīḥ*, vi.59; Abū Dā'ūd, *Sunan* iii.183.

23 In B. and A. 'or.'

24 In D. the last sentences of this paragraph and then the following seven paragraphs are missing.

25 In Z. 'lawful becomes intermixed with something unlawful.'

26 In Z. 'of unspecified objects.'

27 In D. the next two sentences in this paragraph and then the next two paragraphs are missing.

28 In B. and A. 'a problem arises.'

29 Bukhārī, *Ṣaḥīḥ*, p. 1218; Mālik, *Muwaṭṭā'*, v.1218; Ibn Ḥanbal, *Musnad*, iv.531 & iv.286; Ibn Māja in *Dibāja*, iii.516.

30 Bukhārī, *Ṣaḥīḥ*, p. 648; Ibn Ḥanbal, *Musnad*, vi.45-46. This *ḥadīth* was related on the authority of ʿAbd Allāh b. ʿAmr, and the name of the guilty one was Karkara.

31 This sentence and the one that follows it are missing in D.

32 Dārimī, *Sunan*, iii.1649; Ibn Ḥanbal, *Musnad*, xiii.479. Bukhārī, in his *al-Tārīkh al-kabīr*, i.145, related the same on the authority of Qābiṣa.

33 It is interesting to note that Z. explains here that the year in which this was written was 470 AH. See Z.vi.42.

34 Ibn Ḥanbal, *Musnad*, xv.293; Dārimī, *Sunan*, i.1650; Tirmidhī, *Sunan*, v.273-274; Ibn Māja, in *Dibāja*, iv.266.

35 This sentence is missing in D.

36 Ibn Ḥanbal, *Musnad*, v.201; Dārimī, *Sunan*, ii.1335; Shāfiʿī, *Umm*, vii.445.

37 This sentence and the one before it are missing in D.

38 Bukhārī, *Ṣaḥīḥ*, p. 648; Tirmidhī, *Sunan*, iv.139; Ibn Māja in *Dibāja*, iv.111-112; Ibn Ḥanbal, *Musnad*, vi.45-46.

39 Ibn Māja, *Sunan*, iv.111; Mālik, *Muwaṭṭā'*, iii.248; Ibn Ḥanbal, *Musnad*, xiii.243 and xvi.57.

40 From the beginning of the sentence to here, missing in D.

41 Q.v.3.

42 Ibn Māja, in *Dibāja*, iv.404; Ibn Ḥanbal, *Musnad*, xv.152; Dārimī, *Sunan*, iv.1281.

43 In Z. 'number.'

44 Literally, 'a tenth of a tenth.'

45 In A. and B. 'adultery.'

46 In A., B. and D. 'plants and animals.'

47 From here to the end of the sentence missing in Z.

48 Zaylaʿī, *Naṣb al-rāya*, i.154.

49 In B. this sentence is phrased as a statement rather than a question, as the interrogative article (*hal*) is replaced by the affirmative (*qad*).

50 This sentence is missing in D.

51 In A., D. and B. 'lawful.'

52 Q.XLIII.32.

53 'Whatever results from' missing in Z.

54 In D. 'and he returned.'

55 Ibn Ḥanbal, *Musnad*, III.532; Abū Dā'ūd, *Sunan*, v.14; Muslim, *Ṣaḥīḥ*, VIII.58.

56 Missing in D.

57 Tirmidhī, *Sunan*, v.50; Dārimī, *Sunan*, I.334; Tabarānī, *Kabīr*, VIII.278.

58 Q.XVIII.104.

59 The last name is missing in Z.

60 This paragraph is missing in D.

61 Aṭfīyash, *Sharḥ kitāb al-nīl fi-shifā' al-ʿalīl*.

62 Makkī, *Qūt*, II.474.

63 Makkī, *Qūt*, II.474.

64 Tabarānī, *Kabīr*, IX.150; Bayhaqī, *Shuʿab*, IX.411; Darwīsh, *Bughya*, I.424. Bukhārī, in his *Tārīkh al-kabīr*, I.145, related the same on the authority of Qābiṣa.

65 In Z. '... in regard to the buyer and the consumer.'

66 The last part of the sentence is missing in Z.

67 In Z. '... ownership is established by giving over possession of the cash.'

68 Ibn Ḥanbal, *al-Musnad*, II.142, XIII.320 & XIII.323; Muslim, *Ṣaḥīḥ*, v.35; Abū Dā'ūd, *Sunan*, III.456; Tirmidhī, III.565; Ḥākim, *Mustadrak*, II.42.

69 Ibn Māja in *Dibāja*, III.137; Ibn Ḥanbal, *Musnad*, XIII.320; Abū Dā'ūd, *Sunan*, III.457; Tirmidhī, *Sunan*, III.565.

70 This paragraph is missing in D.

71 Ibn Ḥanbal, *Musnad*, v.219; Darwīsh, *Bughya*, x.523.

72 In A. 'have related.'

73 Bukhārī, *Ṣaḥīḥ*, p.55; Muslim, *Ṣaḥīḥ*, VI.57; Tirmidhī, *Sunan*, IV.64; Ibn Ḥanbal, *Musnad*, XIV.118.

74 Abū Dā'ūd, *Sunan*, III.171-172; Ibn Ḥanbal, *Musnad*, x.100, x.123 & x.143; Ibn Māja in *Dibāja*, IV.380; Tirmidhī, *Sunan*, IV.72; Dārimī, *Sunan*, II.1280.

75 Bukhārī, *Ṣaḥīḥ*, p. 535; Muslim, *Ṣaḥīḥ*, VI.69; Ibn Ḥanbal, *Musnad*, I.471 & II.53; Dārimī, *Sunan*, II.1281.

76 Dārimī, *Sunan*, II.1684; Ibn Ḥanbal, *Musnad*, III.347.

77 Iṣfahānī, *Ḥilya*, III.130.

Chapter 3

1 Makkī, *Qūt*, II.484.

2 Makkī, *Qūt*, II.483.

3 Bukhārī, *Ṣaḥīḥ*, p.535; Ibn Ḥanbal, *Musnad*, VII.460.

4 Bukhārī, *Ṣaḥīḥ*, p.754; Muslim, *Ṣaḥīḥ*, VI.118.

5 Bukhārī, *Ṣaḥīḥ*, p.435; Muslim, *Ṣaḥīḥ*, VI.121; Abū Dā'ūd, *Sunan*, IV.95.

6 'Raced each other' missing in D.

7 Muslim, *Ṣaḥīḥ*, VI.1116; Ibn Ḥanbal, *Musnad*, x.398.

8 Q.XLIX.12.

9 Bukhārī, *Ṣaḥīḥ*, p.316; Muslim, *Ṣaḥīḥ*, III.213; Abū Dā'ūd, *Sunan*; Nasā'ī, *Sunan*, IV.159; Ibn Ḥanbal, *Musnad*, x.374. This was

also related in Makkī, *Qūt*, II.313.

10 This sentence and the one following it are missing in D.

11 Tirmidhī, *Sunan*, v.668; Dārimī, *Sunan*, III.1648; Ibn Ḥanbal, *Musnad*, II.347; Bayhaqī, *al-Sunan al-Kubrā*, v.335.

12 The tradition is missing in D. Its provenance and authenticity were discussed in Chapter Two.

13 The last part of this sentence and the following eight sentences are missing in D.

14 'The kind that gives rise to doubt,' missing in Z.

15 Literally, 'the Lord of Lords' (*rabb al-arbāb*).

16 This paragraph is missing in D.

17 Tirmidhī, *Sunan*, IV.601; Abū Dā'ūd, *Sunan*, v.108; Dārimī, *Sunan*, II.1308; Ibn Ḥanbal, *Musnad*, x.123.

18 Bayhaqī, *al-Sunan al-Kubrā*, IX.320.

19 This paragraph and the one that follows it is missing in D.

20 Makkī, *Qūt*, II.480-481.

21 Makkī, *Qūt*, II.460.

22 Makkī, *Qūt*, II.452.

23 In Z. an alternate reading is listed as, 'whom I know to be a soldier.'

24 ʿAbd al-Razzāq, *Muṣannaf*, x.150.

25 ʿAbd al-Razzāq, *Muṣannaf*, x.149; Bayhaqī, *al-Sunan al-Kubrā*, v.335.

26 Iṣfahānī, *Ḥilya*, I.83.

27 In B. and D. 'Khawwāt.'

28 Makkī, *Qūt*, II.463; Ibn Abī Shayba, *Muṣannaf*, XII.208.

29 This sentence and the three that follow it are missing in D.

30 Ibn Sallām, *Kitāb al-amwāl*, pp. 342–343; ʿAbd al-Razzāq, *Muṣannaf*, II.323; Ibn Qutayba, *ʿUyūn al-akhbār*, I.116. The incident is also mentioned in Shaybānī's *al-Sayr al-kabīr* according to Z.VI.89.

31 Hannād, *al-Zuhd*, II. 604.

32 In A. and Z. 'al-Ḥarth.'

33 In D. the tradition ends here. The remainder of the tradition is missing.

34 Bukhārī, *Ṣaḥīḥ*, p.1123; Tirmidhī, *Sunan*, III.448; Nasā'ī, *Sunan*, VI.417; Dārimī, *Sunan*, III.1446; Ibn Ḥanbal, *Musnad*, XII.470.

35 Ṭabarānī, *Kabīr*, XXV.174.

Chapter 4

1 In A., B. and D., 'to me.'

2 According to the commentator, this was one of the questions put to the Imam by Abū Bakr al-Marwazī and recorded in a volume entitled *Masā'il Abī Bakr al-Marwazī*. See Z.VI.96.

3 In B. 'without his saying a word.'

4 In Z. 'in the hand of his counterpart.'

5 In Z. 'one of the jurists did not…'

6 In Z. 'and the other means to return his property to him.'

7 In Z. 'intermixture.'

8 Missing in Z.

9 'To trade with' is missing in A., B. and D.

10 Muḥāsibī, *Makāsib*, p. 71.

11 Ibn Ḥanbal, *Musnad*, xvi.334; Abū Dā'ūd, *Sunan*, iii.407; Dārqutunī, *Sunan*, v.515; Bayhaqī, *al-Sunan al-Kubrā*, v.335; Bannūrī, *Maᶜārif al-Sunan*, i.34-35.

12 Q.xxx.1-3.

13 Tirmidhī, *Sunan*, v.334; Bayhaqī, *Dalā'il*, ii.333.

14 Ṭabarānī, *Kabīr*, iv.469.

15 Ibn Abī Shayba, *Muṣannaf*, xi.467.

16 Ibn ᶜAsākir, *Tārīkh Dimashq*, xxix.138.

17 Ibn Ḥanbal, *Waraᶜ*, p. 103.

18 Bukhārī, *Ṣaḥīḥ*, p. 480; Muslim, *Ṣaḥīḥ*, v.27; Ibn Ḥanbal, *Musnad*, x.477 and xviii.522; Tirmidhī, *Sunan*, iii.657; Dārimī, *Sunan*, iii.1703.

19 Ibn Ḥanbal, *Musnad*, v.218-219; al-Khaṭīb al-Baghdādī, *Tārīkh Baghdād*, xiv.21.

20 Ibn Ḥanbal, *Musnad*, xi.405 & xvii.80; Tirmidhī, *Sunan*, iii.566.

21 Ibn Ḥanbal, *Musnad*, xv.275-278; Ṭabarānī, *Kabīr*, xviii.170; Ibn Abī Shayba, *Muṣannaf*, xi.506.

22 Makkī, *Qūt*, ii.462.

23 Makkī, *Qūt*, ii.460; Ibn Ḥanbal, *Waraᶜ*, pp. 48-49.

24 Q.iii.97.

25 Ibn Ḥanbal, *Waraᶜ*, p. 148.

Chapter 5

1 'Forcibly' missing in D.

2 'Taken as the spoils of war' missing in D.

3 'Reward' instead of cloak in Z.

4 In Z. 'carpets.'

5 In Z. 'distributing the spoils of war.'

6 In B., Z. and A. 'agent.'

7 In Z. 'one is.'

8 In A., B. and D. 'that has given us pause.'

9 In D., A., and B. 'Yazīd b. ᶜAbd al-Malik.'

10 A similar saying was narrated by Muᶜādh b. Jabal. See Iṣfahānī, *Ḥilya*, iii.398; Būṣīrī, *Mukhtaṣar itḥāf al-khiyāra al-mahara*, viii.98; Bukhārī, *al-Tarīkh al-kabīr*, i.236.

11 This saying and the one that follows are missing in D.

12 Bayhaqī, *al-Sunan al-Kubrā*, vi.184; Ibn ᶜAsākir, *Tārīkh Dimashq*, lxiv.374.

13 Dhahabī, *Siyar aᶜlām al-nubala'*, ii.615; Ibn ᶜAsākir, *Tārīkh Dimashq*, lxiv.373; Bayhaqī, al-*Sunan al-Kubrā*, vi.184.

14 Ibn Abī Shayba, *Muṣannaf*, vii.203.

15 Dhahabī, *Siyar aᶜlām al-nubala'*, iii.220; Ibn Saᶜd, *Ṭabaqāt*, iv.140 & 147.

16 Ibn ᶜAsākir, *Tārīkh Dimashq*, xiv.113.

17 Ibn Abī Shayba, *Muṣannaf*, vii.201.

18 ᶜAbd al-Razzāq, *Muṣannaf*, viii.150.

19 Dhahabī, *Siyar aᶜlām al-nubala'*, iii.266; Ibn ᶜAsākir, *Tārīkh Dimashq*, lix.194; Ibn Abī Shayba, *Muṣannaf*, vii.201.

20 Ibn Saᶜd, *Ṭabaqāt*, viii.394.

21 Ibn Saᶜd, *Ṭabaqāt*, vii.129.

22 Ibn Saᶜd, *Ṭabaqāt*, iii.176.

23 A similar incident is related by Muḥibb al-Dīn al-Ṭabarī, *al-Riyāḍ al-naḍira*, II.56 & 388.

24 Hindī, *Kanz al-ʿummāl*, XII.669.

25 Bukhārī, *Ṣaḥīḥ*, p. 426; Dārimī, *Sunan*, XIII.212; Ibn Ḥanbal, *Musnad*, XIII.347; Iṣfahānī, *Ḥilya*, III.186.

26 Bukhārī, *Ṣaḥīḥ*, p. 26 & p. 426; Dārimī, *Sunan*, III.1647.

27 Shāfiʿī, *Umm*, III.146; Bayhaqī, *al-Sunan al-Kubrā*, IV.158; Ibn ʿAsākir, *Tārīkh Dimashq*, XXXVI.193-194.

28 Bukhārī, *Ṣaḥīḥ*, p. 282; Muslim, *Ṣaḥīḥ*, XIII.212; Ibn Ḥanbal, *al-Musnad*, XIII.347; Iṣfahānī, *Ḥilya*, VIII.186.

29 Ṭabarī, *al-Riyāḍ al-naḍira*, I.221; Ibn Saʿd, *Ṭabaqāt*, III.256.

30 In D. 'was not.'

31 This is an allusion to a *ḥadīth*. See Ibn Abī Dunyā, *Iṣlāḥ al-māl*, p. 8.

32 Tirmidhī, *Sunan*, I.6; Nasāʾī, *Sunan*, I.95; Ibn Māja, *Sunan*, I.164; Muslim, *Ṣaḥīḥ*, I.140; al-Khaṭīb al-Baghdādī, *Tārīkh Baghdād*, IV.321; Ibn Ḥajar, *Lisān al-mīzān*, p. 1127; Ibn Ḥajar, *Tahdhīb*, p. 1468.

33 Makkī, *Qūt*, II.489.

34 Makkī, *Qūt*, II.489.

35 Damīrī, *Ḥayāt al-ḥayawān al-kubrā*, I.458. The incident in the preceding paragraph is also mentioned by Damīrī.

36 Makkī, *Qūt*, II.474; Ibn Saʿd, *Ṭabaqāt*, IV.138.

37 In Z. 'ibn Yazīd.'

38 Ibn ʿAsākir, *Tārīkh Dimashq*, XXI.399; Yāfiʿī, *Mirʾāt al-jinān*, II.13; Bayhaqī, *Manāqib Imām al-Shāfiʿī*, II.226.

39 In Z. 'of their income.'

40 Lit. 'the tenth of a tenth.'

41 In D. 'have any compunction about their taking from them.'

42 Missing in B.

43 Sūlī, *Adab al-Kuttāb*, I.190-191; ʿAskarī, *Kitāb al-awāʾil*, pp. 88-89.

44 In Z. 'or give penuriously.'

45 Ibn ʿAsākir, *Tārīkh Dimashq*, XIV.113.

46 In Z. 'and to refrain from raising one's hand (against them).'

47 Missing in Z. all information related to *Kashf al-asrār*, i.e., from '...which is derived from.'

48 In Z. 'whose judges.'

49 In Z. 'is nourished by it'.

50 Suyūṭī, *Tārīkh al-khulafāʾ*, p. 84; Shāfiʿī, *Umm*, V.345.

51 Ibn Sallām, *Kitāb al-amwāl*, pp. 287-288.

52 Ibn Sallām, *Kitāb al-amwāl*, p. 286.

53 In A., D. and B. 'five gardens.'

Chapter 6

1 In Z. 'so that it may be known.'

2 In D. 'some of these two' i.e., texts of censure and texts of reproach.

3 In Z. 'according to what the *Sharīʿa* holds reprehensible.'

4 Haythamī, *Majmaʿ*, V.411; Ṭabarānī, *Kabīr*, XI.39.

5 Ibn Ḥanbal, *Musnad*, V.191

and x.80 and x.290; Tirmidhī, *Sunan*, IV.525 .

6 Ibn Māja in *Dibāja*, I.154.

7 According to the commentator, a similar version of this *ḥadīth* was related by Daylamī (*Firdaws*, I.155) on the authority of ʿUmar (Z.VI.125).

8 Daylamī, *Firdaws*, III.75.

9 This final narration is missing in D.

10 Iṣfahānī, *Ḥilya*, II.273; ʿAbd al-Razzāq, *Muṣannaf*, XI.316.

11 Ibn ʿAbd al-Barr, *Jāmiʿ bayān*, I.636.There is also a *ḥadīth* related by Ibn ʿAdī on the authority of Abū Hurayra in which the Messenger of God says something very similar to this. See Z.VI.127.

12 Ibn ʿAdī, *al-Kāmil*, II.35.

13 Iṣfahānī, *Ḥilya*, III.194; al-Qāḍī ʿAyyāḍ, *Tartīb al-madārik*, IV.76-77.

14 Daylamī, *Firdaws*, III.519. See Z.VI.128.

15 Bukhārī, *al-Tārīkh al-kabīr*, I.443; Ibn Mubārak, *Zuhd*, p. 129.

16 Ibn ʿAsākir, *Tārīkh Dimashq*, LXVIII.197.

17 Ibn Ḥanbal, *Musnad*, II.371; al-Khaṭīb al-Baghdādī, *Tārīkh Baghdād*, II.446.

18 Missing in D.

19 Q.III.187.

20 Q.XIX.59.

21 Q.XIV.38.

22 Ibn ʿAsākir, *Tārīkh Dimashq*, XXII.41; Iṣfahānī, *Ḥilya*, III.141.

23 In D. 'will be lost.'

24 In B. and D. 'ʿAlī.'

25 Iṣfahānī, *Ḥilya*, I.101; Ibn Abī Shayba, *Muṣannaf*, VIII.534.

26 Missing in D.

27 ʿIrāqī points out that this saying is incorrectly attributed to the Messenger of God, pointing to a report by al-Ḥasan that was included by Ibn Abī Dunyā in his *Kitāb al-ṣamt*. See Z.VI.133. Similar reports were narrated by Sufyān al-Thawrī and Yūsuf b. al-Asbāṭ. See Iṣfahānī, *Ḥilya*, VII.46 & VIII.240.

28 This and the following narration are missing in D.

29 Bayhaqī, *Shuʿab*, VI.509.

30 Ṭabarānī, *Kabīr*, XX.96.

31 'To commit more injustices' missing in A. and B. The entire paragraph is missing in D.

32 In Z. 'and supporters' (*al-Anṣār*).

33 In D. 'limit your visits to'.

34 Ḥākim, *al-Mustadrak*, VI.348; Ibn Ḥajar, *Fatḥ al-Bārī*, X.367.

35 Ibn Ḥanbal, *Musnad*, IX.304 & IX.498; Tirmidhī, *Sunan*, III.524.

36 In Z. 'you.'

37 Iṣfahānī, *Ḥilya*, II.166.

38 In A., B. and D. 'excess.'

39 Missing in A., B. and D.

40 Iṣfahānī, *Ḥilya*, V.291; Ibn al-Jawzī, *Muntaẓam*, VIII.295; Ibn ʿAsākir, *Tārīkh Dimashq*, LIII.132; al-Khaṭīb al-Baghdādī, *al-Jāmiʿ li-akhlāq al-rāwī*, I.562.

41 Ibn Abī Dunyā, *al-Zuhd*, p. 185.

42 Mizzī, *Tahdhīb al-kamāl*, XX.474; Dhahabī, *Siyar aʿlām al-nubalā'*, II.351; Ibn ʿAsākir, *Tārīkh*

Dimashq, XLVII.174; Ibn Mubārak, *Zuhd*, I.210.

43 In Z. 'how can one love or not love?'

44 In A., B. and D. 'O Commander of the Faithful!'

45 In A., B. and D. 'O Hishām.'

46 Ibn Khallikān, *Wafayāt*, II.510; Ḥamawī, *Thamarāt al-awrāq*, I.87.

47 Missing in Z.

48 Iṣfahānī, *Ḥilya*, VII.43

49 In A., B. and D. 'even if they were forced.'

50 In Z. 'took flight with.'

51 Ibn Abī Dunyā, *Muḥāsabat al-nafs*, p. 105.

52 The remainder of this paragraph is missing in D.

53 ʿIrāqī said that he was unable to find the source of this particular tradition. The commentator, however, mentions that Tirmidhī related a similar tradition on the authority of Abū Hurayra. See Z.VI.139. Hannād, *Zuhd*, I.327.

54 This is apparently a reference to the Bible at Ezekiel 34:3. 'Ye eat the fat, and ye clothe yourselves with the wool; ye kill those who are fed, but ye feed not the flock.'

55 In B. and D. 'your aloofness from.'

56 Ibn Qutayba, *ʿUyūn al-akhbār*, I.117.

57 Iṣfahānī, *Ḥilya*, V.288.

58 Q.LXXXII.13-14.

59 Q.VII.56.

60 Iṣfahānī, *Ḥilya*, III.161.

61 This paragraph is missing in Z. Iṣfahānī, *Ḥilya*, V.317.

62 In A., B., and D. 'the sharper of your two swords.'

63 Ibn ʿAsākir, *Tārīkh Dimashq*, LI.321; Ibn Qutayba, *ʿUyūn al-akhbār*, II.365; Qayrawānī, *Zuhar al-ādāb*, I.303.

64 Iṣfahānī, *Ḥilya*, IV.46; Ibn Mubārak, *Zuhd*, I.515.

65 Iṣfahānī, *Ḥilya*, IV.4.

66 In Z. *tarfaʿuhu* is added here, meaning that she ascribed the saying to the Messenger of God. This, however, is disputed at length by the commentator. See Z.VI.147-148.

67 According to Zabīdī, VI.147-148, the author erred in ascribing this to ʿĀʾisha. The tradition was, however, related by Quḍāʿī on the authority of Ibn ʿĀʾisha, a well known *muḥaddith* whose narrations were included in the collections of Abū Dāʾūd, Tirmidhī, Nasāʾī, and others. The tradition was also related on the authority of Ibn Masʿūd by Iṣfahānī, *Ḥilya*, IV.121, and by al-Khaṭīb al-Baghdādī in *Tārīkh Baghdād*, IV.277, though, again, there is a question as to whether it was something that Ibn Masʿūd himself said, or whether he heard it from the Messenger of God.

68 Daylamī, *Firdaws*, I.493. According to ʿIrāqī, the narrators of this *ḥadīth* were less than reliable and, for this reason, it appears in none of the authentic collections. See Z.VI.148.

69 Iṣfahānī, *Ḥilya*, II.354.

70 Bayhaqī, *al-Sunan al-Kubrā*, VII.266.

71 The quotation ends here in A., B. and D.

72 Q.xi.113.

73 In Z. 'fitting'

74 In A, B. and D.'it will remain to consider…'

75 Missing in D. In its place, the editor has placed the word 'weapons' in parentheses.

76 In A., B. and D. '…position of avoiding dealings…'

77 In Z. the word used is *irtifāʿ*, which is meaningless in the context of this discussion.

78 This sentence is not included in A., B. or D.

79 Ibn Abī Shayba, *Muṣannaf*, vii.794.

80 This tradition was related by Abū ʿAmr al-Dānī in his *Kitāb al-fitan* and by Daylamī in his *Musnad al-firdaws* (v.100) and, according to ʿIrāqī, the chains of both narrations are weak. See Z.vi.150. See also, Ibn Mubārak, *Zuhd*, i.282.

81 This paragraph is missing in D.

82 Abū Dā'ūd, *Sunan*, iv.55; Ibn Ḥanbal, *Musnad*, v.201-202; Ibn Māja in *Dibāja*, iv.495; Ḥākim, *Mustadrak*, iv.145; Ibn Abī Shayba, *Muṣannaf*, vii.444. In the version of the tradition related by Ibn ʿUmar, the Messenger of God stated, 'May God curse wine and those who drink it, those who pour it, who sell it, who buy it, who make it, who swallow it, who transport it, who receive it, and who live off its profits.'

83 Abū Dā'ūd, *Sunan*, iii.408; Ibn Ḥanbal, *Musnad*, i.439 & ii.162; Ibn Māja in *Dibāja*, iii.236; Tirmidhī, *Sunan*, iii.503; Dārimī, *Sunan*, iii.1650; Nasā'ī, *Sunan*, iii.236.

84 Jābir's version of the tradition was included in the collections of Muslim, *Ṣaḥīḥ* (v.50)and Ibn Ḥanbal, *Musnad* (iv.70), but with the addition of the words at the end, 'They are all the same.' ʿUmar's version of the tradition was related by Ibn Māja, *Sunan* (iii.236). The words of that tradition, however, are somewhat different. 'The last verse to be revealed was the verse about interest; and the Messenger of God, upon him be peace, died before he could explain it to us. So shun all interest, and whatever else is dubious.' Still other versions of this tradition were related by Bukhārī, Nasā'ī, etc.

85 In Z. much of this sentence is missing.

86 This tradition is missing in D.

87 According to ʿIrāqī, the chain of this *ḥadīth*'s transmission, in the collection of Abū Yaʿlā (iii.57) on the authority of Anas, was weak. The commentator, however, cites another version that was related by Ḥākim on the authority of Abū Hurayra. See Z.vi.152.

88 Muslim, *Ṣaḥīḥ*, vi.168; Ibn Ḥanbal, *Musnad*, viii.382.

89 Q.iv.97.

90 See Wāḥidī, *Asbāb al-nuzūl*, p. 180; Tabarānī, *Awsaṭ*, viii.280; Ṭabarī, *Jāmiʿ al-bayān*, ix.100-103.

91 Bayhaqī, *Shuʿab*, xii.40.

92 Ibn Ḥanbal, *Musnad*, iv.5.

93 In Z. *al-marāṣid*.

94 In Z., 'on the roads.'

95 In A., B. and D. 'or from a specific owner.'

96 According to the commentator, this was among the questions asked by Abū Bakr al-Marwazī and recorded by Makkī in *Qūt*. Z.vi.153. See also, Ibn Ḥanbal, *Wara*ʿ, p. 90.

97 In A., B. and D. 'and entering them.'

98 In Z. 'with reeds' (*bi-qaṣb*).

Chapter 7

1 The First, Second and Third Issues are missing in D.

2 In Z. 'it is asked.'

3 In the original, '*al-ḥall*' or '*al-ḥill*.' While I have chosen the first, the commentator would appear to have chosen the second, in which case the sentence would read, 'The [reason for] permission, however, is...'

4 In A. '*taqaddama*'; in B. and Z. '*yaqdumu*.'

5 In A. '*aḥad*'; in B. and Z. '*wāḥid*.'

6 In A. and B. '...except to say that it becomes his [the servant's] property.'

7 This entire section is missing in D.

8 In Z. '*rabṭ*'; in A. and B. '*ḍabṭ*.'

9 In Z. '...if they practice their profession in a shop, but not in order to earn a living.'

10 In Z. 'who wears...'

11 'To him,' not in B.

12 This entire issue is missing in D.

13 In B. '*aqwāl*.'

14 This sentence is missing in B.

15 Missing in Z. 'purpose.'

16 In Z. '*nasīb*,' and in A., B. and D. '*muntasib*'

17 In Z. '*mujāzif*' and in A., B. and D. '*kāthib*.'

18 In A. and B. 'or to someone [else].'

19 In Z. the commentator mentions an alternate text that reads '...as long as it is not used to assist in something unlawful.'

20 In Z. and D. '...in which there is no difficulty.'

21 In Z. '*min qalb*'; and in A., B. and D. '*min qibal*.'

22 In Z. '*li-ʿiwaḍ*'; and in A., B. and D. '*li-gharaḍ*'

23 Bukhārī, *al-Adab al-mufrad*, p. 254; Mālik, *al-Muwaṭṭā'*, v.1334. A slightly different version, 'Give gifts to one another, for gifts erase uneasiness from your hearts,' was related by Tirmidhī, *Sunan*, iv.441; Ibn Ḥanbal, *Musnad*, ix.152; Iṣfahānī, *Ḥilya*, iv.88; Dhahabī, *Mīzān al-iʿtidāl*, iv.246.

24 In A. and D. '... will be called a gift...'

25 In A., B. and D. '*ʿayn*', and in Z. '*nawʿ*'.

26. In A. and D. '*lā kāna lā yuhdā ilayhi*'; in B. '*lā yuhdā ilayhi*,' Z. '*lā mā uhdiya ilayhi*.'

27 In Z. 'a suspicion of.'

28 In A. and B. '*bi'l-wilāya*', in D. '*bi'l-āyāt*', and in Z. '*bi'l-wilāyāt*'.

29 In Z. and D. '... that the

affection will only remain by it [i.e., if the position remains]...'

30 The entire narration is missing in D.

31 Daylamī, *Firdaws*, II.327; Ibn ʿAdī, *al-Kāmil*, II.481; Suyūṭī, *al-Durr al-manthūr*, III.82.

32 Zamakhsharī, *Rabīʿ al-abrār*, V.318; Ṭabarī, *Jāmiʿ al-bayān*, X.321; Wakī, *Akhbār al-quḍā*, I.51.

33 In Z. *tashaffaʿa*; in A., B. and D. *shafaʿa*.

34 Bayhaqī, *Shuʿab*, VII.355.

35 Ibn Abī Shayba, *Muṣannaf*, VII.507.

36 According to ʿIrāqī, this incident was recorded by Shāfiʿī in *Ikhtilāf al-ʿIrāqīyīn*. See Z.VI.162. Mālik, *al-Muwaṭṭā'*, IV.992. The incident was mentioned in greater detail in Chapter Five.

37 In A., D. and Z. *khātūn*.

38 According to ʿIrāqī, this was narrated in Shaybānī's, *al-Sayr al-kabīr* (See Sarakhsī, *Sharh al-sayr al-kabīr*, I.1241); though it was the wife of ʿUmar who sent the perfume. See Z.VI.162.

39 ʿIrāqī explains that while it appears the author attributes this statement to the two mentioned, in fact they both relate the same from the Messenger. Those narrations, however, are weak. See Z.VI.162-163.

40 Bukhārī related this (*Ṣaḥīḥ*, p. 539) in explanation of a chapter title in the Book of Gifts, Chapter of One who Does not Accept a Gift for a Reason. Bukhārī's commentator, Ibn Ḥajar explains that the story about ʿAbd al-ʿAzīz was related by Ibn Saʿd in his *Ṭabaqāt* on the authority of Furāṭ b. Muslim. The *ḥadīth* of the Prophet on the subject was related by Bukhārī, *Ṣaḥīḥ*, p. 537; Tirmidhī, *Sunan*, IV.338; Abū Dā'ūd, *Sunan*, III.517; and Ibn Ḥanbal, *Musnad*, VIII.396 all on the authority of ʿĀ'isha.

41 Bukhārī, *Ṣaḥīḥ*, p .1516; Muslim, *Ṣaḥīḥ*, VI.11; and Ibn Ḥanbal, *Musnad*, XVII.47.

APPENDIX

PERSONS CITED IN THE TEXT—EXCLUDING PROPHETS

AL-ʿABBĀS IBN ʿABD AL-MUṬṬALIB (d. 32/653). He was uncle to the Prophet and his senior by two years. Al-ʿAbbās was known as one of Mecca's leading merchants and financiers. (Ibn Ḥajar, *Iṣāba*, II.263; Ibn al-Athīr, *Usd al-ghāba*, III.163.)

ʿABD ALLĀH IBN ʿĀMIR ibn Kurayz (d. 59/680). A Companion of considerable piety, he was appointed Governor of Basra by his nephew, the Caliph ʿUthmān and, years later, by Muʿāwiya. (Ibn al-Athīr, *Usd al-ghāba*, III.289.)

ʿABD ALLĀH IBN ʿUMAR (d. 73/693). Son of the Caliph ʿUmar ibn al-Khaṭṭāb, he was counted among the most righteous and God-fearing of all the Companions. (Ibn Ḥajar, *Iṣāba*, II.238.)

ʿABD AL-MALIK IBN MARWĀN (d. 86/705). As the fifth in the line of the Umayyad Caliphs, he was responsible for consolidating power for his dynasty, though at the expense of disrupting the lives of many of his most devout citizens. (Ibn Saʿd, *Ṭabaqāt*, V.165-175.)

ABŪ ʿABD ALLĀH AL-ṬŪSĪ, al-Nuʿmān ibn Muḥammad (d. 288/901). He was a narrator of traditions and an ascetic from Khurasan who travelled widely in search of *ḥadīth* material. (Samʿānī, *Ansāb*, I.462.)

ABŪ AYYŪB AL-ANṢĀRĪ (d. 52/672). A Companion and early supporter of the Prophet at Medina, he served as its governor and, years later, was martyred in a campaign against the Byzantines. He was buried outside the gates of Constantinople and his grave is still visited today. (Ibn Ḥajar, *Iṣāba*, I.404-405.)

ABŪ BAKR AL-ṢIDDĪQ (d. 13/634). The first of the four Rightly-Guided Caliphs in Islam, he was the closest of all the Prophet's Companions. (Ibn al-Athīr, *Usd al-ghāba*, III.310-331.)

ABŪ BAKRA (d. 51/671). From his origins as an Abyssinian slave, he became a Companion and one of early Islam's most outstanding examples of moral rectitude. (Ibn al-Athīr, *Usd al-ghāba*, V.149 AND V.334.)

ABŪ AL-DARDĀ' (d. 32/652). A noted Companion and member of the *Ahl al-Ṣuffa*, he is best known for efforts to collect and preserve the text of the Qur'an. (Iṣfahānī, *Ḥilya*, I.208-227.)

ABŪ DHARR, Jundub ibn Junāda (d. 32/652). He was a very pious Companion who was known chiefly for his reticence about people and their society. He was also a transmitter of many traditions. (Ibn ʿAbd al-Barr, *Istiʿāb*, I.252-256.)

ABŪ ḤANĪFA, al-Nuʿmān (d. 150/767). A jurist of the Successor generation, he was the founder of the school of jurisprudence in Kufa that bears his name and which is the first, chronologically, among the four classical Sunni schools. (Ibn Khallikān, *Wafayāt*, V.401-415.)

ABŪ ḤĀZIM, Salama ibn Dīnār (d. 140/757). Father to the famed jurist, Ḥammād, he was numbered among the most pious of the inhabitants of Medina. (Iṣfahānī, *Ḥilya*, III.229-259.)

ABŪ ḤUMAYD AL-SĀʿIDĪ (d. 60/679). A Companion and narrator of traditions who died during the end of Muʿāwiya's caliphate or the early days of Yazīd's. (Ibn Ḥajar, *Taqrīb*, 635.)

ABŪ HURAYRA (d. 58/677). He was one of the most prolific of the Companion narrators, and one who spent a great deal of time with the Messenger of God during the latter years in Medina. (Ibn Ḥajar, *Iṣāba*, IV.200-208.)

ABŪ MŪSĀ AL-ASHʿARĪ (d. 50/670). One of the most influential of the Medinan Companions, he was appointed governor of Basra by ʿUmar. (Ibn al-Athīr, *Usd al-ghāba*, III.364-365.)

ABŪ SĀʿĪD AL-KHUḌARĪ (d. 64/683). Another of the more prolific Companion narrators, Abū Saʿīd was numbered among the most pious of the Medinans. (Ibn Ḥajar, *Iṣāba*, IV.32-33.)

ABŪ THAʿLABA AL-KHUSHANĪ (d. 55/675). A Companion from Medina who pledged his allegiance to the Prophet at the *Bayʿat al-Riḍwān*. Later he moved to Syria where he died. (Ibn al-Athīr, *Usd al-ghāba*, VI.43-44.)

ABŪ ʿUBAYDA IBN AL-JARRĀḤ (d. 18-639). One of the 'Ten Promised Paradise', he was born in Mecca and accompanied the Prophet on all of his expeditions. (Ibn al-Athīr, *Usd al-ghāba*, VI.201-202.)

ʿADĪ IBN ḤĀTIM (d. 68/637). A Companion of the Prophet whose reputation for generosity is nearly without equal among the Arabs. (Ibn al-Athīr, *Usd al-ghāba*, IV.7-10.)

Appendix

AḤMAD IBN ḤANBAL (d. 241/855). A traditionist of the first order from Baghdad, he was the founder of the fourth of the classical Sunni schools of jurisprudence. Like the founders of the other schools, Imam Aḥmad was also renowned for his devotion and piety. (Iṣfahānī, *Ḥilya*, IX.161-234.)

AḤNAF IBN QAYS (d. 67/687). Renowned for his sagacity, he converted to Islam and led his entire tribe, Banū Tamīm, to Islam. (Ibn al-Athīr, *Usd al-ghāba*, I.178-179; Ibn Saʿd, *Ṭabaqāt*, VII.66.)

ʿĀ'ISHA BINT ABĪ BAKR (d. 58/678). She was the wife of the Prophet and an important narrator of traditions dealing with his personal life. She was also numbered among the most learned of all the Companions. (Ibn al-Athīr, *Usd al-ghāba*, IV.186-189.)

AL-ʿALĀ' IBN ZUHAYR al-Azdī (no dates). Son of a tax collector in Ḥulwān who was also a governor of Egypt for five months in 173 A.H. (Al-Kindī, *Kitāb al-wulāh*, 101.)

ʿALĪ IBN ABĪ ṬALIB (d. 40/661). The cousin and son-in-law of the Prophet, he became the fourth of the four Rightly-Guided Caliphs. (Ibn ʿAbd al-Barr, *Istiʿāb*, III.1089-1124.)

ʿALĪ IBN MAʿBAD IBN SHADDĀD (d. 218/833). Originally from Merv, he travelled to Egypt with his father and later studied jurisprudence in the Ḥanbalī school. He was also an accomplished traditionist. (Ibn Ḥajar, *Tahdhīb al-Tahdhīb*, VI.336-337.)

ANAS IBN MĀLIK (d. 93/711). Anas was a Companion and a celebrated narrator who, at an early age, became the personal servant of the Prophet. (Ibn Ḥajar, *Iṣāba*, I.84-85.)

ʿĀTIKA BINT ZAYD IBN ʿAMR IBN NUFAYL ((d. 40/660). She was a poetess from a noble Meccan family, and the wife of the first and the second of the four Rightly-Guided Caliphs, Abū Bakr and then ʿUmar ibn al-Khaṭṭāb. (Ibn ʿAbd al-Barr, *Istiʿāb*, IV.1876-1880; Ibn al-Athīr, *Usd al-ghāba*, VII.181-183.)

AL-AWZĀʿĪ, ʿABD AL-RAḤMĀN (d. 157/774). He was one of the major jurists in Syria during the classical period, and the founder of a school of Sunni jurisprudence named after him which had a following for a few centuries. (Ibn Khallikān, *Wafayāt*, III.127-128.)

BARĪRA (d. 60-64/680-683). She was a Companion and the freed slave of ʿĀ'isha who figures prominently in several important narrations concerning the *Sunna*. (Ibn Ḥajar, *Tahdhīb al-Tahdhīb*, XII.403.)

BISHR IBN AL-ḤĀRITH AL-ḤĀFĪ (d. 227/841). As one who lived an exemplary spiritual life, Bishr is a celebrated figure in Sufi literature. He lived most of his life in Baghdad. (Iṣfahānī, *Ḥilya*, VIII.336–360.)

DHŪ'L-NŪN AL-MIṢRĪ (d. 246/861). An Egyptian by birth, he was a pious and learned man whose teachings about the life of the spirit were adopted widely by the Sufis. (Iṣfahānī, *Ḥilya*, IX.331–395.)

AL-FUḌAYL IBN ʿIYĀḌ (d. 187/803). A man of learning and piety, he studied jurisprudence and traditions with both Abū Ḥanīfa in Kufa and with Sufyān in Mecca. (Dhahabī, *Siyar*, XIII.449.)

ḤABĪB IBN ABĪ THĀBIT (d. 120/738). A jurist of the Successor generation, he was a mufti of Kufa and a figure of exceeding piety. (Dhahabī, *Siyar*, V.288.)

AL-ḤAJJĀJ IBN YŪSUF al-Thaqafī (d. 95/714). A governor of Iraq under the Umayyads, he was responsible for horrible excesses against the populace and their spiritual leadership, many of whom were among the cream of the Successor generation. His atrocities include the bombardment of the holy city of Mecca during the pilgrimage. (Dhahabī, *Siyar*, XII.301; Daynūrī, *Akhbār*, I.314–316; Ibn Kathīr, *Bidāya*, VI.262–266.)

ḤAKĪM IBN JUBAYR (d. no dates). He was a narrator of traditions and a student of Ibrāhīm al-Nakhaʿī at Kufa. (Ibn Saʿd, *Ṭabaqāt*, VI.326.)

ḤAMMĀD IBN SALAMA ibn Dīnār al-Baṣrī (d. 167/784). A conservative jurist and the mufti of Basra, he is credited with contributions to the development of Islamic jurisprudence. (Bukhārī, *Tārīkh*, III.21–23.)

AL-ḤĀRITH AL-MUḤĀSIBĪ (d. 243/857). An early Sufi of Baghdad, he spent his life teaching and writing. His major work, *The Observance of God's Rights*, is said to have been a major influence on Ghazālī, and figured significantly in the way that his *Revival* was written. (Dhahabī, *Siyar*, V.95.)

HĀRŪN AL-RASHĪD (d. 193/809). The fifth and most celebrated of the Abbasid Caliphs in Baghdad who personified the glory of the Caliphate in the Golden Age of Islam. (Tabarī, *Tārīkh*, VIII.230.)

AL-ḤASAN IBN ʿALĪ (d. 49/669). The grandson of the Prophet who laid claim to the caliphate after his father ʿAlī's martyrdom. Following his renunciation of that office in favour of Muʿāwiya, al-Ḥasan lived a quiet life of devotion in Medina. (Ibn ʿAbd al-Barr, *Istiʿāb*, I.383–392.)

AL-ḤASAN AL-BAṢRĪ (d. 110/728). Ḥasan was perhaps one of the best-known scholars of the Successor generation. He was a jurist and a narrator of traditions whose rectitude and devotion attracted for him a vast following. (Iṣfahānī, *Ḥilya*, II.131–161.)

ḤASSĀN IBN ABĪ SINĀN (d. 180/796). A pious man from Basra. (Dhahabī, *Siyar*, II.581.)

ḤĀTIM AL-AṢAMM (d. 237/851). He was a pious man from Balkh known far and wide for his wisdom. (Iṣfahānī, *Ḥilya*, VIII.73–84.)

HISHĀM IBN ʿABD AL-MALIK (d. 125/743). The tenth of the Umayyad caliphs, he was a religious man and showed great respect toward the famous traditionist, al-Zuhrī. (Zirkilī, *Aʿlām*, VIII.86.)

ḤUDHAYFA IBN AL-YAMĀN (d. 36/656). As one of the first to convert to Islam, he was a close and trusted Companion who was also known as the 'Keeper of the Prophet's Secrets'. ʿUmar appointed him governor of Madā'in. (Ibn Ḥajar, *Iṣāba*, I.316–317; Ibn al-Athīr, *Usd al-ghāba*, I.706–708.)

ḤUSAYN IBN ʿALĪ (d. 61/680). The grandson of the Prophet who rose in rebellion against Yazīd ibn Muʿāwiya. He was martyred alongside nearly every member of his immediate family in the Iraqi desert near Karbala. (Dhahabī, *Siyar*, I.225–251.)

IBN ʿABBĀS, ʿABD ALLĀH (d. 68/688). He was the cousin of the Prophet, a narrator of traditions, and a great scholar of the Qur'an. (Iṣfahānī, *Ḥilya*, I.314–329.)

IBN ABĪ LAYLĀ, Muḥammad ibn ʿAbd al-Raḥmān (d. 148/765). A jurist of considerable abilities who served as the qadi of Kufa under both the Umayyads and the Abbasids. (Wakī b. Jarrāḥ, *Akhbār al-quda*, II.406–408; Ibn Saʿd, *Ṭabaqāt*, II.649.)

IBN ABĪ SHUMAYLA, ʿABD AL-RAḤMĀN (no dates). He is known to have been a reliable narrator whose students included Ḥammād ibn Zayd. (Dhahabī, *Kāshif*, II.168.)

IBN MAʿMAR (d. 82/701). He was a military governor in Iraq under the Umayyad Caliph ʿAbd al-Malik. (Ibn al-Jawzī, *Muntaẓam*, VI.25.)

IBN MASʿŪD, ʿABD ALLĀH (d. 32/652). One of the first converts to Islam and one of the closest of all the Companions to the Prophet. He later moved to Kufa where he spent the remainder of his life teaching the Qur'an and its legal implications. (Ibn Ḥajar, *Iṣāba*, II.360–362.)

IBN AL-MUBĀRAK, ʿABD ALLĀH (d. 181/797). A jurist and a narrator of traditions who studied with Abū Ḥanīfa and Mālik ibn Anas. He is best known for his asceticism and his love of jihad. (Iṣfahānī, *Ḥilya*, VIII.162–191.)

IBN SĪRĪN, ABŪ BAKR MUḤAMMAD (d. 110/728). Contemporary and friend of al-Ḥasan al-Baṣrī; he was a jurist and a traditionist of the first order. (Iṣfahānī, *Ḥilya*, II.263–282.)

IBRĀHĪM IBN ADHAM (d. 161/777). He was a jurist who studied with Abū Ḥanīfa, and a man of exceeding piety. (Iṣfahānī, *Ḥilya*, VII.367–395.)

IBRĀHĪM AL-NAKHAʿĪ, Ibn Yazīd (d. 96/715). Ibrāhīm was one of the pillars of the Kufan school of rational jurisprudence that found its most complete expression in the Ḥanafī school. He was a purist with regard to the narration of traditions and a very devout individual. (Iṣfahānī, *Ḥilya*, IV.219–240.)

IBRĀHĪM AL-TAYMĪ, Ibn Yazīd (d. 93/712). A noted narrator of traditions from Kufa and the teacher of al-Aʿmash. (Iṣfahānī, *Ḥilya*, IV.210–219.)

JĀBIR IBN ʿABD ALLĀH AL-ANṢĀRĪ (d. 68–78/687–697). A Companion from Medina and a veteran of the Prophet's campaigns. Jābir was also a prolific narrator of traditions. (Ibn Ḥajar, *Iṣāba*, I.214–215.)

JĀBIR IBN ZAYD (d. 93/712). A famed jurist and scholar of the Qur'an from the Successor generation in Basra, he was exiled to Oman by al-Ḥajjāj. (Iṣfahānī, *Ḥilya*, III.85–92.)

JAʿFAR IBN MUḤAMMAD AL-ṢĀDIQ (d. 148/756). A man of learning and piety, and descended from the family of the Prophet (al-Ḥusayn was his grandfather), the Jaʿfarī Shiʿite sect was named for him. Even so, some of the major figures of the Sunni orthodoxy are numbered among his students, including Abū Ḥanīfa and Mālik ibn Anas. (Ibn Ḥajar, *Tahdhīb al-Tahdhīb*, II.104.)

JUWAYRIYYA BINT AL-ḤĀRITH (d. 50/670). She was wed to the Prophet following the defeat of her tribe, Banū Muṣṭaliq in year five of the Hijra. (Kuḥāla, *Aʿlām al-nisa*, I.227.)

KHALID IBN AL-WALĪD (d. 21/642). A Companion of the Prophet and nephew of the Prophet's wife Maymūna bint al-Ḥārith. His exploits on the field of battle prompted the Prophet to call him the 'Sword of Allāh', and under his leadership the armies of Islam were triumphant at Mecca, Ḥunayn, Iraq and Syria. (Dhahabī, *Siyar*, I.366.)

MAKḤŪL AL-SHĀMĪ, Abū ʿAbd Allāh (d. 112/731). Enslaved as a prisoner of war in Kabul, he was later freed in Damascus where he rose to prominence as a jurist. He is also thought to have authored one of the earliest collections of traditions, *Sunan*. (Shīrazi, Ibn Saᶜd, *Ṭabaqāt*, I.175; Ibn al-Nadīm, *The Fihrist*, 550.)

MĀLIK IBN ANAS (d. 179/795). The founder of the second of the four major schools of Sunni jurisprudence, he emphasized the importance of the customs and practices of the people of Medina as sources for his jurisprudence. (Ibn Khallikān, *Wafayāt*, II.545.)

MĀLIK IBN DĪNĀR (d. 131/748). A famed ascetic from Basra, he made a living from copying the Qur'an. He was an eloquent speaker and relater of oral traditions [*qāṣṣ*]. (Iṣfahānī, *Ḥilya*, II.357-389.)

AL-MANṢŪR ABŪ JAᶜFAR AL-ᶜABBĀSĪ (d. 158/775). The second in the line of the Abbasid caliphs and the one that made Baghdad the seat of the caliphate, he put down rebellions, expanded the empire's borders, and proved himself a gifted politician. (Ibn Kathīr, *Bidāya*, XIII.301-302.)

MARWĀN IBN AL-ḤAKAM (d. 65/675). Born in the lifetime of the Prophet, he moved to Ṭā'if as a child and the two never met. As a cousin to ᶜUthmān, he served as his secretary, and later was governor of Bahrain and then Medina under Muᶜāwiya. For the last ten months of his life, he reigned as the Umayyad Caliph, thus securing the throne for his son and five of his grandsons, and earning for himself the nickname 'The Father of Tyrants' (Abū'l-Jabābira). (Ibn al-Athīr, *Usd al-ghāba*, V.139-141.)

MASRŪQ IBN AL-AJDAᶜ (d. 63/683). He was a traditionist of the Successor generation who lived in Kufa. (Khaṭīb al-Baghdādī, *Tārīkh Baghdād*, XIII.232-235.)

MISWAR IBN MAKHRAMA (d. 64-680). Nephew to ᶜAbd al-Raḥmān ibn ᶜAwf, he was a Companion who was known for his learning and piety. He was martyred by a catapult during the bombardment of Mecca by the army of Yazīd under Ḥusayn ibn Numayr. (Ibn al-Athīr, *Usd al-ghāba*, V.170-171.)

MUᶜĀWIYA IBN ABĪ SUFYĀN (d. 60/680). A Companion, he became the founder of the Umayyad caliphate following his victory at the battle of Ṣiffīn. Under Abū Bakr he led armies against the Byzantines in Syria and was later appointed governor of Syria by ᶜUmar. (Ibn al-Athīr, *Usd al-ghāba*, V.201-204.)

MUGHĪRA IBN SHUᶜBA (d. 50/670). He was a Companion who followed the politics of his times in an astute manner, so that he was appointed governor of Basra under ᶜUthmān and of Kufa under Muᶜāwiya. (Ibn al-Athīr, *Usd al-ghāba*, V.238-240.)

MUḤAMMAD IBN MUQĀTIL (d. 226/841). A noted jurist of Merv, he was also a reliable narrator who related traditions to Bukhārī at Mecca. (Qurashī, *Jawāhir*, I.121.)

MUḤAMMAD IBN ṢĀLIḤ (d. 271/887). A traditionist and pious man from Baghdad, also known as Kalīja, who travelled widely in search of traditions to narrate. He died at Mecca. (Dhahabī, *Siyar*, XII.526.)

MUḤAMMAD IBN SULAYMĀN (d. 173/789). He served as governor of Basra under two Caliphs, al-Mahdī and Hārūn al-Rashīd, and was numbered among the less reliable traditionists. (Dhahabī, *Mīzān*, III.572.)

MUḤAMMAD IBN WĀSIᶜ (d. 123/731). He was a traditionist and a jurist from Basra who was known for his extreme caution in matters of religion. (Iṣfahānī, *Ḥilya*, II.345–357.)

MUḤAMMAD IBN YŪSUF (d. 91/710). The brother of al-Ḥajjāj and an official of the Caliph in Yemen. He was the grandfather of the Umayyad al-Walīd. (Dhahabī, *Siyar*, V.372–374.)

AL-MUKHTĀR AL-THAQAFĪ (d. 67/686). A Shiᶜite extremist of the Successor generation, he opposed the Umayyad caliphate and fought with Ibn Zubayr in the defence of Mecca from Ibn Numayr. Later, however, he opposed Ibn Zubayr and ruled over Kufa in the name of Muḥammad ibn al-Ḥanafiyya, until he was finally defeated by Ibn Zubayr's forces. He was also the brother-in-law of ᶜAbd Allāh ibn ᶜUmar and it was this relationship that he exploited throughout his lifetime. (Dhahabī, *Siyar*, III.538.)

NĀFIᶜ *mawlā* IBN ᶜUMAR (d. 119/143). A jurist and a scholar of traditions from the Successor generation who spent his life in the service of Ibn ᶜUmar, even after he was freed. (Dhahabī, *Siyar*, V.95.)

AL-NAẒẒĀM, ABŪ ISḤĀQ (d. 225/840). A Muᶜtazilite scholar of Baghdad, he was a poet and philosopher whose opinions often offended the orthodox scholars of his times. Thus, his insistence on the need for free thinking led him to take the position that the consensus of the Companions had little validity for those who follow. (Dhahabī, *Siyar*, X.541.)

NUᶜAYM AL-MUJMIR ibn ᶜAbd Allāh (no dates). A narrator of traditions from Medina who spent twenty years in the service of Abū Hurayra, learning traditions from him. Either he or his father was known as a *mujmir* or one who burns incense in mosques. (Ibn Ḥajar, *Taqrīb*, 565; Dhahabī, *Kāshif*, III.207.)

RĀFĪ IBN KHUDAYJ (d. 74/694). He was a Companion from Medina who, as a very young man, presented himself for battle at Badr but was turned back by the Prophet. Rāfī finally had his wish fulfilled at Uḥud, after which he took part in all of the battles for the defence of Islam. Throughout his life he remained a leader of his tribe in Medina. (Ibn al-Athīr, *Usd al-ghāba*, II.232–234.)

SᶜAD IBN ABĪ WAQQĀṢ (d. 55/675). He was one of the 'Ten Promised Paradise' by the Prophet, and one of the most prominent and pious of all the Companions. (Dhahabī, *Siyar*, I.92–124.)

ṢAFIYYA BINT ḤUYAYY ibn Akhṭab (d. 50/670). She was a wife of the Prophet and the daughter of a vanquished Jewish leader at Khaybar. She lived a life of simple piety, and was clearly devoted to the Prophet despite the ill will that greeted her initially from certain of the believers in Medina. (Dhahabī, *Siyar*, II.231–238.)

SAHL AL-TUSTARĪ (d. 283/896). Sahl was an ascetic given to austerity who, especially following his move to Basra, attracted a considerable following. His spiritual experiences and insights, some of which led to controversy, have been preserved in works ascribed to him and to his students. (Dhahabī, *Tārīkh*, XXI.11.)

SAHNŪN IBN SAᶜĪD AL-TANUKHĪ (d. 240/855). A close companion to Imam Mālik, he was a great jurist in his own right. He is best known for his role in preserving the legal opinions and rulings of Imam Mālik in his *al-Mudawwana al-kubrā* (The Greatest Collection). (al-Qāḍī ᶜAyyāḍ, *Tartīb*, IV.45–88.)

SAᶜĪD IBN JUBAYR (d. 95/714). He was a jurist of the Successor generation known equally for his learning as well as his piety. He was martyred by al-Ḥajjaj ibn Yūsuf. (Ibn Saᶜd, *Ṭabaqāt*, VI.178.)

SAᶜĪD IBN AL-MUSAYYAB (d. 94/713). He was one of the most prominent authorities of the Successor generation in Medina on the subjects of the *Sunna* and the law, and his legal opinions formed the basis for much of what later became the Mālikī school of jurisprudence. (Iṣfahānī, *Ḥilya*, II.161–176.)

SALAMA IBN AL-AKWAᶜ (d. 74/694). A Companion of proven valour on the battlefield, he was one of the Medinans who pledged early allegiance to the Prophet, thus opening the way for the Hijra. (Ibn al-Athīr, *Usd al-ghāba*, II.517–518.)

SALMĀN AL-FĀRISĪ (d. 36/656). A Companion of Persian origins who became close to the Prophet and whose practice of Islam became a model for later generations of Sufis. He is perhaps best known as the one who suggested the digging of a trench around Medina as a defensive measure at the time of the Battle of the Trench. (Iṣfahānī, *Ḥilya*, I.185–208.)

SAMNŪN IBN ḤAMZA (d. 298/910). A disciple of Sarī al-Saqaṭī and a poet, he was known as *al-Muḥibb,* the lover, because of his love for God and his unceasing devotion and remembrance. (Dhahabī, *Tārīkh*, XXII.156–157.)

SARĪ AL-SAQAṬĪ (d. 253/867). Sarī began his life as a merchant and a student of *ḥadīth* in Baghdad. After meeting Maᶜrūf al-Karkhī, however, he began to travel the Sufi path and eventually became a very accomplished teacher with a huge following. (Iṣfahānī, *Ḥilya*, X.112–128.)

AL-SHAᶜBĪ, ABŪ ᶜAMR IBN SHARAḤĪL (d. 103/721). He was a famed jurist and narrator of traditions from the Successor generation who also served as a judge in Kufa. He was also a poet and won the admiration of many, including the Caliph ᶜAbd al-Malik. (Khaṭīb al-Baghdādī, *Tārīkh Baghdād*, XII.227–234.)

AL-SHĀFIᶜĪ, MUḤAMMAD IBN IDRĪS (d. 202/820). He was a skilled jurist and the founder of the third of the four Sunni schools of jurisprudence. He studied in Baghdad for a time under Muḥammad al-Shaybānī, in Medina under Mālik ibn Anas, and in Mecca with Sufyān ibn ᶜUyayna before settling in Cairo where he did most of his work, including the first treatise on theoretical jurisprudence (*uṣūl al-fiqh*) entitled *al-Risāla*. (Khaṭīb al-Baghdādī, *Tārīkh Baghdād*, II.56–73.)

SUFYĀN AL-THAWRĪ (d. 166/777). A narrator of traditions and a jurist from Kufa, Sufyān was perhaps best known for his asceticism. His jurisprudence was characterized by its literalist reading of *ḥadīth* sources, and was therefore clearly distinguishable from the jurisprudence of his contemporary, Abū Ḥanīfa. (Dhahabī, *Siyar*, VI.229–279.)

SUFYĀN IBN ᶜUYAYNA (d. 198/814). A student of Zuhrī in *ḥadīth* and endowed with a phenomenal memory, Sufyān is best remembered for preserving the traditionist approach to Islamic jurisprudence in the Hijaz. (Dhahabī, *Siyar*, VIII.545–475.)

SULAYMĀN IBN ᶜABD AL-MALIK IBN MARWĀN (d. 99/717). He was seventh in the line of Umayyad caliphs and, though his rule was brief, it was tyrannical and oppressive. (Dhahabī, *Siyar*, VI.377–383.)

SULAYMĀN IBN AL-TARKHĀN AL-TAYMĪ (d. 43/663). He was a narrator from Basra who was noted for his piety. (Ibn Ḥajar, *Taqrīb*, 252.)

ṬĀWŪS IBN KAYSĀN AL-YAMĀNĪ (d. 106/725). He was a leading scholar of the Successor generation who spent years in the company of his teacher, ᶜAbd Allāh ibn ᶜAbbās. (Ibn Saᶜd, *Ṭabaqāt*, V.391.)

ᶜUBĀDA IBN AL-ṢĀMIT (d. 34/654). A Medinan signatory to the first and second *bayʿat al-ʿUqba,* ʿUbada was one of the first believers and took part in all of the battles of early Islam. He was also one of first five residents of Medina to memorize the Qur'an in its entirety. (Ibn al-Athīr, *Usd al-ghāba,* III.158–160.)

ʿUBAYD ALLĀH IBN ʿUMAR (d. 37/657). He was the youngest of ʿUmar's sons and a celebrated swordsman and rider in the tradition of the desert Arabs. His spontaneous revenge for his father's murder left him at the mercy of the next Caliph ʿUthmān whose decision to forgive him began a long chain of political difficulties. ʿUbayd Allāh fell at the Battle of Ṣiffīn while fighting alongside Muʿāwiya. (Ibn al-Athīr, *Usd al-ghāba,* III.522–523.)

ʿUMAR IBN ʿABD AL-ʿAZĪZ (d. 101/720). Known as the fifth of the Four Rightly-Guided Caliphs, he was the eighth in the line of Umayyad caliphs and the one among them noted for his rectitude and observance of Islamic norms. (Dhahabī, *Siyar,* V.114.)

ʿUMAR IBN AL-KHAṬṬĀB (d. 23/644). The second of the Four Rightly-Guided Caliphs, he was a powerful and influential figure both during the lifetime of the Prophet and after. He was especially known for his personal integrity and devotion to the faith. (Ibn Ḥajar, *Iṣāba,* II.260–261.)

UMM SULAYM BINT MILḤĀN (no dates). She was a Companion from Medina who was known for her devotion to the person of the Prophet. When the Prophet first arrived at Medina, she offered her son, Anas ibn Mālik, then only eight or nine years old, to him as a personal servant. (Ibn al-Athīr, *Usd al-ghāba,* VII.333–334.)

ʿUQBA IBN AL-ḤĀRITH (no dates). A Companion from Mecca who came to Islam following the liberation (*fatḥ*) of that city. He is known for two distasteful incidents: one was mentioned in the text, and the other was his involvement with ʿAbd al-Raḥmān ibn ʿUmar when the two of them were punished by ʿAmr ibn al-ʿĀṣṣ in Egypt for drinking wine. (Ibn al-Athīr, *Usd al-ghāba,* IV.48–49.)

ʿUTHMĀN IBN ʿAFFĀN (d. 35/655). The third of the Four Rightly-Guided Caliphs, he was also the son-in-law of the Prophet. He was a wealthy merchant in Mecca who, upon his conversion to Islam, was steadfast in his generosity to the new community. (Ibn Ḥajar, *Iṣāba,* II.455–456.)

ʿUTHMĀN IBN ZĀ'IDA al-Muqri' (no dates). A Sufi and a narrator of traditions from Kufa and then Rayy. (Ibn Ḥajar, *Taqrīb,* 383.)

WĀBIṢA IBN MAʿBAD al-Asadī (no dates). He was a pious and prudent

Companion who was perhaps best known for his propensity for tears. He lived in Kufa for a time before moving to Raqqa where he died. One of his sons, ʿAbd al-Raḥmān was a jurist who served as the qadi of Raqqa. (Ibn al-Athīr, *Usd al-ghāba*, v.398–399.)

WAHB IBN MUNABBIH (d. 114/732). Known chiefly as a learned convert from Judaism, he was also a narrator of traditions and was one of the first to collect these in writing. (Ibn Khallikān, *Wafayāt*, III.671.)

AL-WALĪD IBN ʿABD AL-MALIK (d. 98/715). The sixth in the line of Umayyad caliphs, he is perhaps best known for his construction of the Umayyad Mosque in Damascus. It was during his reign that Muḥammad ibn al-Qāsim conquered Sind. (Dhahabī, *Siyar*, VI.496–500.)

WUHAYB IBN AL-WARD (d. 153/771). A man of piety and a noted narrator of traditions from Mecca, he was the teacher of Ibn al-Mubārak and others. (Iṣfahānī, *Ḥilya*, VIII.14–162.)

YAḤYĀ IBN MAʿĪN (d. 233/848). A pious contemporary of Aḥmad ibn Ḥanbal's from Baghdad, he was considered the most learned of all *ḥadīth* scholars on the subject of narrators' biographies (*ʿilm al-rijāl*). (Ibn Khallikān, *Wafayāt*, IV.24.)

YAḤYĀ IBN MUʿĀDH (d. 258/872). Yaḥyā was a Sufi from Rayy who travelled throughout Central Asia in order to disseminate his teachings. (Iṣfahānī, *Ḥilya*, X.51–70.)

YAḤYĀ IBN YAḤYĀ (no dates). A man of piety from Mecca and contemporary of Fuḍayl ibn ʿIyāḍ, Ibn ʿUyayna, and Ibn al-Mubārak. (Dhahabī, *Siyar*, X.512.)

YAZĪD IBN ʿABD AL-MALIK (YAZĪD II) (d. 105/724). The ninth of the Umayyad caliphs. (Dhahabī, *Siyar*, VI.279–281.)

YAZĪD IBN MUʿĀWIYA (YAZĪD I) (d. 64/683). The second in the line of Umayyad caliphs and the one whose armies committed unthinkable atrocities, including their laying siege to Mecca, laying waste to Medina, and visiting massacre upon al-Ḥusayn at Karbala. (Dhahabī, *Siyar*, V.279–275.)

YŪSUF IBN ASBĀṬ (d. 199/815). He was a righteous man and a noted narrator of traditions. (Iṣfahānī, *Ḥilya*, VIII.237–253.)

ZAYD IBN THĀBIT (d. 45/665). A Companion from Medina, he is best known as the Scribe of Revelation (*kātib al-waḥy*) for the Prophet and the Companion with the most complete knowledge of the laws of inheritance. (Ibn al-Athīr, *Usd al-ghāba*, II.346–347.)

ZAYNAB BINT JAḤSH AL-ASADĪ (d. 20/641). She was wife to the Prophet and a friend to the poor and needy. She was fond of prayer and fasting, and earned her own money by her own labour so that she could distribute it as charity. (Ibn al-Athīr, *Usd al-ghāba*, VII.126–128.)

ZUBAYDA BINT JAʿFAR (d. 216/832). The wife of the ʿAbbasid caliph, Hārūn al-Rashīd, she is remembered for her charity and for her devotion to the faith. (Khaṭīb al-Baghdādī, *Tārīkh Baghdād*, XIV.433-434.)

AL-ZUBAYR IBN ʿADĪ Abū ʿAbd Allāh al-Ḥamdānī (d. 131/747). He was a narrator of traditions from Kufa and a qadi at Rayy. (Ibn Ḥajar, *Taqrīb*, 214.)

AL-ZUHRĪ, ABŪ BAKR ibn Shihāb, Muḥammad ibn Muslim (d. 124/746). A traditionist and a jurist of the Successor generation who lived in Medina, he was accounted one of the greatest scholars of his time. (Dhahabī, *Siyar*, V.326.)

BIBLIOGRAPHY

ʿAbd al-Bāqī, Muḥammad Fu'ād. *al-Muʿjam al-mufahras li-alfāẓ al-Qur'ān al-Karīm*. Cairo, 1378/1959.

ʿAbd al-Razzāq, Abū Bakr b. Humām al-Sanʿanī. *al-Kitāb al-muṣannaf*. Ed. Ḥabīb al-Raḥmān al-Aʿẓamī. 11 vols. Beirut: al-Maktab al-Islāmī, 1970-1972.

Abou El Fadl, Khalid. *Rebellion and Violence in Islamic Law*. Cambridge, 2001.

———. *Speaking in God's Name: Islamic Law, Authority and Women*. Oxford, 2001.

———. *The Authoritative and Authoritarian in Islamic Discourses*. Virginia, 2002.

Abū Dā'ūd, Sulaymān b. Ashʿath al-Sijistānī. *Sunan*. Ed. ʿIzzat ʿUbayd al-Daʿās. 5 vols. Homs, Syria, 1969–1974.

———. *Kitāb al-marāsīl*. Ed. Shuʿayb Arnauṭ. Beirut, 1408.

Abū Ḥanīfa, al-Nuʿmān b. Thābit. *Kitāb al-āthār*. Karachi, 1410/1990.

Abu Layla, Muhammad. *In Pursuit of Virtue*. London, 1411/1990.

ʿAdawī, Ṣafā al-Ḍawwī Aḥmad al-. *Ihdā' al-dībāja bi-sharḥ sunan Ibn Māja*. 5 vols. Egypt, 1999.

ʿAjlūnī, Ismāʿīl b. Muḥammad al-. *Kashf al-khifā' wa-muzīl al-ilbās ʿammā ishtahara ʿalā alsinat al-nās*. Aleppo, 1351/1933.

ʿAlawānī, Zaynab Ṭāhā. '*Qirā'āt fi-fikr al-Ghazālī al-uṣūlī*', in *Islāmiyyat al-maʿrifa*, 27 (Winter 2001), pp. 121–140.

Anṣārī, Zakariyyā al-. *Asnā al-maṭālib sharḥ rawḍ al-ṭālib*. 6 vols. Egypt, 1313/1896.

———. *al-Ghurar al-bahiyya sharḥ al-buhja*. 11 vols. Beirut, 1997.

Archer, Simon & Rifaat Abdel Karim. *Islamic Finance: Innovation and Growth*. London, 2003.

ʿAskarī, Abū Hilāl al-. *Kitāb al-awā'il*. Riyadh, 1980.

ʿAsqalānī, al-. See under Ibn Ḥajar, Aḥmad b. ʿAlī al-ʿAsqalānī.

Aṭfīyash, Muḥammad b. Yūsuf. *Sharḥ kitāb al-nīl fī shifā' al-ʿalīl*. 17 vols. Beirut/Jeddah, 1973.

ʿAṭṭār, Ḥasan b. Muḥammad, al-. *Ḥāshiyyat al-ʿAṭṭār ʿalā sharḥ Jamʿ al-jawāmiʿ*. 2 vols. Egypt, n.d.

Badawī, ʿAbd al-Raḥmān. *Mu'allafāt al-Ghazālī*. Cairo, 1380/1961.

Baghdādī, al-Khaṭīb al-. See under Khaṭīb al-Baghdādī, al-.
Bahūtī, Manṣūr al-. *Kashshāf al-qināʿ min matn al-iqnāʿ*. 6 vols. Riyadh, n.d.
———. *Sharḥ muntahā al-irādāt*. 3 vols. Beirut, 1416/1996.
Bājī, Abū'l-Walīd Sulaymān, al-. *al-Muntaqā sharḥ al-Muwaṭṭā'*. 7 vols. in 4. Beirut, 1403/1983.
———. *Kitāb al-ḥudūd fī'l-uṣūl*. Ed. Nazīh Ḥammād. Beirut, 1973.
Bannūrī, Muḥammad Yūsuf al-. *Maʿārif al-sunan sharḥ sunan al-Tirmidhī*. 6 vols. Karachi, 1413/1992.
Bayhaqī, Aḥmad b. al-Ḥusayn al-. *Dalā'il al-nubūwwa*. 7 vols. Beirut, 1988.
———. *Kitāb al-sunan al-kubrā*. 2 vols. Beirut, n.d.
———. *Manāqib al-Imām al-Shāfiʿī*. 2 vols. Ed. Aḥmad Ṣaqr. Egypt, 1971.
———. *Shuʿab al-imān*. 14 vols. Ed. Mukhtār Aḥmad al-Nadawī. Riyadh, 2003.
Bazdawī. See under Bukhārī, ʿAbd al-ʿAzīz b. Aḥmad al-.
Bujayramī, Sulaymān b. Muḥammad al-. *Tuḥfat al-ḥabīb ʿalā sharḥ al-khaṭīb*. 4 vols. Beirut, 1995.
Bukhārī, ʿAbd al-ʿAzīz b. Aḥmad al-. *Kashf al-asrār ʿalā uṣūl al-Bazdawī*. 4 vols. Istanbul, 1308/1891.
Bukhārī, Muḥammad b. Ismāʿīl, al-. *al-Adab al-mufrad*. Beirut, 1985/1405. English translation by Yūsuf DeLorenzo. Beirut, 1996.
———. *al-Jāmiʿ al-musnad al-ṣaḥīḥ*. Ed. Muḥammad Tamīm. Beirut, 1995.
———. *al-Tārīkh al-kabīr*. 9 vols. Beirut, n.d.
Būṣīrī, Shihāb al-Dīn, al-. *Mukhtaṣar itḥāf al-khiyāra al-mahara bi-zawā'id al-masānīd al-ʿashara*. 11 vols. Beirut, 1418/1998.
Daḥlān, Muḥammad Iḥsān. *Sirāj al-ṭālibīn sharḥ minhāj al-ʿābidīn ilā jannat Rabb al-ʿĀlamīn*. Jeddah, n.d.
Dāmād, ʿAbd Allāh b. al-Shaykh Muḥammad. *Majmaʿ al-anhur sharḥ multaqā al-abḥur*. Egypt, 1316/1899.
Damīrī, Muḥammad b. Mūsā al-. *Ḥayāt al-ḥayawān al-kubrā*. 2 vols. Cairo, 1956.
Dārimī, Abū Muḥammad, al-. *Sunan*. Ed. Ḥusayn Salīm Asad. 4 vols. Riyadh, 2000/1420.
Dārqutunī, ʿAlī b. ʿUmar. *Sunan*. Ed. ʿAbd Allāh al-Turkī. 5 vols. Beirut, al-Risāla, 2003.
Darwīsh, ʿAbd Allāh. *Bughyat al-rā'id fī taḥqīq majmaʿ al-zawā'id*. 10 vols. Beirut, 1994.
Daylamī, Abū Shujāʿ, al-. *al-Firdaws bi-ma'thūr al-khiṭāb*. 5 vols. Beirut, 1986.
Daynūrī, Abū Ḥanīfa al-. *al-Akhbār al-ṭiwāl*. ed. Jamāl al-Dīn al-Shayyāl. Cairo, 1960.
DeLorenzo, Yusuf Talal. *A Compendium of Legal Opinions on the Operations of Islamic Banks*. 3 vols. London, 1997, 2001.

———. "Shariah Supervision in Modern Islamic Finance," *ABANA Review*, xix, no. 2 (2002).

Dhahabī, Muḥammad b. Aḥmad, al-. *al-Kāshif fī man lahu riwāya fī'l-kutub al-sitta*. Ed. ʿIzzat ʿAlī ʿAṭiyya & Mūsā Muḥammad ʿAlī al-Mūshī. 4 vols. Egypt, n.d.

———. *Mīzān al-iʿtidāl fī naqd al-rijāl*. Ed. ʿAlī Muḥammad al-Bijāwī. 4 vols. Cairo, 1382/1963.

———. *Siyar aʿlām al-nubalā'*. 25 vols. Beirut, 1982.

———. *Tārīkh al-Islām*. Ed. ʿAbd al-Salām. 53 vols. Beirut, 1410/1990.

Encyclopedia of Islam. CD-ROM Edition. 11 vols. Leiden, 2003.

Fārisī, ʿAlā' al-Dīn al-. *al-Iḥsān bi-tartīb Ṣaḥīḥ ibn Ḥibbān*. Ed. Kamāl Yūsuf al-Ḥūt. Beirut, 1987.

———. *al-Fatāwā al-hindiyya (al-ʿālamkīriyya)*. Beirut, 1986.

Ghazālī, Abū Ḥāmid Muḥammad al-.

———. *Faḍā'iḥ al-bāṭiniyya*. Ed. Nādī Faraj Darwīsh. Cairo: al-Maktab al-Thiqāfī, n.d.

———. *Iḥyā' ʿulūm al-dīn*. Ed. ʿAbd Allāh al-Khālidī. 5 vols. Beirut, 1998.

———. *al-Iqtiṣād fī'l-iʿtiqād*. Ed. Ibrāhīm Ākāh Chubūqchī & Ḥusayn Ātāyī. Ankara: Nur Matbaasī, 1962.

———. *Minhāj al-ʿābidīn ilā jannat Rabb al-ʿĀlamīn*. Jeddah, n.d.

———. *al-Mustaṣfā min ʿilm al-uṣūl*. 2 vols. Būlāq, 1322–1325/1905–1907.

———. *al-Tibr al-masbūk fī naṣīḥat al-mulūk*. Beirut, 1409/1988.

———. *al-Wajīz fī fiqh al-Imām al-Shāfiʿī*. 2 vols. Egypt, 1317/1900.

———. *al-Wasīṭ fī'l-madhhab*. Ed. Abū ʿAmr al-Ḥusayn b. ʿUmar. 4 vols. Beirut, 1422/2001.

———. *Abū Ḥāmid al-Ghazālī's al-Mustaṣfā min ʿilm al-uṣūl:* Translation of Volume One by Ahmad Zaki Hammad. Unpublished.

Ḥabbābī, Muḥammad ʿAzīz al-. *Waraqāt ʿan falsafāt Islāmiyya*. Morocco, 1988.

Ḥākim al-Nīsābūrī al-. *al-Mustadrak ʿalā al-Ṣaḥīḥayn*. 4 vols. Hyderabad, 1340/1922.

Ḥalabī, ʿAlī Ḥasan al-. *Mawsūʿat al-aḥādīth wa'l-āthār al-daʿīfa wa'l-mawdūʿa*. 15 vols. Riyadh, 1999.

Ḥamawī, Ibn Ḥijja al-. *Thamarāt al-awrāq*. Ed. Muḥammad Abū al-Faḍl Ibrāhīm. Egypt, 1971.

Ḥammād, Nazīh. *Muʿjam al-muṣṭalaḥāt al-iqtiṣādiyya fī lughat al-fuqahā'*. Virginia, 1995.

Hannād b. al-Sarrī al-Kūfī. *al-Zuhd*. Ed. ʿAbd al-Raḥmān ʿAbd al-Jabbār. 2 vols. Kuwait, 1406.

Ḥaṭṭāb, Abū ʿAbd Allāh Muḥammad al-. *Mawāhib al-jalīl fī sharḥ mukhtaṣar al-khalīl*. Beirut, 1995.

Ḥaydar, ʿAlī. *Durar al-ḥukkām fī sharḥ majallat al-aḥkām*. Beirut, 1991.
Haytamī, Aḥmad b. Muḥammad al-. *al-Fatāwā al-ḥadīthiyya*. 2 vols. Cairo, 1937.
———. *al-Fatāwā al-kubrā al-fiqhiyya*. 4 vols. Cairo, 1357/1938.
———. *Tuḥfat al-muḥtāj ʿalā al-minhāj*. 2 vols. Cairo, 1315/1898.
Haythamī, ʿAlī b. Abī Bakr, al-. *Majmaʿ al-zawā'id wa-manbaʿ al-fawā'id*. 8 vols. Cairo, 1352/1933.
Ḥillī, Abū'l-Qāsim Jaʿfar al-. *al-Mukhtaṣar al-nāfiʿ fī fiqh al-imāmiyya*. Najaf, 1964.
Hindī, ʿAlī al-Muttaqī b. Ḥusām al-Dīn al-. *Kanz al-ʿummāl fī sunan al-aqwāl wa'l-afʿāl*. 18 vols. Beirut, 1985.
Holland, Muhtar. *The Duties of Brotherhood*. London, 1975.
Ibn ʿAbd al-Barr, Yūsuf. *al-Istiʿāb fī maʿrifat al-aṣḥāb*. 4 vols. Ed. ʿAlī al-Bajāwī. Beirut, 1992.
———. *Jāmiʿ bayān al-ʿilm wa-faḍlih*. 2 vols. Saudi Arabia, 1994.
Ibn ʿAbd Rabbih, *al-ʿIqd al-farīd*. Ed. ʿAbd al-Qādir Shahīn. 4 vols. Alexandria, Egypt, 1419/1998.
Ibn ʿAbd al-Salām, ʿIzz al-Dīn. *Qawāʿid al-aḥkām fī maṣāliḥ al-anām*. Beirut, 1990.
Ibn ʿĀbidīn, Muḥammad Amīn. *Radd al-muḥtār ʿalā al-durr al-mukhtār sharḥ tanwīr al-abṣār*. 4 vols. Egypt, 1386/1966.
Ibn Abī Dunyā, ʿAbd Allāh b. Muḥammad. *Iṣlāḥ al-māl*. Ed. Muḥammad ʿAbd al-Qādir ʿAṭā. Lebanon, 1993.
———. *Kitāb muḥāsabat al-nafs*. Ed. Majdī al-Sayyid Ibrāhīm. Cairo, 1987.
———. *Kitāb al-waraʿ*. Ed. Abū ʿAbd Allāh M. al-Ḥamūd. 1 vol. Kuwait, 1988/1408.
———. *al-Zuhd*. Damascus, 1999.
Ibn Abī al-Ḥadīd al-Madā'inī, ʿIzz al-Dīn. *Sharḥ nahj al-balāgha*. Ed. Ḥasan Tamīm. 2 vols. Beirut, 1963.
Ibn Abī Shayba, Abū Bakr. *al-Kitāb al-muṣannaf*. Ed. Muḥammad ʿAwwām. 26 vols. Beirut, 1427/2006.
Ibn ʿAdī, Abū Aḥmad. *al-Kāmil fī ḍuʿafā al-rijāl*. 9 vols. Beirut, 1997.
Ibn Amīr al-Ḥājj. *al-Taqrīr wa'l-taḥbīr*. Egypt, 1316/1899.
Ibn al-ʿArabī, Abū Bakr Muḥammad. *Aḥkām al-Qur'ān*. Ed. ʿAlī Muḥammad al-Bajāwī. 4 vols. Beirut, 1987.
Ibn ʿAsākir, ʿAlī b. al-Ḥasan. *Tārīkh Dimashq*. 80 vols. Beirut, 1998.
Ibn al-Athīr, al-Mubārak b. Muḥammad al-Jazarī, *al-Nihāya fī gharīb al-ḥadīth wa'l-riwāya*. Ed. Abū ʿAbd al-Raḥmān b. ʿUwayḍa. 4 vols. Beirut, 1997.
———. *Usd al-ghāba fī maʿrifa al-ṣaḥāba*. Ed. ʿAlī Aḥmad ʿAbd al-Mawjūd. 8 vols. Beirut, 1415/1994.

Ibn Ḥajar, Aḥmad b. ʿAlī al-ʿAsqalānī. *Bulūgh al-marām min adillat al-aḥkām.* 2 vols. Cairo, 1347/1929.
———. *Fatḥ al-bārī sharḥ Ṣaḥīḥ al-Bukhārī.* Ed. ʿAbd al-ʿAzīz b. Bāz. 13 vols. Beirut, 1414/1994.
———. *al-Iṣāba fī maʿrifat al-ṣaḥāba.* 10 vols. Cairo, 1358/1939.
———. *Lisān al-mīzān.* 8 vols. Cairo, 1996.
———. *al-Maṭālib al-ʿāliya.* 19 vols. Riyadh, 1998.
———. *Tahdhīb al-tahdhīb.* 10 vols. India, 1327/1909.
———. *al-Talkhīṣ al-ḥabīr fī takhrīj aḥādīth sharḥ al-rāfiʿī al-kabīr.* Delhi, 1307/1890.
———. *Taqrīb al-tahdhīb.* Beirut and Damascus, 1406/1986.
Ibn Ḥajja al-Ḥamawī, Abū Bakr. *Thamarāt al-awrāq.* Ed. Muḥammad Abū al-Faḍl Ibrāhım. Egypt, 1971.
Ibn Ḥanbal, Aḥmad b. Muḥammad. *Kitāb al-waraʿ.* Ed. Samīr al-Zuhayrī. Riyadh, 1997.
———. *Kitāb al-zuhd.* Beirut, 1403/1983.
———. *al-Musnad.* Ed. Aḥmad Shākir. 20 vols. Cairo, 1313/1896.
Ibn Ḥazm, Abū Muḥammad ʿAlī. *al-Muḥallā bi'l-āthār.* Ed. ʿAbd al-Ghaffār Sulaymān al-Bandārī. 8 vols. Beirut, n.d.
Ibn al-Humām, Kamāl al-Dīn. *Fatḥ al-qadīr.* 10 vols. Beirut, 2003.
Ibn al-Jawzī. *al-Mawḍūʿāt.* Ed. ʿAbd al-Raḥmān ʿUthmān. 3 vols. Madina, n.d.
———. *al-Muntaẓam fī tārīkh al-mulūk wa'l-umam.* Ed. Muḥammad ʿAbd al-Qādir ʿAṭā'. 19 vols. Beirut, 1412/1992.
Ibn Kathīr, ʿImād al-Dīn. *al-Bidāya wa'l nihāya.* 21 vols. Cairo, 1417/1997.
Ibn Khallikān, Abū al-ʿAbbās Aḥmad. *Wafayāt al-aʿyān wa-anbā' abnā' al-zamān.* Ed. Iḥsān ʿAbbās. 7 vols. Beirut, 1994.
Ibn Māja, al-Qazwīnī. *Sunan.* 2 vols. Cairo, 1313/1896.
Ibn Manẓūr, Jamāl al-Dīn Muḥammad. *Lisān al-ʿArab.* 55 vols. Beirut, 1375/1955.
———. *Mukhtaṣar tārīkh Dimashq li-Ibn ʿAsākir.* Damascus, 1984.
Ibn Mubārak, ʿAbd Allāh al-Marwazī. *al-Zuhd wa'l-raqā'iq.* Ed. Ḥabīb al-Raḥmān al-Aʿẓamī. Beirut, n.d.
Ibn Mufliḥ, Burhān al-Dīn Ibrāhīm. *Kitāb al-furūʿ.* 11 vols. Saudi Arabia, 2003.
———. *al-Mubdiʿ fī sharḥ al-muqniʿ.* Beirut, 1977.
Ibn al-Nadīm, Abū al-Faraj Muḥammad. *The Fihrist.* Edited and translated by Bayard Dodge. Chicago, 1990 (reprint).
Ibn Qayyim, Abū ʿAbd Allāh Muḥammad. *Iʿlām al-muwaqqiʿīn ʿan Rabb al-ʿĀlamīn.* 4 vols. Ed. ʿAbd al-Raḥmān b. al-Wakīl. Cairo, n.d.
Ibn Qudāma, Muwaffaq al-Dīn al-Maqdisī. *al-Mughnī.* 15 vols. Riyadh, n.d.

Ibn Qutayba, ʿAbd Allāh b. Muslim. *ʿUyūn al-akhbār*. Ed. A. al-ʿAdawī. 4 vols. Cairo, 1343-1348/1925-1930.

Ibn Saʿd, Abū ʿAbd Allāh Muḥammad. *Kitāb al-ṭabaqāt al-kubrā*. Ed. Iḥsān ʿAbbās. 8 vols. Beirut, 1968.

Ibn Sallām, Abū ʿAbd Allāh al-Qāsim. *Kitāb al-amwāl*. Ed. Muḥammad Khalīl Harās. Beirut, 1408/1988.

Ibn Taymiyya, Abū al-ʿAbbās Aḥmad. *Majmūʿat al-fatāwā al-kubrā*. 37 vols. Riyadh, 1398/1978.

———. *al-Siyāsa al-sharʿiyya fī iṣlāḥ al-rāʿī wa'l-raʿiyya*. Beirut, 1988.

Iṣfahānī, Abū Nuʿaym, al-. *Ḥilyat al-awliyā' wa-ṭabaqāt al-aṣfiyā'*. 11 vols. Cairo, 1351–1357/1932–1938.

———. *Tārīkh Iṣbahān*. Ed. Sayyid Kusrawī Ḥasan. 2 vols. Beirut, 1990/1410.

Ishbīlī, ʿAbd al-Ḥaqq, al-. *Sharḥ al-aḥkām al-sharʿiyya al-kubra*. Ed. Abū ʿAbd Allāh b. ʿUkāsha. 2 vols. Riyadh, n.d.

Jabrī, Muḥammad ʿĀbid al-. *Arab-Islamic Philosophy: A Contemporary Critique*. Trans. Aziz Abbasi. Texas, 1999.

Jaṣṣāṣ, Abū Bakr Aḥmad b. ʿAlī al-Rāzī al-. *Aḥkām al-Qur'ān*. Ed. Muḥammad Bashīr al-Ghazzī, Kāmil Effendi & Rifʿat al-Kalīsī. 4 vols. Istanbul, 1335/1917.

———. *al-Fuṣūl fī'l-uṣūl*. Ed. ʿAjīl Jāsim al-Nashimī. 2 vols. Kuwait, n.d.

Juwaynī, Abū al-Maʿālī, al-. *al-Burhān fī uṣūl al-fiqh*. Ed. Ṣalāḥ ʿUwaiḍa. 2 vols. Beirut, 1997.

Kāsānī, Abū Bakr b. Masʿūd al-. *Badā'iʿ al-ṣanā'iʿ fī tartīb al-sharā'iʿ*. Ed. ʿAlī Muḥammad Muʿawwaḍ & ʿĀdil Aḥmad ʿAbd al-Mawjūd. 8 vols. Beirut, 1997.

Kashmīrī, Muḥammad Anwar Shāh al-. *Mushkilāt al-Qur'ān*. India, n.d.

Khadduri, Majid. *Islamic Jurisprudence: Shāfiʿī's Risāla*. Baltimore, 1961.

Khaṭīb al-Baghdādī, Abū Bakr Aḥmad al-. *al-Jāmiʿ li-akhlāq al-rāwī*. Ed. Maḥmūd al-Ṭaḥḥān. 2 vols. Riyadh, n.d.

———. *Tārīkh Baghdād*. 15 vols. Beirut, 1407/1986.

Kindī, Abū ʿUmar al-. *Kitāb al-wulāh wa-kitāb al-quḍā*. Ed. Muḥammad Ḥasan Ismāʿīl. Beirut, 2003/1424.

Kuḥāla, ʿUmar. *Aʿlām al-nisā*. 15 vols. Beirut, 1379/1959.

Lane, Edward William. *Arabic-English Lexicon*. 2 vols. Cambridge, 1984.

Makkī, Abū Ṭālib al-. *Qūt al-qulūb fī muʿāmalat al-maḥbūb*. 2 vols. Beirut, 1417/1997.

Mālik b. Anas. *al-Muwaṭṭā'*. Ed. Muṣṭafā al-Aʿzamī. 8 vols. Abu Dhabi, 2004.

Manāwī, ʿAbd al-Ra'ūf, al-. *Fayḍ al-qadīr sharḥ al-Jāmiʿ al-ṣaghīr*. 6 vols. Egypt, 1357/1938.

Mardāwī, ʿAlā' al-Dīn ʿAlī al-. *al-Inṣāf fī maʿrifat al-rājiḥ min al-khilāf.* 8 vols. Egypt, 1374/1955.
Masʿūdī, Abū al-Ḥasan ʿAlī b. al-Ḥusayn al-. *Murūj al-dhahab wa-maʿādin al-jawhar.* Ed. Muḥammad Muḥyi al-Dīn ʿAbd al-Ḥamīd. 6 vols. Cairo, 1966.
Māwardī, Abū al-Ḥasan ʿAlī al-. *al-Aḥkām al-sulṭāniyya wa'l-wilāya al-dīniyya.* Cairo, 1386/1966.
Mawṣilī, Abū Yaʿlā Aḥmad, al-. *al-Musnad.* 13 vols. Damascus, 1984.
al-Mawsūʿa al-fiqhiyya (*Kuwait Fiqh Encyclopedia*). Kuwait: Ministry of Religious Endowments, 1404-1421/1983-2000.
Mizzī, Jamāl al-Dīn Abū al-Ḥajjāj Yūsuf al-. *Tahdhīb al-kamāl fī asmā' al-rijāl.* 35 vols. Ed. Bashshār Maʿrūf. Beirut, n.d.
Morelon, Régis, O. P. *Le Livre du Licite et de l'illicite.* Paris, 1981.
Mubārakpūrī, Muḥammad b. ʿAbd al-Raḥmān al-. *Tuḥfat al-aḥwadhī.* 10 vols. India, 1359/1940.
Muḥāsabī, al-Ḥārith ibn Asad, al-. *al-Makāsib wa'l-waraʿ.* Ed. Nūr Saʿīd. Beirut, 1992.
———. *al-Riʿāya li-ḥuqūq Allāh.* Beirut, n.d.
Mukhtār, Ḥabīb Allāh. *al-Mukhtār sharḥ Kitāb al-āthār.* Karachi, 1412/1991.
Mullā Khusrū, ʿAlī Ḥaydar. *Durar al-ḥukkām fī sharḥ majalla al-aḥkām al-ʿadaliyya.* Baghdad, n.d.
Muslim b. Ḥajjāj al-Nisābūrī. *al-Jāmiʿ al-ṣaḥīḥ.* 4 vols. Beirut, 1415/1995.
Nasafī, ʿAbd Allāh b. Aḥmad al-. *Ṭalabat al-ṭalaba.* Baghdad, 1311.
Nasā'ī, Aḥmad b. Shuʿayb al-. *Sunan.* 5 vols. Beirut, n.d.
———. *Tasmiyat fuqahā' al-amṣār.* Aleppo, 1369.
Nawawī, Muḥyī al-Dīn al-. *al-Majmūʿ sharḥ al-muhadhdhab.* 23 vols. Egypt, 1352/1933.
Nuʿmānī, Muḥammad ʿAbd al-Rashīd al-. *Ibn Māja awr ʿilm-i ḥadīth.* Karachi, 1376/1957.
———. *Lughāt al-Qur'ān.* 4 vols. Karachi, 1994.
———. *Mā tamussu ilayhi al-ḥāja li-man ṭālaʿa Sunan ibn Māja.* Karachi, n.d.
al-Qāḍī ʿAyyāḍ, Abū Faḍl. *Tartīb al-madārik wa-taqrīb al-masālik*, 8 vols. Morocco, vol. 1, 1965, vols. 2-4, 1966-70, vols. 5-8, 1980-83.
Qayrawānī, al-Ḥuṣrī al-. *Zuhar al-ādāb wa-thamar al-albāb.* 4 vols. Beirut, n.d.
Qurashī, ʿAbd al-Qādīr, al-. *al-Jawāhir al-muḍiyya fī ṭabaqāt al-Ḥanafiyya.* 2 vols. Karachi, n.d.
Qurtubī, Abū ʿAbd Allāh b. Muḥammad al-. *al-Jāmiʿ li-aḥkām al-Qur'ān.* 24 vols. Beirut, 1427/2006.
Rāfiʿī, Abū al-Qāsim ʿAbd al-Karīm, al-. *al-ʿAzīz sharḥ al-Wajīz.* 14 vols. Beirut, 1417/1997.

Raḥībānī, Muṣṭafā b. Saʿd al-. *Maṭālib ūlū al-nuhā sharḥ Ghāyat al-muntahā.* 6 vols. Damascus, 1415/1994.

Ramlī, Muḥammad b. Aḥmad. *Nihāyat al-muḥtāj fī sharḥ al-minhāj.* 8 vols. Beirut, 2003.

Raṣṣāʿ, Muḥammad b. Qāsim al-. *Sharḥ Ḥudūd Ibn ʿArafa.* Tunis: al-Maktaba al-ʿilmiyya, 1350/1932.

Rāzī, Fakhr al-Dīn. *al-Maḥṣūl fī ʿilm al-uṣūl.* 6 vols. Beirut, 1414/1982.

Saleh, Nabil A. *Unlawful Gain and Legitimate Profit in Islamic Law.* London: Graham and Trotman, 1992.

Samʿānī, ʿAbd al-Karīm b. Muḥammad al-. *al-Ansāb.* 24 vols. Cairo, 1400/1980.

Samarqandī, Abū al-Layth Naṣr. *ʿUyūn al-masāʾil fī furūʿ al-Ḥanafiyya.* Beirut, 1419/1998.

Ṣanʿānī, Muḥammad b. Ismāʿīl al-. *Subul al-salām sharḥ bulūgh al-marām.* 2 vols. Cairo, n.d.

Sarakhsī, Abū Ḥāmid Muḥammad. *al-Mabsūṭ.* 17 vols. Beirut, 1409/1989.

———. *Sharḥ al-sayr al-kabīr.* 5 vols. Beirut, 1971.

Sayyid, Riḍwān al-. *al-Umma wa'l-jamāʿa wa'l-sulṭa.* Beirut, 1406/1986.

Shabrāwī, Muḥammad Ayman al-. *Fahras aḥādīth kashf al-astār ʿan zawāʾid al-bazzār ʿalā al-kutub al-sitta.* Beirut, 1408/1988.

Shāfiʿī, Muḥammad b. Idrīs al-. *Kitāb al-umm.* 14 vols. Cairo, 1321/1903.

Sharbīnī, Muḥammad al-Khaṭīb al-. *Mughnī al-muḥtāj ilā maʿrifat alfāẓ al-minhāj.* Egypt, 1355/1958.

Shawkānī, Muḥammad b. ʿAlī al-. *Nayl al-awṭār sharḥ muntaqa al-akhbār.* 8 vols. Cairo, 1297/1880.

Shaybānī, Muḥammad b. Ḥasan al-. *Kitāb al-aṣl.* Ed. Abū al-Wafāʾ al-Afghānī. 4 vols. Karachi, 1984.

———. *The Kitab al-Athar of Imam Abu Hanifah.* London: Turath Publishing, 2006.

———. *Kitāb al-ḥujja ʿalā ahl al-madīna.* 2 vols. Lahore, 1981.

Shīrāzī, Abū Isḥāq, al-. *Ṭabaqāt al-fuqahāʾ.* Ed. Iḥsān ʿAbbās. Beirut, 1998.

Sūlī, Muhammad b. Yahyā. *Adab al-Kuttāb.* Ed. Muhammad Buhja. Baghdad, 1341/1922.

Suyūṭī, Jalāl al-Dīn, al-. *al-Durr al-manthūr fī al-tafsīr bi'l-maʾthūr.* 8 vols. Beirut, n.d.

———. *al-Jāmiʿ al-ṣaghīr fī aḥādīth al-bashīr al-nadhīr.* 8 vols. Beirut, 1401/1981.

———. *al-Laʾālī al-maṣnūʿa fī maʿrifat al-aḥādīth al-mawḍūʿa.* Beirut, 1419/1998.

———. *Mufḥamāt al-aqrān fī mubhamāt al-Qurʾān.* Cairo, 1987.

———. *Tārīkh al-khulafāʾ.* Ed. Qāsim al-Shammāʿī al-Rifāʿī & Muḥammad al-ʿUthmānī. Beirut, n.d.

Ṭabarānī, Sulaymān b. Aḥmad al-. *al-Muᶜjam al-awsaṭ*. 10 vols. Cairo, 1415/1995.

———. *al-Muᶜjam al-kabīr*. Ed. Ḥamdī ᶜAbd al-Majīd. 15 vols. Beirut, 1985.

———. *al-Muᶜjam al-ṣaghīr*. 4 vols. Cairo, 1388/1968.

Ṭabarī, Ibn Jarīr al-. *Jāmiᶜ al-bayān fī tawīl āyi al-Qur'ān*. Ed. Aḥmad Shākir. 24 vols. Beirut, 1420/2000.

———. *Tārīkh al-rusul wa'l-mulūk*. 11 vols. Beirut, 1387.

Ṭabarī, Muḥibb al-Dīn Aḥmad. *al-Riyāḍ al-naḍira fī manāqib al-ᶜashara*. 2 vols. Egypt, 1327/1909.

Tanūkhī, Zayn al-Dīn al-Munjī al-. *Nishwār al-muḥāḍara*. Ed. ᶜAbūd al-Shābaḥī. 2 vols. N.p., 1397/1977.

Ṭarazī, Abū al-Fatḥ al-. *al-Mugharrib fī tartīb al-muᶜarrib*. Aleppo, 1402/1982.

Tawḥīdī, al-Ustādh Barq al-. *Fatḥ al-Raḥmān li-aḥādīth al-mīzān*. Pakistan, 1404/1984.

———. *Fatḥ al-khabīr li-aḥādīth al-tārīkh al-kabīr*. Pakistan, 1403/1983.

Tirmidhī, al-Ḥakīm al-. *Nawādir al-wuṣūl fī aḥādīth al-rasūl*. Ed. ᶜAbd al-Raḥmān ᶜUmayra. 4 vols. Beirut, n.d.

Tirmidhī, Muḥammad b. ᶜIsā al-. *Sunan*. Ed. Bashshār Maᶜrūf. 5 vols. Beirut, 1998.

Wāḥidī, ᶜAlī b. Aḥmad al-. *Asbāb al-nuzūl*. Beirut, 1363/1944.

Wakī b. Jarrāḥ, al-Qāḍī Abū Sufyān. *Akhbār al-quḍā*. Ed. ᶜAbd al ᶜAzīz al-Murāghī. 3 vols. Egypt, 1947.

Weiss, Bernard. *The Search for God's Law*. Utah, 1995.

———. *The Spirit of Islamic Law*. Georgia, 1998.

Yāfiᶜī, Abū Muḥammad ᶜAfīf al-Dīn al-. *Mir'āt al-Jinān wa-ᶜibrat al-yaqẓān*. Ed. Khalīl al-Manṣūr. Beirut, 1997/1417.

Yaqubi, Muhammad Nizam. *Fatāwā al-Imām al-Ghazālī*. PhD diss., University of Wales, 2003.

Zabīdī, al-Murtaḍā al-. *Itḥāf al-sādat al-muttaqīn bi-sharḥ asrār Iḥyā' ᶜulūm al-dīn*. 10 vols. Cairo, 1311/1894.

Zamakhsharī, Maḥmūd b. ᶜUmar al-. *al-Kashshāf ᶜan ḥaqā'iq ghawāmiḍ al-tanzīl wa-ᶜuyūn al-aqāwīl fī wujūh al-ta'wīl*. 6 vols. Riyadh, 1998.

———. *Rabīᶜ al-abrār wa-fuṣūṣ al-akhbār*. Ed. ᶜAbd al-Majīd Diyāb & Ramaḍān ᶜAbd al-Tawwāb. 2 vols. Cairo, 1992–.

Zarkashī, Muḥammad b. Bahādur al-. *al-Baḥr al-muḥīṭ*. 6 vols. Kuwait, 1992.

———. *al-Manthūr fī'l-qawāᶜid*. Ed. Fā'iq Aḥmad Maḥmūd. Kuwait, 1402/1982.

Zaylaᶜī, ᶜAbd Allāh b. Yūsuf al-. *Naṣb al-rāya fī takhrīj aḥādīth al-hidāya*. Ed. Muḥammad Yūsuf al-Bannūrī. 4 vols. Cairo, 1357/1938.

———. *Tabyīn al-ḥaqā'iq sharḥ kanz al-daqā'iq*. 6 vols. Cairo, 1313/1895.

Ziriklī, Khayr al-Dīn. *al-Aᶜlām*. 9 vols. Beirut, 2002.

INDEX TO QUR'ĀNIC QUOTATIONS

INDEX

Index

Index